PRACTICU

ECONOMICS

PRACTICUM

Janice Boucher Breuer

University of South Carolina

ECONOMICS

PRINCIPLES AND TOOLS

ARTHUR O'SULLIVAN
STEVEN M. SHEFFRIN

Prentice Hall, Upper Saddle River, New Jersey 07458

Dedicated to my son, J. Martin, and my daughter, Lena.

Acquisitions editor: Rod Banister
Associate editor: Gladys Soto
Project editor: Richard Bretan
Printer: Banta Book Group

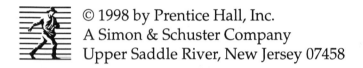

© 1998 by Prentice Hall, Inc.
A Simon & Schuster Company
Upper Saddle River, New Jersey 07458

Printed in the United States of America

10 9 8 7 6 5 4 3 2 1

ISBN 0-13-975269-2

Prentice-Hall International (UK) Limited, *London*
Prentice-Hall of Australia Pty. Limited, *Sydney*
Prentice-Hall Canada Inc., *Toronto*
Prentice-Hall Hispanoamericana, S.A., *Mexico*
Prentice-Hall of India Private Limited, *New Delhi*
Prentice-Hall of Japan, Inc., *Tokyo*
Simon & Schuster Asia Pte. Ltd., *Singapore*
Editora Prentice-Hall do Brasil, Ltda., *Rio de Janeiro*

Table of Contents

PREFACE

About the practicum...

This study guide has been designed especially for you as a student of economics. I have chosen to label the book a "practicum" instead of a "study guide" to emphasize that it is a place where you can practice the material that you have learned. The practicum is designed to promote your comprehension of economic principles and your ability to apply them to different problems since these are the skills that you will be required to use when you take an economics exam and other economics courses.

The practicum is different from any other economics principles study guide for a few reasons. First, it contains a section on performance enhancing tips (PETS). The PETS are tips that may help you through some of the rougher material in each chapter as well as with some basic principles that are used over and over again throughout the course. Second, the practicum is different from other study guides because it contains an answer key to the practice exam multiple choice questions and to the essay questions. For the multiple choice questions, the correct answer is explained in detail and explanations are given for why the other options are not correct. In this way, you learn a lot more because you learn not only why an answer is right but why other answers are wrong. This should help you when it comes time to take an exam. The practicum also provides detailed answers to the essay questions. Finally, since your professor may use terms different than those used in text, equivalent terms that your professor may use have been put in parentheses. For example, some professors use the term "resources" to mean land, labor, and capital whereas other professors use the term "factors of production."

The practicum is not a tool to help you memorize economic principles, nor should it be used as a tool for memorization. It has been my experience as an instructor that students who understand basic economic principles perform much better than students who attempt to learn by memorizing material.

Some words of wisdom...

When I was a sophomore at the University of Delaware, I took my first principles of economics course in the Spring of 1980. I had heard from my roommates and other classmates that economics was a very difficult course, made only more difficult because the professor who was to be teaching the course, Professor Harry Hutchinson, was supposedly very hard on the students. Naturally, I was scared since it seemed like there was a real possibility that this might be one course that I (and a lot of other students) might fail. Much to my surprise, I actually liked economics and thought Professor Hutchinson was a great teacher. In fact, I ended up majoring in economics and going onto graduate school to earn a Ph.D. in it! The words of wisdom that I'd like to impart to you I owe a great deal to Professor Hutchinson. These are words of wisdom I share every semester with the students I teach at the University of South Carolina.

#1   Attend class.

Don't think to yourself "I don't have to attend class to learn; I can learn this material by reading the textbook." First, professors cover material in class that they will put on the exam. This means two things: (1) professors may include material in their lectures that is not in the textbook and test you on it; and (2) material not covered in class will probably not show up on the exam. By attending class, you will have a better idea about what to spend time studying and what not to, and your study time will be more focussed and, thus, more productive.

#2   Take notes in class and recopy them within three days after each class.

For me, recopying my notes was the most useful practice for learning that I engaged in during my college and graduate school career. Recopying notes forces you to review the material and confront any points on which you are not clear. You learn by recopying your notes. Also, by recopying your notes, you will have a well-organized, clear set of notes from which to study. And, that makes studying much easier.

When you recopy your notes, elaborate on major points from the lecture and supplement them with relevant material from the text. Write down questions about the material directly in your notes so that you can ask the professor later. Use colored pens, stars, stickers, or whatever else you want to make your notes unique.

#3   Read or, at least, skim the assigned chapter(s) to be covered in each class before the class meets. Within three days after class, reread the chapter(s).

#4   Jump the gun with studying.

Begin studying for the exam four to five days prior to the exam date. You'd be surprised how much easier it is to learn when you don't feel pressured for time. Plus, the extra time to study gives you an opportunity to review the material more than once or twice and to work through the practicum. You'll also have time to meet with your professor and ask questions about material which gives you trouble.

#5   Do things in reverse.

When your professor works through an example in class for which an "increase" is considered, work through the reverse case of a "decrease." When you are working through the practice exam multiple choice questions and essay questions in the practicum, it may also be useful for you to consider the reverse of each question. For example, if the multiple choice question asks you to consider an "increase," instead consider a "decrease" and then figure out whether there is any correct answer or how an answer would have to be modified to be correct. You should do likewise for questions where you are asked to consider a "rightward" shift in a curve, or a "negative" relationship, or which statement is "true."

#6   Meet with your professor to discuss material that you have trouble with.

All of these words of wisdom may be summed up as:

Expect to work hard if you want to do well. Hard work, in this course, or any course, usually has its rewards.

In my experience as a student and then later as a professor who has interacted with students, I have observed firsthand how hard work has transformed a D student into a C or B student and a C student into a B or A student.

ACKNOWLEDGEMENTS

There are a number of people who I would like to acknowledge for their participation throughout the preparation of this practicum. I would like to thank my husband for giving me some quiet nights and weekends to work on the practicum and my parents for giving me a quiet place and a quiet week in Arizona to work on the practicum. I would like to thank Francisco Veiga for preparing the graphs and formatting the text for me. I would like to thank my students over the past ten years for exposing me to their questions, travails, and triumphs in learning economics. I would also like to thank the many economics professors that I had as an undergraduate student at the University of Delaware and as a graduate student at the University of North Carolina-Chapel Hill. I would especially like to name Professor Harry Hutchinson, Professor Stanley Black, Professor Randy Nelson, Professor Knox Lovell, and Professor Dennis Appleyard. Finally, I'd like to thank the staff at Prentice Hall for their effort in helping me pull this off.

CHAPTER 1
INTRODUCTION AND APPENDIX

I.   OVERVIEW

In this chapter, you will be introduced to economics. You will also be introduced to basic graphing principles and the formula for a slope and for calculating a percentage change. You will learn about the basic economic problem of scarcity and see how it is represented with a graph. You will learn about the resources a society has that enable it to produce goods and services (output). You will learn what a market is. You will also learn about some of the terms that economists use and some of the techniques they use for thinking about problems a society, an individual, or a firm faces.

II.   CHECKLIST

By the end of this chapter, you should be able to:

√   Explain the concept of scarcity.
√   Use the production possibilities curve to reflect scarcity.
√   List the resources or factors of production a society has that enable it to produce goods and services.
√   Describe what it means for a society to be producing at a point inside, along, and outside the production possibilities curve.
√   Define a market and explain why it exists.
√   Describe the usefulness of making assumptions.
√   Explain what is meant by "ceteris paribus."
√   Draw a picture of a graph with a positive slope and a negative slope.
√   Compute the slope of a graph.
√   Determine what will cause a graph to shift and in what direction and what will cause a movement along a graph.
√   Compute a percentage change and use it to make other calculations.

III.   KEY TERMS

Economics: the study of the choices made by people who are faced with scarcity.
Scarcity: a situation in which resources are limited and can be used in different ways, so we must sacrifice one thing for another.
Factors of production: the resources used to produce goods and services.
Natural resources: things created by acts of nature and used to produce goods and services.
Labor: the human effort used to produce goods and services, including both physical and mental effort.
Physical capital: objects made by humans and used to produce goods and services.
Human capital: the knowledge and skills acquired by a worker through education and experience and used to produce goods and services.
Entrepreneurship is the effort used to coordinate the production and sale of goods and services.
Production possibilities curve: a curve that shows the possible combinations of goods and services available to an economy, given that all productive resources are fully employed and efficiently utilized.

1

Microeconomics: the study of the choices made by consumers, firms, and government and how these decisions affect the market for a particular good or service.

Market: an arrangement that allows buyers and sellers to exchange things: a buyer exchanges money for a product, while a seller exchanges a product for money.

Macroeconomics: the study of the nation's economy as a whole.

Variable: a measure of something that can take on different values.

Ceteris paribus: Latin for "other variables are held fixed."

IV.   PERFORMANCE ENHANCING TIPS (PETS)

<u>PET #1</u>

A graph of the relationship between X and Y (use whatever variables you like) will SHIFT when other variables, like Z, G, and J (use whatever variables you like), which are relevant to the relationship between X and Y change. Changes in the variables, X and Y, that are being graphed will NOT cause a shift of the curve but, instead, will cause a MOVEMENT along the curve.

As your textbook discusses in the appendix to Chapter 1, a graph shows the relationship between two variables while holding fixed or constant (i.e., the "ceteris paribus" condition) other variables that are relevant to the relationship being graphed.

Generically speaking, a graph of the relationship between X and Y holds other variables, like Z, G, J, etc., that are relevant to the relationship between X and Y fixed. That is, the relationship assumed to hold between X and Y is based on the current state of other variables believed to be relevant to X and Y. The relationship between X and Y is drawn for today, and what the values of Z, G, and J are today, not, one year later. For example, a graph of the relationship between age and income-earning potential holds constant other variables, like level of education, skills, and perhaps even whether the government administration is Republican or Democrat, at the time the relationship is drawn.

Suppose graph A below labelled "A" was drawn for you during your senior year in high school when you had not yet decided whether you wanted to attend college.

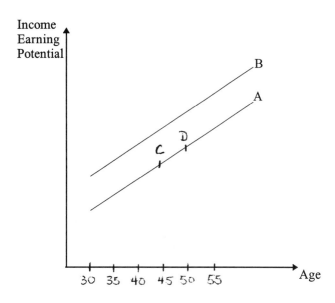

The graph shows that, as you get older, your income earning potential will rise.

Now, draw the graph assuming that you have graduated from college. You should expect that your income earning potential, *for any and every age*, will be higher since you are now more educated. How could you represent this with the graph? Since your income earning potential will be higher after you have graduated from college than if you had not graduated from college, graph A would be shifted up, to the left. This is represented by the graph labelled B. Now, notice that, when you compare your income earning potential at *any and every* age, it is higher, which is consistent with the assumption that more education leads to higher income earning potential, regardless of age. That is, the graph shows that, at age 30, the income earning potential of the college graduate exceeds that of the high school graduate. The same is true at age 40, 50, and so on.

Suppose you are told that the earth's temperature had increased by 1 degree since the graph had been drawn. What would this do to the graph? Nothing. The change in the earth's temperature is not a variable that is relevant to the relationship between age and income earning potential. Therefore, its change will not cause a shift in the curve.

Suppose you are asked what happens to the curve when age increases? Since age is graphed on one of the axes, a change in age is simply represented by a movement along the curve, say, from point C to D, as age increases. An increase in age should NOT be represented by a shift in the curve. A shift in the curve can only occur when some other variable, besides age or income earning potential, that is relevant to the relationship, changes.

PET #2

The numeric value computed from a slope can be a very informative piece of information, especially when debating economic policy. For example, a statement like "an increase in the budget deficit will raise interest rates" may be agreed to be true, but what is the magnitude (or numeric value) of this relationship? Is it big or small? If it is very small, perhaps policymakers needn't worry about the effects of the budget deficit on interest rates. Similarly, a statement like "an increase in the unemployment rate will bring inflation down" may be agreed to be true, but what is the magnitude (or numeric value) of this relationship?

Is it big or small? If it is very big, then a country that has a high rate of inflation may be willing to sacrifice an increase in its unemployment rate in order to bring down inflation. Otherwise, maybe not.

An easy way to compare the slopes of two graphs of the same relationship is to draw them as below, where both of them start from the same value on the X or Y axis. Then, consider the *same change* in the value on either the X or Y axis:

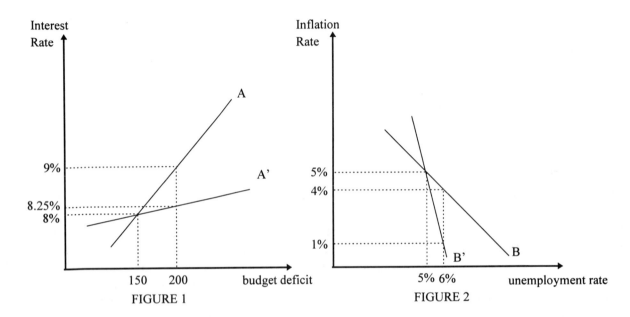

FIGURE 1   FIGURE 2

Is the slope of A or A' bigger in Figure 1? For the same $50 billion increase in the budget deficit, the interest rate rises by 1% along graph A (slope = 1%/$50 billion) and by 0.25% along graph A' (slope = 0.25%/$50 billion). That is, a $50 billion increase in the budget deficit will cause the interest rate to rise by 1% (and vice-versa for a decrease). Along graph A', a $50 billion increase in the budget deficit will cause the interest rate to rise by 0.25% (and vice-versa for a decrease). Along graph A, the interest rate is more responsive (or sensitive) to the change in the budget deficit than along graph A'.

Is the slope of B or B' bigger in Figure 2? In this case, the slope of each graph is negative and so "bigger" means in "absolute" terms (i.e., ignore the negative sign). For the same 1% increase in the unemployment rate, along graph B', the reduction in inflation is bigger. Inflation falls by 4% compared to 1% along graph B. That is, the slope of graph B' is 4%/1% and along graph B is 1%/1%.

V.   PRACTICE EXAM: MULTIPLE CHOICE

1.   Which one of the following does **NOT** represent the concept of "scarcity"?

a.   a decision by your parents to put more of their savings to fund college expenses and less to life insurance.
b.   public policy in the state of Washington to reduce timber production so that more wildlife species will be preserved.
c.   a decision by a company to increase advertising expense for a new board game by decreasing its budget for telephone expense.

d.   a decision to commit more time to perfecting your volleyball serve and more time to perfecting your tennis serve.
e.   a decision by a student to spend more time studying and less time partying.

2.   Which one of the following would **NOT** be considered a resource or factor of production?

a.   a conveyor belt.
b.   a financial analyst with a B.A. degree.
c.   tin.
d.   a new house.
e.   a computer.

3.   Which one of the following would cause the production possibilities curve (PPC) to shift to the *left*?

a.   a technological advancement.
b.   an increase in the skill level of workers.
c.   a deterioration in the interstate highway system.
d.   a discovery of more oil.
e.   an increase in the amount of plant and equipment.

4.   Which one of the following would **NOT** cause a rightward shift in the production possibilities curve (PPC)?

a.   an increase in the utilization of workers.
b.   an increase in the pool of labor available to work.
c.   a technological breakthrough.
d.   a newer stock of physical capital.
e.   all of the above will cause a rightward shift in the PPC.

5.   Which one of the following statements is true?

a.   the production possibilities curve is positively sloped, which shows that, as society wants to produce more of one good, it must produce less of another.
b.   the production possibilities curve is negatively sloped because, with a limited set of resources, society can only produce more of one good by taking resources out of producing another good.
c.   at a point outside the production possibilities curve, resources are fully employed.
d.   at a point inside the production possibilities curve, resources are efficiently used.
e.   a movement along the production possibilities curve shows that society can produce more of both goods.

6.   Which one of the following statements is the most accurate?

a.   "If I increase the amount of time spent reading my economics textbook and working through the study guide, my course grade in economics should improve."
b.   "If the U.S. budget deficit were reduced, then interest rates would be lower."
c.   "If the tax on cigarettes were increased, fewer packages of cigarettes would be sold."
d.   "If my company lowers the price of its product, it should sell more, assuming that our competitors don't do likewise."

e.   "Lower interest rates will lead to consumers taking out more car loans."

7.   Which one of the following illustrates a negative (inverse) relationship between two variables?

a.   as auto insurance rates decrease, the number of automobile purchases remains unchanged.
b.   as patrol cars out on the road increase, highway speeding decreases.
c.   as highway speeding decreases, highway fatalities decrease.
d.   as drunken driving increases, auto insurance rates increase.
e.   (b) and (c).

8.   Consider a graph of grade point average versus hours studied. Which one of the following would be assumed held constant in such a graph?

a.   number of classes attended.
b.   grade point average.
c.   hours studied.
d.   phases of the moon.
e.   all of the above are held constant.

9.   Which one of the following statements about the graph below is true? The graph shows the relationship between household spending and personal income.

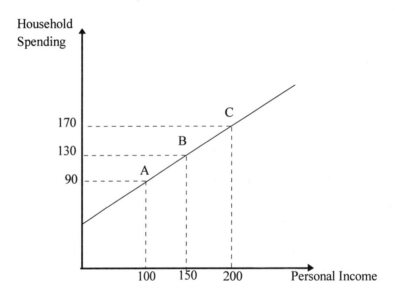

a.   the slope is calculated at point A as 90/100 = 0.90.
b.   the slope is negative.
c.   an increase in personal income taxes would shift the curve up, to the left.
d.   an increase in interest rates would shift the curve up, to the left.
e.   the slope is 0.80.

10.   Which one of the following statements is true about the graph below? The graph shows the relationship between the average cost of production and the quantity of output produced.

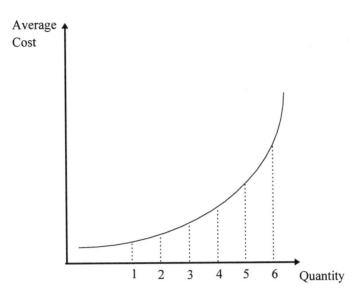

a.   the average cost of production is increasing at a decreasing rate.
b.   if the quantity of output produced increases, the curve will shift to the right.
c.   the average cost of production is increasing at an increasing rate.
d.   the slope of the average cost of production is constant.
e.   the average cost of production curve is negatively sloped.

11.   Suppose you volunteer at a local food bank and find that, for every additional 100 brochures you send out seeking financial donations, the food bank sees an increase in the donations received of $1,500. If you convince the executive director of the food bank to send out 200 more brochures this year than last year, by how much can you expect donations to change by?

a. $3,000.
b. $750.
c. $30.
d. $135.
e.   cannot be determined from the information given.

12.   Suppose you go out to dinner with your friends and your bill comes to $12. You thought the service that the table waiter provided was adequate, so you decide to leave a tip of 15%. What would be the amount of your tip?

a. $1.25.
b. $1.80.
c. $2.40.
d. $1.50.
e. $0.18.

VI.   PRACTICE EXAM: ESSAY QUESTIONS

1.   Consider a society that is producing two types of goods: birdhouses and pianos. Explain what happens in a society if a decision is made to produce more birdhouses.

2.   Suppose you hear a commentator on the radio state that, when interest rates fall, the stock market tends to rise. Draw a picture of such a relationship. Describe the slope. What factors would cause a movement along the graph? What factors might cause a shift in the graph?

VII.   ANSWER KEY: MULTIPLE CHOICE

1.   Correct Answer: d.

Discussion: This statement does not represent the concept of scarcity because it does not reflect any sacrifice or trade-off. That is, you have decided to commit *more* of your limited amount of time to *both* activities. Thus, you are not giving up anything. Of course, you will obviously have to cut back time on other activities (perhaps to sleeping, studying, shopping, or whatever), but such trade-offs are not expressed in the answer.

Statements a, b, and c all represent the concept of scarcity. Statement a represents the concept of scarcity because it reflects a sacrifice or trade-off made by your parents. Their decision to put more of their savings toward college expenses means that they will have less savings to devote to life insurance. That is, while your parents have to give up some funding of life insurance, in return, they are able to increase funding for college expenses. Statement b represents the concept of scarcity because it reflects a sacrifice or trade-off made by legislators representing the state's interests. The sacrifice is that some timber companies will be put out of business. In return, more wildlife species will be preserved. Statement c represents the concept of scarcity because it reflects a sacrifice or trade-off made by a business. The sacrifice is that its telephone budget will be reduced. In return, the company will be able to beef up its advertising expenses for the new board game.

Note: while there is a sacrifice, there is also something earned in return. Perhaps another way to think of sacrifice is "trade-off" whereby something must be given up in order to obtain more of something else.

2.   Correct Answer: d.

Discussion: A resource or factor of production is any good, service, or talent that enables a society to produce output -- other goods and services. A new house does not enable society to produce more of other goods and services.

Statements a, b, c, and e are all examples of factors of production. A conveyor belt is physical capital. It may be used by a factory in its production process. A financial analyst is both labor and human capital. The financial analyst provides physical and mental effort on the job and also brings with him or her skills acquired through formal education. Tin is a natural resource. It may be used in many different production processes -- bottling, sheeting, etc. A computer may be used in the production process of a service like banking or in manufacturing.

3.   Correct Answer: c.

Discussion: A leftward shift in the PPC means that society can now produce *fewer* goods and services of all types. This occurs because its resources or factors of production have, for whatever reason, been depleted. A deterioration in the interstate highway system is a reduction in the physical capital resource that society uses to (indirectly) produce all types of goods and services.

Statements a, b, d, and e are all examples that would be represented by shifting the production possibilities curve to the right. A technological advancement makes it easier for society to produce more goods and services with its *existing* set of natural resources. An increase in the skill level of workers is an increase in the factor of production "human capital." More skilled workers tend to be more productive. That is, workers are able to produce more while on the job. A discovery of more oil is an increase in the factor of production "natural resources." With more natural resources available for production, more goods and services can be produced. An increase in the amount of plant and equipment is an increase in a society's capital stock which enables it to produce more of all types of goods and services. All of these would be represented with a rightward shift in the PPC. A rightward shift shows that society is able to produce more of all types of goods and services.

4.   Correct Answer: a.

Discussion: An increase in the utilization of workers implies that workers must have been idle or underutilized prior to the increase. This is represented by being at a point inside the PPC. When the utilization of workers (or, for that matter, production facilities) is increased, society moves from a point inside the PPC toward a point on the PPC. There is no shift in the PPC. Notice that society, in this case, does not face a trade-off. It can produce more of both types of goods.

Statements b, c, and d will all cause a rightward shift in the production possibilities curve, not a movement to the PPC. An increase in the pool of labor available to work is an increase in the factor of production labor. With more labor available to work, more goods and services can be produced. This would be represented by a rightward shift in the PPC. A technological breakthrough enables a society with its given set of resources (factors of production) to produce more goods and services. This would be represented by a rightward shift in the PPC. A newer stock of physical capital enables society to produce more than before because its physical capital (equipment, factories, etc.) is not as old and, therefore, as subject to breakdown. This would be represented by a rightward shift in the PPC. Statement e cannot be correct since answer a is correct.

5.   Correct Answer: b.

Discussion: Statement b is true. The production possibilities curve is negatively sloped which shows that, in order to produce more of one good, less of another good must be produced. The reason this trade-off arises is because when society has a limited set of resources that are fully employed and efficiently used, the only way it can physically produce more of one good is to take resources out of the production of another good. Thus, production of the other good must necessarily decline.

Statements a, c, d, and e are all false. Statement a is false because the production possibilities curve is not positively sloped; it is negatively sloped. Statement c is false because a point outside the production possibilities curve represents a combination of goods and services that is unattainable given society's current set of resources and its current state of technology. Society does not currently have enough resources to produce at a point outside the production possibilities curve. Thus, the issue of full employment is moot. Statement d is false because a point inside the production possibilities curve reflects a society that is either underutilizing its resources (there is some "idleness") or is not using its resources efficiently. If society were using its resources efficiently and the resoucres were fully employed, a point on the production possibilities curve would be attained. Statement e is false because a movement along the production possibilities curve reflects a trade-off which means that more of one good can be produced but only at the expense of reducing production of another good.

6.   Correct answer: d.

Discussion: Statement d is the most accurate because it is the only statement that qualifies the relationship between the two variables, price and amount sold. For example, without the qualifier, a company may lower its price but find that its sales do not increase. This situation may arise because the company's competitors may also lower their price, making it harder for the company to sell more even though it has lowered its price. The qualifier, in effect, holds fixed other variables that may be relevant to the relationship between price and amount sold. The qualifier thus makes more clear what the expected relationship is between the two variables.

Statements a, b, and c are not as accurate as statement d because none of these answers ahderes to the "ceteris paribus" condition of holding other variables fixed that might also be important to a relationship between two variables. Statement a would be more accurate if it was qualified with a clause like "assuming that I continue to attend class regularly and take and recopy my notes." That is, even if you spend more time reading the textbook and using the study guide, if you decide, at the same time, to skip class and stop taking notes, you may not see any improvement in your grade at all. Statement b would be more accurate if it was qualified with a clause like "assuming that the central bank decides not to raise interest rates." That is, a lower budget deficit may not necessarily lead to lower interest rates if something else happens in the economy to change them. Statement c would be more accurate if it was qualified with a clause like "assuming tobacco companies do not increase their advertising and/or do not lower the price they charge for a pack of cigarettes." That is, an increased tax on cigarettes may not have the desired effect of reducing the packages of cigarettes sold if tobacco producers respond by, say, lowering the price they charge for a pack of cigarettes.

7.   Correct Answer: b.

Discussion: Statement b is the only response that shows a negative (or inverse) relationship. A negative relationship exists when one variable increases and the other decreases or when one variable decreases and the other increases. In statement b, as patrol cars out on the road increase, highway speeding decreases.

Statements a, c, and d do not illustrate a negative relationship. Statement a indicates that there is no relationship between auto insurance rate decreases and automobile purchases. Statement c illustrates a positive relationship. Even though both variables are decreasing, they move in the same direction. That is, you could also say that, as highway speeding increases, highway fatalities increase. In either case, there is a positive (or direct) relationship between both variables. Statement d, for the reason just mentioned, illustrates a positive relationship between drunken driving and auto insurance rates. Statement e cannot be correct because statement c is not correct.

8.   Correct Answer: a.

Discussion: Number of classes attended is the only variable being held constant in this example. Since the graph will show a picture of grade point average versus hours studied, these variables will be on the axes of the graph. Suppose that grade point average is graphed on the vertical axis and hours studied on the horizontal axis; you should expect the graph to have a positive slope. Suppose it is drawn assuming that the full number of classes is attended. Now, if the number of classes attended drops, what would happen to the position of the graph? It would shift down, to the right, indicating that, for a given number of hours studied, the grade point average will, in all cases, be lower.

Statements b and c are not correct because they are the variables being graphed and, therefore, are subject to change. Statement d is not correct because the phases of the moon are not relevant to the relationship between the two variables so it doesn't matter whether it is assumed to be held constant or not. Statement e is not correct because the number of classes attended is held constant, as stated in a. It is reasonable to assume that this variable is relevant to the relationship between grade point average and number of hours spent studying.

9.   Correct answer: e.

Discussion: A slope is calculated by taking two points on a curve and computing the change in the variable on the vertical axis (the rise) and dividing it by the change in the variable on the horizontal axis (the run). Taking any two points on the diagram (A to B, B to C, A to C) will produce a slope of 0.80.

Statement a is not correct because a slope cannot be computed by using a single point on a graph. Remember this! Statement b is not correct because the graph shows a positive slope -- that is, as personal income increases, household spending rises (A to B) and, as personal income decreases, household spending decreases (B to A). Statement c is not correct because an increase in personal income taxes would be expected to lower the level of household spending for every level of personal income. This would be represented by shifting the curve down, to the right. Statement d is not correct because an increase in interest rates would be expected to lower the level of household spending for every level of personal income. This, too, would be represented by shifting the curve down, to the right.

10.   Correct Answer: c.

Discussion: The average cost of production is increasing at an increasing rate. You can figure this out by comparing several points on the graph. Compare the change in the average cost of production from an increase in output of one unit from 1 to 2 units to the change in the cost of production from an increase in output of 5 to 6 units. You will see, even without numbers, that the change in the average cost of production will be greater when output increases by one unit from 5 to 6 than when output increases one unit from 1 to 2. Alternatively, you could look at the change in the average cost of production as you move from producing 1 unit to 2 units to 3 units, and so on. Again, you will see that the average cost of production increases by more when going from producing 2 to 3 units than from 1 to 2 units. Thus, the average cost of production is increasing at an increasing rate.

Statement a is not correct because the average cost of production is increasing at an increasing rate, as explained above. Statement b is not correct. As the quantity of output increases (or decreases), this would be represented by a movement along the curve, not a shift in it. Remember that a shift in a curve only occurs when a variable that is relevant to the relationship to the two being graphed changes. When a variable on the axis itself changes, this is represented by a movement along the curve. Statement d is not correct because the average cost of production is increasing at an increasing rate. If the slope were constant, then the change in the average cost of production from producing 1 to 2 units, compared to 5 to 6 units would be exactly the same (as it would from 2 to 3 units, as well). Statement e is not correct because the graph is positively sloped. The graph shows that, as output increases, the average cost of production increases (and vice-versa).

11.   Correct answer: a.

Discussion: The information in the question reveals that the change in donations received is $1,500 for every 100 additional brochures mailed out. That is, every 1 additional brochure sent out returns $15 in donations. ($1500 donations/100 brochures = $15 donations/1 brochure). So, if the food bank mails out 200 more brochures, it can expect to raise $15 per brochure X 200 brochures = $3,000.

Statements b, c, and d are not correct based on the explanation above. Statement e is not correct because there is enough information to figure out the answer.

12.   Correct Answer: b.

Discussion: You can use a few methods for calculating the tip. You could multiply $12 by 0.15 (15/100) which would yield $1.80. If you don't have a calculator or want to double check your answer, you could compute 10% of $12 which is $1.20. Since 10% of $12 is $1.20, 5% of $12 must be $0.60 (half of $1.20). Then, add $1.20 + $0.60 to get $1.80.

Statements a, c, d, and e are all incorrect. Statement a reflects a tip of just a nickel over a 10% tip. Statement c reflects a tip of 20% ($12 X 0.20 = $2.40). Statement d reflects a tip of [($1.50/$12)]X100 = 12.5%. Statement e reflects a tip of 1.5% ($12 X 0.015 = $0.18).

VIII. ANSWER KEY: ESSAY QUESTIONS

1.   If the society decides that it wants to produce more birdhouses, then it must give up (sacrifice) the production of some pianos. Since the resources that a society has available to help produce output are scarce (limited, fixed amount) at a point in time, the only way the society can produce more birdhouses would be to cut back piano production. By cutting back piano production, the society frees up resources from producing pianos and can then allocate those resources (labor, capital, etc.) into birdhouse production. However, if the amount of resources available to the society were to increase, then these new resources could be devoted to producing more birdhouses without having to cut back on piano production.

2.   The commentator is pointing out a relationship between two variables -- the interest rates and stock prices. The stated relationship is negative since the two variables move in opposite directions. That is, when interest rates fall, stock prices rise and vice-versa. Thus, a graph of the relationship should have a negative slope. Factors that would cause a movement along the graph are the two variables that would be labelled on each axis which are the interest rate and stock prices. Of course, there are other factors that could affect interest rates and stock prices. Such factors are held constant (not permitted to change) when drawing the relationship between interest rates and stock prices. For example, one factor that might be held constant is whether the president is a Republican or Democrat. If the relationship is drawn based on the current party of the president (Democrat), the graph may shift (be further to the right or left) when the party changes to Republican (assuming the party of the president is relevant to the relationship between interest rates and stock prices). Another factor that might be held constant is the unemployment rate. That is, the relationship is drawn assuming a certain unemployment rate. If the unemployment rate were to change (assuming it is relevant to the relationship between interest rates and stock prices), the graph may shift.

Take It to the Net

We invite you to visit the O'Sullivan/Sheffrin page on the Prentice Hall Web site at:

http://www.prenhall.com/osullivan/

for this chapter's World Wide Web exercise.

CHAPTER 2
KEY PRINCIPLES IN ECONOMICS

I.   OVERVIEW

In this chapter, you will learn fundamental economic principles that will be used throughout this course. You will learn that decisions made by a household, business, or government generally involve an opportunity cost; choosing one option means that other options must be given up or sacrificed or foregone. You will learn about the marginal principle. The marginal principle can be used to guide decisions. It requires that the marginal benefit be compared to the marginal cost of undertaking an activity. You will learn about the principle of diminishing returns. The principle of diminishing returns means that more and more effort devoted to an activity leads to smaller and smaller increases (or improvements) in the activity. Diminishing returns arise when more and more effort is exerted but there is no change in other factors which affect the activity. You will learn about the spillover principle. The spillover principle means that the benefits and costs of an activity may "spill over" to other parties not directly involved in the activity. Lastly, you will learn about the reality principle. The reality principle requires that you think in "inflation-adjusted" terms. That is, you must always consider the effects of rising prices (inflation) on your income, pay raises, and interest and dividend earnings from financial investments, as well as on your debt. A true picture of the national economy also requires that you think of its performance in inflation-adjusted terms.

II.   CHECKLIST

By the end of this chapter, you should be able to do the following:

√   Evaluate the opportunity cost that is encountered when choosing an activity (e.g., attending a party on Saturday night, furthering your education, opening up a new factory, building more schools, cutting tax rates).

√   Use the production possibilities curve to compute the opportunity cost of producing one good or bundles of goods instead of another.

√   Explain why opportunity costs increase in moving either up or down the production possibilities curve.

√   Use marginal analysis to decide the level at which an activity should be undertaken.

√   Explain why picking an activity level where "marginal benefit" = "marginal cost" is the best choice.

√   Explain why fixed costs are not relevant for marginal analysis, i.e., why it is that fixed costs do not matter in selecting an activity level.

√   Explain the circumstances under which diminishing returns occur and under what circumstances it does not occur.

√   Explain the spillover principle and give examples of spillover benefits and spillover costs.

√   Use the reality principle to assess how well off you are based on the income you earn, any pay raises you might get, or any interest earnings you might receive from financial investments.

√   Use the reality principle to get a true picture of the state of the economy.

√   Explain the difference between nominal and real variables.

III. KEY TERMS

Marginal benefit: the extra benefit resulting from a small increase in some activity.

Marginal cost: the additional cost resulting from a small increase in some activity.

Fixed costs: costs that do not change as the level of an activity changes.

Variable costs: costs that change as the level of an activity changes.

Explicit costs: costs in the form of actual cash payments.

Implicit costs: the opportunity cost of non-purchased inputs.

Economic cost: the sum of explicit and implicit costs.

Short Run: a period of time over which one or more factors of production is fixed; in most cases, a period of time over which a firm cannot modify an existing facility or build a new one.

Long run: a period of time long enough that a firm can change all the factors of production, meaning that a firm can modify its existing production facility or build a new one.

Diminishing returns: as one input increases while holding the other inputs are held fixed, output increases, but at a decreasing rate.

Spillover or externality: a cost or benefit experienced by people who are external to the decision about how much of a good to produce or consume.

Nominal value: the face value of a sum of money.

Real value: the value of a sum of money in terms of the quantity of goods the money can buy.

IV.   PERFORMANCE ENHANCING TIPS (PETS)

PET #1

Throughout this course, it is wise to always consider the best foregone alternative (option that is given up) when a household, firm, or government makes a decision. An understanding of what is being given up in order to have something else may alter your opinion about the proper course of action.

For example, suppose that a political candidate is proposing that tax rates be cut. What opportunity costs might arise if the proposal is adopted? On the surface, you might think that a tax cut is great because your take-home pay will be higher and allow you to buy more goods and services (assuming prices don't rise; remember the reality principle). However, as with most decisions, there is a cost -- something that is given up. In this case, a tax cut means that the government has less money to spend. So, the government may have to cut funding for space programs, or education, or highway repair, or police protection, or whatever. These are opportunity costs of the tax cut. Which one of these government programs is the "best" foregone alternative depends on your viewpoint. If you value good schools, then the cut in education would be considered the opportunity cost associated with the tax cut. As you can see, debate over the opportunity costs of the proposal to cut taxes can lead to quite a lively discussion and may mean that not everybody agrees that a tax cut is such a good thing.

PET #2

*When you see the term "marginal," you should always think of computing the **change** in a variable. Computing the change requires that you have some numeric value before the change and some numeric value after the change. The difference between the two is the change in the variable.*

For example, suppose you have computed the revenue that your company earns from selling 5,000 jewelry boxes is $100,000. Furthermore, you have forecasted that, if the company sells 6,000 jewelry boxes, the revenue will be $108,000. What is the addition to revenue (marginal) revenue? It is $8,000 (for 1,000 more boxes). Suppose that the cost of producing 5,000 jewelry boxes is $90,000 and you forecast that the cost of producing 6,000 boxes will be $95,000. What is the addition to cost (marginal cost) associated with producing 1,000 more jewelry boxes? It is $5,000.

Now, use the marginal principle to answer whether your company would be better off by increasing production by 1,000 boxes. Since the marginal revenue (benefit to the company) is $8,000 and the marginal cost (cost to the company) is $5,000, the marginal principle dictates that production be increased since the marginal benefit exceeds the marginal cost. That is, the company will add more to its revenue than it will incur in costs by raising production. This means that the company's profits will increase.

PET #3

*The marginal cost or marginal benefit associated with **fixed** costs or fixed benefits are zero. When costs and/or benefits are fixed, the change in the costs or benefits must, by definition, be zero. This is why fixed costs and benefits are not considered when using the marginal principle to decide the best activity level.*

For example, suppose that the fixed costs of operating a factory are the rent and interest on loans (debt) that it must pay every month. Suppose these fixed costs total $3,400 per month. Consider the other monthly costs of operating a factory, including paying employees and paying for raw materials. Suppose these costs are $6,600. If the factory decides to increase production, it must hire more employees and purchase more raw materials. Suppose these costs rise to $8,900. What about rent and interest? Do they change when the company decides to produce more? No, they are fixed costs. So, what is the *marginal* cost associated with increasing production? All you have to do is compute the change in costs -- the cost of rent and interest on loans went from $3,400 to $3,400, which is a change of zero. There is no addition to fixed costs and, thus, no marginal cost associated with them. The costs of employees and raw materials has increased from $6,600 to $8,900, which is an increase of $2,300. The change in costs or marginal cost associated with increasing production is $0 + $2,300 = $2,300.

PET #4

*Diminishing marginal returns means that, as an activity level (such as production) is **increased**, it increases but at a **decreasing** rate. Just because the term "diminishing" is used does NOT mean that an activity level (such as production) decreases or diminishes.*

For example, which table below illustrates the principle of diminishing returns?

Table A		Table B	
# of workers	Output	# of workers	Output
1	100	1	100
2	98	2	110
3	95	3	117
4	91	4	122

The correct answer is Table B. In Table B, output is increasing as more workers are hired. However, the rate at which output is increasing is decreasing. Output increases by 10 units (110-100) from hiring one additional worker, then by 7 units (117-110), and then by 5 (122-117). In Table A, output is decreasing as more workers are hired. This is not the definition of diminishing marginal returns.

PET #5

*Compare the inflation rate to the rate of change in any **nominal** variable to determine whether it has increased, decreased, or remained unchanged in **real** terms.*

For example, suppose your boss gives you a raise of 15% for the coming year. You may be quite happy about this until one of your economist friends points out that inflation is expected to be 18% this year. In this case, while your nominal income will grow by 15%, your real income (inflation-adjusted) will be expected to decrease by 3% (15%-18%). Maybe you should go back to your boss and ask for a bigger raise!

For another example, suppose that you invested $1,000 in the stock market at the beginning of this year. At the end of the year, your investment is now worth $1,200. What is the percent return on your investment? In nominal terms, it is 20% = [(1,200 - 1,000)/1,000] X 100. What is the percent increase in real terms? First, you'll need the inflation rate for that year. Suppose inflation was 4%. Then, in real terms, your investment has increased in value by 16% (20% - 4%).

V.   PRACTICE EXAM: MULTIPLE CHOICE QUESTIONS

1.   The "bowed out" shape of the production possibilities curve (PPC) arises because:

a.   as we move farther inside the PPC, an economy loses increasing amounts of both goods.
b.   the opportunity cost associated with a move from a point on the PPC to a point outside the PPC increases in terms of what must be given up to get there.
c.   to continue to get the same increment in the production of a particular good requires that more and more of the other good be given up.
d.   since resources are scarce, producing more of one good means we must produce less of another.
e.   none of the above.

2.   Based on the diagram below, which statement is correct?

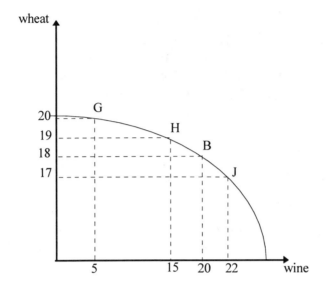

a.   moving from G to H incurs an opportunity cost of 1 bushel of wheat.
b.   as the economy moves along the PPC, more wheat can be obtained along with more wine.
c.   the opportunity cost of moving from G to H to B increases while the opportunity cost of moving from B to H to G decreases.
d.   moving from H to B incurs an opportunity cost of 5 barrels of wine.
e.   moving from G to J entails no opportunity cost.

3.   Which one of the following is an example of a fixed cost?

a.   electricity.
b.   raw materials.
c.   telephone.
d.   supplies.
e.   rent.

4.   Suppose you are debating whether to open up your own pet shop. Which one of the following is an example of an implicit cost?

a.   cost of fish tanks.
b.   cost of a computerized bookkeeping system.
c.   cost of your time spent setting up the shop and monitoring it.
d.   costs for sales clerks.
e.   cost of pet food.

5.   Suppose Fred computes the marginal benefit of working one more hour as a salesclerk in an electronics store to be $7.75. However, by working one more hour, he must give up the opportunity to attend a *free* one-hour workshop on how to start your own business. However, Fred believes he will learn a lot by attending the workshop. Based on this information, which one of the following statements is correct?

a.   Fred should work one more hour in the electronics shop since the workshop is free.

b.   Fred should not work that one more hour in the electronics shop if the implicit value of what he will learn by attending the workshop is $25.00.

c.   Fred should not work that one more hour in the electronics shop if the implicit value of what he will learn by attending the workshop is $5.00.

d.   Fred should work one more hour in the electronics shop if the implicit value of what he will earn by attending the workshop is $5.00.

e.   (b) and (d) are correct statements.

6.   Use the table below to answer the following question.

# of workers	Output
1	5
2	15
3	30
4	37
5	40
6	38

Diminishing returns occur:

a.   between the first and second worker.
b.   between the second and third worker.
c.   between the third and fourth worker.
d.   between the fourth and fifth worker.
e.   between the fifth and sixth worker.

7.   Which one of the following statements is true?

a.   diminishing returns occur when a firm can change the amount of all of the factors of production it uses.

b.   if Helena finds that the marginal benefit of eating an ice cream cone is equal to the marginal cost of eating an ice cream cone, then Helena would be better off to eat one more ice cream cone.

c.   the short run is defined as a period during which some workers are idle.

d.   the production possibilities curve is positively sloped.

e.   none of the above are true statements.

8.   Which one of the following activities is least likely to generate a spillover?

a.   wearing perfume.
b.   smoking a cigarette.
c.   reading a comic book.
d.   picking up trash from the roadside.
e.   repainting the exterior of your house.

9.   Suppose that your boss just informed you that you will be receiving a raise of 8% for this coming year. Suppose further that you have heard economic forecasts that the inflation rate for this coming year will be 9%. Based on this information, you might think to yourself:

a.   "Wow, they must really like me -- I'm effectively getting a 17% pay raise! I need to call home and tell Mom!"
b.   "Gee, thanks for the raise, but the raise isn't actually a raise at all since my real income will decline by 1%."
c.   "This isn't much of a raise, but at least my real income will increase by 1%."
d.   "Well, this isn't really a raise -- my real income is going to decline by 0.72%."
e.   "This isn't really a raise -- my real income is going to decline by 7.2%."

10.   Suppose an old high school friend calls you up and desperately pleads to borrow $1,000 from you. You've been out working for a few years and have a little bundle in savings and decide that this is a good friend who really needs your help. So, you lend him $1,000 with the promise that he pays you the $1,000 back, without interest, at the end of the year. In one year after you are paid back:

a.   In real terms, the money you will be paid back will be worth less than $1,000 if inflation was greater than 0%.
b.   In real terms, the money you will be paid back will be worth more than $1,000 if inflation was greater than 0%.
c.   In real and nominal terms, you will be paid back $1,000.
d.   In nominal terms, the money you will be paid back will be worth less than $1,000 if inflation was greater than 0%.
e.   In nominal terms, the money you will be paid back will be worth more than $1,000 if inflation was greater than 0%.

VI.   PRACTICE EXAM: ESSAY QUESTIONS

1.   Explain what happens when a country decides to move from one point on its production possibilities curve to another. Be sure to discuss opportunity cost and the allocation of scarce resources.

2.   What advice would you give to a friend who has received two job offers, both which offer the same starting salary of $30,000 and the same benefits package. The jobs are basically the same. However, one job is located in Boston and the other job in Columbia, S.C.

VII.   ANSWER KEY: MULTIPLE CHOICE QUESTIONS

1.   Correct Answer: c.

Discussion: The bowed-out shape of the PPC reflects increasing opportunity costs (which arise because resources are not equally-well adapted to producing one good as another). Statement c is the only one that expresses that opportunity costs are increasing, i.e., that more and more of one good must be given up in order to get back the same increment (say, 1 unit) of the other good. For example, to produce 1 more motorboat may require that an economy give up producing 100 rolls of carpet; if the economy wants to produce 1 more boat, the economy now has to give up producing 125 rolls of carpet; and if the economy wants to produce yet 1 more motorboat, the economy now has to give up producing 175 rolls of carpet.

The question asks about the bowed-out shape of the PPC and so requires an answer that addresses a movement along the PPC, not to or from it. Statements a and b are incorrect because they address movements from a point not on the PPC to a point on it (or vice-versa), neither of which deals with a movement along the PPC. Statement d is incorrect because it only explains why the PPC has a negative slope, not why it has a bowed-out shape. Statement e is incorrect because answer c is correct.

2.   Correct answer: a.

Discussion: Opportunity cost is measured by how much is given up or sacrificed. In this case, the graph shows that in moving from G to H, the economy foregoes producing (reduces production by) 1 bushel of wheat. In return, however, the economy is able to produce 10 more barrels of wine.

Statement b is incorrect because it is not true that, as the economy moves along the PPC, more wheat can be obtained along with more wine. The concept of opportunity cost means that the economy can only have more wheat if it produces less wine (and vice-versa). Statement c is incorrect because increasing opportunity costs are encountered moving in both directions along the PPC. To see this, note that, as the economy moves from G to H, it must give up producing 1 bushel of wheat but gets back 10 barrels of wine. As the economy moves from H to B, it must give up 1 bushel of wheat, but this time only gets back 5 barrels of wine. That is, it is more costly to produce wine because less is gotten back in return for the same 1 bushel of wheat. Thus, opportunity costs of producing more wine are increasing as the economy moves from G to H to B. If the economy moves from B to H to G, opportunity costs will also be increasing. To see this, note that, as the economy moves from B to H, it must give up producing 5 barrels of wine, while it gets back 1 bushel of wheat. In moving from H to G, the economy must now give up 10 barrels of wine while still only getting back 1 bushel of wheat. This just means that producing wheat has become more costly (i.e., the opportunity cost has increased). Statement d is not correct. Opportunity cost is measured by how much is given up; in moving from H to B, the economy has gotten back (not given up) 5 barrels of wine. Statement e is not correct because there is an opportunity cost; the opportunity cost is 3 bushels of wheat.

3.   Correct answer: e.

Discussion: Rent is the only example of a cost that will not change with a firm's production level. That is, whether a firm produces 0, 1, or 1,000,000 skateboards, will not change the cost of the rent the firm pays for the production facility, for example.

Electricity, raw materials, telephone, and supplies are all examples of costs that will change with a firm's production level. The more a firm produces, the more electricity it will need to operate the factory, the more raw materials it will need to produce the product, the more telephone calls it will have to make to coordinate distribution and sales, and the more supplies (packaging, etc.) it will need in production.

4.   Correct Answer: c.

Discussion: An implicit cost is a cost for which a check does not have to be written. The cost of your time spent setting up the shop and monitoring it is time that you, as owner, could have spent elsewhere, perhaps working for a company. While you will be compensated for your time as shop owner through any profits the pet shop makes, you are not explicitly paid for your time, i.e., there is not a set salary or wage per hour.

Fish tanks, a computerized bookkeeping system, sales clerks, and pet food are all expenses that you must explicitly write a check for. They are explicit costs that arise from operating a pet shop.

5.   Correct answer: e.

Discussion: Statement e is correct because statements b and d are both correct. Statement b is correct because the marginal cost of not working one more hour (or of attending the workshop) is $7.75, i.e., Fred will give up $7.75 by attending the workshop. However, Fred will benefit. The marginal benefit of using that one hour to attend the workshop has a value of $25.00. In this case, the marginal benefit of attending the workshop exceeds the marginal cost of attending the workshop so Fred would be better off by attending the workshop. Statement d is also correct but for the reverse reasons. In this case, if Fred assesses the marginal benefit of the one hour of attending the workshop at $5.00, the marginal benefit exceeds the marginal cost of attending the workshop ($7.75 loss in wages from not working that one hour). Here, Fred would be better off working and not attending the workshop.

Statement a is not correct. Even though the workshop is free, it does not meann that there is no benefit to attending it. Thus, it is not correct to compare the marginal cost of attending the workshop of $7.75 to a zero benefit.   Statement c is not correct. If the marginal benefit of attending the one-hour workshop is $5.00 and the marginal cost of attending it is $7.75 (loss in wages from not working that one hour), then Fred would be better off working that one hour. Here, the marginal benefit of attending the workshop is less than the marginal cost of attending the workshop. So, the workshop should not be attended. Statements b and d are both correct; however, option (e) allows you to pick both statements so that it is the correct answer.

6.   Correct answer: c.

Discussion: Diminishing returns occur when the addition of one more input (a worker in this example) adds less to output than the previous worker. Between the third and fourth worker, output increases by 7 units but had previously increased by 15 units (from 15 to 30). Thus, diminishing returns have set in.

Statement a is incorrect. Output has increased by 10 units from hiring one more worker but diminishing returns cannot yet be inferred until you are able to make one more comparison. Statement b is incorrect because, in this case, output has increased by 15 units from hiring one more worker (2 to 3 workers) and had previously increased by 10 units. This is an example of output increasing at an *increasing* rate, not a decreasing rate as is true of diminishing returns. (See PET #4.) Statement d is not correct because the point at which diminishing returns has set in is where the rate of increase in output slows down; this happens between the third and fourth worker, not the fourth and fifth worker. While statement d does show that the addition to output is decreasing (it had been 7 units from the previous worker and is now 3), it is not the point at which diminishing returns has set in. Statement e is not correct because output actually *decreases* by hiring one more worker. That is, output goes from 40 units to 38 units (-2) by hiring one more worker. This is not an example of diminishing returns (see PET #4).

7.   Correct answer: e.

Discussion: Statements a, b, c, and d are not true.

Statement a is incorrect because diminishing returns occur because a firm CANNOT change the amount of all of the factors of production it uses. Statement b is incorrect because, if Helena found the marginal benefit to eating an ice cream cone just equal to the marginal cost, then she is as well-off (or happy) as she can be. She should neither eat one more ice cream cone nor one fewer. She is eating just the right amount. Statement c is incorrect by definition. The short run is a time period during which a firm is not able to change the level of all of the factors of production that it uses to produce output. Statement d is incorrect because the production possibilities curve is negatively sloped.

8.   Correct answer: c.

Discussion: Statement c is correct because it is the only activity that does not generate any benefits or costs to those who are not reading the comic book. That is, reading a comic book does not impose a cost or those around you, nor does it create a benefit for those around you.

Wearing perfume can generate a spillover cost to others who are allergic to perfume or are bothered by the scent. The same is true for smoking a cigarette. Picking up trash from the roadside can generate a spillover benefit to others who use the road. They get to enjoy a more picturesque roadtrip. Repainting the exterior of your house can generate a spillover benefit for your neighbors. The benefit is that they don't have to look at a rundown-looking house. Also, by keeping up the appearance of your house, you may help to keep the property values in your neighborhood from declining.

9.   Correct answer: b.

Discussion: Since your nominal income is going to grow by 8% but prices are expected to go up by 9%, then in real terms, your income will decline by 1% (8% - 9%). (See PET #5.)

Statement a is not correct. This statement assumes that you have added the two numbers. It is not correct to add the growth rate of your nominal income and the inflation rate to determine the effect on your real income. Statement c is not correct. This statement assumes that you should take the inflation rate and subtract the growth rate of the nominal variable. This is not correct; it is the other way around. Statements d and e are not correct. These statements assume that you have multiplied the numbers which is not the correct method for computing the real value of a variable.

10.   Correct answer: a.

Discussion: If you have agreed to be paid back $1,000 without interest and inflation is greater than 0%, then, in real terms, your $1,000 will be worth less than $1,000. In other words, your $1,000 will not be able to buy as much as it had the year before if inflation was greater than 0%. You should note that, in nominal terms, you are still getting back $1,000 but, in real terms, you are getting back less than $1,000.

Statement b is incorrect. If inflation is greater than 0%, then the $1,000 you are paid back will not be able to buy as much as the year before. Thus, in real terms, the money you will be paid back is less than $1,000. Statement c is not correct. In nominal terms, you will be receiving $1,000. However, in real terms, you may be getting back more or less than $1,000 depending on whether prices have fallen (deflation) or risen (inflation). Statement d is not correct because, in nominal terms, you will be getting back $1,000. Statement e is not correct because, again, you will be getting back $1,000 in nominal terms. Inflation affects how much you earn in real terms, not nominal terms.

VIII.   ANSWER KEY: ESSAY QUESTIONS

1.   When a country moves from one point on its production possibilities curve to another, it has made a decision to produce fewer units of one good (e.g., apparel) and more of another (e.g., electronics). The country faces an opportunity cost -- the opportunity cost is that the country must cut back on production of apparel goods if it wants to produce more electronics. This is because resources are scarce. In order to produce more electronics, more resources -- land, labor, capital -- will have to be devoted to the electronics industry which means that there will be fewer resources available to produce apparel goods. That is, there will be a re-allocation of resources from the apparel industry to the electronics industry. With fewer resources avaiable to the apparel industry, apparel production will contract; the opposite will happen in the electronics industry. While the movement along the production possibilities curve assumes that resources remain fully employed (and efficiently used), there may be an adjustment phase (setting up new factory floors, training apparel workers to work in the electronics industry) during which some resources may become idle.

2.   The advice I would give to my friend would be to consider the cost of living in Boston compared to that in Columbia, S.C. That is, I would have her consider the price of food, rent, clothing, etc., in the one city compared to the other in determining which job offer provides the higher "real" salary. Since Boston is known to be a very expensive city and Columbia is in the Southeast, where the cost of living is typically lower than in the Northeast, I would suggest to my friend that, in real terms, the salary offer from the company in Columbia is better than the other offer. I would suggest to my friend that, if she really wants to live in Boston, she tell the company that they will have to offer a higher nominal salary to entice her to work for them.

Take It to the Net

We invite you to visit the O'Sullivan/Sheffrin page on the Prentice Hall Web site at:

http://www.prenhall.com/osullivan/

for this chapter's World Wide Web exercise.

CHAPTER 3
MARKETS AND THE GOVERNMENT IN THE GLOBAL ECONOMY

I. OVERVIEW

In this chapter, you will learn what markets are. You will learn that markets exist because people find it easier and mutually beneficial to specialize in producing certain types of goods, and to exchange what they have produced with what others have produced, than to produce for all of their own needs. You will learn that specialization and exchange can increase the set and amount of goods and services that each participating party may ultimately acquire. You will learn about comparative advantage which is an application of the principle of opportunity cost. You will learn that comparative advantage can be used to determine which goods and services households, firms, and countries should specialize in, i.e., produce, and which they should exchange. You will learn that households, firms, the government, and foreign countries all participate in markets as both buyers and sellers. You will learn what role the government plays in a market-based economy. You will also learn of different methods the government uses to finance its activities. You will learn about the differences between a market-based economy and a centrally planned economy. You will learn that international trade may also be based on comparative advantage and that it, too, can be mutually beneficial. You will also learn about different types of trade protection and that trade protection inhibits international trade based on comparative advantage. You will learn about the foreign exchange market, what an exchange rate is, and how to convert the dollar price of a good or service to a foreign currency price, and vice-versa.

II. CHECKLIST

By the end of this chapter, you should be able to do the following:

√   Explain why specialization and exchange can benefit all participating parties.
√   Determine comparative advantage by comparing opportunity costs of production.
√   List the different markets of exchange and explain in which market who is doing the buying and who is doing the selling.
√   Explain the roles government plays in a market-based economy.
√   List different methods of taxation and define what they are.
√   List different types of trade protection and define what they are.
√   Define an exchange rate and use it to convert the dollar price of a good or service to a foreign currency price, and vice-versa.

III. KEY TERMS

Absolute advantage: the ability of one person or nation to produce a particular good at a lower absolute cost than another person or nation.
Comparative advantage: the ability of one person or nation to produce a good at an opportunity cost that is lower than the opportunity cost of another person or nation.
Market system: a system under which individuals and firms use markets to facilitate the exchange of money and products.

25

Benefit-tax approach: the idea a person's tax liability should depend on how much he or she benefits from government programs.

Horizontal equity: the notion that people in similar economic circumstances should pay similar taxes.

Vertical equity: the notion that people with higher income or wealth should pay higher taxes.

Mixed economy: an economic system under which government plays an important role, including the regulation of markets, where most economic decisions are made.

Centrally planned economy: an economy in which a government bureaucracy decides how much of each good to produce, how to produce the goods, and how to allocate the products among consumers.

Transition: the process of shifting from a centrally planned economy toward a mixed economic system, with markets playing a greater role in the economy.

Privatizing: the process of selling state firms to individuals.

Export: a good produced in the "home" country (for example, the U.S.) and sold in another country.

Import: a good produced in a foreign Country And purchased by residents of the "home" country (for example, the U.S.).

Multinational corporation: an organization that produces and sells goods and services throughout the world.

Worldwide sourcing: the practice of buying components for a product from nations throughout the world.

Barriers to trade: rules that restricts the free flow of goods between nations, including **tariffs** (taxes on imports), **quotas** (limits on total imports), **voluntary export restraints** (agreements between governments to limit imports), and **nontariff trade barriers** (subtle practices that hinder trade).

General Agreement on Tariffs and Trade (GATT): an international agreement that has lowered trade barriers between the U.S. and other nations.

World Trade Organization (WTO): the new organization that oversees GATT and other international trade agreements.

North American Free Trade Agreement (NAFTA): an international agreement that lowers barriers to trade between the United States, Mexico, and Canada (signed in 1994).

European Union: an organization of European nations that has reduced trade barriers within Europe.

Exchange rate: the price at which currencies trade for one another.

Foreign exchange market: a market in which people to exchange one currency for another.

IV.   PERFORMANCE ENHANCING TIPS (PETS)

<u>PET #1</u>

Opportunity cost calculations used to determine comparative advantage should be based on a per unit comparison.

Suppose you are given the following information:

	Country A	Country B
Wood products	10/hour	8/hour
High-tech products	15/hour	4/hour

The information in the table tells you that Country A can produce 10 units of wood products in one hour (with its resources) and 15 units of high-tech products in one hour.   Country B can produce 8 units of wood products in one hour (with its resources) and 4 units of high-tech products in one hour.   How can this information be used to determine which country has a comparative advantage in wood production and which country has a comparative advantage in high-tech production?

As a side point, you may wish to note that Country A has an absolute advantage in the production of both wood and high-tech products since it can produce more per hour of either good than can Country B. But, absolute advantage does NOT determine the basis for trade.

The easiest way to compute comparative advantage is to determine what the opportunity cost of production is for each good for each country, on a per unit basis. To do this, you must first answer how much Country A must give up if it were to specialize in the production of wood. For every additional hour of effort devoted to producing wood products, Country A would give up the production of 15 units of high-tech products. (Of course, it is then able to produce 10 more units of wood products.) On a per unit basis, Country A must give up 1.5 units of high-tech products for each 1 unit of wood products = (15 high-tech products/hour)/(10 wood products/hour) = 1.5 high-tech products/1 wood product. You would read this as "for Country A, the opportunity cost of 1 wood product is 1.5 high-tech products." For Country B, for every additional hour of effort devoted to producing wood products, it must give up 4 units of high-tech products. (Of course, it is then able to produce 8 more units of wood products.) On a per unit basis, Country B must give up 0.5 units of high-tech products for each 1 unit of wood products = (4 high-tech products/hour)/(8 wood products/hour). You would read this as "for Country B, the opportunity cost of 1 wood product is 0.5 high-tech products." Thus, Country B has the lower opportunity cost of producing wood products since it has to give up fewer high-tech products.

Since Country B has the lower opportunity cost of wood production, it should specialize in wood production. (Wood production is "less costly" in Country B than in Country A.) If this is true, then it must also be true that Country A has the lower opportunity cost of high-tech production and, thus, should specialize in producing high-tech goods.

Let's see if this is true using the numbers from the table above. For Country A, the opportunity cost of producing more high-tech products is that, for every additional hour of producing high-tech products, it must give up producing 10 units of wood products. (Of course, it is then able to produce 15 more units of high-tech products.) On a per unit basis, Country A must give up 0.67 wood products for every 1 high-tech product = (10 wood products/hour)/(15 high-tech products per hour). You would read this as "for Country A, the opportunity cost of 1 high-tech product is 0.67 wood products." For Country B, the opportunity cost of producing more high-tech products is that, for every additional hour of producing high-tech products, it must give up producing 8 units of wood products. (Of course, it is then able to produce 4 more units of high-tech products.) On a per unit basis, Country B must give up 2 wood products for every one unit of high-tech products = (8 wood products/hour)/(4 high-tech products/hour). Thus, Country A has the lower opportunity cost of producing high-tech products since it has to give up fewer wood products. (High-tech production is "less costly" in Country A than in Country B.)

PET #2

Household savings helps to fund firms' purchases of machinery, buildings, equipment, and technology (physical capital).

This performance enhancing tip may not be especially useful in this chapter, but when you get to the chapters on Macroeconomics, it will be important to remember.

PET #3

If a government spends more for its programs than it collects in taxes, it finances its overspending by borrowing money from households, firms, and foreign countries. The government borrows by selling securities (bonds or IOUs) to households, firms, and foreign countries who in turn lend their saving to the government. The government, of course, promises to pay back the lenders with interest.

PET #4

Trade protection increases the price a country pays for goods it imports from other countries.

Your textbook mentions different types of trade protection -- tariffs, quotas, and nontariff barriers, all of which act to raise the price of the goods and services that a country imports from other countries.

PET #5

The exchange rate is the price of one currency in terms of another. It can be thought of just like the price of any good or service.

Think about the price of any good or service, say a painting priced at $200, i.e., $200/painting. The item in the denominator is what is being priced. So too for an exchange rate. Suppose the exchange rate is expressed as 0.50 U.S. dollars/1 German mark. In this case, the currency that is being priced is the mark. Its price is 50 cents. The inverse of this exchange rate would be 2 German marks/$1 U.S. dollar. Now, the currency that is being priced is the dollar. One dollar is priced at (or costs) 2 German marks.

If the price of a painting rises, we would say the painting has appreciated in value. If the price of a painting falls, we would say the painting has depreciated in value. So too for an exchange rate. If the exchange rate decreased from 0.50 U.S. dollars/1 German mark to 0.40 U.S. dollars/1 German mark, we would say that the mark has depreciated since it now worth 40 cents instead of 50 cents. If the German mark has depreciated against the dollar, then it must be true that the U.S. dollar has appreciated. To see this, the inverse of 0.40 US dollars/1 German mark is 2.5 German marks/1 U.S. dollar. Thus, the dollar has appreciated in value since it is now worth 2.5 marks instead of 2 marks.

V.   PRACTICE EXAM: MULTIPLE CHOICE QUESTIONS

1.   Which one of the following is true of a corporation?

a.   it is owned by a single individual.
b.   it is owned by two or more partners.
c.   it is owned by stockholders.
d.   it is held in trust.
e.   it is owned by a bank.

2.   Which one of the following statements is **NOT** true for the United States?

a.   70% of all firms are proprietorships.
b.   the major sources of tax revenue for the federal government are corporate income taxes.

c.   three-fourths (75%) of income earned by households comes from wages and salaries.
d.   one of the three biggest spending programs for states is education.
e.   the two biggest federal government spending programs are income security and national defense.

3.   Which one of the following is **NOT** a role of the government?

a.   redistributing income from richer households to poorer households.
b.   providing national defense, parks, and public safety, among other things.
c.   regulating businesses.
d.   making international trade policy.
e.   all of the above are roles of the government.

4.   Under a vertically equitable tax system:

a.   every household would pay the same dollar amount of taxes. For example, every household would be required to pay $2,500.
b.   every household would pay the same percentage of their income in taxes. For example, every household would be required to pay 15% of their income in taxes.
c.   wealthier households would pay a higher percentage of their incomes in taxes. For example, wealthier households would be required to pay 35% of their income in taxes whereas poorer households would pay 10% of their income in taxes.
d.   every household would pay taxes based on the amount of government services they used over a year.
e.   every household would pay taxes based on a three-year average of their income.

5.   Suppose a state has in place a 5% sales tax. Further, suppose for that year, businesses throughout the state have collectively made $100,000,000 (100 million) in sales. How much in sales tax revenues will be collected by the government?

a. $50,000,000.
b. $5,000,000.
c. $500,000.
d. $50,000.
e. $500,000,000.

6.   The U.S. economy is referred to as a(n):

a.   laissez-faire economy.
b.   centrally planned economy.
c.   equitable economy.
d.   mixed economy.
e.   de facto economy.

7.   Use the table below to answer the following question.

	Country A	Country B
Toys	50 per day	20 per day
Ships	2 per day	1 per day

Which country has the comparative advantage in producing toys, and which country has the comparative advantage in producing ships?

a.   Country A has the comparative advantage in producing both toys and ships.
b.   Country B has the comparative advantage in producing both toys and ships.
c.   Country A has the comparative advantage in producing toys and Country B has the comparative advantage in producing ships.
d.   Country B has the comparative advantage in producing toys and Country A has the comparative advantage in producing ships.
e.   Need information on exchange rates to answer the question.

8.   Which one of the following is **NOT** an example of a trade barrier?

a.   tariffs.
b.   quotas.
c.   health and safety laws.
d.   the General Agreement on Tariffs and Trade.
e.   slow and inefficient customs systems.

9.   Which one of the following statements is correct?

a.   The top three trading partners of the U.S. are Australia, Canada, and Poland.
b.   NAFTA is a free-trade agreement between Canada, Mexico, and the United States.
c.   The countries of the European Union plan on joining the governments of all of the participating countries into one federal government.
d.   The Smoot-Hawley Tariff Act raised the average tariff in the U.S. by 150%.
e.   all of the above are correct statements.

10.   Suppose that you are going to buy a cuckoo clock from Germany and the German mark price for the clock is 250 marks. If the current exchange rate is 2 marks/U.S. dollar, you will pay $_____. If the exchange rate changes to 1.8 marks/U.S. dollar, the _____ will have depreciated.

a. $125; dollar.
b. $125; mark.
c. $500; dollar.
d. $500; mark.
e. $250; dollar.

VI.   PRACTICE EXAM: ESSAY QUESTIONS

1.   What purposes do taxes serve, what types of taxes are there, and what effects do taxes have on people's behavior?

2.   What roles does a government play in a mixed economy?

VII.   ANSWER KEY: MULTIPLE CHOICE QUESTIONS

1.   Correct answer: c.

Discussion: A corporation is owned by those individuals who have purchased stock in the corporation. They are the stockholders, and they effectively own the company. Stockholders are paid dividends on the shares of stock they own. This is sort of like earning interest, except that dividend payments do not necessarily offer the same yield every quarter or every year as would be typical with an investment in an interest-bearing asset.

Statement a would be true if the question was about a sole proprietorship. Statement b would be true if the question was about a partnerhsip. Statement d is an irrelevant concept. Statement e is incorrect because a corporation is owned by stockholders, not a bank.

2.   Correct answer: b.

Discussion: Statement b is not true. The major sources of tax revenues for the federal government are personal income and payroll taxes.

Statements, a, c, d, and e are all true for the U.S.

3.   Correct answer: e.

Discussion: All of the above statements are listed in your textbook as roles of the government. The book includes one more role which is the role of taxing.

Statements a, b, c, and d are all true statements.

4.   Correct answer: c.

Discussion: A vertically equitable tax system (sometimes called a "progressive" tax system) is one in which the wealthier citizens pay a higher percentage of income in taxes than do the poorer citizens. This type of tax system reduces to some extent the differences in income between the citizens of a country.

Statement a is an example of a tax system in which every household is assessed a lump-sum fee that they must pay regardless of their income or family size. Statement b is an example of a horizontally equitable tax system (sometimes referred to as a flat tax). Statement d is an example that applies the benefit-tax approach to assessing taxes. Statement e computes taxes paid by an individual based on the last three years' worth of income.

5.   Correct Answer: b.

Discussion: To compute the amount collected in sales tax revenues, multiply 100,000,000 times (5/100) or (0.05). This equals $5,000,000.

Statement a would be correct if the sales tax rate was 50%. Statement c would be correct if the sales tax rate was 0.5% (or a half percent). Statement d would be correct if the sales tax rate was 0.05%. Statement e would be correct if the sales tax rate was 500%.

6.   Correct answer: d.

Discussion: The U.S. economy is a mixed economy because production and consumption decisions are carried out largely by the private sector with the government playing a smaller role.

Statement a is not correct because a laissez-faire economy is one in which the government plays no role at all. Statement b is not correct because a centrally planned economy is one in which the government makes the production and consumption decisions for the economy. Statement c and e are not correct -- they are made-up terms.

7.   Correct answer: c.

Discussion: Country A must give up 50 toys to produce 2 ships. On a per unit basis, Country A must give up 25 toys to produce 1 ship. On the other hand, Country B must give up 20 toys to produce 1 ship. Since Country B has to give up fewer toys to produce 1 ship, Country B incurs a smaller opportunity cost of building one more ship. That is, it is less costly to produce a ship in Country B than in Country A. So, Country B should produce ships, which means Country A should produce toys. The two countries will be able to acquire more of both goods by trading or exchanging toys for ships and vice-versa.

Statement a is not correct. It would be correct if the question had been "which country has an absolute advantage in toy production and which in ship production?" The table shows that Country A can produce more toys and more ships per day than can Country B. However, this is not the concept of comparative advantage. Statement b is not correct for similar reasons just mentioned. Statement d is not correct because it is the other way around -- Country A has a comparative advantage in toy production and Country B in ship building. Statement e is not correct because comparative advantage can be computed using the table of numbers given.

8.   Correct answer: d.

Discussion: The General Agreement on Tariffs and Trade (GATT) is an agreement between countries to work together to reduce tariff rates amongst themselves.

A tariff is a tax on an imported good which raises the price that a country must pay to buy it from another country. This acts as a trade barrier. A quota is a restriction on the quantity of imports of a particular good that a country may purchase from another country. It is also a trade barrier and acts to raise the price of the imported good. Health and safety laws are nontariff trade barriers. These laws may effectively make it more difficult for a country to import a product from another country. For example, the health and safety laws of European countries restrict them from importing hormone-fed beef. This meant that they could not buy hormone-fed beef from the U.S. Slow and inefficient customs laws also act as a trade barrier. For example, if a product must pass through several layers of administration and paperwork before being admitted into the importing country, this raises the cost of the good and, thus, its price. This effectively makes it harder and more expensive for the importing country to buy the good and more of a hassle for the exporting country to deliver its products to another country.

9.   Correct answer: b.

Discussion: NAFTA is the North American Free Trade Agreement. It is an agreement to eliminate all tariffs and trade barriers between the U.S., Canada, and Mexico.

Statement a is incorrect because the top three trading partners of the U.S. are Canada, Mexico, and Japan. Statement c is incorrect; the countries of the European Union are planning on having completely free trade and a single currency. Statement d is incorrect because the Smoot-Hawley Tariff Act raises tariffs an average of 59%. Statement e is not correct because not all of the statements are true.

10.   Correct answer: a.

Discussion: To figure out the dollar price of the clock, the mark price must be converted to dollars using the exchange rate. Since the exchange rate is expressed as marks/dollar, you can determine the dollar price by multiplying 250 marks X (1 dollar/2 marks) = $125. (The marks in the numerator and denominator cancel each other out.) Since the exchange rate is expressed as marks/dollar, it is best to think of the exchange rate as the price of a dollar. Since the exchange rate has changed from 2 marks/dollar to 1.8 marks/dollar, the price of a dollar has decreased (See PET #5), i.e., the dollar has depreciated (which also means that the mark must have appreciated).

Statement b is not correct because the mark appreciated, not depreciated. Statement c is not correct because the conversion of the mark price of the clock to a dollar price leads to a price of $125, not $500. Statement d is not correct for the reasons mentioned for b and c. Statement e is not correct because the dollar price of the clock is $125, not $250.

VIII.   ANSWER KEY: ESSAY QUESTIONS

1.   Taxes serve the purpose of paying for goods and services that a society may collectively want to have but which may be too expensive to pay for on an individual basis. By pooling money collected from households and corporations across the country, goods like national defense, highways and bridges, prisons, national parks, school buildings, etc., may be easier to pay for. Taxes also serve a purpose of funding the poorer segments of society or those who have fallen on hard times. For example, your tax dollars may be used to fund unemployment compensation, drug rehabilitation, health care, etc. So, your tax dollars not only pay for goods and services from which you might directly benefit but also pay for goods and services which you may or may not ever use. There are three basic types of taxes: taxes on households/workers, taxes on corporations, and excise taxes which are taxes on specific goods like gasoline, cigarettes, and imported goods. Households/workers pay personal income taxes, social security taxes, payroll taxes, sales taxes, and property taxes, to name a few. Corporations pay corporate income taxes, payroll taxes, sales taxes, and property taxes as well, to name a few. Households and corporations, to the extent that they purchase goods that have an excise tax levied on them, also pay taxes to the government. Taxes can distort people's behavior by altering the actual price that they pay for a good or service or for providing a good or service. A higher personal income tax rate may cause people to spend less and/or save more. A tax on gasoline may cause people to use gasoline more frugally. A tax on air travel may cause people to be less likely to fly to get somewhere. A city property tax may cause fewer people to want to live in the city. A tax on paper may cause a publishing company to be more likely to produce electronic versions of their product than paper versions.

2.   A government plays several roles in a mixed economy. It provides goods and services like parks, public safety, consumer information, museums, etc., to its citizens.   A government also redistributes income from richer citizens to poorer citizens. This is done in the interest of creating a more equitable distribution of income. In order for the government to be able to provide goods and services and transfer income from richer citizens to poorer citizens, it must collect taxes. A government also regulates business practices for different reasons. A government may regulate an industry to ensure that it doesn't impose undue hazards on its citizens (nuclear fuel); a government may regulate an industry to ensure that its citizens aren't charged an unfair price for the product (utilities or cable industry); or a government may regulate industries to ensure that its citizens are not being sold unsafe products (automobiles, food, medicine). Finally, a government enacts trade policy. A government may set the rules of the game that are used between countries that engage in trading goods and services with each other. It should also be mentioned that a government establishes a legal system to assign and enforce property rights. This makes it easier for consumers and businesses to interact.

Take It to the Net

We invite you to visit the O'Sullivan/Sheffrin page on the Prentice Hall Web site at:

http://www.prenhall.com/osullivan/

for this chapter's World Wide Web exercise.

CHAPTER 4
SUPPLY, DEMAND, AND MARKET EQUILIBRIUM

I.   OVERVIEW

In this chapter, you will learn about two basic economic constructs: demand and supply. These two constructs can be used to answer questions like: what might happen to housing prices in a subdivision if a new mall is built near the subdivision? what might happen to the price of a share of a health services company when the government revamps the health care system? what might happen to the price of bread when former Soviet-bloc countries begin to trade with the U.S.? what might happen to the price of tea when the price of coffee rises? Not only can demand and supply be used to guide your thinking about what will happen to prices, it can also be used to guide your thinking about whether more or less will be bought and sold. In this chapter, you will learn how to use graphs of demand and supply to determine what happens to a market price and the quantity bought and sold. Thus, in this chapter it is imperative that you familiarize yourself with shifts of a curve versus movements along a curve (see Chapter 1 of Practicum).

II.   CHECKLIST

By the end of this chapter, you should be able to do the following:

√   Explain the Law of Demand and the Law of Supply (for both price increases and price decreases).
√   Understand what will cause a movement along a demand or supply curve and what will cause the curves to shift.
√   Explain what happens to equilibrium price and equilibrium quantity when:

> demand increases (shifts right)
> demand decreases (shifts left)
> supply increases (shifts right)
> supply decreases (shifts left)

√   Explain whether you can determine for certain what happens to equilibrium price and equilibrium quantity when demand and/or supply both shift.
√   List factors that will cause demand to shift (and in which direction).
√   List factors that will cause supply to shift (and in which direction).
√   Explain what causes a shortage and what causes a surplus and be able to depict them with a supply and demand graph.

III.   KEY TERMS

Perfectly competitive market: a market with a very large number of firms, each of which produces the same standardized product and is so small that it does not affect the market price of the good it produces.
Demand curve: a curve showing the relationship between price and the quantity that consumers are willing to buy during a particular time period.
Law of demand: the lower the price, the larger the quantity demanded.
Substitution Effect: The change in consumption resulting from a change in the price of one good relative to the price of other goods.

Income Effect: The change in consumption resulting from an increase in the consumer's real income.

Normal good: a good for which an increase in income *increases* demand.

Inferior good: a good for which an increase in income *decreases* demand.

Market equilibrium: a situation in which the quantity of a product demanded equals the quantity supplied, so there is no pressure to change the price.

Change in quantity demanded: a change in quantity resulting from a change in the price of the good; causes movement along a demand curve.

Change in demand: a change in quantity resulting from a change in something other than the price of the good; causes the entire demand curve to shift.

Substitutes: two goods for which an increase in the price of one good increases the demand for the other good.

Complements: two goods for which an increase in the price of one good decreases the demand for the other good.

Supply curve: a curve showing the relationship between price and the quantity that producers are willing to sell during a particular time period.

Law of supply: the higher the price, the larger the quantity supplied.

Change in quantity supplied: a change in quantity resulting from a change in the price of the good; causes movement along a supply curve.

Change in supply: a change in quantity resulting from a change in something other than the price of the good; causes the entire supply curve to shift.

Shortage: a situation in which consumers are willing to buy more than producers are willing to sell.

Surplus: a situation in which producers are willing to sell more than consumers are willing to buy.

IV.   PERFORMANCE ENHANCING TIPS (PETS)

PET #1

Since price is a variable on the axis of a graph of the demand and supply of a particular good, a change in the price will NOT cause the demand or supply curve for that good to shift but will instead be represented by a movement along the demand and supply curves.

Remember from Chapter 1 of the Practicum that in a graph of Y and X, where Y and X are drawn on either axis, changes in Y or X will not cause the curve(s) to shift but instead cause movements along the curve. It may be wise to review practice question 8 and PET #1 from Chapter 1 to reinforce your memory of this principle.

PET #2

*When the price of good X rises (falls), the **quantity demanded** falls (rises). Do NOT say that the demand falls (rises) since this means the whole curve shifts left (right).*

For example, suppose you read on the exam a statement that says, "What happens in the market for peanut butter when the price of peanut butter falls?" One of the test options might be "the demand for peanut butter increases." This is not the correct answer. A statement like "the demand for peanut butter increases" would be represented by shifting the whole demand curve out to the right. However, since the price of peanut butter has fallen and is a variable on the axis for which the demand and supply of peanut butter are drawn, the decline in the price of peanut butter will be represented by moving along the demand curve. As the price of peanut butter falls, the *quantity of peanut butter demanded* increases. This would be the correct answer.

PET #3

*When the price of good X rises (falls), the **quantity supplied** rises (falls). Do NOT say that the supply rises (falls) since this means the whole supply curve shifts right (left).*

For example, suppose you read on the exam a statement that says, "What happens in the market for jelly when the price of jelly falls?" One of the test options might be "the supply of jelly decreases." This is not the correct answer. A statement like "the supply of jelly decreases" would be represented by shifting the whole supply curve to the left. However, since the price of jelly has fallen and is a variable on the axis for which the demand and supply of jelly are drawn, the decline in the price of jelly will be represented by moving along the supply curve. As the price of jelly falls, the *quantity of jelly supplied* decreases. This would be the correct answer.

PET #4

A rightward shift in the demand curve can be expressed in the following ways:

    (a)   at every price, the quantity demanded that buyers want is now higher.
    (b)   at every quantity demanded, the price buyers would be willing to pay is now higher.

To see this, look at the two graphs below. Demand curve (a) corresponds to statement (a) because, at every price, the quantity demand is now higher. Demand curve (b) corresponds to statement (b) because, at every quantity demanded, the price buyers would be willing to pay is now higher. In both cases, the demand curve is further to the right after the shift than before.

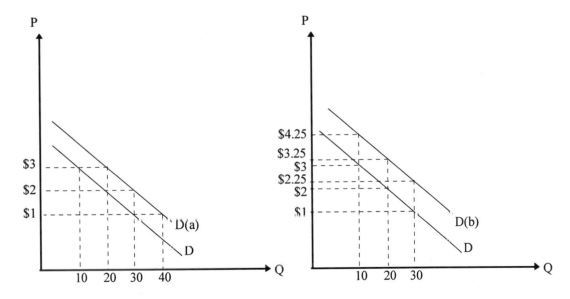

You should be able to rewrite statements (a) and (b) for a leftward shift in demand.

PET #5

A rightward shift in the supply curve can be expressed in the following ways:

(a)   at every price, the quantity that producers are willing to supply is now higher.

(b)   at every quantity supplied, the price at which producers would be willing to sell is now lower.

To see this, look at the two graphs below. Supply curve (a) corresponds to statement (a) and supply curve (b) corresponds to statement (b). In both cases, the supply curve is further to the right after the shift than before.

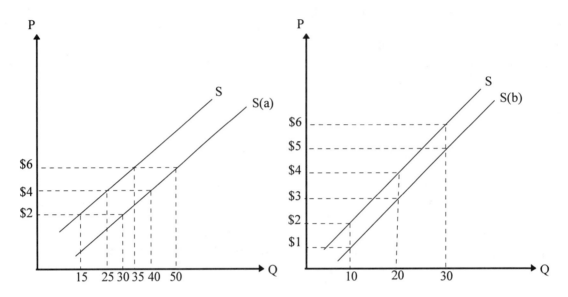

You should be able to rewrite statements (a) and (b) for a leftward shift in supply.

PET #6

Factors other than a change in the price of good X may cause the demand and/or supply curves to shift to the right or left. These factors can be remembered with the simple mnemonic: P.I.N.T.E.O.

	For Demand	**For Supply**
P -	prices of related goods	prices of related goods
I -	income	input prices
N -	number of buyers (population)	number of producers
T -	tastes	technology
E -	expectations	expectations
O -	other (advertising, fads, etc.)	other (weather, strikes, taxes on producers, etc.)

While this mnemonic should help you if basic logic fails you during an exam (perhaps due to exam-induced stress), you should not simply memorize these lists. They should make sense to you. So, for example, if there is a technological improvement in producing computer chips, it should make sense that the technological improvement makes production of chips more efficient and less costly, which you would represent by shifting the supply curve for computer chips to the right. That is, supply increases.

Likewise, it should make sense to you that, when the price of peanut butter goes up, the demand for jelly (a complement) will decrease, which you would represent by shifting the demand curve for jelly to the left. You should work through different examples of each to ensure that your logic is correct.

PET #7

When you are asked to consider the effects of a shift in demand together with a shift in supply, you should first consider the directional effects on price and quantity of each shift individually. Then, you should assess whether the shifts move price in opposite directions and whether the shift moves quantity in opposite directions. If the shifts do, you will be unable to determine (without further information) the ultimate effect on price and quantity.

To see why this is so, look at the table below and read the discussion following it. You may want to draw a graph of each shift listed below to assure yourself that the table is correct.

Shift	Effect on Price	Effect on Quantity
Demand increases (shifts right)	Price rises	Quantity rises
Demand decreases (shifts left)	Price falls	Quantity falls
Supply increases (shifts right)	Price falls	Quantity rises
Supply decreases (shifts left)	Price rises	Quantity falls

Suppose you are given a test question that asks what happens in the market for bicycles when rollerblading becomes the rage and when the price of aluminum used in making bicycles increases.

First, you must categorize the rollerblading rage as one of the four shift factors above and the increased price of aluminum as one of the four shift factors above. The rollerblading rage would be categorized as a leftward shift in the demand for *bicycles* and the increased price of aluminum as a leftward shift in the supply of bicycles. Since rollerblading and bicycling are substitutes, the increased rollerblading rage might decrease the demand for bicycles (leftward shift) which, is to say that, at every price, the quantity demanded would now be lower. Since aluminum is an input into bicycles, the increased price of aluminum makes bicycle production more costly which is to say that, at every quantity supplied, the price that producers would be willing to accept would be higher (to cover their costs). That is, the supply of bicycles decreases (shifts left).

Now, the decrease in demand for bicycles will lower the equilibrium price and quantity of bicycles. The decrease in the supply of bicycles will raise the equilibrium price and lower the equilibrium quantity of bicycles. In this case, the two shifts move price in the opposite direction but have the same directional effect on the equilibrium quantity. Therefore, you can only answer for sure what happens to the equilibrium quantity. (It falls.) If you knew the magnitudes of the shifts in demand and supply, you would be able to answer what happens to the equilibrium price.

V.   PRACTICE EXAM: MULTIPLE CHOICE QUESTIONS

1.   Which one of the following statements is correct about the Law of Demand?

a. as the price of oranges decreases, the demand for oranges increases.
b. as the price of oranges increases, the demand for oranges increases.
c. as the price of oranges decreases, the quantity of oranges demanded increases.
d. as the price of oranges increases, the quantity of oranges demanded increases.
e. as the price of oranges decreases, the demand for oranges shifts left.

2. Consider the market for flavored mineral water. If the price of soda (a substitute for flavored mineral water) increases, which one of the following might be an outcome?

a. the demand for soda will decrease.
b. the demand for mineral water will increase (shift right).
c. the price of mineral water will fall.
d. the equilibrium quantity of mineral water will fall.
e. (b) and (c).

3. Which one of the following statements is correct about the Law of Supply?

a. as the price of dogbones decreases, the supply of dogbones increases.
b. as the price of dogbones increases, the supply of dogbones increases.
c. as the price of dogbones decreases, the quantity of dogbones supplied decreases.
d. as the price of dogbones increases, the quantity of dogbones supplied decreases.
e. as the price of dogbones increases, the supply of dogbones shifts right.

4. Consider the market for mattresses. If the price of foam used in making mattresses declines, which one of the following might be an outcome?

a. the supply of mattresses will increase (shift right).
b. the demand for mattresses will increase.
c. the price of mattresses will rise.
d. there will be a shortage of mattresses.
e. (a) and (b).

5. Which one of the following would **NOT** cause the supply of bananas to decrease?

a. a technological advance in banana production.
b. a decrease in the number of producers of bananas.
c. an increase in the price of a fertilizer used in growing bananas.
d. a severe rain shortage.
e. a tax placed on banana producers.

6. Which one of the following would **NOT** cause the demand for walking shoes to increase?

a. an advertising campaign that says walking is good for your health.
b. an increase in income.
c. a decrease in the price of rubber used in producing walking shoes.
d. an increased preference for walking rather than running.
e. all of the above will cause the demand for walking shoes to increase.

7.   Consider the market for chocolate candy. What is the effect on the equilibrium price and equilibrium quantity of a decrease in demand for and an increase in the supply of chocolate candy?

a.   equilibrium price rises; equilibrium quantity falls.
b.   equilibrium price falls; equilibrium quantity rises.
c.   equilibrium price = ?; equilibrium quantity falls.
d.   equilibrium price rises; equilibrium quantity rises.
e.   equilibrium price falls; equilibrium quantity = ?.

8.   Use the graph below to answer the following question.

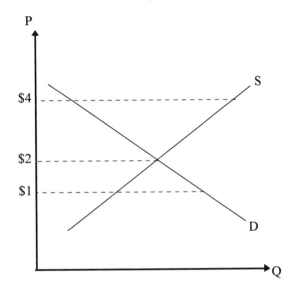

Which one of the following statements is true about the graph?

a.   there is a shortage at a price of $4.
b.   there is a surplus at a price of $4.
c.   at a current price of $1, there is pressure for the equilibrium price to fall.
d.   if the price fell from $4 to $2, quantity supplied would increase.
e.   if the price fell from $4 to $2, demand would shift right.

9.   Pretend that you are an economic detective and are given the following clues about the market for wine: the price of wine rose and the equilibrium quantity of wine declined. In writing your investigative report, which one of the following would you conclude might be responsible for the outcome?

a.   a decrease in the demand for wine.
b.   a decrease in the supply of wine.
c.   an increase in the demand for wine.
d.   an increase in the supply of wine.
e.   a decrease in the demand for wine and an increase in the supply of wine.

10.   The U.S. imports a lot of cars from Japan. Suppose that the price of steel that Japan uses in making cars declines. What effect might this have in the U.S. market for cars?

a.   the supply of Japanese-made cars to the U.S. will decrease.
b.   the price of Japanese-made cars sold in the U.S. will decrease.
c.   the price of Japanese-made cars sold in the U.S. will increase.
d.   the demand for Japanese-made cars will increase.
e.   the quantity of Japanese-made cars sold in the U.S. will decrease.

11.   Which one of the following statements would be true of an increase in demand for cameras?

a.   equilibrium price rises and the supply of cameras increases.
b.   equilibrium price rises and the supply of cameras decreases.
c.   equilibrium price falls and the quantity of cameras supplied decreases.
d.   equilibrium price rises and the quantity of cameras supplied increases.
e.   equilibrium price falls and the supply of cameras falls.

VI.   PRACTICE EXAM: ESSAY QUESTIONS

1.   Consider the market for athletic wear. Describe what happens to demand, supply, quantity demanded, quantity supplied, equilibrium price and equilibrium quantity when the price of spandex used in making athletic wear rises and at the same time a fitness craze sweeps the country, thanks in part, to Richard Simmons. Do not simply draw graphs. Write in complete sentences as you describe what happens.

2.   Consider the market for American-made cheese. Suppose that the current equilibrium price is $1 per pound. Suppose that the French develop a preference for American-made cheese. Describe what would be true in the market if, after this development, the price remained at $1. Would this be an equilibrium price? Why or why not? What would eventually happen in the market for American-made cheese?

VII.   ANSWER KEY: MULTIPLE CHOICE QUESTIONS

1.   Correct Answer: c.

Discussion: The law of demand expresses an inverse or negative relationship between the price of a good and the quantity demanded (holding other factors constant). Thus, when the price of X rises, the quantity of X demanded falls and when the price of X falls, the quantity of X demanded rises.

Statement a is incorrect because demand does not increase (which would be represented by the demand curve shifting right). The law of demand is about a movement along a demand curve, not a shift in the curve. Statement b and e are incorrect for similar reasons. Statement d is incorrect because it infers a positive relationship between price and quantity demanded.

2.   Correct answer: b.

Discussion: Since mineral water and soda are substitutes, when the price of soda rises, consumers may switch to buying mineral water instead. Thus, the demand for mineral water increases, represented by a rightward shift in demand.

Statement a is incorrect because the price of soda is not a shift factor in the market for soda; a fall in the price of soda causes a movement along the demand curve for soda and, thus, causes the quantity of soda demanded (not the Demand) to decrease. Statement c is not correct because when the demand for mineral water increases, the price of mineral water will rise. Statement d is not correct because when the demand for mineral water increases, the equilibrium quantity will rise. Statement e is not correct because statement a is not correct.

3.   Correct answer: c.

Discussion: The Law of Supply states that there is a positive relationship between the price of X and the quantity of X supplied, holding other factors constant. This means that, when the price of X increases, the quantity of X supplied increases and when the price of X decreases, the quantity of X supplied decreases. Statement c describes a positive relationship between the price of dogbones and the quantity of dogbones supplied.

Statements a, b, and e are incorrect because a change in the price of dogbones will not cause the supply curve to shift in either direction but rather cause a movement along the supply curve (quantity supplied changes).   Statement d is not correct because there is a positive relationship between the price and quantity supplied, not a negative relationship as implied in statement d.

4.   Correct answer: a.

Discussion: Foam is an input into mattresses. When the price of foam decreases, it makes mattress production less costly. This would be represented by shifting the supply of mattresses to the right, i.e., supply increasing.

Statement b is not correct because the price of foam will not shift the demand for mattresses. What will happen, however, is that, as the supply of mattresses increases, which will cause the price of mattresses to fall, the quantity of mattresses demanded will rise in response. Thus, b would have been correct if it had said "quantity demanded." Statement c is not correct because an increase in the supply of mattresses caused by the decrease in the price of foam will decrease the price of mattresses. Statement d is not correct because there is no reason given to think a shortage would occur. Statement e is not correct because statement b is not correct.

5.   Correct answer: a.

Discussion: A technological advance in banana production would increase the supply of bananas, not decrease it.

Statements b, c, d, and e are all factors that would cause the supply of bananas to decrease. A decrease in the number of producers would obviously reduce the supply of bananas. An increase in the price of fertilizer raises the cost of producing bananas and would be represented by a leftward shift in supply, i.e., supply decreases. A severe rain shortage would obviously reduce the banana crop and, thus, decrease the supply of bananas. A tax on banana growers has the effect of raising the cost of doing business. This acts just like an increase in the price of fertilizer, i.e., the supply of bananas would shift left (decrease).

6.   Correct answer: c.

Discussion: A decrease in the price of rubber used in producing walking shoes will lower the cost of producing walking shoes and cause the supply of walking shoes to increase, not the demand. However, quantity demanded would rise since the lower cost of production would translate to a lower price of walking shoes which would raise the quantity of walking shoes demanded (movement along the demand curve).

Statements a, b, and d would lead to an increase in the demand for walking shoes. However, it may be worth noting that, if walking shoes are considered inferior goods, then an increase in income would actually reduce the demand for walking shoes. Statement e is not correct because statement c should have been selected.

7.   Correct answer: e.

Discussion: A decrease in demand for chocolate candy will lower the equilibrium price and lower the equilibrium quantity. An increase in the supply of chocolate candy will lower the equilibrium price and raise the equilibrium quantity. You can see these two cases by drawing graphs of them, separately. Since the demand and supply shifts only push the price in the same direction, price will decline for sure. However, the demand and supply shifts push the equilibrium quantity in opposite directions, so the effect is not known for certain.

8.   Correct answer: b.

At a price of $4, the quantity supplied exceeds the quantity demanded which is the case of a surplus. Just take the price of $4 and draw a line over to the demand and supply curves and then drop those points down to the quantity axis. You will see that the quantity supplied exceeds the quantity demanded.

Discussion: Statement a is not correct because there is not a shortage but rather a surplus. Statement c is not correct because there would be pressure for the price to rise to the equilibrium price of $2. In fact, at a price of $1, there is a shortage. Statement d is not correct because, if the price fell from $4 to $2, the quantity supplied would decrease. Statement e is not correct because, if the price fell from $4 to $2, the quantity demanded (not demand) would increase.

9.   Correct answer: b.

A decrease in the supply of wine is represented by shifting the supply curve to the left. A leftward shift in supply raises the equilibrium price and reduces the equilibrium quantity. You can see this by drawing a graph where supply shifts to the left and sketching out what happens to the equilibrium price and quantity.

Statement b is not correct because a decrease in demand would reduce the equilibrium price and reduce the equilibrium quantity. Statement c is not correct because an increase in demand would raise the equilibrium price and raise the equilibrium quantity. Statement d is not correct because an increase in supply would lower the equilibrium price and raise the equilibrium quantity. Statement e is not correct because the effects of these two shifts will have an uncertain effect on price but lower the equilibrium quantity for certain.

10.   Correct answer: b.

Discussion: A decrease in the price of steel reduces the cost of manufacturing cars and, thus, increases the supply of Japanese-made cars. The increase in supply of Japanese-made cars will lower the price that American buyers pay for the cars. You can see this by drawing a graph where supply shifts to the right along the demand curve.

Statement a is not correct because the supply will increase, not decrease. Statement c is not correct because the price will decrease, not increase. Statement d is not correct because the event will not cause demand to shift; quantity demanded will, however, rise. Statement e is not correct because the quantity of cars sold in the U.S. will increase, not decrease.

11.   Correct answer: d.

Discussion: An increase in the demand for cameras would be represented by shifting the demand curve to the right. The increase in demand raises the equilibrium price and quantity. As the equilibrium price rises, there is a movement along the supply curve which shows that the quantity supplied increases. You may wish to draw a graph to see this.

Statement a is not correct because the supply curve for cameras does not shift to the right; the quantity of cameras supplied increases.   Statement b is not correct because the supply curve does not shift. Statement c is not correct because the equilibrium price rises, not falls, and the quantity of cameras increases, not decreases. Statement e is not correct because the price of cameras rises and because the supply curve does not shift.

VIII.   ANSWER KEY: ESSAY QUESTIONS

1.   I will analyze the two events of an increase in the price of spandex and the fitness craze separately for their effect on the equilibrium price and quantity of athletic wear. Then, I will consider the combined effect of the two events on price and quantity. First, the increase in the price of spandex used in making athletic wear is an increase in an input price. As such, the increased input price raises the cost of producing athletic wear at every quantity supplied. This can be represented by shifting the supply curve of athletic wear to the left. The shift reflects that, at every quantity supplied, the price that producers would be willing to accept in order to produce various amounts of athletic wear is now higher. By itself, this raises the equilibrium price of athletic wear and lowers the equilibrium quantity. (Notice that the price increase caused by supply shifting left will cause a *movement along the demand curve* which means that the *quantity* of athletic wear demanded will decrease). The fitness craze spawned in part by Richard Simmons will increase the demand for athletic wear. That is, at every price, the quantity demanded will now be higher than before. An increase in demand is represented by shifting the demand curve for athletic wear to the right. By itself, the rightward shift raises the price of athletic wear and increases the equilibrium quantity. (Notice that the price increase caused by demand shifting right will cause a *movement along the supply curve* which means that the *quantity* of athletic wear supplied will increase.)

When the effects of the shifts in demand and supply are combined, we know for certain that the equilibrium price will increase since both events cause price to increase. However, we do not know for sure what the effect is on the equilibrium quantity since, in the first case, the equilibrium quantity declines but, in the second case, the equilibrium quantity rises.

2.   An increased preference by the French for American-made cheese would mean that there would be an increase in the demand for American-made cheese. This would be represented by shifting the demand curve for American-made cheese to the right, as the graph below shows. At every price, the quantity demanded is now higher (or at every quantity, the price that buyers would be willing to pay is now higher). If the price remained at $1 (rather than rising as it should), there would be a shortage of American-made cheese. That is, if the price remained at $1, the new quantity demanded would now exceed the quantity supplied at a price of $1. This would not be an equilibrium price any more. The shortage should not persist for too long because the shortage creates upward pressure on the price of cheese. Eventually, the price of cheese will rise to a new equilibrium price which is above $1. As the price rises, two things happen to eliminate the shortage. (1) As the price rises, the quantity supplied increases as the arrows along the supply curve indicate (Law of Supply; movement along supply curve); this helps eliminate the shortage. (2) As the price rises, the quantity demanded decreases as the arrows along the demand curve indicate (Law of Demand; movement along demand curve); this too helps eliminate the shortage. Eventually, a new equilibrium price will be reached where the new quantity supplied is equal to the new quantity demanded.

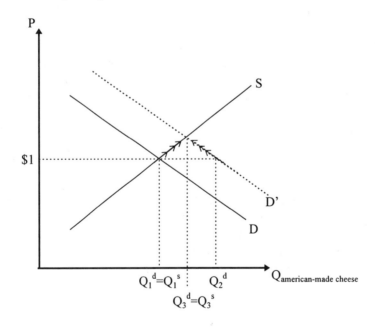

Take It to the Net

---

for this chapter's World Wide Web exercise.

CHAPTER 5
ELASTICITY - A MEASURE OF RESPONSIVENESS

I.   OVERVIEW

In this chapter, you will learn about the elasticity of demand and the elasticity of supply. Price elasticities can be used to compute by how much, in percentage terms, quantity demanded and quantity supplied of a good will change in response to an X% change in the price of that good. You will also learn that the elasticity of demand can be used to figure out what will happen to the total revenue of a firm when it lowers or raises the price of one of its products or services by X%. You will learn that the elasticity of demand and supply can be used to determine by what percentage the equilibrium price of a good will change when either demand or supply shifts. You will learn why the elasticity of demand for some products is very high and for others very low and you will learn what factors affect the elasticity of demand. You will learn that the concept of elasticity has important applications for business decisionmaking or policymaking. Since you will be using formulas that require that you compute percentage changes, you may wish to review appendix 1 of the text and the Basic Algebra chapter of the practicum.

II.   CHECKLIST

By the end of this chapter, you should be able to:

√   Explain in words what the elasticity of demand and supply are.
√   Use formulas to compute the elasticity of demand and supply.
√   Use the elasticity of demand and supply to figure out the percentage price change for a given percentage quantity change.
√   Use the elasticity of demand and supply to figure out the percentage quantity change for a given percentage price change.
√   Use the elasticity of demand to determine what happens to the total revenue of a firm when it raises or lowers the price of one of its products.
√   Use the elasticity of demand to determine whether a particular policy enacted by the government will have the desired effects.
√   Use the elasticity of demand and supply to determine what happens to the equilibrium price when demand or supply shifts.

III.   KEY TERMS

Price elasticity of demand: a measure of the responsiveness of the quantity demanded to changes in price; computed by dividing the percentage change in quantity demanded by the percentage change in price.
Price elasticity of supply: a measure of the responsiveness of the quantity supplied to changes in price; computed by dividing the percentage change in quantity supplied by the percentage change in price.

and from the appendix:

Income elasticity of demand: a measure of the responsiveness of the quantity demanded to changes in consumer income; computed by dividing the percentage change in the quantity demanded by the percentage change in income.

Cross elasticity of demand: a measure of the responsiveness of the quantity demanded to changes in the price of a related good; computed by dividing the percentage change in the quantity demanded of one good (X) by the percentage change in the price of another good (Y).

IV. PERFORMANCE ENHANCING TIPS (PETS)

PET #1

Elasticities are quoted on a "per unit basis."

Maybe this statement doesn't make sense quite yet, but it will after you look at the following example. Suppose you are told that the elasticity of demand is 2. What does that mean? You know that the elasticity of demand (E_d) for good X is given by the formula $\%\Delta Q^d_x/\%\Delta P_x$. You may think that, when you are given the number 2, all you have is the number in the numerator. Since, 2 is equal to 2/1, you do have a number for the numerator and denominator of the elasticity of demand formula. The number in the denominator is 1. Thus, an elasticity of demand of 2 means that a 1% increase in the price of good X leads to a 2% decline in the quantity of good X demanded. Once you know the elasticity of demand on a per unit basis, you can also scale up or down the percentage changes in price and quantity but keeping the proportion equal to 2. For example, you could say that with an elasticity of demand of 2, a 10% increase in the price of good X leads to a 20% decline in the quantity of good X demanded.

PET #2

For any formula, if you are given two of three missing components, you can always figure out the third component. Likewise for three of four, four of five, and so on.

This performance enhancing tip will prove useful in this chapter as you apply it to elasticities and will also prove useful in other chapters of this textbook.

Let's see how this works by applying it to the elasticity of demand. Suppose you are told that the elasticity of demand is 0.5 and that a firm is considering reducing the price of one of its products by 10%. Can you determine by how much quantity demanded would change? All of you have to do is plug the numbers that you are given into the formula:

$$E_d = \%\Delta Q^d_x/\%\Delta P_x$$
$$0.5 = \%\Delta Q^d_x/10$$
$$0.5 \times 10 = \%\Delta Q^d_x$$
$$5 = \%\Delta Q^d_x$$

Thus, a 10% reduction in the price of the product will lead to a 5% increase in the quantity of the good demanded.

Let's try another example. Suppose you are told that the elasticity of demand is 4 and that a firm wants to increase the quantity it sells by 20%. By how much must it lower price in order to generate a 20% increase in the quantity it sells? The elasticity formula could be rewritten to solve for $\%\Delta P_x$ as:

$$\%\Delta P_x = \%\Delta Q^d_x/E_d$$

$\%\Delta P_X = 20/4$
$\%\Delta P_X = 5$

Thus, the firm would have to lower the price of the product by 5% in order to generate a 20% increase in quantity demanded.

<u>PET #3</u>

Lowering the price of a good does not always lower the total revenue that a firm will earn nor does raising the price of a good always increase the total revenue that a firm will earn.

Let's see why the statement above is true. First, total revenue is computed as price X quantity demanded. In order to understand the effect on total revenue of a given percentage price change, you must also know by how much quantity demanded will change in percentage terms. Obviously, a lower price will reduce total revenue but only if the quantity demanded does not increase but instead remains the same (no change). Likewise, a higher price will raise total revenue but only if the quantity demanded does not decrease but remains the same (no change). However, it is usually the case that, when the price of a good is lowered, the quantity demanded increases and, when the price of a good is raised, the quantity demanded declines. In the case of a lower price, the lower price by itself reduces total revenue but, since quantity demanded will increase, this will tend to raise total revenue. In the case of a price increase, the higher price will by itself raise total revenue but, since quantity demanded will fall, this will tend to decrease total revenue. Thus, the combined effects on price and quantity must be determined.

Suppose you are told that the elasticity of demand is 2 and that a firm is going to raise the price of its product by 5%. What will be the effect on total revenue? With an elasticity of demand of 2, the percentage change in quantity demanded can be figured out. It will decrease by 10% (See PET #2). The net effect on revenue is based on a comparison of the percentage change in price to the percentage change in quantity demanded. A 5% increase in the price by itself would **raise** total revenue by 5%. A 10% decrease in the quantity demanded would by itself **reduce** total revenue by 10%. The combined effect depends on which one dominates. Since the 10% reduction is bigger in magnitude than the 5% increase, total revenue will decline.

V.   PRACTICE EXAM: MULTIPLE CHOICE QUESTIONS

1.   Which one of the following is the correct formula for the elasticity of demand?

a. $\Delta P_X / \Delta Q^d_X$
b. $\%\Delta Q^d_X / \%\Delta P_X$
c. $\Delta Q^d_X / \Delta P_X$
d. $\%\Delta P_X / \%\Delta Q^d_X + \%\Delta Q^s_X$
e. $\%\Delta P_X / \%\Delta Q^d_X$

2.   Suppose the elasticity of demand for bowling is 1.5 and the manager of the bowling alley decides to raise the price of a game by 5%. By what percentage will quantity demanded change?

a.   decline by 7.5%.

b.   rise by 7.5%.
c.   decline by 3%.
d.   rise by 3%.
e.   not enough information to answer the question.

3.   Suppose the government wants to reduce teenage smoking by 50%. Suppose further that the government knows that the teenage elasticity of demand for a pack of cigarettes is 2. By what percentage would the government have to increase the price of a pack of cigarettes (through a tax) in order to cut teenage smoking by 50%?

a.   100%.
b.   25%.
c.   50%.
d.   250%.
e.   20%.

4.   Which one of the following defines an inelastic demand?

a. $E_d > 1$
b. $E_d = 1$
c. $E_d < 1$
d. $E_d > 0$
e. $E_d < 0$

5.   Which one of the following factors would reduce the elasticity of demand for a particular product?

a.   more time to shop around.
b.   no close substitutes.
c.   big part of budget.
d.   luxury item.
e.   all of the above reduce the elasticity of demand.

6.   Which one of the following goods would you characterize as being the most elastic?

a.   insulin.
b.   coffee.
c.   cigarettes.
d.   gasoline.
e.   cookies.

7.   Suppose the elasticity of demand for flowers at a local florist is estimated to be 4, as computed by a savvy economics student. If the florist raises the price of flowers by 5%, then:

a.   the revenue earned by the florist will decline.
b.   the quantity of flowers sold by the florist will decline by 1.25%.
c.   the quantity of flowers sold by the florist will decline by 0.2%.
d.   the quantity of flowers sold by the florist will decline by 20%.

e.   (a) and (d).

8.   Total revenue _____ when the price of a good increases and its demand is inelastic, and total revenue _____ when the price of a good decreases and its demand is elastic.

a.   increases/increases
b.   increases/decreases
c.   increases/does not change
d.   decreases/decreases
e.   decreases/increases

9.   What is the elasticity of supply of cows if the price of a cow increases from $500 to $550 and the quantity supplied rises from 100,000 to 130,000? (Do not use the midpoint formula).

a.   3.33.
b.   3.0.
c.   5.0.
d.   6.0.
e.   cannot be determined without information on percentages.

10.   Suppose that the supply of tweed jackets increases by 20%. Further, suppose that the elasticity of demand for tweed jackets is 1 and the elasticity of supply is 4. What will happen to the equilibrium price of tweed jackets?

a.   rise by 8%.
b.   fall by 8%.
c.   rise by 4%.
d.   fall by 4%.
e.   fall by 5%.

VI.   PRACTICE EXAM: ESSAY QUESTIONS

1.   Discuss the short- and long-run effects of a government policy of imposing a tax that would raise the price of oil and gasoline by 20% assuming that the elasticity of demand for oil is currently estimated to be 0.5 and the elasticity of demand for gasoline to be 1.2. Be sure to address what factors might alter the elasticity numbers over time.

2.   Suppose that you are an economic consultant for a large company that produces and sells lollipops that are shaped as the faces of Hollywood celebrities. The company has shops in the major cities around the Country And also sells by mail-order catalog. As an economic consultant, you have estimated the elasticity of demand for store-bought lollipops to be 0.75 and the elasticity of demand for mail-order lollipops to be 3. What advice would you give to the president of the company if she wanted to increase revenue from the shops and through mail orders? Now, suppose that the price of sugar increases causing a 20% reduction in the supply of celebrity lollipops. What information would you need to compute the effect of the reduction in supply on the equilibrium price?

VII. ANSWER KEY: MULTIPLE CHOICE QUESTIONS

1.   Correct answer: b.

Discussion: The elasticity of demand is the percentage change in the quantity of good X demanded by the percentage change in its price.

Statement a is not correct because it is not expressed in percentage changes (but rather absolute changes) and has the numerator and denominator reversed. Statement c is not correct because it is expressed in absolute changes. Statement d is not correct because the elasticity of supply does not enter the formula. Statement e is not correct because the numerator and denominator should be reversed.

2.   Correct answer: a.

Discussion: A rise in the price will always reduce the quantity demanded, so first you must look for an answer that has quantity demanded declining. The percentage change in quantity demanded is computed by multiplying E_d times $\%\Delta P = 1.5 \times 5 = 7.5$.

Statement b is not correct because the quantity demanded will decline, not increase, when the price rises. Statement c and d are wrong based on the formula. Statement e is not correct because there is enough information to answer the question.

3.   Correct answer: b.

Discussion: Since you are given the elasticity of demand and a desired percentage change in the quantity demanded, you can figure out the percentage change in price as $\%\Delta P_X = \%\Delta Q^d_X/E_d$. Thus, $\%\Delta P_X = 50\%/2 = 25\%$.

Statement a is not correct because the two numbers should not be multiplied. Statement c would only be correct if the elasticity of demand were 1. Statement d is not correct; it is off by a factor of 10. Statement e is also not correct.

4.   Correct answer: c.

Discussion: An inelastic demand is defined as one for which E_d is less than 1, which means that a 1% increase in price reduces the quantity demanded by less than 1% (and vice-versa for a price decrease).

Statement a defines an elastic demand. Statement b defines a unitary elastic demand. Statements d and e are not correct because elasticity is defined with respect to 1, not zero.

5.   Correct answer: b.

Discussion: When there are no close substitutes for a product, that makes the demand for it more inelastic. That is, the price of the good can be raised by a big percentage but quantity demanded will not respond by very much because there are not close substitutes that consumers could switch their purchases to. This describes a good that has an inelastic demand.

If consumers have more time to shop around, they are more likely to compare prices. This means that consumers will be more sensitive to price changes, i.e., demand will be more elastic. If a good is a big part of a consumer's budget, a small change in the price will have a bigger impact on his or her budget. Thus, consumers will be more likely to greatly reduce their purchases of the good even if its price goes up a little bit. This defines demand to be more elastic. (You may want to think about the effects on budget and spending if the price of a pen goes up by 10% to the price of housing going up by 10%). Luxury items, because they are not necessities, tend to have a more elastic demand. Since a, c, and d are likely to raise the elasticity of demand (make it more elastic), statement e cannot be correct.

6.   Correct answer: e.

Discussion: Cookies are the only good that are not a "necessity." Goods that are not a necessity tend to have a more elastic demand.

Insulin is a necessary good to a diabetic; no matter how much the price of insulin increases, the purchases of insulin will not drop. In this case, the elasticity of demand for insulin is likely to be zero. The same, to a lesser degree, is true of gasoline. People must have transportation to their jobs, the grocery store, etc. Thus, gasoline is more of a necessity than cookies. A similar story can be told for coffee. Most people cannot seem to get through the day without at least one cup of coffee which makes coffee more of a necessity than cookies. Cigarettes have an addictive property which means that price increases will have less of an effect of reducing consumption than for a non-addictive good. Thus, cookies are likely to have a higher elasticity of demand than cigarettes.

7.   Correct answer: e.

Discussion: When the elasticity of demand is greater than 1, an X% price change will cause a greater than X% change in quantity demanded. In this case, the florist has chosen to raise, not lower, the price of flowers. With an elasticity of demand of 4, the 5% point increase in the price will lead to a 20% point decline in the quantity of flowers sold. Thus, statement d is correct. At the same time, since the percentage change in the price increase is swamped by the percentage reduction in the quantity of flowers sold, the revenue earned by the florist will drop. Thus, statement a is correct, too.

Statement b is not correct; the effect on quantity is not determined by dividing 5 by 4 but instead multiplying the two numbers. Statement c is not correct because it is off by a factor of 10.

8.   Correct answer: a.

Discussion: With an inelastic demand, the percentage rise (in this case) in the price of the good is greater than the percentage reduction in the quantity demanded, which means that, on net, total revenue (p X q) will increase. With an elastic demand, the percentage drop (in this case) will be less than the percentage increase in the quantity of the good demanded. (Remember price and quantity demanded move in opposite directions.) Thus, on net, total revenue will rise.

Statement b is not correct; it would have been correct if the second part of the question asked what happened to total revenue when the price of a good with an elastic demand was increased. Statement c is not correct; only a unitary elasticity of demand leads to no change in total revenue when price is raised or lowered. Statement d is not correct; it would have been correct if the question had asked what happens to total revenue when price is decreased and demand is inelastic and what happens to total revenue when price is increased and demand is elastic. Statement e is not correct; it would have been correct if the first part of the question had asked what happens to total revenue when price is decreased and demand is inelastic.

9.   Correct answer: b.

Discussion: The percentage change in the price of a cow is 10% [($550-500)/500]X100 and the percentage change in the quantity of cows supplied is 30% [(130,000-100,000)/100,000]X100. The elasticity of supply is computed as the percentage change in the quantity supplied divided by the percentage change in the price which is 30%/10% = 3.

For the reasoning just mentioned, statements a, c, and d are not correct. Statement e is not correct because you are given information that allows you to compute percentage changes.

10.   Correct answer: d.

Discussion: Since the supply of tweed jackets has increased, you should be looking for an answer that has the price of tweed jackets declining. The formula used to compute the percentage change in the equilibrium price is to take the percentage shift in supply (or demand, if that had been the question) and divide it by the sum of the elasticity of supply and demand. Thus, the percentage change in the equilibrium price will be 20%/(1 + 4) = 20%/5 = 4%.

Statements a and c cannot be correct because a supply increase causes a drop in the equilibrium price (see Chapter 4 for review if you don't remember this). Statements b and e are not correct because the formula gives an answer of 4%.

VIII. ANSWER KEY: ESSAY QUESTIONS

1.   Since the currently estimated elasticity of demand for oil is 0.5, a 20% increase in the price of oil will reduce the quantity demanded by 10% (0.5 X 20%), at least in the short run. The tax revenue collected by the government on oil will, however, increase. The tax revenue will increase because the percentage increase in the price of oil dominates the percentage decrease in the quantity demanded. For gasoline, a 20% increase in its price will reduce the quantity demanded by 24% (1.2 X 20%), at least in the short run. In the short run, the 20% increase in the price of gasoline is much more effective at reducing consumer use of gasoline than is the 20% increase in the price of oil at reducing consumer use of oil (compare 10% to 24%). However, the tax revenue collected on gasoline sales will actually decline because the percentage decrease in the quantity demanded outweighs the percentage increase in the price. Thus, on balance, tax revenue collected by the government on gasoline will decline. While in the short run it may be difficult to find substitutes for oil or gasoline, in the long run, consumers may be able to modify their spending behavior. They may find substitutes for oil or gasoline (perhaps because innovative companies will invent products like methanol or battery-run automobiles). Thus, in the long run, the estimated elasticities may increase. In fact, if the elasticity for oil increased above 1, then the tax increase of 20% would end up lowering the tax revenue collected by the government on oil consumption.

2.   The advice I would give to the president of the celebrity lollipop company is this: raise the price of lollipops purchased in shops throughout the country and lower the price of lollipops purchased through mail-order catalogs. However, be aware that, eventually, when consumers become aware of the

price difference, you may see your revenue from the stores decline (rather than rise after you have raised the price), but your revenue from mail orders may eventually increase by more than originally estimated. This may happen because customers from the store-bought shops may begin to purchase by mail order. That is, they will have found an almost identical substitute for the store-bought lollipops.

If the price of sugar rises, the supply of celebrity lollipops will decrease (shift left). The decreased supply will raise the price of a store-bought and mail-order lollipops. In order to know by how much the equilibrium prices would rise, you would need information on the elasticity of supply of store-bought and mail-order lollipops (in addition to the elasticity of demand) as well as on the percentage reduction in the supply of each type of lollipop. For example, if the supply of mail-order lollipops dropped by 40% and the elasticity of supply is 1 and you are given that the elasticity of demand is 3, then the equilibrium price will change by 40%/(1+3) = 40%/4 = 10%.

Take It to the Net

We invite you to visit the O'Sullivan/Sheffrin page on the Prentice Hall Web site at:

http://www.prenhall.com/osullivan/

for this chapter's World Wide Web exercise.

CHAPTER 6
GOVERNMENT INTERVENTION IN MARKETS

I.   OVERVIEW

In this chapter, you will learn about whether the interaction of consumers and producers leads to an efficient or inefficient outcome. You will learn that, when inefficient outcomes arise, the government may step in, in an effort to promote a better outcome. You will also learn why a government may intervene in a market that is already efficient and what effects it may create. You will learn that spillover benefits and costs generally create an inefficient outcome, either for producers or consumers. You will examine the effects of government price-setting policies such as rent control and dairy price supports on equilibrium price, quantities, and efficiency. You will also examine the effects of government restrictions on quantity such as quotas, voluntary export restraints, and licensing agreements. You will learn that there are always winners and losers of price-setting and quantity-restricting policies. You will see that there is an interface between economics and politics. You will learn about the difference between public and private goods and that there may be a role for the government in delivering public goods to the market.

II.   CHECKLIST

By the end of this chapter, you should be able to:

√   Use a graph of demand and supply to show why, in the absence of spillover benefits and costs at the equilibrium price and quantity, neither a consumer nor a producer could benefit from there being one more transaction.
√   Explain what an efficient market outcome is and what an inefficient market outcome is.
√   Explain what a maximum price (price ceiling) policy is and the effects it creates on price, quantity demanded, and quantity supplied. Be able to discuss any other consequences that might arise from the policy.
√   List some real world examples of price ceilings.
√   Explain what a minimum price (price floor or price support) policy is and the effects it creates on price, quantity demanded and quantity supplied. You should also be able to discuss any other consequences that might arise from the policy.
√   List some real world examples of price supports.
√   Identify who "wins" and who "loses" under different government policies.
√   Define a public good and contrast it to a private good.
√   Explain the free-rider and chump problems.
√   List some real world examples of public goods.

III.   KEY TERMS

Inefficient market: a market in which there is an additional transaction that would benefit a buyer, a seller, and any third parties affected by the transaction.
Efficient market: a market in which there are *no* additional transactions that would benefit a buyer, a seller, and any third parties affected by the transactions.
Imperfectly competitive market: a market in which firms are large enough that they affect market prices.

Invisible hand: the phenomenon that leads individual consumers and producers to the market equilibrium, which is efficient in some circumstances.

Price ceiling: a maximum price; transactions above the maximum price are outlawed.

Price floor: a minimum price; transactions below the maximum price are outlawed.

Rent control: a policy under which the government specifies a maximum rent that is below the equilibrium rent.

Price support: a policy under which the government specifies a minimum price above the equilibrium price.

Taxi medallion: a license to operate a taxi.

Import ban: a law that prohibits the importation of a particular good.

Spillover benefit: the benefit from a good experienced by people who do not decide how much of the good to produce or consume.

Public good: a good that is available for everyone to consume, regardless of who pays and who doesn't.

Private good: a good that is consumed by a single person or household.

Free-rider problem: each person will try to get the benefit of a public good without paying for it, trying to get a free ride at the expense of others.

IV.   PERFORMANCE ENHANCING TIPS (PETS)

PET #1

The prices corresponding to the quantities demanded and supplied along the demand and supply curves can be used to measure the marginal benefit to society of consuming and the marginal cost to society of producing at various quantities.

Look at the graph below for the market for apples.

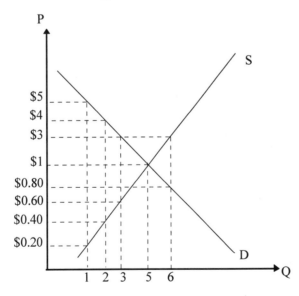

The demand curve can be used to infer what the marginal benefit is to a consumer from buying one more apple. The marginal benefit is simply measured by the price a consumer would be willing to pay to buy one more apple. Thus, the marginal benefit of the first apple (benefit to the consumer from buying the first apple) is $5; the marginal benefit of the second apple (benefit to the consumer from buying the second apple) is $4; and so on.

The supply curve can be used to infer what the marginal cost is from producing one more apple. The marginal cost of the first apple (cost to the producer of producing the first apple) is $0.20. The marginal cost of the second apple (cost to the producer of producing the second apple) is $0.40; and so on.

Notice that the marginal benefit of the third apple is $3 which exceeds the marginal cost of producing the third apple, $0.60. Thus, at a quantity of 3 apples, producers could profit by producing the third apple since consumers would be willing to pay $3. So producers should produce more apples.

Now, compare the marginal benefit of the sixth apple to the marginal cost. The marginal benefit is $0.80 while the marginal cost is $3.00. Thus, at a quantity of six apples, the marginal cost exceeds the marginal benefit, so it would not make sense for producers to produce an apple for which nobody is willing to pay them enough to cover the marginal cost of production.

At equilibrium, the marginal benefit of the fifth apple is $1 and equal to the marginal cost of producing the fifth apple. This is the efficient outcome; neither more nor fewer apples should be produced.

PET #2

Maximum prices (price ceilings) that are set below the equilibrium price create a shortage where quantity demanded exceeds quantity supplied. A price ceiling set above the equilibrium price is ineffective.

To see this, compare the two graphs below. Graph A illustrates a price ceiling set below the equilibrium price and graph B, a price ceiling set above the equilibrium price. Remember that a price ceiling is a government-controlled price above which the equilibrium price may not rise.

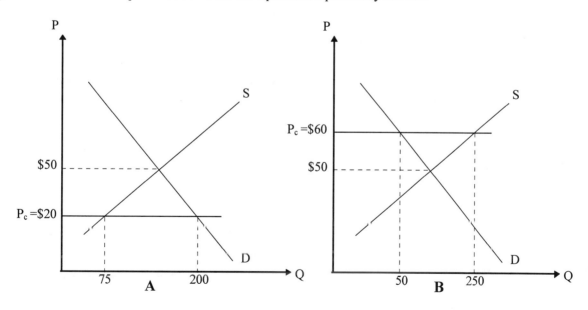

In graph A, at a price of $20, the quantity demanded is 200 units and the quantity supplied is 75 units. Thus, there is a shortage of 125 units. If the government removed the price ceiling, the price would rise to

$50 and the shortage would be eliminated as quantity demanded would decline and quantity supplied would increase (movements along the curves).

In graph B, at a price ceiling of $60, the quantity demanded is 50 units and the quantity supplied is 250 units. However, the equilibrium (or market-determined) price is $50. Thus, there is no tendency for the price to rise above the government-imposed price of $60, so the price ceiling, in this case, is not effective.

PET #3

Minimum prices (price floors or price supports) that are set above the equilibrium price create a surplus where quantity supplied exceeds quantity demanded. A price floor set below the equilibrium price is ineffective.

To see this, compare the two graphs below. Graph A illustrates a price floor set above the equilibrium price and graph B, a price floor set below the equilibrium price. Remember that a price floor is a government-controlled price below which the equilibrium price may not fall.

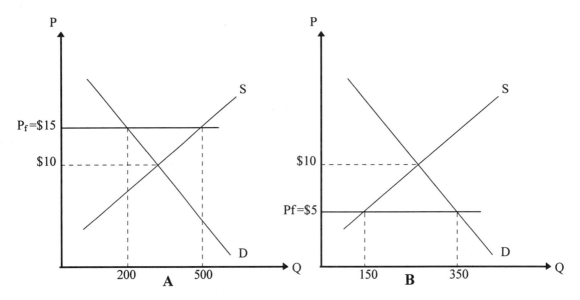

In graph A, at a price floor of $15, the quantity demanded is 200 units and the quantity supplied is 500 units. Thus, there is a surplus of 300 units. If the government removed the price floor, the price would fall to $10 and the surplus would be eliminated as quantity demanded would rise and quantity supplied would decrease (movements along the curves).

In graph B, at a price floor of $5, the quantity demanded is 350 units and the quantity supplied is 150 units. However, the equilibrium (or market-determined) price is $10. Thus, there is no tendency for the price to fall below $10 and so the price floor of $5 is not effective.

V.   PRACTICE EXAM: MULTIPLE CHOICE QUESTIONS

1.   An efficient market outcome is one in which:

a.   the marginal benefit to consumers exceeds the marginal costs to producers.
b.   there are spillover benefits but no spillover costs.
c.   there are no free-rider problems.
d.   a third party can benefit from a transaction.
e.   no buyer, seller, or third party can benefit from any further transactions.

2.   Consider the graph below depicting the market for guitars.

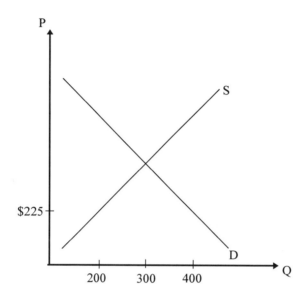

Which one of the following statements is true?

a.   At a quantity of 400, the marginal benefit of a guitar exceeds the marginal cost.
b.   At a quantity of 200, the marginal benefit of a guitar exceeds the marginal cost.
c.   If the price was $225 per guitar, there would be a surplus of guitars.
d.   One more consumer could be better off if 299 guitars were produced instead of 300.
e.   (b) and (c).

3.   Who is responsible for the metaphor of the "invisible hand"?

a.   Adam Smith.
b.   Art O'Sullivan.
c.   John Maynard Keynes.
d.   Milton Friedman.
e.   Steven Sheffrin.

4.   Suppose the government sets a maximum price (price ceiling) for pacemakers (a medical device that monitors the beats per minute of the heart). The maximum price is set at $1,299 and the equilibrium price is $1,750. Which one of the following would **NOT** be a likely result?

a.   consumers may bribe their doctors for pacemakers or be willing to pay special hook-up fees.
b.   a surplus would develop.
c.   the quality of pacemakers may decline.

d.   the quanity of pacemakers supplied may decline in the long run.
e.   all of the above would be likely to develop.

5.   Suppose the government sets a minimum price (price floor) for cheese of $1.25 per pound. Based on the diagram below, which one of the following statements is correct?

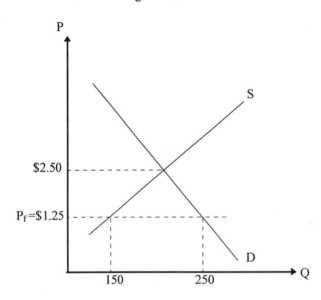

a.   there will be a surplus of 100 pounds of cheese.
b.   there will be a shortage of 100 pounds of cheese.
c.   at $1.25, the marginal cost of production exceeds the marginal benefit of consumption.
d.   the price floor is ineffective.
e.   supply will decrease.

6.   Which one of the following is an effect of a minimum price (price floor) that is set above the equilibrium price?

a.   quantity supplied increases.
b.   quantity demanded decreases.
c.   an inefficient outcome is produced.
d.   suppliers win and consumers lose.
e.   all of the above are effects of a minimum price.

7.   Which one of the following is **NOT** an example of a quantity restriction (control)?

a.   a quota on aircraft imports.
b.   a voluntary export restraint on automobiles.
c.   subsidized housing.
d.   licensing liquor stores.
e.   a ban on oil imports.

8.   Suppose you were debating whether to become a hotdog vendor in your town. You estimate that you can sell 40,000 hotdogs a year at a price of $2. You estimate the opportunity cost of your time to be

$10,000 per year. You figure that you will operate the business for the next two years at which point you will go back to school. If you become a hotdog vendor, you must pay for a vending license. The license costs $200,000. Assume that you have $200,000 from an inheritance to pay for the license. The $200,000 is in a checking account earning 3% interest per year. Which one of the following would be your best strategy?

a.   buy the license and become a hotdog vendor since you'll make $80,000 a year.
b.   do not buy the license since it costs too much.
c.   buy the license and become a hotdog vendor if you expect that in two years you can sell the license for $250,000.
d.   leave the $200,000 in the bank since you'll earn more in interest than working as a hotdog vendor.
e.   do not buy the license but put the $200,000 into a mutual fund that earns 10% interest per year.

9.   Which one of the following would be an effect of the U.S. government imposing a quota on imports of, say, automobiles?

a.   the price of imported automobiles will increase.
b.   the quantity of automobiles supplied by the foreign source will increase.
c.   the quantity of automobiles demanded will increase.
d.   employment in the U.S. automobile industry will decrease.
e.   a surplus of foreign-made automobiles will be created in the U.S.

10.   Which one of the following would **NOT** be an example of a public good?

a.   preservation of endangered species.
b.   federally-subsidized flu shots that cost $5.
c.   national defense.
d.   a city park.
e.   a bridge.

11.   Which one of the following statements is true of public goods?

a.   they are generally paid for through taxes.
b.   it is impractical to exclude people who don't pay for them from using them.
c.   they are available for everyone to consume.
d.   they are associated with the free-rider problem.
e.   all of the above are true of public goods.

12.   Which one of the following methods is the best way to overcome the free-rider problem?

a.   ask people to make voluntary contributions.
b.   tax people.
c.   impose a price support.
d.   subsidize the users of the good/program.
e.   institute government-sponsored advertising campaigns for the good.

VI.   PRACTICE EXAM: ESSAY QUESTIONS

1.   Suppose that you are a lobbyist for the textile industry. Assume the industry is perfectly competitive and has no spillover benefits or costs associated with it. What government favors might you seek for your industry? Who will benefit if you are awarded a government favor? Who will be hurt? Will an efficient outcome occur if your lobbying is effective? Explain.

2.   First, explain why a bridge is a public good. Also, why is it that some cities collect tolls for using a bridge? Second, explain why a rent-controlled apartment may not turn out to be as inexpensive as you may have thought based on the monthly payment?

VII.   ANSWER KEY: MULTIPLE CHOICE QUESTIONS

1.   Correct answer: e.

Discussion: Statement e is correct because it is the only statement that points out that no further transactions can make anybody else better off. This defines an efficient outcome.

Statement a is not correct. If the marginal benefit to consumers from consuming good Z exceeds the marginal costs to producers of producing good Z, then producers could make consumers better off by producing more and consumers could make producers better off by paying them. Since the marginal benefit of consumers exceeds the marginal costs of production, that means they would be willing to pay more than what it costs the producers to produce. This is just an application of the marginal principle from Chapter 2. Statement b is not correct because spillover benefits lead to inefficient outcomes, just as do spillover costs. Statement c is not correct because the absence of a free-rider problem does not define whether an outcome will be efficient or not. Statement d is not correct because, if a third party can benefit from a transaction, the outcome must not currently be the efficient one.

2.   Correct answer: b.

Discussion: At a quantity of 200, the marginal benefit is determined by drawing a line from the quantity level up to the demand curve and then over to the price line. The corresponding price is a measure of the marginal benefit of the 200th guitar. The marginal cost is determined by drawing a line from the quantity level up to the supply curve and then over to the price line. The corresponding price is a measure of the marginal cost of the 200th guitar. As you can see, the marginal benefit is greater than the marginal cost.

Statement a is not correct because the marginal cost exceeds the marginal benefit of the 400th guitar. Statement c is not correct because a price of $225 leads to a shortage, not a surplus. Statement d is not correct because the equilibrium quantity of 300 guitars is the efficient outcome, so nobody could be made better off by producing fewer (or even more) guitars. Statement e is not correct because statement c is not correct.

3.   Correct answer: a.

Discussion: Adam Smith, who wrote the Wealth of Nations is responsible for the metaphor of the "invisible hand" which is just that people acting in their own self-interest can frequently lead to outcomes in which all participating parties benefit.

None of the other statements are correct. In fact, O'Sullivan and Sheffrin are the authors of your textbook.

4.   Correct answer: b.

Discussion: A maximum price that is set below the equilibrium price creates a shortage, not a surplus.

Since a maximum price set below the equilibrium price creates a shortage, several consequences emerge. One is that people may bribe their doctors with monetary or non-monetary gifts so that they can be one of the recipients of the limited supply of pacemakers. Second, the quality of pacemakers may decline because the shortage or excess demand for pacemakers doesn't give an incentive to the producers to produce a better product. They know that they can sell what they produce because, if one buyer makes demands on them, another buyer will be ready to pay the $1,299 for the pacemaker. Third, the quantity of pacemakers supplied may decline in the long run as pacemaker manufacturers decide that it is not as profitable to produce pacemakers (because of the government-imposed price) and so they may decide to produce other medical devices or get out of the business altogether.

5.   Correct answer: d.

Discussion: Since the price floor is set below the equilibrium price, it is ineffective. Remember that a price floor is a government-imposed price below which the price may not drop. By market forces, the price will naturally rest at $1.50.

Statements a and b are not correct because the price floor is ineffective, so neither a surplus, nor shortage will emerge. An equilibrium where quantity demanded = quantity supplied at a price of $1.50 will emerge. Statement c is not correct because the quantity supplied and quantity demanded at $1.25 are different, which means you can't compare the marginal benefit to the marginal cost. You have to look at the same quantity level for both demand and supply. Statement e is not correct because an ineffective price floor does not have the effect of decreasing supply (supply shifting left).

6.   Correct answer: e.

Discussion: A minimum price set above the equilibrium price creates a surplus. It does so by raising the price above the equilibrium. As the price is increased, quantity supplied increases (movement along the supply curve, Law of Supply) and quantity demanded decreases (movement along the demand curve, Law of Demand). An inefficient outcome is produced because we are no longer at the equilibrium level of output which is where marginal benefit equals marginal cost. Suppliers win because they get a higher price for their product but consumers lose because they have to pay a higher price for it.

7.   Correct answer: c.

Discussion: Subsidized housing is housing that is provided to people at a price below the market price.

Quotas, voluntary export restraints, licenses, and bans all restrict or limit the quantity of a good to various degrees.

8.   Correct answer: c.

Discussion: Your income over two years, after accounting for the opportunity cost of your time, will be $140,000, which is equal to [($2 X 40,0000) - $10,000] X 2 years. Plus, you will make $250,000 when you sell the license in two years. So, in total, you will have made $390,000 in two years. However, you had an expense of $200,000 to pay for the license. Thus, your profit across the two years is $190,000.

Statement a is not correct because you should not just consider how much you will make each year. You have to factor in the costs of your time and the license as well as earnings from selling the license. Statement b is not correct for similar reasons. Statement d is not correct because, if you leave the $200,000 in the bank for 2 years, you will earn $12,000 in interest, or $6,000 each year (200,000 X 3%). This is less than the $190,000 you could earn if you opened the hotdog stand. Statement e is not correct because, if you put the $200,000 in a mutual fund for two years, you will earn $40,000, or $20,000 each year ($200,000 X 10%).

9.   Correct answer: a.

Discussion: A quota restricts the supply of imports and, thus, reduces the overall supply of automobiles in the U.S. market. This raises the price of automobiles.

Statement b is not correct because the quota reduces the quantity of automobiles supplied by the foreign source, not increases it.   Statement c is not correct because, as the price increases, the quantity of automobiles demanded will decrease not increase. Statement d is not correct because employment in the U.S. automobile industry will increase as they increase production some to make up for the reduction from the foreign source. Statement e is not correct because a shortage of foreign-made automobiles will be created in the U.S.

10.   Correct answer: b.

Discussion: Flu shots are rival in consumption. The flu shot that I get means that somebody else can't have the exact same flu shot that I got. Each individual "consumes" their own flu shot. It is also excludable; if you don't pay for a flu shot, you can't get a flu shot.

By contrast, preservation of an endangered species, a bridge, or a city park, or national defense is something that I can consume (use, get enjoyment out of) while at the same time, so can somebody else. Also, if I want a bridge or preservation of an endangered species or city park or national defense and pay for it myself, other people can consume (use, enjoy) it even if they don't pay for it.

11.   Correct answer: e.

Discussion: All of the above are characteristics of public good.

12.   Correct answer: b.

Discussion: The free-rider problem means that people recognize that they will be able to use a good without having to pay for it because they figure others will pay for it. Thus, a tax will force all people to indirectly pay for the good.

Voluntary contributions will not overcome the free-rider problem.   Nobody will make a voluntary contribution; they'll be waiting for other people to make contributions so that the good will be provided and then they can use it without having paid anything for it. A price support won't work and isn't related to the free-rider problem. Subsidizing users of the good/program makes no sense since that means the government would be paying the free-riders to use it. This is the reverse of a tax. An advertising campaign won't work either.

VIII. ANSWER KEY: ESSAY QUESTIONS

1.   If I were a lobbyist for the textile industry, I would probably seek out government favors that would lead to a higher, government-supported price for textiles. There are numerous government policies that could create a higher price for textiles. First, a minimum price policy (price support) which establishes a price below which the price of textiles may not fall and is above the equilibrium price would certainly generate a higher price for textiles and make the industry executives happy as they would see their profits rise (assuming nothing else happened to hurt profits). Second, any form of quantity restriction, be it a quota or ban on imports of textiles from foreign countries, a quota on domestic industry output, or collecting a fee (paid for by textile producers) for a license to produce textiles, would ultimately reduce the textile industry output (supply of textiles would shift left) and the price of textiles would rise. A quota or ban on imports might also benefit employment in the textile industry since the loss of textiles due to a ban or quota on imports might mean that domestic industries might increase their production (and employment) to make up for the loss. While a fee for a license might lead to a higher price for textiles, the textile producers who are already in the industry may not be happy about having to pay the fee. The lobbyist might be smarter to ask that any new textile producers would have to buy a license in order to produce.

Of course, any of these schemes will likely hurt consumers who ultimately end up having to pay a higher price for clothing made from textiles. (Obviously, clothing makers who buy textiles will also have to pay a higher price for textiles which they will pass on to consumers). Consumers may also find that the supply of clothing is smaller than before the lobbying. Producers of textiles would be the winners because they would see the profits of their companies increase as the price they earned on the sales of textiles would be higher. However, the producers would have to factor into their profit calculation the expense of retaining a lobbyist. If the lobbyist is very expensive, the producers may not make a profit after all.

An efficient outcome will not occur if the lobbying is successful. The price will be higher than the equilibrium price that would have occurred under a market-determined outcome, and the quantity available to consumers will be lower than that under a market-determined outcome.

2.   A bridge is a public good because it satisfies the two criteria that determine a public good: non-rivalry and non-excludability. A bridge is a good that is non-rival in consumption because my use of the bridge does not restrict or eliminate somebody else's use of the bridge. The bridge is available for anybody to use. A bridge is also non-excludable, meaning that it is impractical to exclude people who don't pay for the bridge from using it. For example, if I want a bridge built across a river so it is quicker for me to get to work and I pay $1,000,000 to have the bridge built, it is going to be very difficult to exclude other commuters from using the bridge. Some cities collect tolls on their bridges as a way of getting those who use the bridge to pay proportionately more for it. Most citizens of a city pay for a bridge through their taxes; if they must also pay a toll to use the bridge, then those who use it the most will be paying more for the bridge than those who hardly use it.

A rent-controlled apartment may not turn out to be as inexpensive as the stated monthly payment suggests because of hidden fees. The apartment owners might add on some extra (rather costly) fees since they know there are lots of other people who would be willing to pay more than the rent-controlled price for the apartment. Thus, the apartment owners are just trying to rent to that person who is willing to pay what the true (market-determined or equilibrium) rental price would be. Alternatively, while the rent for the apartment may be controlled and, therefore, seem low relative to other rental rates around the city, the quality of the apartment may be pretty bad. The apartment may be very run down, poorly heated, with poor plumbing and peeling paint. Thus, while you may end up paying at the rent-controlled rate, you're paying for what you get. In this sense, even though your monthly payment may be low, you're not really reaping the benefits that you might have imagined (low monthly fee for a quality apartment).

Take It to the Net

We invite you to visit the O'Sullivan/Sheffrin page on the Prentice Hall Web site at:

http://www.prenhall.com/osullivan/

for this chapter's World Wide Web exercise.

CHAPTER 7
CONSUMER CHOICE

I.   OVERVIEW

In this chapter, you will learn about factors that affect an individual's decision about how much of a particular product or products to consume (or buy). Thus, you will consider an individual demand curve (instead of a market demand curve as in Chapters 4 and 5). You will learn about income and substitution effects. You will re-encounter the principle of opportunity cost, the reality principle which requires that you think in inflation-adjusted terms, and the marginal principle. You will learn about utility and marginal utility (economists way of measuring the satisfaction that consumers receive from the consumption of goods). You will learn about the law of diminishing marginal utility and the utility-maximizing rule. You will learn about consumer surplus and how to measure it using a demand curve.

II.   CHECKLIST

By the end of the chapter, you should be able to:

√   Apply the principle of opportunity cost to consumption decisions.
√   Explain the income and substitution effects that result from a change in the price of a good.
√   Explain why each point on an individual demand curve represents a point at which the marginal benefit of consuming (using) a good equals the marginal cost to the consumer.
√   Explain the law of diminishing marginal utility and represent it with a graph.
√   Explain why consumers are willing to pay a higher price for consuming the first unit of a good than for any subsequent units.
√   Explain the utility-maximizing rule and use it to decide whether a consumer should increase or decrease the consumption of one good and decrease or increase the consumption of another.
√   Define consumer surplus and measure it using a graph.
√   Explain why increases in price reduce consumer surplus and vice-versa.

III.   KEY TERMS

Individual demand curve: a curve that shows the relationship between the price of a good and the quantity that a single consumer is willing to buy (the quantity demanded).
Substitution effect: the change in consumption resulting from a change in the price of one good relative to the price of other goods.
Real income: consumer's income measured in terms of the goods it can buy.
Normal good: a good for which the demand increases as real income rises.
Inferior good: a good for which demand decreases as real income rises.
Income Effect: the change in consumption resulting from an increase in the consumer's real income.
Utility: the satisfaction or pleasure the consumer experiences when he or she consumes a good, measured as the number of **utils**.
Marginal utility: the change in utility for one additional unit of the good.
Law of diminishing marginal utility: as the consumption of a particular good increases, marginal utility decreases.

Utility-maximizing rule: pick the affordable combination of consumer goods that makes the marginal utility per dollar spent on one good equal to that of a second good.

Consumer surplus: the difference between the maximum amount a consumer is willing to pay for a product and the price the consumer pays for the product.

IV.   PERFORMANCE ENHANCING TIPS (PETS)

PET #1

*When you see the term "marginal," you should always think of computing the **change** in a variable. Computing the change requires that you have some numeric value before the change and some numeric value after the change. The difference between the two is the change in the variable.*

You have seen this PET in Chapter 2 of the Practicum, but it is repeated again here because you will use it in this chapter to compute marginal utility.

Marginal utility is the change in utility or utils from increasing consumption (or cutting back on consumption) by one more unit of a good. The change in utility or utils is a way of measuring the change in satisfaction or benefits or "happiness" that consumers receive from consuming that one more unit of the good.

Use the table below to fill in the marginal utility reaped from buying potato chips.

Bags of Potato Chips	Utility	Marginal Utility
1	50 utils	
2	90 utils	
3	120 utils	
4	140 utils	
5	150 utils	
6	120 utils	

The marginal utility (change in utility) associated with consuming the first bag of potato chips is 50 utils since 0 bags of potato chips yields 0 utility. The total utility associated with consuming two bags of potato chips is 90 utils which means that the change in utility (marginal utility) from consuming the second bag of potato chips is 40 utils. The marginal utility for the third bag is computed similarly as 30 utils, 20 utils for the fourth bag, and 10 utils for the fifth bag. However, the sixth bag actually *reduces* total utility from 150 to 120, so the marginal utility is negative = -30. A rational consumer obviously would not consume any more than 5 bags of potato chips since that would reduce his overall level of satisfaction.

PET #2

*Diminishing marginal utility means that the utility (or satisfaction) from consuming more and more of a good **increases** but at a **decreasing** rate. Just because the term "diminishing" is used does NOT mean that the level of utility (satisfaction) decreases or diminishes.*

In Chapter 2, you encountered the principle of diminishing marginal returns or diminishing marginal output. In this chapter, the principle is applied to utility. In fact, if you look at the table above, assuming you've now filled in the correct numbers, you will see that the numbers in the table reflect diminishing marginal utility. The marginal utility declines from 50 to 40 to 30 to 20 to 10 utils. The numbers are just a way of expressing that an individual gets less and less satisfaction from eating more and more bags of potato chips.

PET #3

The rule of utility-maximization is a marginal benefit-marginal cost comparison. If there is not an equality in the expression, then a consumer can rearrange his consumption choices and be better off (get more utility).

The rule of utility-maximization can be expressed two ways:

(i)   [Marginal Utility of Good X/Price of X]=[Marginal Utility of Good Y/Price of Y]

which can be rearranged as (see Basic Algebra appendixr of the Practicum if you need review):

(ii)   [Marginal Utility of Good X/Marginal Utility of Good Y]=[Price of Good X/Price of Good Y].

The first expression compares the marginal utility per unit price paid of good X to good Y. It says that the marginal utility (or marginal benefit) per unit of cost to the consumer of good X is equal to the marginal utility (or marginal benefit) per unit of cost to the consumer of good Y. If the equality sign was replaced with a > sign, then the marginal utility per unit price paid for good X would be greater than the marginal utility per unit price paid for good Y. Thus, a consumer could be better off (receive more utility) by re-arranging his budget to consume more of good X and less of good Y (or vice-versa if the equality sign were replaced with a < sign).

The second expression compares the relative marginal utility of good X to good Y to the relative price paid for good X to good Y. Remember that, to the consumer, the price paid for one unit of a good represents the marginal cost to the consumer. The second expression says that the relative marginal utility (or marginal benefit) of good X to good Y is equal to the relative marginal cost to the consumer of good X to good Y. If the equality sign was replaced with a > sign, then the marginal utility of good X relative to good Y would be greater than the relative marginal cost of good X to good Y. Since the relative marginal benefit of good X is greater than the relative marginal cost of good X, a consumer could be better of by rearranging his budget to consume more of good X and less of good Y (or vice-versa if the equality sign were replaced with a < sign).

PET #4

The utility-maximizing rule is based on a consumer having a given budget (income) and facing fixed prices of the goods. A bigger budget (income) or changes in the price of the goods the consumer typically purchases could alter the quantities that a consumer would select based on the utility-maximizing rule.

Suppose based on the utility-maximizing rule, you decide to buy one chicken-salad sandwich and three sodas a day. Suppose that the price of a chicken salad sandwich is $2.00 and the price of a soda is $0.50. Furthermore, the marginal utility you receive from the one and only chicken salad sandwich is 8 utils and the marginal utility you receive from the additional third soda is 2 utils. Are you maximizing your *total* utility? Let's see:

Using (i) from PET #3 above:

8 utils/$2.00 = 2 utils/$0.50
4 = 4.

Using (ii) from PET #3 above:

8 utils/2 utils = $2.00/$0.50
4 = 4.

Thus, you are maximizing your total utility (for the given prices and your given income) by consuming one sandwich and three sodas since the two ratios are equal.

Now, suppose the price of a soda goes up to $1 but you continue to consume one chicken salad sandwich and three sodas. What would happen to the conditions above? Let's see:

Using (i) from PET #3 above:

8 utils/$2.00 = 4 utils/$1.00
4 > 2.

This means that the marginal benefit per unit cost of one more chicken salad sandwich is greater than the marginal benefit per unit cost of one more soda. Thus, the consumer could be better off by increasing his consumption of chicken salad sandwiches and reducing his consumption of sodas.

Using (ii) from PET #3 above:

8 utils/2 utils = $2.00/$1.00
4 > 2.

This means that the marginal utility of chicken salad sandwiches relative to sodas is greater than the marginal cost of chicken salad sandwiches relative to sodas. Thus, the consumer could be better off by increasing his consumption of chicken salad sandwiches and reducing his consumption of sodas since he receives relatively more benefits than costs from chicken salad sandwiches.

Both of these examples illustrate what you probably already know: an increase in the price of a good (relative to others) will lead to a reduction in the amount consumed for a given income, tastes, etc.

Now, suppose that rather than the price of the goods changing, the income of the consumer changes. Let's suppose that the consumer gets an increase in his income. What will happen? Without any price changes, the *ratio* of prices will still be 4. However, since the consumer now has more income, he can consume more of *both* goods. When he does this, what will happen to the marginal utility of the goods? They will decline. Diminishing marginal utility tells you that, as more of a good is consumed, the addition to utility (marginal utility) of consuming one more unit of that good declines. Thus, for example, a consumer may now consume 3 chicken salad sandwiches and 6 sodas a day. The third chicken salad sandwich may now yield a marginal utility of 4 utils and the sixth soda may now yield a marginal utility of 1 util. However, it is no accident that the ratio of marginal utilities remains at 4. The utility-maximizing rule dictates that the consumer consume chicken salad sandwiches and sodas until the *ratio* of marginal utilities is equal to the ratio of the prices. Since the ratio of prices hasn't changed, the *ratio* of the marginal utilities must still be 4 even though the quantities consumed (and the respective marginal utilities) have changed.

PET #5

Consumer surplus is measured as the area underneath the demand curve but above the price line. It is measured using the formula for the area of a triangle which is 1/2 X base X height of triangle.

Suppose you were asked to compute the consumer surplus based on the graph below assuming the price is $5.

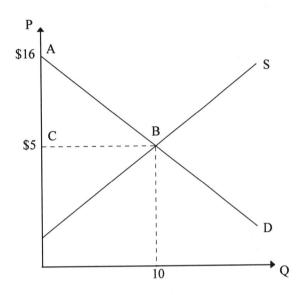

The triangle is marked off by the letters ABC. The base of the triangle is 10 units. The height of the triangle is ($16-$5) = $9.
Thus, the area of consumer surplus is 1/2 X 10 units X $9/unit = $45.

V.   PRACTICE EXAM: MULTIPLE CHOICE QUESTIONS

1.   Suppose you are given a monthly income of $200 to spend on food while at college. Further, suppose the price of a single-serving pizza is $4 and the price of a deli-sandwich is $2. Which one of the following consumption combinations is possible given these prices and income?

a.   40 pizzas, 50 sandwiches.
b.   15 pizzas, 80 sandwiches.
c.   20 pizzas, 60 sandwiches.
d.   10 pizzas, 100 sandwiches.
e.   50 pizzas, 20 sandwiches.

2.   When the price of a normal good declines, the quantity demanded increases because:

a.   the opportunity cost of consuming the good declines.

b.   a consumer's real income increases and this enables him to buy more.
c.   the consumer's marginal utility of the good increases.
d.   the good is worth more.
e.   (a) and (b).

3.   When the price of an inferior good declines,

a.   the substitution effect works to increase the quantity demanded and the income effect works to reduce the quantity demanded.
b.   the substitution and income effects both work to increase the quantity demanded.
c.   the substitution effect works to decrease the quantity demanded and the income effect works to increase the quantity demanded.
d.   the substitution and income effects both work to decrease the quantity demanded.
e.   the income effect dominates the substitution effect.

4.   Which one of the following would be the best example of an inferior good?

a.   steak.
b.   lobster.
c.   a cruise.
d.   macaroni and cheese.
e.   jewelry.

5.   Which one of the following could explain the observation that the U.S. buys more automobiles per year than Japan?

a.   differences in preferences/tastes for driving versus taking mass transit.
b.   a lower price of gasoline in the U.S. relative to Japan.
c.   a bigger population in the U.S.
d.   mass transit is safer in Japan than in the U.S.
e.   all of the above.

6.   Which one of the statements based on the following table is true?

Number of Sweaters Purchased	Total Utility
1	25 utils
2	40 utils
3	50 utils
4	55 utils
5	58 utils

a.   the marginal utility of the fifth sweater is 33 utils (58-25).
b.   total utility is diminishing.
c.   total utility is increasing but at a decreasing rate.
d.   marginal utility is negative.
e.   marginal utility cannot be computed without more information.

7.   Which one of the following terms is used in economics to describe the satisfaction that individuals receive from their consumption of goods and services?

a.   utility.
b.   opportunity cost.
c.   totality.
d.   plaisir.
e.   hedonity.

8.   Use the utility-maximizing rule and the information below to determine the correct answer.

Marginal utility of 1 shrimp = 10
Marginal utility of 1 strawberry = 5
Price of 1 shrimp = $0.25
Price of 1 strawberry = $0.10

Based on this information, a consumer:

a.   is maximizing his or her utility.
b.   should eat more strawberries and fewer shrimp.
c.   should eat more shrimp and fewer strawberries.
d.   is minimizing his or her utility.
e.   (b) and (d).

9.   Suppose you are given the following information:

price of an ice cream cone = $1.50
price of french fries = $0.75

Which one of the following statements is true given the information above?

a.   If a consumer is maximizing utility, then the marginal utility of an ice cream cone/marginal utility
        of french fries = 0.50.
b.   If a consumer is maximizing utility, then the marginal utility of an ice cream cone/marginal utility
        of french fries = 2.00.
c.   A consumer will maximize utility by eating 2 bags of french fries for every ice cream cone.
d.   With an income of $600 a month, a consumer could eat 300 ice cream cones and 400 bags of french
        fries.
e.   (b) and (d).

10.   Which one of the following statements is **NOT** true of a demand curve? Assume a normal good.

a.   it is negatively sloped.
b.   it will shift right as more consumers desire to buy the good.
c.   it is the sum of the quantities demanded by all consumers at various prices of the good.
d.   an increased preference for the good will shift the demand curve to the left.
e.   every point on the demand curve satisfies the marginal principle.

11.   Which one of the following statements is true based on the graph below?

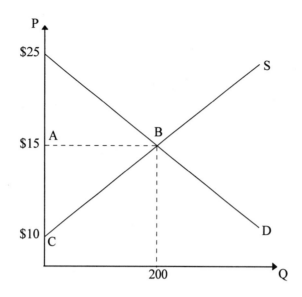

a.   Consumer surplus is measured by the triangle ABC.
b.   Consumer surplus equals $1,000.
c.   Consumer surplus will decrease if the price decreases.
d.   Consumer surplus will increase if the demand curve shifts to the right and the price increases.
e.   Consumer surplus will increase if the demand curve shifts to the left and the price increases.

VI.   PRACTICE EXAM: ESSAY QUESTIONS

1.   Explain the income and substitution effects for a normal good and for an inferior good.

2.   Suppose that you are a member of a book club for which you have paid an annual subscription fee of $30. As a member, you may purchase books for $1 a book and no more than 12 books per year. Using economic principles, explain how you might decide how many books to buy.

VII.   ANSWER KEY: MULTIPLE CHOICE

1.   Correct answer: c.

Discussion: The cost of 20 pizzas is $80 and the cost of 60 sandwiches is $120. The sum of these equals the monthly income of $200.

Statements a, b, d, and e are all combinations of pizzas and sandwiches that require more than $200.

2.   Correct answer: e.

Discussion: Statement e is correct because (a) is just a way of restating the substitution effect and (b) is just a way of restating the income effect.

Statement c is not correct because the *marginal* utility of increasing consumption (quantity demanded) would actually decline. More and more of a good adds progressively less to total utility which is to say that marginal utility declines as more is consumed. This is the law of diminishing marginal utility. Statement d is not correct because when the price of the good drops, it is worth less, not more. Statements a and b are both correct.

3.   Correct answer: a.

Discussion: For an inferior or normal good, the substitution effect *always* works to increase the quantity demanded. That is, when the price of a good drops, the quantity demanded will always rise regardless of whether the good is a normal or inferior good. However, the income effect works differently for an inferior good than for a normal good. First, the income effect arises because, when the price of a good drops, the real income of the consumer increases. Now, whether the income effect increases the quantity demanded or reduces the quantity demanded depends on whether the good is normal or inferior. Since the good is inferior, an increase in real income will reduce the quantity demanded.

Statement b would be correct if the question had asked about a normal good. Statement c is not correct because, when the price of a good drops, the substitution effect does not work to decrease quantity demanded but, rather, increase it. Also, with an inferior good, the income effect works to reduce quantity demanded, not increase it. Statement d is not correct because the substitution effect works to increase the quantity demanded. Statement e is not correct because it is not known whether the income effect dominates the substitution effect.

4.   Correct answer: d.

Discussion: When income increases, the consumption of macaroni and cheese is the most likely of the options listed to decrease.

Steak, lobster, jewelry, and a cruise are all goods for which the amount consumed would be most likely to increase when income increases.

5.   Correct answer: e.

Discussion: Statement a means that U.S. consumers simply prefer driving automobiles over mass transit as compared to the Japanese. This would translate in the observation that the U.S. buys more automobiles than Japan does. A lower price of gasoline in the U.S. means that it is less costly to drive an automobile in the U.S. than in Japan. Since gasoline is a complementary good to automobiles, the lower price of gasoline translates to a stronger demand for automobiles in the U.S. A bigger population in the U.S. than in Japan means that there is a bigger market or more buyers for automobiles than in Japan. This too, could explain why the U.S. buys more automobiles than Japan. If mass transit is safer in Japan than in the U.S, the Japanese would be more inclined to use mass transit than would Americans. In other words, Americans would be less inclined to use mass transit and, thus, more inclined to drive automobiles. This too, could explain why the U.S. buys more automobiles than Japan.

6.   Correct answer: c.

Discussion: This question requires that you compute the marginal utility associated with each sweater purchased. Thus, the marginal utility from the first sweater is 25 utils. The marginal utility or addition to utility from the second sweater is 15 utils (40-25); from the third sweater is 10 utils (50-40); from the fourth sweater is 5 utils (55-50); and from the fifth sweater is 3 utils (58-55). Thus, while total utility is increasing (from 25 to 58), it is increasing at a decreasing rate. Marginal utility is diminishing.

Statement a is not correct because the marginal utility from the fifth sweater is measured by asking what the addition to utility is from buying the fifth sweater. Thus, the correct answer would be 3 utils. Statement b is not correct because total utility is increasing; marginal utility is diminishing. Statement d is not correct because in no case is marginal utility computed to be negative. Statement e is not correct because you can compute marginal utility from the table.

7.   Correct answer: a.

Discussion: Utility is the term used to describe the satisfaction or enjoyment individuals receive from the consumption of goods and services.

While opportunity cost is an economic concept, it is not the term used to describe satisfaction from consumption. Totality, plaisir (french for pleasure), and hedonity are not correct.

8.   Correct answer: b.

Discussion: The ratio of the marginal utility of 1 shrimp to the price of 1 shrimp is 40 and the ratio of the marginal utility of one strawberry to the price of one strawberry is 50. Since the marginal utility per unit cost to the consumer of a strawberry is greater than for shrimp, the consumer could be made better off by consuming more strawberries and fewer shrimp.

Statement a is not correct. For the consumer to be maximizing utility, the ratios mentioned above would have to be equal to each other. (See PET #3.) Statement c is not correct since it should be the other way around. Statement d is not correct; while we know the consumer is not maximizing his utility, we can't say (without other information) whether the consumer is minimizing his utility. Statement e is not correct because statement d is not correct.

9.   Correct answer: e.

Discussion: Statement b is correct because the ratio of the price of an ice cream cone/price of french fries is 2. Thus, the ratio of the marginal utility of an ice cream cone/marginal utility of french fries must be equal to 2. (See PET #3.) Statement d is also correct because, if the consumer buys 200 ice cream cones at a price of $1.50 per cone, he spends $300 and has $300 remaining to spend on french fries. At a price of $0.75 per bag of french fries, the consumer can by 400 bags of fries with the remaining $300 from his income.

Statement a is not correct because the ratio is 2/1 not 1/2 (= 0.50). Statement c is not correct because the utility-maximizing rule only tells you about the ratio of the marginal utilities, not about the ratio at which ice cream cones and french fries would be eaten to maximize utility. For example, a 2/1 ratio of marginal utilities might correspond to 100 ice cream cones and 600 french fries which is a ratio of 6 bags of french fries/1 ice cream cone.

10.   Correct answer: d.

Discussion: An increased preference for a good will shift the demand curve for it to the right.

Statement a is true based on the Law of Demand. Statement b is true because more consumers increase the demand for a good. Statement c is true because a demand curve is representative of the market. Statement e is also true.

11.   Correct answer: b.

Discussion: Consumer surplus is measured using the formula for a triangle which is 1/2*base*height. In this case, the base is 200 units and the height is $10. Thus, the consumer surplus is 1/2*200units*$10/unit = $1,000.

Statement a is not correct; consumer surplus is measured by the triangle ADE. Statement c is not correct because consumer surplus increases when the price paid for the good decreases. (Draw in a lower price line). Statement d is not correct because you don't know what will happen to consumer surplus. On the one hand, the rightward shift will increase consumer surplus (draw a demand curve further to the right), but on the other hand, the price increase will decrease consumer surplus (draw in a higher price line). Statement e cannot be correct because a leftward shift in demand would decrease consumer surplus (draw a demand curve further to the left) as would a price increase (draw in a higher price line). Thus, consumer surplus would necessarily decrease.

VIII.   ANSWER KEY: ESSAY QUESTIONS

1.   Normal Good: When the price of a good drops, there are two effects: (1) the substitution effect, and (2) the income effect. The substitution effect means that, as the price of a good drops, the opportunity cost of purchasing it is now lower and so consumers are more inclined to buy more of the good. Thus, the price drop increases the quantity demanded (vice-versa for a price increase). The income effect occurs because, as the price of a good drops, a consumer is now able to purchase more of the good because his "real" income has increased. For example, if the price of a pair of shoes was $30 and they dropped to $15, a consumer could buy twice as many pairs of shoes as before, given the same nominal income. That is, the consumer's real income has increased. For a normal good, the price-drop induced increase in real income will increase the amount of the good that the consumer buys. The income effect also works in reverse. If the price increased rather than decreased, the consumer's real income would decline, and he would buy fewer units of the good.

Inferior Good: The substitution effect described above for a normal good is also present for an inferior good. Thus, the substitution effect works exactly as explained above. However, the income effect works differently. For an inferior good, as the price of the good drops and the consumer's real income thus rises, the consumer will now buy less of the good because it is an inferior good. Generic sodas or toilet paper are good examples of inferior goods. If, instead, the price of the good increased, the substitution effect would act to reduce the purchases of the good by the consumer. However, the real income effect would, in this case, lead to an increase in the quantity demanded for the good by the consumer.

2.   In order to decide how many books to buy, I would have to compute the marginal utility (addition to utility) I received from buying successively more and more books. I would also consider, in my mind, the opportunity cost of buying a book. The opportunity cost might be that I am able to buy fewer and fewer classical music tapes. I would then translate that opportunity cost into a loss of marginal utility. I would

have to know what the marginal utility that I would lose would be of giving up the purchase of classical music tapes. I would also have to know what the price of a classical music tape was. For example, suppose I received 15 utils from the third book and, correspondingly, given that I purchased three books, I am able to purchase twenty classical music tapes where the twentieth classical music tape yields 10 utils. Further, suppose that the price of a classical music tape is $5. In this case, the marginal utility of the fifth book/price of book = 5 and the marginal utility of twentieth tape/price of tape = 4. Thus, I would benefit by buying more books and fewer tapes since I will receive a relatively bigger addition to utility (per unit price paid) from more books than I will lose from cutting back on my purchases of classical music tapes.

Take It to the Net

We invite you to visit the O'Sullivan/Sheffrin page on the Prentice Hall Web site at:

http://www.prenhall.com/osullivan/

for this chapter's World Wide Web exercise.

APPENDIX TO CHAPTER 7: CONSUMER CHOICE USING INDIFFERENCE CURVES

I.   OVERVIEW

In the appendix to Chapter 7, you will see a more graphical depiction of consumer choice. You will use budget lines and indifference curves which are just ways of representing income constraints for given prices of goods and services and preferences. You will also see how an individual demand curve is derived.

II.   CHECKLIST

By the end of this appendix, you should be able to:

√   Draw a budget line assuming different prices for the goods under consideration.
√   Define the slope of the budget line and explain why it is equal to the price of the good on the horizontal axis divided by the price of the good on the vertical axis.
√   Define an indifference curve and explain the relationship of an indifference curve to one above it and one below it.
√   Define the marginal rate of substitution.
√   Explain why the indifference curve becomes flatter as you move down along the curve.
√   Draw a graph of a budget line and indifference curve and find the utility-maximizing point.
√   Explain why the utility-maximizing point is the point of tangency between the budget line and the indifference curve and why non-tangency points are not utility maximizing.
√   Derive a demand curve by changing the slope of the budget line and finding new utility-maximizing points.

III.   KEY TERMS

Consumer's budget set: a set of points that includes all the combinations of two goods that a consumer can afford, given the consumer's income and the prices of the two goods.
Budget line: the line connecting all the combinations of two goods that exhaust a consumer's budget.
Indifference curve: the set of combinations of two goods that generate the same level of utility or satisfaction.
Marginal rate of substitution (MRS): the rate at which a consumer is willing to substitute one good for another.

IV.   PERFORMANCE ENHANCING TIPS (PETS)

PET #1

The ratio of two variables can increase because the variable in the numerator gets bigger or because the variable in the denominator gets smaller. The ratio of two variables can decrease because the variable in the numerator gets smaller or because the variable in the denominator gets bigger.

For example, suppose the ratio of the marginal utility of good X to the marginal utility of good Y (MU_x/MU_y) is 4. Now, suppose a consumer consumes more of good X. Based on the law of diminishing marginal utility, the marginal utility of good X will decline. This means that the ratio, (MU_x/MU_y), will decrease from the value of 4. Suppose instead that the consumer consumes less of good Y. Based on the law of diminishing marginal utility (in reverse now because the consumer is consuming less, not more), the marginal utility of good Y will increase. This too, means that the ratio, (MU_x/MU_y), will decrease.

PET #2

The slope of the budget line is the ratio of the price of good X (good on the horizontal axis) to the price of good Y (good on the vertical axis) which is also equal to the ratio of the change in good Y divided by the change in good X.

Suppose the price of a single-serving pizza is $4 and the price of a deli sandwich is $2. Further, suppose a consumer has a budget/income of $200. If the consumer buys 20 pizzas, she will spend $80 and have $120 remaining to spend on sandwiches. Thus, she could buy 60 sandwiches. If the consumer decides to buy 30 pizzas, she will spend $120 and have $80 remaining to spend on sandwiches. Thus, she could buy 40 sandwiches. The change in the quantity of pizzas is +10 and the change in the quantity of deli sandwiches is -20.

Notice that the ratio of the price of a pizza to a sandwich is ($4/pizza)/($2/sandwich) = 2 sandwiches/1 pizza. Also, notice that, based on the numbers above, the change in the quantity of sandwiches divided by the change in the quantity of pizzas is 20/10 = 2 sandwiches/1 pizza (allowing for a negative sign since the consumer must trade-off sandwiches for pizzas).

V.   PRACTICE EXAM: MULTIPLE CHOICE QUESTIONS

1.   Which one of the following is true of indifference curves?

a.   they represent the combination of two goods that generate the same level of income.
b.   combinations of goods above the indifference curve generate more satisfaction.
c.   a lower point along an indifference curve yields less satisfaction than a higher point.
d.   the slope of the indifference curve gets bigger (steeper) as you move down the indifference curve.
e.   (b) and (c).

2.   Which one of the following statements is true assuming the marginal rate of substitution between good G and good H is equal to 3?

a.   an increase in the consumption of good G and a decrease in the consumption of good H will increase the marginal rate of substitution.
b.   if the ratio of the price of good G to the price of good H is 4, then a consumer is maximizing his utility.
c.   an increase in the consumption of good G and an increase in the consumption of good H will increase the marginal rate of substitution.
d.   a decrease in the consumption of good G and an increase in the consumption of good H will increase the marginal rate of substitution.

e.   a decrease in income will reduce the marginal rate of substitution.

3.   Which one of the points in the graph below is associated with utility maximization?

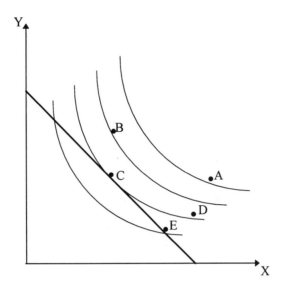

a.   point A.
b.   point B.
c.   point C.
d.   point D.
e.   point E.

4.   Suppose you are given the following information:

marginal utility of 1 cup coffee = 20 utils
marginal utility of 1 can soda = 10 utils
price of 1 cup of coffee = $1.00

What would the price of one can of soda have to be in order for the consumer to maximize his utility?

a. $0.50.
b. $2.00.
c. $5.00.
d. $200.
e.   cannot be answered without information on consumer's income/budget.

VI.   PRACTICE EXAM: ESSAY QUESTION

1.   Given the following information, draw a budget line for the consumer. Be sure to label the axes and provide a number for the vertical and horizontal intercepts.

        Income = $1,000/month.

Price of 1 pound of steak = $4.00
Price of 1 pound of potatoes = $0.50

Now, draw several indifference curves into the picture, being sure to draw one that represents utility maximization. Describe what is true at the utility-maximizing point. Describe why points on the other indifference curves do not represent utility maximization.

VII.   ANSWER KEY: MULTIPLE CHOICE

1.   Correct answer: b.

Discussion: An indifference curve that is further to the right than another represents a higher level of satisfaction. The reason is that a curve that is further to the right shows that more of good X can be had for every level of good Y or, alternatively, that more of good Y can be had for every level of good X. (See PET #3 of Chapter 1 of Practicum.)

Statement a is not correct; it would be correct if "income" was replaced with "utility" or "satisfaction." Statement c is not correct because a point on the same indifference curve, whether it is higher or lower, yields the same level of satisfaction.   Statement d is not correct because the slope of the indifference curve gets flatter as you move down the indifference curve. This happens because, as you move down the indifference curve, more of good X (the good on the horizontal axis) is being consumed and less of good Y (the good on the vertical axis) is being consumed. Thus, the marginal utility (addition to utility) of good X is declining and that of good Y is increasing. Since the slope of the indifference curve is MU_x/MU_y, the slope is getting smaller or flatter.

2.   Correct answer: d.

Discussion: A decrease in the consumption of good G will increase the marginal utility of good G (law of diminishing marginal utility in reverse because consumption of good G is decreasing, not increasing). An increase in the consumption of good H will decrease the marginal utility of good H. Since the question asks about MU_G/MU_H, this number will increase.

Statement a is not correct because the marginal rate of substitution would decrease. Statement b is not correct; for utility maximization the price ratio would have to be 3. Statement c is not correct because the marginal rate of substitution is defined with respect to trade-offs in consumption of one good relative to another. Statement c allows for an increase in the consumption of both goods. Statement e is not correct because income does not affect the marginal rate of substitution (which is the slope of the indifference curve).

3.   Correct answer: c.

Discussion: At point c, the indifference curve is tangent to the budget line. The tangency means that the marginal rate of substitution between good X and good Y is equal to the price ratio of good X to good Y.

Points A, B, D, and E are not tangencies. Points A and B are unattainable given the current income of the consumer. Point D is on the same indifference curve as point C but is not the tangency point. Point E is on a lower indifference curve than point C and, thus, cannot be utility maximizing given the consumer's current income.

4.   Correct answer: a.

Discussion: The marginal utility of 1 cup of coffee/marginal utility of 1 can of soda is 2 (20/10). Thus, the price of 1 cup of coffee/price of 1 can of soda must also be 2. Since the price of 1 cup of coffee is $1, a can of soda must cost $0.50 for utility maximization to prevail.

Based on the above, statements b, c, and d cannot be correct. Statement e is not correct because you do not need information on the consumer's budget to determine the condition for utility maximization.

VIII.   ANSWER KEY: ESSAY QUESTION

1.   My drawing puts potatoes on the vertical axis and steak on the horizontal axis. With an income of $1,000, 2,000 pounds of potatoes could be purchased in one month if no steak was purchased. With an income of $1000, 250 pounds of steak could be purchased in one month if no potatoes were purchased. Thus, the vertical intercept is 2,000 pounds of potatoes and the horizontal intercept is 250 pounds of steak. The slope of the budget line is given by the ratio of the price of steak to the price of potatoes. Thus, the slope of the budget line is 8 pounds of potatoes/1 steak. You can also figure out the slope of the budget line by taking two points (end points since you have information on them) and calculating the change in pounds of potatoes consumed and pound of steak consumed. The change in pounds of potatoes consumed is (2,000 - 0) and the change in pounds of steak consumed is (250 - 0). Using the formula for a slope of rise/run, the slope of the budget line would be 8 pounds of potatoes/1 pound of steak.

The utility-maximizing point is found where the slope of the indifference curve is tangent to the budget line. This occurs at point A. At this point, the marginal utility of steak/marginal utility of potatoes = price of steak/price of potatoes. A consumer cannot get to a higher indifference curve, like point B, since his income does not allow him to afford that combination of goods. A point like point C is on a lower indifference curve than point A and, thus, not one that achieves the highest level of utility (satisfaction).

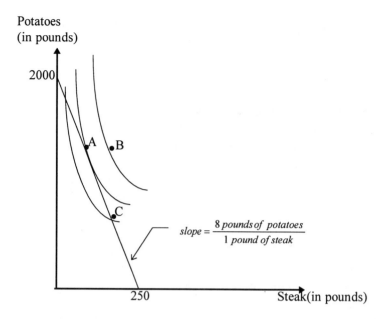

Take It to the Net

We invite you to visit the O'Sullivan/Sheffrin page on the Prentice Hall Web site at:

http://www.prenhall.com/osullivan/

for this chapter's World Wide Web exercise.

CHAPTER 8
THE FIRM'S SHORT-RUN AND LONG-RUN COST CURVES

I.   OVERVIEW

In this chapter, you will learn about the costs a firm incurs when it produces output. You will learn that there are fixed costs and variable costs, and explicit and implicit costs of production. You will learn that a firm's marginal cost changes as it produces more and more (or less and less) output. You will also learn about a firm's short- and long-run average costs. You will learn that the short and the long run are different time horizons that a firm considers when making decisions about how much to produce, whether to build another plant, hire more workers, or cut back production. You will re-encounter the concept of diminishing returns which is a short-run concept. You will learn about economies and diseconomies of scale which are long-run concepts.

II.   CHECKLIST

By the end of this chapter, you should be able to:

√   Explain the difference between explicit and implicit costs.
√   Give some examples of explicit costs and implicit costs.
√   Explain the difference between accounting profit and economic profit.
√   Explain the difference between the short run and the long run.
√   Explain the difference between variable and fixed costs and why, in the long run, all costs are variable.
√   Give some examples of variable costs and fixed costs.
√   Explain why diminishing returns cause marginal cost in the short run to increase.
√   Draw a short-run average fixed cost curve and a short-run average variable cost curve and explain their shape.
√   Draw a long-run average cost curve and explain its shape.
√   Draw a short-run marginal cost curve and explain its shape.
√   Explain the relationship between marginal cost and the average cost curves.
√   Explain what causes economies and diseconomies of scale.
√   Define a firm's minimum efficient scale and represent it with a graph.

III.   KEY TERMS

Short run for microeconomics: a period of time over which the number of firms in an industry is fixed and existing firms cannot change their production facilities.
Long run for microeconomics: a period of time over which the number of firms in an industry can change and firms can change their production facility.
Short-run marginal cost (SMC): the change in total cost resulting from a one-unit increase in output from an existing production facility.
Short-run average total cost (SATC): short-run total cost divided by the quantity of output.
Fixed cost: costs that do not depend on the quantity produced.
Average fixed cost (AFC): fixed cost divided by the quantity produced.
Variable costs: costs that vary as the firm changes its output.

Short-run average variable cost (SAVC): variable cost divided by the quantity produced.
Indivisible input: an input that cannot be scaled down to produce a small quantity of output.
Long-run average cost (LAC): total cost divided by the quantity of output when the firm can choose a production facility of any size.
Economies of scale: a situation in which an increase in the quantity produced decreases the long-run average cost of production.
Minimum efficient scale: the output at which the long-run average cost curve becomes horizontal.
Diseconomies of scale: a situation in which an increase in the quantity produced increases the long-run average cost of production.
Explicit costs: the firm's actual cash payments for its inputs.
Implicit costs: the opportunity costs of non-purchased inputs.
Economic cost: the sum of explicit and implicit costs.

IV.   PERFORMANCE ENHANCING TIPS (PETS)

PET #1

For any formula, if you are given two of three components, you can always figure out the third component. Likewise for three of four, four of five, and so on.

You encountered this PET in Chapter 5 where it was applied to the elasticity of demand. In this chapter, you can apply it to total, variable, and fixed costs, average total, average variable, and average fixed costs, and output. Let's see how.

Suppose you are told that the total cost of producing 100 units of output is $2,000. What is the average total cost? The average total cost (ATC) is computed using:

$$ATC = \text{Total Cost/Output}$$

Since you have two of the three components to the formula, you can figure out the third component. Thus, the average total cost would be $2,000/100 units = $20/unit.

Now, suppose you are told that the average total cost is $20/unit and that the output level is 100 units. What is the total cost (TC)? The formula above can be rearranged as below to figure out the total cost:

$$TC = ATC \times \text{Output}$$

Thus, the total cost would be $20/unit X 100 units = $2,000.

Next, suppose you are told that the average total cost is $20/unit and that the total cost is $2,000. How many units of output (Q) must the firm be producing? The formulas above can be rearranged as below to figure out the output of the firm:

$$Q = \text{Total Cost/Average Total Cost}$$

Thus, the firm must be producing $2,000/($20/unit) = 100 units.

The same is true for computing variable costs (total or average) and fixed costs (total or average).

You can also apply this PET to the relationship between short-run total cost, variable cost, and fixed cost, and to the relationship between short-run average total cost, average variable cost, and average fixed cost.

For example, suppose you are told that the variable cost of producing 100 units of output is $1,500 and the fixed cost of producing 100 units of output is $500. What is the short-run total cost?

The short-run total cost is the sum of the two:

Total Cost = variable cost + fixed cost

Thus, the total cost is $2,000.

Based on the information above, the average variable cost would be $1,500/100 units = $15/unit and the average fixed cost would be $500/100 units $5/unit. Thus, the average total cost would be:

Average total cost = average variable cost + average fixed cost

Thus, the average total cost would be $15/unit + $5/unit = $20/ unit.

PET #2

Short-run marginal cost is computed by calculating the change in (or addition to) the short-run total cost as output increases by one unit. Since the short-run total cost is the sum of variable cost plus fixed cost, and since fixed costs do not change as the level of output changes, then marginal cost can also be computed by calculating the change in the short-run variable cost as output increases by one unit.

Suppose you are told that the variable cost of producing 10 units of output is $250 and that the fixed cost of producing 10 units of output is $100. Further, you are told that the variable cost of producing 11 units of output is $275. Since fixed costs are fixed, the fixed cost of producing 11 units of output remains at $100. What is the total cost of producing 10 units of output? Of 11 units of output? What is the marginal cost of the 11th unit of output?

Total cost of producing 10 units of output is $250 + $100 = $350.

Total cost of producing 11 units of output is $275 + $100 = $375.

The marginal cost (addition to cost) of producing one more unit of output, the 11th unit, is equal to the change in total cost which is also equal to the change in the variable cost. Let's see why:

Marginal Cost of 11th unit = Change in total cost = change in variable cost + change in fixed cost.

The change in total cost is $375 - $350 = $25.
The change in variable cost is $275 - $250 = $25.
The change in fixed cost is $100 - $100 = $0.

Notice that the sum of the change in the variable cost plus the change in the fixed cost equals $25. This is because fixed costs do not change as output changes. That is, the marginal cost associated with fixed inputs is zero. Thus, in the short run, the marginal cost can also be computed as the change in the variable cost.

Remember that in the long run, all costs are variable costs. There are no "fixed" costs.

PET #3

When marginal cost is less than average total (or average variable) cost, average total (or average variable) cost will decrease. When marginal cost is greater than average total (or average variable) cost, average total (or average variable) cost will increase.

Suppose that you are told that the average total cost of producing 300 units of output is $60 and that the marginal cost of producing the 301st unit of output is $65. Will the average total cost of producing 301 units of output be greater or less than $60?

Since the marginal cost of increasing output by one unit to 301 units is greater than the average cost of producing the previous 300 units, then the average cost of producing 301 units will increase.

V.   PRACTICE EXAM: MULTIPLE CHOICE QUESTIONS

1.   Which one of the following would be considered an implicit cost by a firm?

a.   monthly electricity bill.
b.   monthly rent for use of a warehouse.
c.   weekly wages paid to workers.
d.   foregone interest income because an entrepreneur must use her own money to start up a business.
e.   payment for installation of a fax line.

2.   In the long run, a firm can:

a.   alter the number of workers it hires.
b.   alter the amount of raw materials it uses.
c.   alter the size of the factory.
d.   open up new factories or close down factories.
e.   all of the above.

3.   Which one of the following statements is true?

a.   short-run total cost = variable cost - fixed cost.
b.   short-run total cost = variable cost + fixed cost.
c.   average total cost = average variable cost/average fixed cost.
d.   fixed cost = average fixed cost/output.
e.   average variable cost = variable cost X output.

4.   Which one of the following explains why a firm's short-run marginal cost increases as it produces more and more output?

a.   diminishing returns.
b.   diseconomies of scale.
c.   increasing returns to scale.
d.   diminishing marginal utility.
e.   diseconomies of scope.

5.   Which one of the following statements is true?

a.   a firm's short-run average variable cost first increases and then decreases as output increases.
b.   a firm's short-run average total cost curve is shaped like a "W."
c.   a firm's average fixed cost always decreases as output increases.
d.   average variable cost increases as output increases because each additional worker becomes less and less productive in the short run.
e.   (c) and (d).

6.   Use the following information to answer the question below.

output = 250 units
fixed cost = $1,000
average variable cost = $6 per unit
average total cost = $10 per unit
marginal cost = $12

Which one of the following statements is true based on the information above?

a.   average fixed cost = $4 per unit and total cost = $25,000.
b.   variable cost = $1,500 and average fixed cost = $4 per unit.
c.   variable cost = $2,500 and total cost = $1,500.
d.   average fixed cost = $4 per unit and total cost = $22.
e.   total cost = $1,006 and variable cost = $18.

7.   Use the following information to answer the question below.

output = 100 units
average fixed cost = $3 per unit
short-run total cost = $800
marginal cost = $60

The firm's total variable cost must be:

a. $500.
b. $770.
c. $77.
d. $7,700.
e.   cannot be calculated without more information.

8.   Use the graph below to answer the following question.

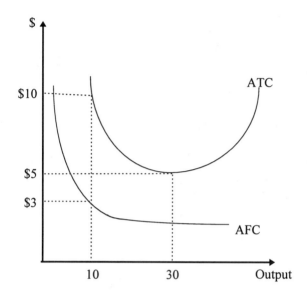

Which one of the following statements is true?

a.   the average variable cost of producing 10 units of output is $13 per unit.
b.   the total cost of producing 30 units of output is $5.
c.   the variable cost of producing 10 units of output is $70.
d.   the marginal cost of producing 30 units of output must be less than $5.
e.   none of the above are true.

9.   Which one of the following defines the long-run average cost of production?

a.   total cost divided by the quantity of output when the firm cannot alter the number of workers it hires.
b.   total cost divided by the quantity of output when the firm can choose a production facility of any size.
c.   total cost multiplied by the quantity of output when the firm can choose a production facility of any size.
d.   total cost divided by the quantity of output when the firm cannot alter the size of its facilities.
e.   total cost divided by the quantity of output when the firm cannot change the number of factories it operates.

10.   Which one of the following is a reason for economies of scale?

a.   specialization.
b.   diminishing returns.
c.   divisible inputs.
d.   rising marginal costs.
e.   comparative advantage.

11.   Which one of the following is **NOT** an example of an indivisible input?

a.   an industrial mold for a giant bowl of jello.
b.   a large cargo ship.
c.   "clean rooms" used by a computer-chip maker.
d.   an expensive piece of medical equipment.
e.   all of the above are examples of indivisible inputs.

12.   Which one of the following statements is **NOT** true?

a.   the minimum efficient scale for production is that output level where average costs are neither increasing nor decreasing, i.e., the long-run average cost curve is horizontal.
b.   diseconomies of scale may arise from the use of indivisible inputs.
c.   diseconomies of scale may occur because of coordination problems that arise as more and more output is produced.
d.   diseconomies of scale may occur because input costs increase as a firm produces more and more output.
e.   in the long run, a firm does not encounter diminishing returns.

VI.   PRACTICE EXAM: ESSAY QUESTIONS

1.   Explain why specialization can lead to economies of scale.

2.   Distinguish diminishing returns from diseconomies of scale.

VII.   ANSWER KEY: MULTIPLE CHOICE QUESTIONS

1.   Correct answer: d.

Discussion: An implicit cost is a cost for which there is not an explicit payment by check or money. Your textbook lists two types of implicit costs -- the cost of a business owner's time and the cost of a business owner's use of his or her own funds (financial capital). Implicit costs should be included when figuring up economic profit. However, they are not included when figuring up accounting profit.

Statements a, b, c, and e are all examples of explicit costs.

2.   Correct answer: e.

Discussion: The long run is defined as a period of time over which a firm is able to choose the combination of workers, raw materials, size of the factory, and number of factories to operate in order to produce output at the least per unit cost (average cost).

Statements a, b, c, and d are all factors of production that can be altered in the long run. In the short run, however, generally speaking, only the number of workers and the amount of raw material a firm uses can be altered. The size of the factory along with the number of factories currently in operation cannot simply be changed on short notice (say, one week).

3.   Correct answer: b.

Discussion: Short-run total cost is the sum of variable cost plus fixed cost. That's why its referred to as "total."

Statement a is not correct because total cost is the sum of, not the difference between, variable cost and fixed cost. Statement c is not correct. It would have been correct if it had read "average total cost = average variable cost + average fixed cost." Statement d is not correct. It would have been correct if it had read "fixed cost = average fixed cost X output." Statement e is not correct. It would have been correct if it had read "average variable cost = variable cost/output." (See PET #1 for review.)

4.   Correct answer: a.

Discussion: Diminishing returns means that each additional worker that is hired to produce more output is less productive than the workers hired before him. Thus, it becomes more costly to the firm to get that worker to produce the same level of output as the previous workers. A way to think about it is that that worker would have to work more hours than the other workers (and, therefore, be paid overtime) in order to produce the same amount of output as the other workers are producing.

Diseconomies of scale is a long-run concept. Increasing returns to scale is not a term you have encountered, nor is diseconomies of scope. Diminishing marginal utility is a concept related to consumer "satisfaction" not a firm's cost of production.

5.   Correct answer: e.

Discussion: Statement c is correct because fixed costs do not change with the level of output. Since average fixed cost is calculated as fixed cost/output, as output increases, average fixed cost must decline. (The number in the denominator gets bigger but the number in the numerator does not change). Statement d is also correct. It is another way of stating that diminishing returns gives rise to increasing average variable cost (as well as increasing marginal cost).

Statement a is not correct because average total cost first decreases and then increases as output increases. Statement b is not correct; a firm's average total cost curve is shaped like a "U." Statements c and d are both correct, which is why statement e is the answer.

6.   Correct answer: b.

Discussion: Variable cost is computed by multiplying average variable cost by the output level = $6 per unit X 250 units = $1,500. Average fixed cost is computed by dividing fixed cost by the output level = $1,000/250 units = $4/unit.

Statement a is not correct because total cost is $2,500, not $25,000. Total cost can be computed from figuring out variable cost (as above) which is $1,500 and adding to it the fixed cost of $1,000. Statement c is not correct based on the discussion. Statement d is not correct because total cost is not $22. (Total cost is not the sum of marginal cost plus average total cost). Statement e is not correct because total cost is not $1,006 and variable cost is not $18.

7.   Correct answer: a.

Discussion: To arrive at the correct answer, you must compute fixed cost using average fixed cost and output. Fixed cost = $3 per unit X 100 units = $300. Then, you can compute variable cost from the difference between total cost and fixed cost = $800 - $300 = $500.

Statements b, c, and d are not correct based on the above discussion. Statement e is not correct because there is enough information (i.e., you don't need to know average variable cost) to compute total variable cost.

8.   Correct answer: c.

Discussion: The graph shows the average total cost and average fixed cost associated with different levels of production. Since the average total cost of 10 units of output is $10 per unit and the average fixed cost is $3 per unit, the average variable cost must be $7 per unit. Since the average variable cost is $7 per unit, the variable cost must be $7 per unit X 10 units = $70.

Statement a is not correct because the average variable cost is $7 per unit. Statement b is not correct. It would have been correct if it stated that the *average* total cost of production was $5. Statement d is not correct because average total cost is increasing beyond 30 units of output. If the average cost is increasing, the marginal cost must be greater than the average cost of $5, not less than $5. Statement e is not correct because statement c is correct.

9.   Correct answer: b.

Discussion: Statement b is correct; it indicates a long-run concept since the production facility's size can be changed and because an average cost is computed by dividing a total cost by an output level.

Statements a, d, and e are not correct because they imply short-run concepts where the firm has some fixed factors of production that cannot be changed. Statement c is not correct because average cost is not computed by multiplying total cost by the output level.

10.   Correct answer: a.

Discussion: When workers are able to specialize in the tasks that they do, they become more productive. They know how to do a task well and they don't have to spend time switching from task to task. Statement b is not correct; diminishing returns give rise to increasing marginal (and variable and total) costs of production. Statement c is not correct; indivisible inputs give rise to economies of scale, not divisible inputs. Statement d is not correct because, with economies of scale, marginal costs will be decreasing or not changing. Statement e is not a concept that is applied to economies of scale.

11.   Correct answer: e.

Discussion: Indivisible inputs are those inputs that cannot be divided up to accommodate low levels of production. For example, a piece of medical equipment must be purchased by a hospital regardless of whether they will use it for one patient, two patients, twenty patients, or one thousand patients. The same is true of an industrial mold, a large cargo ship, and clean rooms used by a computer chip maker. Can you think of other examples?

12.   Correct answer: b.

Discussion: Statement b is the only statement that is not true. Indivisible inputs give rise to economies of scale, not diseconomies of scale. All of the other statements are true.

VIII.   ANSWER KEY: ESSAY QUESTIONS

1.   Specialization is a long-run concept. In the long run, a firm is able to alter the amount of equipment each worker has to work with and the amount of space within which each worker works. Thus, in the long run, with more equipment and more space to work, workers can specialize at a task. This means that they can now spend more time on one task (rather than having to move between tasks). This makes workers more productive because time is not lost as workers move between tasks. Thus, each worker is able to produce more output per hour than before. Also, since workers spend more time on the same task, they learn to do the task more efficiently and, thus, can produce more output per hour than before. Since more output per hour is being produced by the workers and their wages have not changed, the average cost per unit of output will decline in the long run. Economies of scale is defined as a declining average cost as output increases.

2.   Diminishing returns is a short-run concept and arises because one (or more) of the factors of production with which a firm produces output is fixed, i.e., the amount is not able to be changed in the short run. Typically, plant and equipment are considered the fixed factors of production. Since the amount of plant and equipment is fixed, if a firm wants to produce more output, it must hire more workers but cannot alter the amount of plant and equipment. Consequently, more and more workers are jammed into factory floor space and may have to waste time waiting for a piece of equipment to use to finish their task. What this means is that each additional worker that is hired by the firm will produce less output per hour than the previous worker. This is the definition of diminishing returns.

Diseconomies of scale is a long-run concept and arises because of coordination problems and increasing input costs when a firm gets bigger and bigger (produces more and more output). Diseconomies of scale is defined as an increase in long-run average cost as output increases. This is the reverse of economies of scale. Coordination problems can contribute to the average cost of production increasing as output increases. Coordination problems may arise because of layers of bureaucracy or management that a business decision must pass through before actually being executed and/or because of personnel problems. Also, as a firm produces more and more output, it increases its demand for inputs which can put upward pressure on the price of inputs. This can thereby contribute to an increase in the average cost of production.

Take It to the Net

We invite you to visit the O'Sullivan/Sheffrin page on the Prentice Hall Web site at:

http://www.prenhall.com/osullivan/

for this chapter's World Wide Web exercise.

CHAPTER 9
PERFECT COMPETITION IN THE SHORT RUN

I.   OVERVIEW

In this chapter, you will learn about the four different types of market structure. However, in this chapter, you will focus on the perfectly competitive market structure and the characteristics that describe it. You will learn how a firm decides how much output to produce in a perfectly competitive market. You will use the cost concepts and cost curves that you learned about in the previous chapter together with a revenue and marginal revenue curve. You will re-encounter the marginal principle and apply it to determining the level of output that will maximize a firm's profit. You will learn about the factors that influence a firm's decision to either shut down its operation or to continue it even in the face of losses. You will learn what factors might contribute to entry to or exit from a perfectly competitive market. You will see how entry and exit affect the profit levels of the firms that are already operating in the market. You will also see how an industry supply curve is derived from individual firms' collective decisions about how much to produce at various prices. You will learn about producer surplus which is analogous to the concept of consumer surplus that you learned about in Chapter 7. You will see that the interaction of supply and demand in a perfectly competitive market structure in which there are no spillover costs or benefits creates an efficient outcome.

II.   CHECKLIST

By the end of this chapter, you should be able to:

√   List the characteristics of a perfectly competitive market structure.
√   Give some real world examples of a perfectly competitive market structure.
√   Define total and marginal revenue and represent them with a graph.
√   Explain the difference between economic profit and accounting profit.
√   Explain why marginal revenue equals price in a perfectly competitive market.
√   Explain why the rule of picking an output level where price (marginal revenue) equals marginal cost maximizes a firm's profit.
√   Use a graph to pick the profit-maximizing output level and represent profit on the graph.
√   Explain when a firm would, in the short run, decide to shut down its operation and when, in the long run, it would decide to shut down its operation.
√   Explain what would happen in a perfectly competitive market to the typical firm earning zero economic profit when there is an increase in market demand (and vice-versa).
√   Use graphs to show what would happen in a perfectly competitive market to the typical firm earning zero economic profit when there is an increase in market demand (and vice-versa).
√   Define producer surplus and represent it with a graph.
√   Use market demand and supply curve to explain market efficiency and to show why maximum and minimum prices do not lead to efficiency.

III.   KEY TERMS

Perfectly competitive market: a market with a very large number of firms, each of which produces the same standardized product and takes the market price as given.

Total revenue: the money the firm gets by selling its product; equal to the price times the quantity sold.

Operating cost: the cost incurred by operating as opposed to shutting down a production facility.

Sunk cost: the cost a firm has already paid or has agreed to pay some time in the future.

Shut-down price: the price at which the firm is indifferent between operating and shutting down.

Firm's short-run supply curve: a curve showing the relationship between price and the quantity of output supplied by a firm.

Short-run industry supply curve: a curve showing the relationship between price and the quantity of output supplied by an entire industry.

Short-run supply curve: a curve showing the relationship between price and quantity supplied in the short run (the number of firms is fixed and firms cannot change their production facilities).

Short-run marginal cost: the change in cost from producing just one more unit of output in an existing facility.

Economic profit: total revenue minus the total economic cost (the sum of explicit and implicit costs).

Accounting profit: total revenue minus explicit costs.

Normal accounting profit: an accounting profit equal to the firm's implicit costs.

Total value of a market: The sum of the net benefits experienced by consumers and producers; equal to the sum of consumer surplus and producer surplus.

Producer surplus: the difference between the market price of a product and the minimum amount a producer is willing to accept for that product. Alternatively, the difference between the market price and the marginal cost of production.

IV.   PERFORMANCE ENHANCING TIPS (PETS)

PET #1

Price and marginal revenue are the same number for a firm in a perfectly competitive market structure.

Let's explore why price and marginal revenue are the same number in for a firm in a perfectly competitive market structure. In perfect competition, a firm is a price taker which means that it does not have to lower the price of its product to sell more of it. It can sell all that it wants at the going price. This means that, as a firm sells more and more units of its output, it continues to get the same price for its output.

For example, suppose the price of output was $2 per unit. If a firm sells one unit, the total revenue it receives is $2. If a firm sells two units, the total revenue it receives is $4. If a firm sells three units, the total revenue it receives is $6, and so on. Now, what is the marginal revenue (or addition to revenue) from selling one more unit? When the firm sells two units instead of one, it adds $2 to its total revenue ($4 - $2). When the firm sells three units instead of two, it adds $2 to its total revenue ($6 - $4), and so on. Thus, marginal revenue and price are the same for a firm in a perfectly competitive market structure.

PET #2

The rule of picking an output level where price is equal to marginal cost in order to maximize profit can also be expressed as picking an output level where marginal revenue is equal to marginal cost. This happens because, in a perfectly competitive market structure, marginal revenue and price are the same number.

In the next few chapters, the rule for maximizing profits that you will encounter is to pick an output level where marginal revenue is equal to marginal cost (instead of where price is equal to marginal cost). But, it is really the same rule that you have learned in this, chapter and the same rationale for why the rule maximizes a firm's profit applies. It may be better to remember the rule as marginal revenue = marginal cost instead of price = marginal cost as long as you understand that price and marginal revenue are the same for a firm operating in a perfectly competitive market.

PET #3

*Firms that earn zero economic profit can continue to operate. This is because a firm earning zero **economic** profit can be earning a positive **accounting** profit. The positive accounting profit is what a firm may use to fund projects that will allow it to continue to operate in the future.*

V.   PRACTICE EXAM: MULTIPLE CHOICE QUESTIONS

1.   Which one of the following is **NOT** a characteristic of a perfectly competitive market structure?

a.   very large number of firms.
b.   standardized (or homogeneous) product.
c.   barriers to entry.
d.   no control over price.
e.   all of the above are characteristics of a perfectly competitive market structure.

2.   Which one of the following would be an example of a perfectly competitive industry?

a.   restaurants.
b.   hog farmers.
c.   aircraft industry.
d.   auto dealerships.
e.   patented sheetworking tools.

3.   Use the information below to answer the following question.

    quantity sold = 500,000 units
    price = $1.00 per unit
    explicit costs = $400,000
    implicit costs = $150,000

Based on this information, the firm is:

a.   earning positive economic profit of $100,000.
b.   earning zero economic profit.
c.   earning positive accounting profit of $100,000.
d.   making an economic loss (negative economic profit) of $50,000.
e.   (c) and (d).

4.   A firm can maximize its profits by picking an output level where:

a.   price > average variable costs.
b.   price > average total costs.
c.   marginal revenue = marginal cost.
d.   price = average variable cost.
e.   (b) and (c).

5.   Which one of the following statements is always true of a firm in a perfectly competitive market?

a.   price = marginal revenue.
b.   price = marginal cost.
c.   price = total revenue.
d.   average total cost = average variable cost.
e.   economic profit is positive.

6.   Use the graph below to answer the following question.

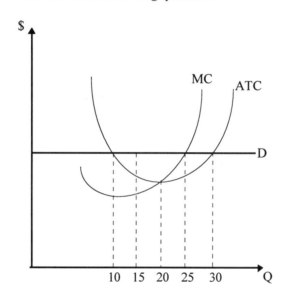

The output level that will maximize the firm's profit is:

a.   10 units.
b.   15 units.
c.   20 units.
d.   25 units.
e.   30 units.

7.   Use the diagram below to compute the profit that the firm is earning.

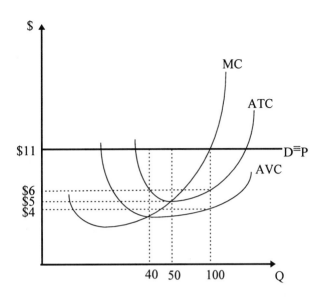

The firm's profit is:

a. $0.
b. $500.
c. $300.
d. $200.
e. $700.

8.   Which one of the following statements is correct based on the following information?

        price = $5.00 per unit
        quantity = 200 units
        total variable cost = $400
        total fixed cost = $800
        marginal cost = $5.00

a.   the firm is making a loss but should, in the short run, continue to operate.
b.   the firm is making a loss and should shut down its operation.
c.   the firm is making a profit of $600.
d.   the firm is making zero profit.
e.   price is greater than average total cost.

9.   Which one of the following statements is correct based on the graph below?

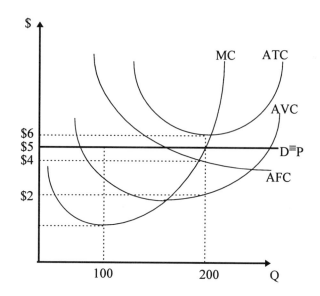

a.   the firm is making a loss but should, in the short run, continue to operate.
b.   the firm is making a loss and should shut down its operation in the short run.
c.   the firm is making a profit of $600.
d.   the firm is making zero profit.
e.   price is greater than average total cost.

10.   Which one of the following statements is true?

a.   in the short run, if a firm shuts down, it will have zero revenue and zero costs.
b.   a firm should shut down if price is greater than average variable cost but less than average total cost.
c.   a firm can maximize its profits by producing an output level where price equals marginal revenue.
d.   in the short run, if a firm shuts down, it will have a loss equal to the amount of its sunk (or fixed) costs.
e.   none of the above.

11.   Suppose all firms in a perfectly competitive industry are currently earning zero economic profit. Assume the price of output is $10 per unit. Now, suppose that consumer demand for the industry's product declines. Which one of the following would be least likely to occur?

a.   firms may begin to earn a negative economic profit in the short run.
b.   price will decline.
c.   marginal costs will rise.
d.   some firms will exit the industry.
e.   producer surplus will decrease in the short run.

12.   In the graph below, producer surplus is measured by the area:

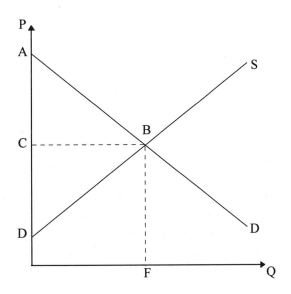

a.   ABC.
b.   ABD.
c.   CBD.
d.   OCBF.
e.   OBF.

13.   Based on the graph below, which one of the following prices is the efficient price (the one that maximizes total market value)?

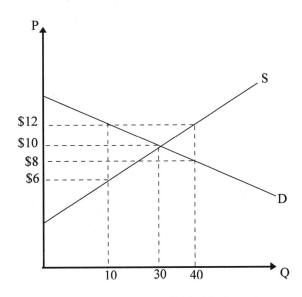

a. $12.
b. $10.
c. $8.
d. $25.
e. $0.

VI.   PRACTICE EXAM: ESSAY QUESTIONS

1.   Briefly explain why it is profit maximizing for a firm to produce output up until the point at which marginal revenue equals marginal cost.

2.   Suppose, after graduation, you take a job in a factory in Chile that produces faux leather shoes. One day, your boss comes in and says, "This factory isn't operating at a profit, so we can minimize our losses by closing up shop." Yikes! You didn't think you'd lose your job that quickly. Your boss continues talking and states that the company is having to pay 300,000 pesos a month for rent, interest on debt, and other non-avoidable costs. He also says that it costs 150,000 pesos a month just to pay you and all the other workers, including paying for the raw materials, to produce the shoes. He states that, at current production of 5,000 boxes of shoes a month, the company can only expect to get 40 pesos per box of shoes. Do you agree with your boss that the company should close up shop? Why or why not?

VII.   ANSWER KEY: MULTIPLE CHOICE

1.   Correct answer: c.

Discussion: Barriers to entry characterize an oligopolistic and monopolist market structure.

A perfectly competitive market structure is one in which there are a very large number of firms each producing a very small portion of overall industry output. The product produced is said to be "standardized" or "homogeneous," which means that consumers don't perceive very much of a difference in buying from one producer than any other. Since there are so many firms providing such a small portion of industry output, the firms have no control over price; it is dictated by the market forces of supply and demand. Firms are said to be "price takers."

2.   Correct answer: b.

Discussion: Hog farmers are many and produce a fairly standardized product, the hog.

Pizzerias are an example of a monopolistically competitive market structure since they produce a slightly differentiated product. The same may be true of auto dealerships (although auto manufacturers are considered to be an oligopoly). The aircraft industry is an example of an oligopolistic market structure since there are few firms in the industry that typically operate with economies of scale. A firm that has a patent typically has a monopoly. Thus, patented sheetworking tools are an example of a monopoly.

3.   Correct answer: e.

Discussion: The total revenue that the firm is earning is $500,000 ($5 X 100,000 units). The economic cost is $550,000 (= $400,000 + $150,000). Thus, economic profit is -$50,000. That is, the firm is earning a loss.

The accounting profit that the firm is earning is equal to $100,000 ($500,000 - $400,000). Thus statements c and d are both correct. Statements a and b are not correct because the firm is making negative economic profit.

4.   Correct answer: c.

Discussion: The rule for maximizing profits is to pick an output level where marginal revenue equals marginal cost. There is only one output level where this is true. When a firm follows this principle, it may make positive profit, zero profit, or even a negative profit (in which case we'd say that the firm would be minimizing its losses) but this is the best the firm can do. To assure yourself that this condition will maximize a firm's profit, consider the two other possibilities: (1) marginal revenue > marginal cost and (2) marginal revenue < marginal cost. If condition (1) is true, then a firm could add more to its revenue than to its costs by producing one more unit of output. This means that the firm's profits would increase if it produced more output. Thus, the firm could not yet be maximizing profits. If condition (2) is true, then a firm is adding more to its costs than to its revenue by producing the additional output. By producing this output level, the firm would be cutting into its profits and would be better off reducing production.

Statement a is not correct because there are a number of output levels where this would be true and, thus, the rule would offer no guidance about which output level to pick. The same is true of statement b. Statement d is not correct, but it is the condition that would say that a firm is indifferent between shutting down and remaining open in the short run. Statement e is not correct because statement b is not correct.

5.   Correct answer: a.

Discussion: For a perfectly competitive firm which is a price taker, the firm's revenue from selling each additional unit of output, its marginal revenue, will always equal price.

Statement b is not correct since firms can in the short run earn positive or negative economic profit. Statement c is not correct; total revenue is equal to price X quantity. Statement d is not correct since a firm also has fixed costs. Statement e is not correct because a firm does not always earn positive economic profit.

6.   Correct answer: d.

Discussion: The output level that a profit-maximizing firm will choose is the output level where marginal revenue (price) equals marginal cost. This occurs at an output level of 25 units (where the price and marginal cost curves intersect).

Statements a, b, c, and e are all incorrect based on the above method for finding a firm's profit-maximizing level of output.

7.   Correct answer: b.

Discussion: The profit is determined by first selecting the output level that a profit maximizing firm will choose. The profit-maximizing output level is where marginal revenue (price) equals marginal cost. This occurs at an output level of 100 units. Given that output level, the average total cost of 100 units of output is $6 and the price is $11. Thus, profit is equal to ($11 X 100) - ($6 X 100) = $500.

Statements a, c, d, and e are all incorrect based on the above method for finding and calculating a firm's profit.

8.   Correct answer: a.

The firm's total revenue from operating would be $1,000 ($5 X 200 units). The firm's total cost would be $400 + $800 = $1,200. If the firm operates, it will make a loss of $200. This is less than the firm would lose if it shut down its operation.

If the firm shut down its operation, it would not earn any revenue but would still have to pay for its fixed costs. Thus, the firm would lose $800. Thus, statement b is not correct. Statement c and d are not correct because the firm is not earning a profit. Statement e is not correct because average total cost is $1,200/200 units = $6. Thus, price is less than average total cost which is why the firm is making a loss. Notice that, since price is equal to marginal cost, the firm is doing the best it can, i.e., minimizing its losses.

9.   Correct answer: a.

Discussion: This question is a graphical representation of question (8). To answer this question, you must first establish what the profit-maximizing output level of the firm is. It is found where price and marginal cost are equal (intersect) which is at an output level of 200 units. The average total cost of producing 200 units is $6. The average variable cost of producing 200 units is $2. The average fixed cost is $4. Since price exceeds average variable cost, the firm should continue to operate even though it will earn a loss of $200.

In order to answer the question, you could also calculate the total cost of producing 200 units of output as $1,200 and the revenue as $1,000. Thus, the firm will lose $200. Then, you could calculate how much the firm will lose if it shuts down. If it shuts down, it will have to pay its fixed costs which can be read off the graph by taking the average fixed cost of $4 and multiplying it by the output level of 200 units. Thus, the firm's loss would be $800.

Statements b, c, d, and e are all incorrect for the same reasons mentioned in the answer to question (8).

10.   Correct answer: d.

Discussion: If a firm shuts down in the short run, it will have no revenue to offset the sunk or fixed costs that it must continue to pay. Thus, the firm will lose an amount equal to its sunk or fixed costs.

Statement a is not correct because, if a firm shuts down in the short run, it will still have some costs to pay. Statement b is not correct. It would have been correct if it had said that a firm should remain open if price is greater than average variable cost but less than average total cost. Statement c is not correct because a perfectly competitive firm maximizes its profits by producing an output level where price (or marginal revenue) equals marginal cost. Statement e is not correct because statement d is correct.

11.   Correct answer: c.

Discussion: If demand declines, as you learned in Chapter 4, this would cause price to decline. Thus, statement b is likely to occur. As the price of the product declines, firms that were initially earning zero economic profit will see price drop below their average total cost. This will cause them to make a loss (negative economic profit) in the short run. Thus, statement a is likely to occur. As firms earn negative economic profit, there will be exit from the industry. Thus, statement d is likely to occur. As price declines, the profit-maximizing output level for firms will change -- it will decrease. That is, firms will produce less output. Since both price and output have declined, producer surplus must necessarily decline. (The effect on consumer surplus would be ambiguous since the price decline would raise consumer surplus but the quantity decline would reduce it). Thus, statement e is likely to occur. Statement c is least likely to occur because, as a firm produces less output, its marginal cost of production will decline.

12.   Correct answer: c.

Discussion: Producer surplus is measured as the area below the price line but above the supply curve out to the equilibrium level of output. CBD satisfies this area.

Statement a (area ABC) is a measure of consumer surplus. Statement b (area ABD) is a measure of total market value (consumer surplus + producer surplus). Statement d (area OCBF) measures price X quantity for the industry (market). Statement e area (OBF) does not correspond to anything.

13.   Correct answer: b.

Discussion: The efficient price is the equilibrium price which is $10. This is the price at which quantity demanded = quantity supplied. It is also the price that maximizes the sum of consumer + producer surplus.

None of the other prices are equilibrium prices, which means that transactions between buyers and sellers could be rearranged to make both parties better off. For example, at a price of $12, producers would being willing to sell 40 units of output. However, at price of $12, consumers would only be willing to buy 10 units. Since producers can only sell what consumers are willing to buy, producers would be able to sell 10 units of output. The marginal cost of production of the 10th unit is less than $12 but the marginal benefit of the 10th unit (read off the demand curve) is $12, society could be made better off. Producers will gain by selling more than 10 units (as long as the marginal cost of production is less than the price received for the good) and consumers will gain because they will be able to get more of the good at a lower price.

VIII.   ANSWER KEY: ESSAY QUESTIONS

1.   Note: P = price, MR = marginal revenue, MC = marginal cost.

When a firm produces output up to that level at which MR = MC, it is always adding more to revenue than it is to costs, and, thus, adding something (however small) to its profits. If a firm produced at an output level at which MR < MC, the firm is actually taking away from its profits because some of the output costs more to produce than it can be sold for. If a firm produces output where MR > MC, it could continue to expand production and though adding more to cost, could add even more to revenue, thereby adding to its profits. Thus, a firm maximizes profits where MR = MC.

2.   Based on short-run analysis, you should disagree with your boss:

The costs of closing up shop in the short run are 300,000 pesos (due to fixed costs). That is, 300,000 pesos must be paid regardless of whether the factory produces no shoes or some shoes. This is the loss the firm would sustain in the short run if it were to close up shop. If the factory were to continue current operation, it could produce 5,000 boxes of shoes and earn revenue of 200,000 pesos which could offset some of the fixed costs. However, by producing, the company would incur another cost -- variable costs in the amount of 150,000 pesos. On net, there is a positive difference of 50,000 pesos between revenue and variable costs. This positive difference can help pay for fixed costs so that, if the firm continues to operate, its losses will be 250,000 pesos (Revenue - Fixed Costs - Variable Costs) instead of 300,000 (fixed costs).

You might also point out that, if the company is planning on closing the factory temporarily, it might make customers mad, which can have deleterious effects on future sales. Moreover, if the company temporarily lays off workers, they may go find work elsewhere and, thus, the company might face some retraining and re-hiring (or search) costs when they re-open the factory.

On the other hand, if the company is planning on closing the factory permanently, i.e., in the long run, perhaps because of a perceived permanent downturn in demand for faux leather shoes, then your advice may be different. You may advise the company to close the factory and sell its assets (to cover some of its fixed costs, like interest on debt). Also, by closing the factory, the company may be able to avoid fixed costs like rent as well.

Take It to the Net

We invite you to visit the O'Sullivan/Sheffrin page on the Prentice Hall Web site at:

http://www.prenhall.com/osullivan/

for this chapter's World Wide Web exercise.

CHAPTER 10
LONG-RUN SUPPLY AND MARKET DYNAMICS

I.   OVERVIEW

In this chapter, you will revisit the distinction between the short and long run and learn how, in the long run, the quantity supplied is more responsive to changes in price than in the short run. You will see that this occurs because, in the long run, firms can enter and exit the industry (in a perfectly competitive market structure) and alter the size of their production facilities. You will learn about how changes in demand affect the price of a product differently in the short run than in the long run. You will also learn about increasing, decreasing, and constant cost industries which are determined by how productive inputs are as more firms enter (or exit) an industry and how the price of inputs changes as more firms enter (or exit) an industry. You will compare the slope of a short-run supply curve to the slope of a long-run supply curve and compute the elasticities of supply of each.

II.   CHECKLIST

By the end of this chapter, you should be able to:

√   Explain the difference between the short and the long run.
√   Explain what causes firms to enter and exit an industry in a perfectly competitive market structure.
√   Compare what happens to the quantity supplied by a market as the price of the product increases (or decreases), in the short and the long run, and compare the difference.
√   Explain what causes a supply curve to be positively sloped and explain what would cause it to be more steeply sloped.
√   Explain the difference between increasing, decreasing, and constant cost industries and illustrate the difference using a graph of the long-run supply curve.
√   Compute total and average costs of production for various output levels.
√   Compute elasticities of supply.

III.   KEY TERMS

Long-run supply curve: a curve showing the relationship between price and quantity supplied in the long run.
Increasing-cost industry: an industry in which the average cost of production increases as the industry grows, so the long-run supply curve is positively sloped.
Constant-cost industry: an industry in which the average cost of production is constant, so the long run supply curve is horizontal.
Decreasing-cost industry: an industry in which the average cost of production decreases as the industry grows.

IV.   PERFORMANCE ENHANCING TIPS (PETS)

PET #1

The long-run supply curve is flatter than the short-run supply curve. This means that quantity supplied is more responsive to a given price change in the long run than is quantity supplied in the short run.

Compare the slope of supply curve (a) to supply curve (b) in the diagram below.

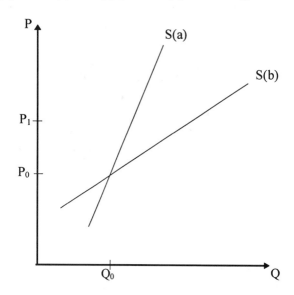

Supply curve (b) is flatter than supply curve (a). What does this mean in practical terms? Let's examine the response of quantity supplied to the same change in price along the two different supply curves. Draw a line from price Po across to the supply curves. Where the price line intersects the supply curves, draw a vertical line down to the quantity axis and mark this as the quantity supplied at price Po along graph (a) and (b). You will notice that, at this price, the quantity supplied in the short and long run is the same amount.

Now, draw a line from price Pl across to the supply curves. Where the price line intersects the supply curves, draw vertical lines down to the quantity axis and mark these as the quantity supplied at price Pl along graphs (a) and (b). Compare the changes in the quantity supplied along supply curves (a) and (b). You will see that, as the price increases, the quantity supplied increases more along supply curve (b) than along supply curve (a).   That means that quantity supplied is more responsive to price in the long run than in the short run. Why does this occur? It occurs because, in the long run, as the price of a good increases, more firms enter the industry (attracted by profits due to the higher price) and existing firms may have expanded the size of their facility thus enabling them to produce more. Therefore, for any given price increase, more is willingly supplied by firms.

PET #2

An increase in demand raises the price of a good by less in the long run than in the short run. A decrease in demand lowers the price of a good by less in the long run than in the short run.

To see this, draw an increase in demand (rightward shift in the demand curve) in the graph below.

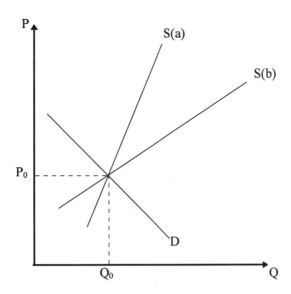

Now, mark the new equilibrium prices along the short-run supply curve (a) and along the long-run supply curve (b). Compare the change in the price from the initial price of Po along the two supply curves. What do you see? You should see that the price has increased by less along supply curve (b) -- the flat, long-run supply curve than it has increased along supply curve (a).

Why does this occur? In the long run, remember that, in response to a price increase, more firms enter the industry and existing firms will expand the size of their facility; the higher price creates economic profits which motivate entry and expansion in the industry. Thus, in the long run, the industry is better able to satisfy the increased demand for their product. Buyers do not have to bid as fiercely against each other for the ability to purchase the product and, thus, the price of the product does not rise by as much.

You should work through a decrease in demand on your own.

V.   PRACTICE EXAM: MULTIPLE CHOICE QUESTIONS

1.   Which one of the following is the definition of the long run?

a.   a period of time over which the demand for a product can increase or decrease.
b.   a period of time over which firms can enter and exit an industry.
c.   a period of time over which firms can alter the size of their production facility.
d.   a period of time over which the price of inputs used by an industry remains constant.
e.   (b) and (c).

2.   Suppose that the total cost to a typical firm of producing five-foot-high artificial Christmas trees is $3,000. Suppose the typical firm produces 500 artificial Christmas trees per season. Further, suppose that there are 600 firms in the industry. What is the average cost per Christmas tree and what is the total industry output?

a. $6; 30,000.
b. $3,000; 30,000.

c. $6; 500.
d. $6; 3,000.
e. $0.10; 30,000.

3.   Suppose the average cost of producing a set of golf clubs is $225. Suppose the price at which producers can sell a set of golf clubs is $230. Based on the information you are given, which one of the following best describes the industry response?

a.   firms will exit the industry because the economic profit per set of golf clubs is so small.
b.   firms will enter the industry because there are positive economic profits to be earned.
c.   the quantity of golf clubs supplied by the industry will remain unchanged.
d.   demand for golf clubs will increase.
e.   the cost of graphite used in making golf clubs will increase.

4.   Which one of the following explains why, in the long run, the average cost of production may increase as an industry expands (produces more output)?

a.   rising input prices.
b.   rising productivity of inputs.
c.   falling input prices.
d.   increasing fixed costs.
e.   (a) and (b).

5.   Suppose that a typical farmer sells 10,000 bushels of peaches each season and that the total revenue he earns is $100,000. Further, suppose that the average cost of producing 10,000 bushels is $12 per bushel. Based on this information, which one of the following statements is correct?

a.   there are positive economic profits and farmers will enter the industry.
b.   there are negative economic profits and some farmers will leave the industry.
c.   the average cost of production is rising.
d.   the elasticity of supply is 1.2.
e.   cannot be answered without information on price per bushel.

6.   Which one of the following statements is NOT true?

a.   an increasing cost industry has a positively sloped long-run supply curve.
b.   the long-run average cost of production depends, in part, on how productive inputs are.
c.   a constant cost industry has a horizontal long-run supply curve.
d.   diminishing returns explains why the average cost of production decreases in the long run.
e.   all of the above statements are true.

7.   Consider the taxi industry which is assumed to be a constant cost industry. If the demand for taxi services decreases, in the short run, the price for taxi services will _____ and, in the long run, the price for taxi services will _____.

a.   increase; decrease.
b.   decrease; decrease.

c.   decrease; remain unchanged.
d.   remain unchanged; decrease.
e.   none of the above.

8.   Use the following information to answer the question below.

Initial equilibrium price = $10
New equilibrium price = $15
Initial equilibrium quantity supplied (short and long run) = 1,000 units
New equilibrium quantity supplied in short run = 1,250
New equilibrium quantity supplied in long run = 2,000 units

The short-run elasticity of supply is _____ and the long-run elasticity of supply is _____.
a.   5/250; 5/1,000.
b.   5; 20.
c.   0.50; 2.0.
d.   2; 0.50.
e.   0.25; 0.20.

9.   Economic profit is defined as:

a.   total revenue - implicit costs.
b.   total revenue - explicit costs.
c.   total revenue - implicit costs - explicit costs.
d.   total revenue + implicit costs + explicit costs.
e.   explicit costs - total revenue.

10.   The graph below depicts the situation for a typical firm in a perfectly competitive market structure. Based on the graph, which would be the most likely industry response? Assume the industry is an increasing cost industry.

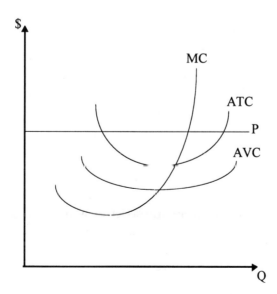

a.   there will be entry into the industry.
b.   existing firms will expand their production facilities.
c.   the prices of inputs will rise.
d.   the skill level of the workforce will decline.
e.   all of the above.

VI.   PRACTICE EXAM: ESSAY QUESTIONS

1.   Explain why the long-run supply curve is flatter than the short-run supply curve.

2.   Consider the market for beef. Suppose that the demand for beef declines because of health concerns. Explain what will happen to the price and quantity of beef supplied in the short and long run assuming the industry is an increasing cost industry.

VII.   ANSWER KEY: MULTIPLE CHOICE QUESTIONS

1.   Correct answer: e.

Discussion: The long run is a period of time over which new firms can enter the industry (to capture positive economic profits) or exit the industry (to cut their losses). Over a longer period of time, firms already in the industry can also alter the size of their production facilities; they may wish to expand their operation if economic profits increase, or they may wish to shut down some of their operation if they begin to incur losses.

Statements a and d are not correct because the long run is not defined with respect to changes in demand or changes in input prices. Statements b and c are both correct, which is why statement e is the correct answer.

2.   Correct answer: a.

Discussion: The average cost of production of the typical firm is computed by dividing the total cost of production by the firm's output level. (You may wish to review PET #1 from Chapter 8 of the P Practicum). In this case, the average cost is $6 = ($3,000/500 units). Since each firm produces 500 Christmas trees and there are currently 600 firms in the industry, total industry output is 30,000 trees (500 X 600).

Statements b - e cannot be correct based on the calculations above.

3.   Correct answer: b.

Discussion: Since the price that producers can get for a set of golf clubs exceeds the average cost of production by $5, firms will earn $5 of economic profit per set of golf clubs. That is, they will be earning positive economic profit. The positive economic profit will attract other firms into the industry. Entry will stop when economic profit is driven to zero.

Statement a is not correct; any positive economic profit is considered to motivate entry into an industry. Statement c is not correct because the positive economic profit will prompt entry into the industry and, thus, lead to an increase in the quantity supplied. Statement d is not correct because there is nothing in the information given that gives a reason why the demand for golf clubs will increase. Statement e is not necessarily correct; it depends on whether the golf club industry is an increasing, decreasing or constant cost industry. If the industry is an increasing cost industry, then the price of graphite will likely increase. However, if the industry is a decreasing or constant cost industry, the price of graphite may actually decrease or not change at all as more golf club producers demand more graphite.

4.   Correct answer: a.

Discussion: As an industry expands (produces more output), the demand for inputs increases. This increase in demand for inputs can put upward pressure on the price of inputs and thereby lead to a rise in the cost of the price of inputs. This, in turn, would raise a firm's average cost of production.

Statement b is not correct. Rising productivity would actually decrease the average cost of production, not increase it. Statement c is not correct since falling input prices would actually decrease the average cost of production. Statement d is not correct because, in the long run, there are no costs that are considered as fixed costs. Statement e is not correct because statement b is not correct.

5.   Correct answer: b.

Discussion: In this question, you must determine whether the typical farmer is making a positive, zero, or negative economic profit. You can determine the profit situation of the farmer by either calculating the price per bushel that the typical farmer receives for his peaches or the total cost of producing 10,000 bushels. Once you have made either one of these calculations, you can determine whether there is entry or exit into the industry. The price per bushel can be calculated by dividing total revenue by the number of bushels sold. Since the total revenue is $100,000 and the number of bushels sold is 10,000, the price per bushel is $10. With the average cost of production being $12, the typical farmer will lose $2 on every bushel sold. Alternatively, you could have calculated the total cost of producing 10,000 bushels as $120,000 ($12 X 10,000). In this case, the farmer will lose $20,000 for the lot of 10,000 bushels sold (i.e., $2 for every bushel sold). With either calculation, you should see that the farmer will not be making a positive economic profit. The long-run industry response to negative economic profits is for firms (farmers, in this case) to leave the industry.

Statement a is not correct based on the reasoning above. Statement c is not necessarily correct; it depends on whether the industry is an increasing, decreasing, or constant cost industry. If the industry is an increasing cost industry, as firms *exit*, there will be less demand for inputs and the price of inputs would drop. This would mean that the average cost of production would decrease. If the industry is a constant cost industry, the exit of firms will have no effect on the input prices and the average cost of production would remain constant. If the industry is a decreasing cost industry, as firms *exit*, the cost of inputs will rise which will raise the average cost of production. Statement d is not correct because you are not given enough information to calculate an elasticity of supply. In order to calculate an elasticity, you would need changes in prices and quantity supplied from which you could compute percentage changes. Statement e is not correct because you are given enough information to answer the question.

6.   Correct answer: d.

Discussion: Statement d is correct because it is the only statement that is NOT true. Remember that diminishing returns are a short-run phenomenon. They arise because a firm, in the short run, cannot alter the size of the capital stock (plant and equipment) that it uses to produce output. On the other hand, average costs of production that decrease in the long run is a long-run phenomenon and is a result of entry/exit and alteration of plant size.

Statements a, b, and c are all true. Since statement d is not true, statement e cannot be the correct answer.

7.   Correct answer: c.

Discussion: The key to answering this question correctly is to know what the shape of the long-run supply curve is when the industry is a constant cost industry. A constant cost industry has a horizontal supply curve. Thus, when demand decreases (shifts left) and moves along a horizontal supply curve, the price of the good will not change from its initial price. However, in the short run, the supply curve is positively sloped. Thus, a decrease in demand will lead to a lower price for the good in the short run.

Statements a and d should be ruled out. From Chapters 4 and 5, you should know that a decrease in demand will lower the price of a good, not increase it or leave it unchanged. Statement b is not correct because, in the long run, the price of the good will remain unchanged, not decrease. Statement e is not correct because statement c is correct.

8.   Correct answer: c.

Discussion: The elasticity of supply is computed as the percentage change in the quantity supplied divided by the percentage change in the price. (You may wish to review Chapter 5 of the Practicum). The percentage change in the quantity supplied in the short run is $[(1,250 - 1,000)/1,000]X\ 100 = 25\%$. The percentage change in the quantity supplied in the long run is $[(2,000 - 1,000)/1,000]X100 = 100\%$. The percentage change in the price is $[(\$15 - \$10)/\$10]X100 = 50\%$. Thus, the elasticity of supply in the short run is $25\%/50\% = \frac{1}{2} = 0.50$ and the elasticity of supply in the long run is $100\%/50\% = 10/5 = 2$.

Statements a, b, d, and e cannot be correct based on the calculations above.

9.   Correct answer: c.

Discussion: Economic profit considers implicit costs of production -- that is, costs for which there is no direct or explicit outlay by the firm. An owner of a firm's cost of time is an opportunity cost for which there is no direct payment. Thus, it is an implicit cost and should be used in calculating a firm's economic profit. On the other hand, accounting profit, as you may recall from Chapter 8, is the difference between total revenue and explicit costs.

Statement a is not correct because economic profit is calculated by considering both explicit and implicit costs, not just implicit costs. Statement b is not correct because it is a measure of accounting profit, not economic profit. Statement d is not correct because economic profit is the difference between total revenue and implicit and explicit costs, not the sum of these. Statement e is not correct because profit is calculated by subtracting costs from revenue, not vice-versa.

10.   Correct answer: e.

Discussion: The graph for this question shows that the typical firm is earning positive economic profit. In order to determine this, you must first choose the profit-maximizing output level of the firm. Remember from Chapter 9 that the profit-maximizing rule is to produce at an output level where marginal revenue equals marginal cost. For a perfectly competitive firm, price and marginal revenue are identical numerically. Thus, the profit-maximizing output level is found where the price (marginal revenue) and marginal cost curves intersect. Find this point on the graph and then draw a vertical line down to the quantity axis. This quantity is the profit-maximizing output level. You may wish to label it q*.

Now, you must determine whether the firm is earning a positive, zero, or negative economic profit. To do this, find the average cost of production of producing q* and compare it to the price. The average cost of production is found by drawing a vertical line up from q* to the average cost curve and then over to the $ axis. As you can see, the average cost is less than the price which means that the typical firm is making positive economic profit.

Now that you have determined that the typical firm is making a positive economic profit, you should know that this will attract entry into the industry, lead to expansion of existing firms, put upward pressure on the price of inputs as more are demanded as the industry grows (in an increasing cost industry) and also lead to a decline in the skill level of workers. As the industry grows and produces more output, it will have to hire more workers. However, the firms will not be able to hire the cream of the crop as these workers are already employed in the industry. Thus, firms will end up hiring less skilled (and, therefore, less productive) workers.

Since statements a - d are all true of an increasing cost industry earning positive economic profit, statement e is the correct answer.

VIII.   ANSWER KEY: ESSAY QUESTIONS

1.   The long-run supply curve and the short-run supply curve both show the relationship between the price of a good and the quantity supplied. However, the time period considered for the relationship is different. In the short run, the number of firms producing for the industry is fixed as is the current size of each firm's facility. In the long run, the number of firms producing for the industry can change as firms enter or exit the industry and the size of the facilities of existing firms can be altered. This means that in the long run, the total industry output can be much more responsive to a price change than in the short run. For example, when the price of a good increases (because of an increase in demand), the short run output response of the industry is constrained by how many firms are already producing for the industry and the current size of their operation. A given amount of firms with a given plant size can only produce so much more In response to a higher price for the output they produce. However, in the long run, a higher price may lure more firms into the industry as well as motivate some firms to alter the size of their operation. Thus, a higher price may elicit a bigger increase in output in the long run than in the short run. Graphically, this would be represented by a supply curve that is flatter for the long run (and, thus, steeper for the short run). You may want to take a look at PET #1 of this chapter to inspect the difference between the long and short-run supply curves.

2.   An increasing cost industry has a long-run supply curve that is positively sloped. Of course, the short-run supply curve is also positively sloped. However, the long-run supply curve is flatter (more

elastic) than the short-run supply curve as the graph below illustrates. A decline in the demand for beef would be represented by a leftward shift in the supply curve. The reduced demand for beef will, in the short and long run, lead to a lower price of beef as the graph shows. However, in the short run, the price drop will be bigger than in the long run. The graph also shows that the equilibrium quantity of beef will decline. It will decline by more in the long run than in the short run.

The drop in demand for beef will, in the short run, cause some firms to shut down their operation altogether. Other firms will continue to operate, but they cannot change the size of the capital stock (and, thus, their fixed costs) that they operate with. In the long run, some firms will make a decision to exit the industry as they sustain losses, whereas other firms that remain will likely reduce the size of their operation (lay off workers, shut down some factories, etc). In the long run, the number of firms in the industry will decline and the size of their facility will likely decrease.

Take It to the Net

We invite you to visit the O'Sullivan/Sheffrin page on the Prentice Hall Web site at:

http://www.prenhall.com/osullivan/

for this chapter's World Wide Web exercise.

CHAPTER 11
MONOPOLY AND PRICE DISCRIMINATION

I.   OVERVIEW

In this chapter, you will learn about the market structure of monopoly in which there is a single supplier of output to a market. You will learn about what gives rise to a monopoly. You will learn how a monopolist chooses the profit-maximizing level of output and determines the price at which it will sell the output. You will learn that, in contrast to a perfectly competitive market structure, price and marginal revenue are different for a monopolist and that a monopolist typically earns positive economic profit. You will learn about the costs and benefits to society of a monopoly. You will learn about the behavior of price discrimination which a monopolist may undertake. You will learn that price discrimination is the practice of charging different prices to different groups of customers for the same product and that the elasticity of demand can be used to decide which group of customers should be charged a higher price.

II.   CHECKLIST

By the end of this chapter, you should be able to:

√   Describe the characteristics of a monopoly.
√   List factors that would give rise to a monopoly.
√   List some real world examples of a monopoly.
√   Explain why marginal revenue is less than price for a monopolist but equal to price for a perfectly competitive firm.
√   Use a graph to depict the profit-maximizing output level a monopolist would produce, the price that would be charged for the product, and the profit the monopolist would earn.
√   Discuss and compare the relationship of price, marginal revenue, marginal cost, and average cost for a profit-maximizing monopolist.
√   Compare the price and output decisions of a monopolist to a perfectly competitive firm.
√   Explain rent seeking.
√   Discuss the trade-offs that occur when a patent is granted to a firm which gives the firm monopoly power.
√   Describe the conditions that make it possible for a firm to price discriminate.
√   Describe how a price discrimination scheme works and which group of customers would be charged a higher price.

III.   KEY TERMS

Dumping: the practice under which a firm charges a lower price in a foreign market than in the domestic market.
Franchise or license scheme: a policy under which the government picks a single firm to sell a particular product.
Monopoly: a market in which a single firm serves the entire market.
Natural monopoly: a market in which there are large economies of scale, so a single firm will be profitable but a pair of firms would lose money.

Patent: the exclusive right to sell a particular good for some period of time.

Price discrimination: the process under which a firm divides consumers into two or more groups and picks a different price for each group.

Rent seeking: the process under which a firm spends money to persuade the government to erect barriers to entry and pick the firm as the monopolist.

Unnatural monopoly: a monopoly resulting from artificial barriers that prevent additional firms from entering a market.

IV.   PERFORMANCE ENHANCING TIPS (PETS)

PET #1

The profit-maximizing rule for a monopolist (as for any firm) is to produce an output level where marginal revenue equals marginal cost.

Remember that marginal revenue is the addition to revenue from selling one more unit of output and marginal cost is the addition to cost from producing one more unit of output. As long as the addition to revenue (marginal revenue) exceeds the addition to cost (marginal cost), the monopolist will add to its profits. Thus, the monopolist will maximize its profits by continuing to produce and sell output until marginal revenue is just equal to marginal cost. Beyond that output level, profits will actually be smaller (not maximized).

PET #2

For a profit-maximizing monopolist, the price of its output will be greater than the marginal cost.

This performance enhancing tip is based on two principles: (1) the addition to revenue (marginal revenue) that a monopolist earns from selling one more unit of output is less than the price it receives for selling that one more unit of output, (see your textbook for a good explanation); and (2) a profit-maximizing firm produces an output level where marginal revenue equals marginal cost. Statement (1) says that price > marginal revenue. Statement (2) says that marginal revenue equals marginal cost. Thus, it must be the case that, for a monopolist, price > marginal cost.

PET #3

A monopolist produces an output level that is less than a perfectly competitive industry would produce and charges a price that is higher than would prevail under perfect competition.

Under perfect competition, a profit-maximizing firm produces an output level where marginal revenue equals marginal cost, just as does a monopolist. However, for a perfectly competitive firm, marginal revenue and price are identical. This means that a profit-maximizing firm in a perfectly competitive market also ends up producing an output level where price is equal to marginal cost. This is not true of a monopolist as PET #2 discusses. This is the reason that a monopolist will produce a lower output level and charge a higher price for its output than it would if it were a perfectly competitive firm.

To see this, look at the graph below.

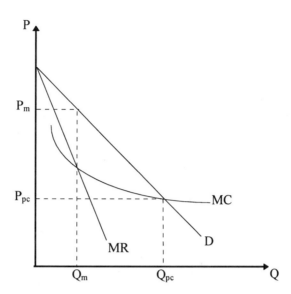

The monopolist will produce output level Qm which is where marginal revenue and marginal cost are equal. The monopolist will decide on a price for output level Qm by using the demand curve. At output level Qm, the demand curve dictates that the price be Pm. Now, suppose the monopolist were to behave as a perfectly competitive firm. It would produce an output level where price equals marginal cost and charge a price dictated by the demand curve for that output level. Price equals marginal cost where the demand and marginal cost curves intersect. The output level in this case would be Qpc. The price charged would be read off the demand curve corresponding to output level Qpc which is Ppc. As the graph shows, the monopolist's price exceeds what would be charged by a perfectly competitive firm and produces an output level that is less than would be produced under perfect competition.

V.   PRACTICE EXAM: MULTIPLE CHOICE QUESTIONS

1.   Which one of the following characteristics is true of a monopoly?

a.   a large number of firms in the industry.
b.   barriers to entry into the industry.
c.   firm acts as a price taker.
d.   price equals marginal revenue.
e.   all of the above.

2.   Which one of the following would NOT be an example of a monopoly?

a.   a patent granted to a computer company.
b.   a franchise awarded to a food service on campus.
c.   American Medical Association.
d.   Major League Baseball.
e.   all of the above.

3.   A monopolist maximizes profit by picking the output level where:

a.   marginal revenue = marginal cost.
b.   price = marginal revenue.
c.   price = marginal cost.
d.   price > average cost.
e.   price = average cost.

4.   Which one of the following is true for a monopolist?

a.   freedom of entry.
b.   price > marginal revenue.
c.   produces a socially efficient output level.
d.   is unable to price discriminate.
e.   earns zero economic profit in the long run.

5.   Use the diagram below to select the profit-maximizing output level that a monopolist would choose.

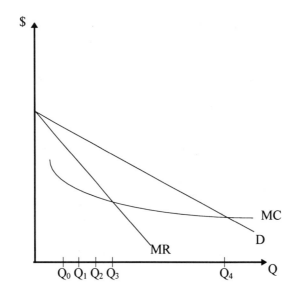

a. Q_0
b. Q_1
c. Q_2
d. Q_3
e. Q_4

6.   If the average cost curve is horizontal, say at $2 per unit of output, then:

a.   marginal cost = $2.
b.   marginal cost = $0.
c.   marginal cost > $2.
d.   marginal cost = $1.
e.   cannot be determined with information given.

7.   Suppose the price at which a monopolist is selling its output is $12 and the marginal revenue associated with selling the last unit of output is $9. Further, suppose the marginal cost of the last unit of output sold is $10. Which one of the following best describes what the monopolist should do?

a.   increase output and raise price.
b.   increase output and lower price.
c.   decrease output and lower price.
d.   decrease output and raise price.
e.   shut down.

8.   Which one of the following is a cost of a monopoly?

a.   price consumers pay is higher than they would under perfect competition.
b.   output is less than under perfect competition.
c.   rent seeking leads to loss in output in other industries.
d.   consumer surplus is less than under perfect competition.
e.   all of the above.

9.   Which one of the following is a benefit to consumers of a patent-generated monopoly?

a.   rent seeking.
b.   innovation.
c.   deadweight loss.
d.   monopoly profits.
e.   price discrimination.

10.   Which one of the following would NOT be a good example of price discrimination?

a.   rebates on washer/dryer combos.
b.   no-fee checking to bank customers that keep $500 or more in their checking accounts.
c.   restaurant discounts to early bird (before 5:00 pm) diners.
d.   coupons for drycleaning.
e.   senior citizen discount for popcorn at the movies.

11.   The practice of price discrimination:

a.   occurs when a monopolist sells a product below the marginal cost of production.
b.   increases a monopolist's revenue.
c.   will always increase a monopolist's profit.
d.   does not require that a firm have control over the price at which it sells its output.
e.   is to charge a higher price to the high elasticity demand group of customers and a lower price to the low elasticity demand group of customers.

VI.   PRACTICE EXAM: ESSAY QUESTIONS

1.   Discuss the cost and benefits to society of a monopoly that is created because a patent is granted for the product the firm produces.

2.   Explain whether a monopoly could increase its revenue *and* its profits by charging different prices to different groups of customers. You may wish to give a numerical example to illustrate your point.

VII.   ANSWER KEY: MULTIPLE CHOICE QUESTIONS

1.   Correct answer: b.

Discussion: A monopolistic market structure is characterized by barriers to entry -- some barriers are artificial (or government created) and others arise naturally (as will be discussed in Chapter 12).

Statements a, c, and d are all characteristics of a perfectly competitive market structure.

2.   Correct answer: e.

Discussion: Monopolies can be created by patents (which in the U.S. are awarded for 20 years without an annual renewal fee), franchise and licensing schemes, industrial, sports, and other associations that restrict the number of firms in the market.

3.   Correct answer: a.

Discussion: A monopolist (or any type of firm) will maximize profits by producing an output level where marginal revenue = marginal cost (see PET #1 of this chapter for review).

Statement b describes the relationship between price and marginal revenue for a perfectly competitive firm. Statement c is another version of the profit-maximizing condition for a perfectly competitive firm. Statement d would ensure profit greater than zero but not necessarily the biggest (maximized) profit. Statement e would ensure zero economic profit.

4.   Correct answer: b.

Discussion: A monopolist (unlike a perfectly competitive firm) must lower the price of its output to all of its customers in order to sell more to a few more customers. This means that the price the monopolist receives from selling the last unit of output is not the addition to revenue (marginal revenue) from selling the last unit of output. The marginal revenue from selling the last unit will be less than the price the firm receives on that last unit because while the firm gets paid $X for the last unit of output, it loses revenue from lowering the price to the previous customers who were paying the higher price. The sum of these two effects makes the marginal revenue earned on the last unit of output sold less than the price received on the last unit of output sold.

Statement a is not correct because a monopolist does not face freedom of entry but rather barriers to entry. Statement c is not correct because a monopolist produces a socially *inefficient* output level (it produces too little output). Statement d is not correct because a monopolist may be able to price discriminate.   Statement e is not correct because a monopolist earns positive economic profit in the long run.

5.   Correct answer: d.

Discussion: A profit-maximizing monopolist picks an output level where marginal revenue equals marginal cost (which occurs where these two curves intersect). The output level at the intersection of these two curves is Q_3.

Statements a, b, c, and e are all output levels corresponding to other intersection points. The output level where the demand and marginal cost curves intersect is the output level that would be set if price = marginal cost was the rule the monopolist followed. This would be a socially efficient output level.

6.   Correct answer: a.

Discussion: When the average cost curve is horizontal, it means that the average cost per unit of output is not changing as more and more output is produced. If the average cost is not changing,. it must be the case that the marginal cost is equal to the average cost. (Your book gives an example using your GPA which is an average of the grades you made in the courses you've already taken. If your GPA is 3.0 and you get a B (= 3.0) on a course you take in the summer (the marginal course), your GPA (average) will remain at 3.0).

Statements b and d are for a marginal cost that is less than the average cost. If this were the case, then the average cost would be "pulled down" or decline and, thus, not remain constant. Statement c is for a marginal cost that exceeds the average cost; in this case, the average cost would be "pulled up" or increase and, thus, not remain constant.   Statement e is not correct because you are given enough information to get an answer.

7.   Correct answer: d.

Discussion: Since marginal cost > marginal revenue, the monopolist is not maximizing its profits and, in fact, is producing too much output. If the monopolist is producing too much output, then, based on the demand curve, he is charging a price below the profit-maximizing price. Thus, the monopolist should reduce his output level until marginal revenue = marginal cost. By reducing the output level, the monopolist moves back along the demand curve to a higher price for his output.

Statements a and b are not correct because, if the monopolist increased his output level, he would continue adding more to his costs than to his revenue and profits would decline. Statement c is not correct because the monopolist should not lower but raise price. Statement e is not correct because there is no information that tells you whether the monopolist should shut down.

8.   Correct answer: e.

Discussion: A monopolist charges a higher price and produces less output than would arise under perfect competition.   This is costly to consumers (see your textbook, PET #3, and essay #1 for further discussion). This also means that consumer surplus (a measure of the benefits to consumers from their purchases) is smaller under a monopolistic market structure than a perfectly competitive one. Monopolies, which often arise as a result of rent seeking undertaken by lobbyists, also entail an opportunity cost to society in that the lobbyists could be employed elsewhere, thereby adding to output in other industries which consumers could, in turn, purchase.

9.   Correct answer: b.

Discussion: The awarding of a patent to a firm grants the firm monopoly status (at least for 20 years). The monopoly status means the firm is assured of making positive economic profit. The profit incentive then motivates the firm to actually produce and market the product, thereby making it available to consumers. Without the assurance of profit, the firm may not undertake production of the product and, thus, consumers would lose out on innovative new products.

Statements a and c are costs of a monopoly. Statement d is a benefit to the monopolist but not to consumers. Statement e is not necessarily a benefit to consumers; price discrimination by a monopolist might lead the monopolist to charge some groups of customers a higher price than other groups.

10.   Correct answer: e.

Discussion: One of the conditions necessary for price discrimination to work is that it not be possible for customers to resell (or buy for others) the product that is being discounted. In the case of senior citizen discounts for popcorn at movie theaters, the senior citizen can easily purchase the popcorn and then, once inside the movie theater, share it or give it to his or her companion(s) who may not be senior citizens.

Statements a - d are all examples of price discrimination that are practiced. Your book also lists similar examples.

11.   Correct answer: b.

Discussion: Price discrimination is the practice of charging different groups of customers different prices for the same product with the intent of increasing a firm's revenue.

Statement a is not correct because it is not the definition of price discrimination. Statement c is not correct because a monopolist's profits will not necessarily increase with price discrimination if the cost of serving two or more different customer groups increases. Thus, while price discrimination would raise revenue, it may also raise a monopolist's costs and, thus, lead to lower, not higher, profit. Statement d is not correct because price discrimination requires that a firm have some control over the price at which it sells its output. Statement e is not correct; it is actually the reverse. A higher price should be charged to the low elasticity of demand customers and a lower price to the high elasticity of demand customers.

VIII. ANSWER KEY: ESSAY QUESTIONS

1.   The costs to society of a monopoly is that consumers are charged a higher price for the product than they would if entry into the industry could occur as in perfect competition. Also, the industry output under a monopolist is less than would occur if the industry operated as a perfectly competitive one. Thus, society loses on two accounts -- customers pay a higher price for the output and there are some customers who don't get to purchase the output because not enough is produced. This means that consumer surplus is lower under a monopolistic market structure than under a perfectly competitive

market structure.   Also, rent-seeking behavior is likely to occur and this entails an opportunity cost to society. Rent seeking occurs because, in general, firms prefer to be protected from competition so that they can thereby earn positive economic profits indefinitely.   Thus, a firm might hire lobbyists to go to Washington, DC in the hopes that the lobbyists will be able to get the firm some form of protection from competition, i.e., status as a monopoly.   The time and effort of the lobbyists, however, entails an opportunity cost in that the lobbyists could be employed in other industries, thereby increasing output elsewhere that consumers could purchase.

Of course, there are benefits to the monopolist (a member of society, too).   The monopolist earns positive economic profit (at least for the life of the patent).   Also, with patent-generated monopolies, a society at least gets the benefit that new products will be produced instead of none at all.   That is, innovation benefits society.   For example, a new drug that benefits cancer may not be produced unless a patent which ensures the innovating firm positive economic profits is granted.   That is, a firm with the technology to produce a new drug may choose not to if they know that, as soon as they produce it, other firms will enter the market and drive economic profits to zero.

The problem with patent granting is that the government does not always know which products will be produced even without a patent.   Thus, the government may inadvertently grant monopoly status and, thus, monopoly profits to a firm that does not otherwise truly need the assurance of monopoly profits to produce the product.   In this way, society loses for the reasons mentioned above.

2.   A monopolist that charges different prices to different customers is practicing price discrimination. First, consider the revenue from a monopolist that is not practicing price discrimination. Suppose the monopolist charges a price of $10 per unit of output and sells 2,000 units. The total revenue earned by the monopolist is $20,000. Price discrimination by the monopolist will be possible if three conditions are met: (1) the firm has some control over the price at which it sells its output; (2) different groups of customers must be willing to pay a different price for the same product; (3) resale is not possible. Assuming these conditions are met, a monopolist may wish to split its customer base into two groups (although more than two is also an option).   The two groups are established based on the differences in the responsiveness to price changes. Assume one group is very price conscious. That is, a lower price will induce them to buy substantially more and a higher price will induce them to buy substantially less. This is just a way of saying that, for this group, the elasticity of demand is high (exceeds 1). The second group is not as price conscious. While a lower price will induce them to buy more, they will not be inclined to buy much more and, while a higher price will induce them to buy less, they will not be inclined to cut back their purchases very much. This is just a way of saying that, for this group, the elasticity of demand is not very high (is less than 1).

Suppose the elasticities of demand for the price conscious group is 2 and for the "price inconscious" group is 0.4. Based on the differences in the elasticities of demand, the firm's total revenue could actually be greater than $20,000 using the following pricing scheme: charge a price higher than $10 (say, 10% higher) to the low elasticity demand group and charge a price lower than $10 (say, 10% lower) to the high elasticity demand group. What will happen is the following:

> For the group charged the 10% higher price, the quantity sold will, using the elasticity of demand of 0.4, decline by 4%. However, total revenue will still increase because the increase in price in percentage terms exceeds the decrease in quantity demanded in percentage terms. (See Chapter 5 for review.)

For the group charged the 10% lower price, the quantity sold will, using the elasticity of demand of 2, increase by 20%. However, total revenue will increase because the increase in the quantity sold in percentage terms exceeds the decrease in the price in percentage terms. (See Chapter 5 for review.)

Since both price changes lead to an increase in total revenue, the firm will see its total revenue increase above $20,000.

While the example I used assumed that the monopolist raised price to the low elasticity demand group by the same percentage as it lowered price to the high elasticity demand group, a monopolist could raise and lower the price to the different groups of customers by different percentages and still see its profits increase.

One thing to mention is that, while the price discrimination scheme increased the total revenue of the firm, we cannot be sure what happens to the profits of the firm without knowing how or if the total cost of serving two different groups of customers has changed. If the cost does not change, then the price discrimination scheme will increase total revenue and profits. However, it may be possible that the costs increase by more than the revenue increases and, thus, the firm could end up making less in profit, but more in revenue.

Take It to the Net

We invite you to visit the O'Sullivan/Sheffrin page on the Prentice Hall Web site at:

http://www.prenhall.com/osullivan/

for this chapter's World Wide Web exercise.

CHAPTER 12
ENTRY DECISIONS: NATURAL MONOPOLY
AND MONOPOLISTIC COMPETITION

I.   OVERVIEW

In this chapter, you will learn about what a firm considers before deciding to enter a particular industry. You will learn that, in the case of industries with very high fixed costs of start up, often only one firm will enter the industry. This is the case of a natural monopoly. You will learn that in the case of industries with low fixed costs of start up, there is often a great deal of entry and, thus, competition amongst firms. This is the case of monopolistic competition. You will learn how firms already in an industry are affected by the entry of new firms into the industry. You will learn why natural monopolies are typically regulated by the government. You will learn that the government regulation comes in the form of an "average cost pricing policy" which is aimed at achieving a more socially efficient outcome than would arise under an unregulated situation. You will learn that an average cost pricing policy ensures a natural monopoly a guaranteed profit but reduces the incentive for the monopoly to keep its costs of production low.

II.   CHECKLIST

By the end of this chapter, you should be able to:

√   Explain what gives rise to a natural monopoly.
√   List some real world examples of natural monopolies.
√   Explain why natural monopolies are often regulated.
√   Explain a natural monopoly's reaction to regulation.
√   Describe the objective and policy used in regulating natural monopolies.
√   Use a graph to show how an average cost pricing policy works.
√   List the characteristics of a monopolistically competitive market structure.
√   List some real world examples of firms that operate under monopolistic competition.
√   Explain the profit-maximizing rule for a monopolistically competitive firm and depict it with a graph for both the short and the long run.
√   Discuss the relationship between price, marginal revenue, marginal cost, and average cost of a firm in a monopolistically competitive market structure.
√   Discuss the costs and benefits to a monopolistically competitive market structure.
√   Explain what motivates firms to enter a monopolistically competitive market structure.
√   Describe what happens to the price, output, and profits of firms in a monopolistically competitive market structure in the long run.

III.   KEY TERMS

Entrepreneur: a person who has an idea for a business and then coordinates the production and sale of goods and services, taking risks in the process.
Natural monopoly: a market in which the entry of a second firm would make price less than average cost, so a single firm serves the entire market.

Average-cost pricing policy: a regulatory policy under which the government picks the point on the demand curve at which price equals average cost.

Monopolistic competition: a situation in which each firm has a *monopoly* in selling its own differentiated product, but *competes* with other firms selling similar products.

IV.   PERFORMANCE ENHANCING TIPS (PETS)

<u>PET #1</u>

The profit-maximizing rule for a natural monopoly is to produce an output level where marginal revenue is equal to marginal cost.

This is just PET #1 from Chapter 11 restated for a natural monopoly. You may want to review PET #1 from Chapter 11 since it provides a more detailed explanation of the PET. You may also want to review PET #2 and PET #3 from Chapter 11 since they also apply to a natural monopoly.

<u>PET #2</u>

An average cost pricing policy lowers the price that consumers would pay compared to an unregulated situation and increases the output produced compared to an unregulated situation.

To see this, look at the graph below.

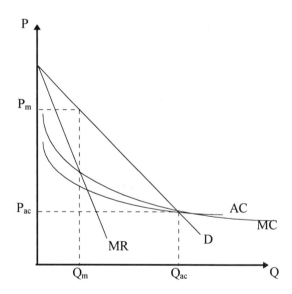

An unregulated natural monopoly would produce an output level where marginal revenue equals marginal cost and charge a price based on what the demand curve would support for that output level. In the graph below, the unregulated natural monopoly would produce an output level Q_m and charge a price P_m.

An average cost pricing policy dictates that the price of output equal the average cost to produce it. This occurs at the intersection of the demand (price) and average cost curves. The graph shows that the output level corresponding to price = average cost is Q_{ac}. Of course, the price associated with this output level (read off of the demand curve) is P_{ac}.

Since $P_{ac} < P_m$ and $Q_{ac} > Q_m$, the average cost pricing policy moves closer to a socially efficient outcome.

PET #3

A monopolistically competitive firm maximizes its profit by producing at an output level where marginal revenue equals marginal cost.

The same reasoning discussed in PET #1 of Chapter 11 applies to a monopolistically competitive firm as well. You may want to review it if you are not comfortable with the principle.

PET #4

The entry of firms into a monopolistically competitive market structure causes the demand curves of all firms to shift to the left since each firm now gets a smaller piece of the consumer market. Since the demand curves shift to the left, the marginal revenue curves also shift to the left.

Since the demand and marginal revenue curves of monopolistically competitive firms shift as entry occurs in the industry, the profit-maximizing output level and corresponding price the firms will charge will also change.

V.   PRACTICE EXAM: MULTIPLE CHOICE QUESTIONS

1.   Which one of the following gives rise to a natural monopoly?

a.   patents.
b.   increasing average costs of production.
c.   economies of scale.
d.   inelastic market demand.
e.   competition.

2.   Which one of the following would be the best example of a natural monopoly?

a.   video rental stores.
b.   wheat farming.
c.   oil refineries.
d.   sewerage treatment.
e.   auto dealerships.

3.   The average cost curve of a natural monopoly is best described as:

a.   L-shaped.
b.   J-shaped.
c.   U-shaped.
d.   W-shaped.

e.   S-shaped.

4.   Based on the graph below, the output level a profit-maximizing natural monopoly would produce is
        _____ and the output level a regulated natural monopoly would produce is _____.

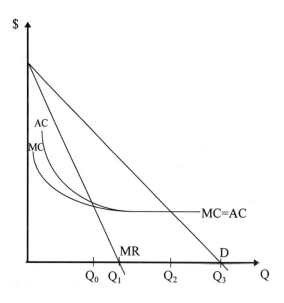

a. $Q_0; Q_1$.
b. $Q_1; Q_2$.
c. $Q_0; Q_2$.
d. $Q_1; Q_3$.
e. $Q_2; Q_3$.

5.   Based on the diagram below, the price a profit-maximizing natural monopoly would charge for its
        output is _____ and the price a regulated natural monopoly would charge is _____.

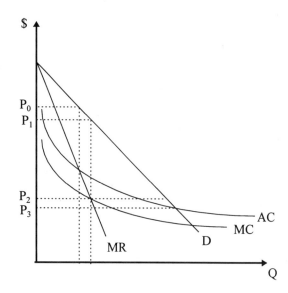

a. P_0; P_1.
b. P_1; P_2.
c. P_0; P_2.
d. P_1; P_3.
e. P_2; P_3.

6.   Which one of the following statements is NOT true of an average-cost-pricing policy:

a.   it will create zero economic profit.
b.   it is established where the demand curve intersects the average cost curve.
c.   it creates little incentive for the monopolist to control costs.
d.   it leads to a higher price than would be charged by an unregulated monopolist.
e.   it leads to more output being produced than would arise if the monopoly was not regulated.

7.   Which one of the following would NOT be a characteristic of a monopolistically competitive market structure?

a.   a homogeneous product.
b.   many firms in the industry.
c.   slight control over price.
d.   no artificial barriers to entry.
e.   all of the above are characteristics of a monopolistically competitive market structure.

8.   Which one of the following would NOT differentiate one product from another under monopolistic competition?

a.   location.
b.   special services that go along with the purchase of a product.
c.   economies of scale.
d.   physical characteristics.
e.   product image.

9.   In the long run, firms in a monopolistically competitive market structure:

a.   earn zero economic profit.
b.   produce an output level where price = marginal cost.
c.   do not produce output at minimum average cost.
d.   produce an output level where marginal revenue = marginal cost.
e.   a, c, and d are true.

10.   Under monopolistic competition, entry typically causes price to _____ and profits to _____.

a.   decrease; decrease.
b.   decrease; increase.
c.   increase; increase.
d.   increase; decrease.
e.   decrease; remain unchanged.

11.   Government elimination of artificial barriers to entry can be expected to:

a.   lead to more competition.
b.   lead to improved service.
c.   lead to a lower price for output
d.   lead to lower profits.
e.   all of the above.

12.   Which one of the following would be the best example of a monopolistically competitive firm?

a.   sugar farmer.
b.   railway transportation.
c.   Italian restaurants.
d.   drug company.
e.   food service at a national park.

VI.   PRACTICE EXAM: ESSAY QUESTIONS

1.   Public utilities such as electricity are referred to as natural monopolies and are often subject to regulation by a state authority (the "Public Regulatory Commission"). Explain why a public utility such as electricity is referred to as a "natural monopoly." Explain how and why an average cost pricing policy is applied to public utility. Discuss the effects of the policy on the price and output the utility sells at and produces. Discuss how the policy affects the utility's profits and costs.

2.   Consider a small city's drycleaning market which is monopolistically competitive. Currently, the typical drycleaner is charging $5 an item. The average cost of drycleaning is $2. The typical drycleaner cleans 1,000 items per week. (Each customer drops off approximately 4 items). Suppose a new drycleaner was to enter the market. Explain what would happen to the price, average cost, output, and profit of a typical drycleaner. Discuss the costs and benefits to consumers of having a drycleaning market that is monopolistically competitive.

VII.   ANSWER KEY: MULTIPLE CHOICE QUESTIONS

1.   Correct answer: c.

Discussion: Economies of scale (average cost declining over large ranges of output) arise because the fixed costs of starting up a business are very high. This typically occurs if the business requires the use of indivisible inputs.

Statement a is not correct because a patent creates an unnatural or artificial monopoly. Statement b is not correct; decreasing average costs over a large range of output characterize a natural monopoly. Statement d is not correct because demand has nothing to do with market structure. Statement e is not correct; monopolies are characterized by barriers to entry and, hence, the absence of competition.

2.   Correct answer: d.

Discussion: Natural monopolies typically arise because of the use of indivisible inputs and high fixed costs of start up. A natural monopoly is where there is a single supplier of a good or service. Sewage treatment is a good example of a natural monopoly.

Since there are typically more than one video rental store per town and because the costs of start up are low, video rental stores are best characterized as monopolistically competitive firms. Wheat farmers produce a homogeneous product and serve a very small portion of the overall market. They also have little control over the price at which they can sell their wheat. Wheat farmers are thus best characterized as perfectly competitive firms. Auto dealerships have a lot in common with video rental stores and are thus characterized as monopolistically competitive firms. While oil refineries may have a high fixed cost of start up and require the use of indivisible inputs, there is typically more than one oil refining company that services a country. In Chapter 13, you will see that an oil refinery is best characterized as an oligopolistic firm.

3.   Correct answer: a.

Discussion: The average cost of production of a natural monopoly is very high at low levels of output. As output expands, average costs drop and continue to decline over large ranges of output. In fact, average costs typically are constant over large ranges of output. Thus, an average cost curve would be L-shaped.

A J-shaped average cost curve would indicate that average costs of production are low at low levels of output and then increase as output expands. A U-shaped average cost curve is typical of short-run analysis. W- and S-shaped cost curves have not been addressed in your textbook.

4.   Correct answer: a.

Discussion: An unregulated natural monopoly produces where marginal revenue = marginal cost (the two curves intersect). This occurs at output level Q_0. A regulated natural monopoly produces where price = average cost (demand and average cost curves intersect). This occurs at output level Q_1. Thus, statement a is the only correct answer.

5.   Correct answer: d.

Discussion: To arrive at the correct answer, you must first establish at what output level a profit-maximizing natural monopoly will produce. Once you have determined that output level, you read up to the demand curve and over to the price line to establish the price the natural monopolist would charge. In this case, the profit-maximizing output level occurs where marginal revenue = marginal cost (they intersect) and the price is P_1. For a regulated natural monopoly, price is set equal to average cost. This occurs where the demand and average cost curves intersect. At this point, read over to the vertical axis and that will be the price the regulator sets. In this case, it is P_3. Thus, statement d is the only correct option.

6.   Correct answer: d.

Discussion: One of the aims of an average-cost-pricing policy is to lower the price that customers must pay for the product or service. Thus, an average-cost-pricing policy leads to a lower price, not a higher price than would be charged by an unregulated monopolist.

Statements a, b, c, and e are all true of an average-cost-pricing policy. Since the policy sets price = average cost, the monopoly earns zero economic profit. This price-setting policy can be depicted where demand and the average cost curves intersect. Since the regulated monopolist's price will always be set equal to average costs, it has no incentive to hold down its costs. The monopolist knows that, whatever costs they incur, they will always be covered by the pricing policy. Another aim of the average cost pricing policy is to force the monopolist to serve as many customers as possible. Thus, the policy will increase the output of the monopolist.

7.   Correct answer: a.

Discussion: A monopolistically competitive market structure is characterized by product differentiation, real or perceived. A homogeneous product is virtually identical (apples, sugar, wheat, etc.) and is characteristic of a perfectly competitive market structure.

In a monopolistically competitive market structure, there is still a lot of competition and, hence, there are many firms in the industry. However, the firm does have some control over the price it sets. Furthermore, the are no artificial barriers to entry, which is why there is a lot of competition.

8.   Correct answer: c.

Discussion: Economies of scale typically characterize monopolies, particularly natural monopolies. Statements a, b, d, and e are all factors that can cause similar products to be differentiated from one another.

9.   Correct answer: e.

Discussion: In the long run, competition in the monopolistically competitive market structure leads to entry up until the point at which it is no longer desirable. This occurs where zero economic profits are being earned by the firms in the industry. Monopolistically competitive firms do not produce at minimum average cost because they serve a small portion of the market and because their profit-maximizing strategy is to set marginal revenue = marginal cost. As just mentioned, the profit-maximizing strategy of any firm is to set marginal revenue = marginal cost. Thus, statements a, c, and d are true of a monopolistically competitive market structure.

Statement b describes a version of the profit-maximizing rule that a perfectly competitive firm could use.

10.   Correct answer: a.

Discussion: Competition in a monopolistically competitive market structure is what leads to a lower price for the firms' output. This acts to reduce firms' profits. Also, the average cost of production typically rises for monopolistically competitive firms. This too acts to reduce firms' profits. Thus, statement a is the only correct option.

11.   Correct answer: e.

Discussion: Studies have shown that, when the government steps in to remove artificial barriers to entry and thereby promote competition amongst firms that all of the above will result.

12.   Correct answer: c.

Discussion: Statement c is the best example because there are many Italian restaurants each with their own characteristics that differentiate them from each other. Furthermore, entry into the restaurant business is very open.

A sugar farmer is an example of a perfectly competitive firm. Railway transportation is an example of a natural monopoly. A drug company is an example of a patent-generated monopoly. Food service at a national park is an example of a license-generated monopoly.

VIII. ANSWER KEY: ESSAY QUESTIONS

1.   A public utility, such as electricity, is an example of a natural monopoly. A natural monopoly occurs when there is a single supplier of the output to the market because any more than one firm in the industry would not be profitable. The reason that more than one firm would not be profitable is that a natural monopoly is characterized by very high fixed start-up costs and, thus, very high average costs at low levels of output. This means that, with more than one firm in the market, each firm would have only a portion of the overall market and, thus, would produce for a smaller portion of the market. However, since average costs of production are very high at low levels of output and since each firm is producing for only a portion of the market, each firm will face a very high average cost of production. The firms may not be able to extract a price from their customers that is high enough to cover the costs of providing a service to them and, thus, each firm will earn negative economic profit. Faced with this prospect, firms typically choose not to enter an industry with high fixed costs of start up where one firm is already present. In other words, the market supports only one firm in the industry. Since this type of monopoly arises naturally, i.e., without the government offering franchises, patents, etc., it is referred to as a natural monopoly.

An average cost pricing policy is often used in the interest of creating a more socially efficient outcome -- that is, where price is lower and output higher than would arise if the monopolist were unregulated. Under an average cost pricing policy, the regulatory commission effectively sets a price equal to the monopolist's average cost of production and requires that the electric company serve all customers willing to pay the price. In terms of a graph, the regulatory commission forces the utility to produce an output level where the demand and average cost curves intersect. Since price is set equal to average cost, the electric company earns zero economic profit (but positive accounting profit). The average cost pricing policy creates a disincentive for the utility to minimize its costs of production. The reason the disincentive is created is that the utility knows that the regulated price will be set based on the utility's average cost of production; the utility's average cost of production will always be covered, so the utility is always assured of at least zero economic profit, no less. Thus, the utility does not have an incentive to keep costs of production low as would an unregulated firm that desires to maximize profits.

2.   In a monopolistically competitive market, there is ease of entry. The ease of entry, however, means that there will be a lot of competition for customers amongst the firms. Thus, firms that are currently making positive economic profit face the threat of entry by entrepreneurs who believe that they, too, could make a profit in the industry. In fact, entry in a monopolistically competitive market structure typically occurs up until the point at which firms are making zero economic profit. At this point, there is no incentive for more entry into the market.

In the case of the drycleaning business of the small city, the typical drycleaner is making $2,000 in profit per week based on the approximately 250 customers served (1,000 items per week/4 items dropped off per customer). If a new drycleaner enters the market, there will be some competition from him. This means several things. First, the existing drycleaners may have to lower the price of their service in order to hold on to their customer base. Since the new drycleaner will likely take away customers from the existing drycleaners, their demand curves (and marginal revenue curves) will shift to the left. However, the lower price charged by the drycleaners will mean that they may not lose as many customers as anticipated. Second, because the existing drycleaners will be serving fewer customers (less output), the average cost of serving each customer will rise. (Remember that average costs decline as output increases and vice-versa, i.e., average costs increase as output declines). Third, since the drycleaners will be charging a lower price for their service and incurring a higher average cost of production, the drycleaners' profits will be reduced. In the end, entry into the small city's drycleaning business will stop when economic profits are driven to zero.

There are costs and benefits to the drycleaning business operating under a monopolistically competitive market structure. With ease of entry, there will be a lot of drycleaners serving the market, each with their own level of customer service, location, etc. Thus, in a monopolistically competitive market structure, customers get the benefits of being able to select from a variety of slightly differentiated products and services. Also, customers will likely see that the travel time to the drycleaner they patronize will decrease since more drycleaners in the city means more locations being serviced. The customers also benefit in that competition typically leads to a lower price for the product or service being purchased. The cost to society of a monopolistically competitive market is that the average cost of production is higher. From an efficiency standpoint, this is a cost to society since it would be better off if the drycleaners could produce where average cost is minimized and, correspondingly, the price consumers pay would be the lowest possible. Of course, competition leads to price being reduced to some degree.

Take It to the Net

We invite you to visit the O'Sullivan/Sheffrin page on the Prentice Hall Web site at:

http://www.prenhall.com/osullivan/

for this chapter's World Wide Web exercise.

CHAPTER 13
OLIGOPOLY AND ANTI-TRUST POLICY

I.   OVERVIEW

In this chapter, you will learn about the market structure of oligopoly. You will learn about the characteristics of an oligopoly and what gives rise to an oligopoly. You will also learn how oligopolists make pricing decisions. You will learn that oligopolists act strategically, anticipating the actions of their competitors in response to their own pricing decisions. You will learn that oligopolists may enter into price-fixing schemes, price-matching schemes, price leadership, mergers and trusts, or practice entry deterrence in an attempt to avoid the consequences of competition. You will use a game tree to analyze the choices and probable strategic outcomes of oligopolists. You will also learn about the kinked demand curve that oligopolists may face. You will learn about contestable markets. You will also learn about an "insecure" monopolist and the steps they may take to deter entry by other firms. You will learn what role anti-trust policy as well as trade policy play in regulating the behavior of oligopolists so that they do not enter into anti-competitive agreements. You will also learn how deregulation has affected some oligopolistic industries.

II.   CHECKLIST

By the end of this chapter you should be able to:

√   Describe the characteristics of an oligopoly.
√   Explain what gives rise to an oligopoly.
√   List some real world examples of an oligopolistic market structure.
√   Discuss the duopolists' (2-firm oligopoly) dilemma.
√   Discuss and explain the rationale for price-fixing schemes, price-matching schemes, price leadership, predatory pricing, and mergers and trusts. Discuss why such schemes are often likely to break down.
√   Use a game tree to determine what the likely pricing outcome will be between duopolists.
√   Explain why oligopolists face a kinked demand curve.
√   Explain the behavior of an insecure monopolist.
√   Define a concentration ratio and discuss how it might be used to establish whether an oligopoly exists.
√   List some of the major pieces of anti-trust legislation and explain their purpose.

III.   KEY TERMS

Oligopoly: a market served by a few firms.
Concentration ratio: a measure of the degree of concentration in a market; the four-firm concentration ratio is the percentage of output produced by the four largest firms.
Cartel: a group of firms that coordinate their pricing decisions, often by charging the same price.
Price fixing: an arrangement in which two firms coordinate their pricing decisions.
Game tree: a visual representation of the consequences of different strategies.
Dominant strategy: an action that is the best choice under all circumstances.

Duopolists' dilemma: a situation in which both firms would be better off if they picked the high price, but each one picks the low price.

Guaranteed price matching: a scheme under which a firm guarantees that it will match a lower price by a competitor; also known as a "meet-the-competition" policy.

Grim-trigger: a strategy under which a firm responds to underpricing by picking a price so low that each firm makes zero economic profit.

Tit-for-tat: a strategy under which the one firm starts out with the cartel price and then picks whatever price the other firm picked in the previous period.

Price leadership: an arrangement under which one firm picks a price and other firms in the market match the leader's price.

Kinked-demand model: a model under which firms in an oligopoly match price reductions by other firms but do not match price increases.

Insecure monopolist: a monopolist who faces the possibility that a second firm will enter the market.

Entry Deterrence: a scheme under which a firm increases its output and accepts a lower price to deter other firms from entering the market.

Contestable market: a market in which the costs of entering and leaving are very low, so the firms in the market are constantly threatened by the entry of new firms.

Trust: an arrangement under which the owners of several companies transfer their decision-making powers to a small group of trustees, who then make decisions for all the firms in the trust.

Merger: a process in which two or more firms combine their operations.

Predatory pricing: a pricing scheme under which a firm decreases its price to drive a rival out of business, and increases the price when the other firm disappears.

IV.   PERFORMANCE ENHANCING TIPS

PET #1

The oligopolists' (or duopolists') dilemma is that each firm knows that by choosing to sell its output at a high price, the competition will sell at a lower price and, thus, undercut the high-priced firm's profits. Thus, each firm chooses to sell at the low price but in so doing, each firm ends up with a profit below what they could earn if they collectively agreed to the high price.

The dilemma thus creates an incentive for the oligopolists to collude -- devise pricing schemes that lead to the high price outcome for all firms. However, such schemes are often illegal under anti-trust policy.

PET #2

Cartels and other price-fixing schemes create the incentive for one or more of the participating firms to cheat (undercut the agreed upon price). The cheater is tempted to cheat because his firm's profits will increase at the expense of the other cartel members.

Because of the temptation to cheat, cartels and other price-fixing schemes are often hard to sustain unless there is some enforcement mechanism or punishment that deters the cheater(s) from cheating.

V.   PRACTICE EXAM: MULTIPLE CHOICE QUESTIONS

1.   Which one of the following is an example of an oligopolistic industry?

a.   aircraft and parts.
b.   video rental stores.
c.   apple growers.
d.   sewage and water treatment.
e.   clothing stores.

2.   Which one of the following would NOT be true of an oligopolistic market structure?

a.   each firm sells a similar product or service.
b.   each firm is a price taker.
c.   economies of scale in production.
d.   a firm may carry out a big advertising campaign.
e.   a few firms serve the market.

3.   A cartel is:

a.   an industrial association in which research and development is shared.
b.   the firm in the industry that sets the going price.
c.   a policy designed to prevent mergers that produce a concentration ratio greater than 40%.
d.   a group of firms that coordinate their pricing decisions, often by charging the same price.
e.   an industry watchdog group that monitors the price of output to ensure that consumers are not being ripped off.

4.   Which one of the following statements is true?

a.   cartels and price fixing are legal in the U.S.
b.   a four-firm concentration ratio is the percentage of industry profits earned by the four biggest firms.
c.   a kinked demand curve is flatter (more elastic) below the kink than above.
d.   a grim-trigger strategy is when a firm prices its output so low that the competition makes losses and, thus, is driven out of the market.
e.   free-trade policy promotes competition.

5.   Suppose you are given the following information on a two-firm oligopoly (duopoly).
      Firm A will earn $5,000 in profit if it charges a price of $10 and Firm B charges a price of $10; Firm B will earn $5,000 in profit.
      Firm A will earn $2,000 in profit if it charges a price of $10 and Firm B charges a price of $7; Firm B will earn $6,000 in profit.
      Firm A will earn $6,000 in profit if it charges a price of $7 and Firm B charges a price of $10; Firm B will earn B will earn $2,000 in profit.
      Firm A will earn $3,000 in profit if it charges a price of $7 and Firm B charges a price of $7; Firm B will earn $2,000 in profit.

If Firm A must pick the price at which it sells its output without knowing what price Firm B will pick and Firm B must pick the price at which it sells its output without knowing what price Firm A will pick, at what price combination will Firms A and B ultimately sell?

a. $10; $10.
b. $10; $7.
c. $7; $10.
d. $7; $7.
e.   cannot be determined without further information.

6.   The rational outcome of a guaranteed price matching or "meet-the-competition" policy is that:

a.   both firms will sell at the low price.
b.   one firm will sell at a high price until the competition sells at a low price; then it will sell at the low price.
c.   both firms will sell at the high price.
d.   consumers are fooled into thinking the price matching scheme will protect them from high prices.
e.   (c) and (d).

7.   Which one of the following is NOT a retaliation strategy that firms would apply to one that cheated on a price-fixing scheme by selling at a price below the agreed-upon fixed price?

a.   all other firms sell at the same low price as the cheating firm.
b.   all other firms sell at a price that ensures zero economic profit for all firms.
c.   each period, all other firms sell at the price picked by the cheater in the previous period.
d.   all other firms collect a penalty fee from the cheater.
e.   all of the above are retaliation schemes used by oligopolists.

8.   Which one of the following statements is NOT true?

a.   a firm that chooses to cheat on a price-fixing scheme should consider the short-term gain in profits from cheating versus the long-term loss in profits from being punished.
b.   the duopoly-pricing strategy leads to negative economic profits.
c.   cartels may break down because of the incentive to cheat.
d.   price leadership arrangements are an implicit price-fixing scheme.
e.   all of the above are true statements.

9.   Which one of the following statements is NOT true?

a.   a monopolist may act like a firm in a market with many firms, picking a low price and earning a small profit so as to deter entry and thereby guarantee profits for the longer term.
b.   a contestable market is one in which firms can enter and leave the market without incurring large costs.
c.   a firm can increase its share of the market by forming a trust.
d.   predatory pricing forces the predator and the prey to incur losses.
e.   mergers are illegal under anti-trust law.

10.   Which one of the following statements is true of anti-trust legislation?

a.   The Sherman Act made it illegal to monopolize a market or to engage in practices that resulted in a "restraint of trade."
b.   The Federal Competition Commission was established to enforce anti-trust laws.
c.   The Clayton Act outlawed all stock-purchase mergers.
d.   The Hart-Scott-Rodino Act extended anti-trust legislation to corporations.
e.   The Robinson-Patman Act encouraged selling products at "unreasonably low prices" since consumers would benefit.

11.   The purpose of anti-trust laws is to:

a.   promote competition.
b.   reduce the price that consumers pay for output.
c.   protect domestic firms from foreign trade.
d.   ensure that firms do not avoid paying income taxes.
e.   (a) and (b).

VI.   PRACTICE EXAM: ESSAY QUESTIONS

1.   Explain why the duopolists' dilemma often leads to price-fixing schemes. Be sure to discuss a number of different price-fixing schemes and what may cause them to break down. Also discuss the enforcement mechanisms that the duopolists might undertake to ensure that a price-fixing scheme does not break down.

2.   Suppose you ran the only bakery in town and were currently very profitable. What things might you consider if you wanted to ensure that you continued to enjoy the same success in the future?

VII.   ANSWER KEY: MULTIPLE CHOICE QUESTIONS

1.   Correct answer: a.

Discussion: Aircraft and parts are examples of oligopolistic market structures. Video rental stores and clothing stores are examples of monopolistically competitive market structures. Apple growers are an example of a perfectly competitive market structure and sewage and water treatment is an example of a natural monopoly.

2.   Correct answer: b.

Discussion: In an oligopolistic market structure, firms have some control over price and act strategically in setting price. That means that each firm considers the reaction of the other firms to the price that it may choose to sell its output. Firms are price takers in a perfectly competitive market structure.

Statements a, c, d, and e are all true of an oligopolistic market structure.

3.   Correct answer: d.

Discussion: A cartel is a group of firms that get together to agree to fix the price at which they sell their output. The purpose of the agreement is to ensure higher profits for all firms than if they acted independently.

Statements a, b, c, and e are all incorrect. Statement b is the definition of a price leader.

4.   Correct answer: e.

Discussion: Free trade is a policy that does not prohibit foreign firms from selling in the domestic market. As such, free-trade policy promotes competition and works to achieve some of the same objectives as anti-trust policy.

Statement a is not correct. Price-fixing agreements are illegal in the U.S. Statement b is not correct. A four-firm concentration ratio is the percentage of industry output that the four biggest firms in the industry produce. Statement c is not correct. The kinked demand curve is flatter (more elastic) above the kink than below. This is because when a firm raises its price (above the kink point), it will lose a lot of customers. This is just a way of saying quantity demanded is very responsive to price above the kink. Statement d is not correct because a grim-trigger strategy is not designed to lead to losses for firms but rather zero economic profits.

5.   Correct answer: d.

Discussion: The duopolist's dilemma means that the two firms end up both picking the low price even though it is not the price at which each firm's profits would be maximized. The reasoning is as follows: Firm A knows that, if it picks the high price, Firm B will pick the low price since that way, Firm B will get bigger profits. Thus, Firm A does not have the incentive to pick the high price. For the same reasoning, Firm B knows that, if it picks the high price, Firm A will pick the low price since, that way, Firm A will get bigger profits. Thus, Firm B will not choose the high price. So, if both firms have to pick the price at which they will sell output without knowledge of what price the other has selected, they will both end up picking the low price.

6.   Correct answer: e.

Discussion: A guaranteed price-matching strategy never actually has to be enacted by the firm that sets the policy. This is because both firms will end up selling at the high price. Thus, consumers may think that they are being protected when in fact the protection is just an "empty promise." The reason the policy leads to a high price by both firms is that, once the competitor sees the other firm selling at the high price (albeit with the price-matching policy), the other firm is now able to select the price that will guarantee it the biggest profit. That price is the higher price, so both firms end up being able to sell at the higher price.

7.   Correct answer: d.

Discussion: Statement d is not correct. The book does not discuss any scenario in which firms are able to impose and effectively collect penalties from the cheater.

Statement a is the definition of a duopoly price retaliation strategy. Statement b is the definition of the grim-trigger retaliation strategy. Statement c is the definition of a tit-for-tat pricing strategy. Statement e cannot be correct because statement d is not correct.

8.   Correct answer: b.

Discussion: A duopoly-price strategy leads to smaller profits than would arise under a price-fixing agreement. Predatory pricing, on the other hand, leads to negative economic profits.

Statements a, c, and d are all true.

9.   Correct answer: e.

Discussion: Not all mergers are illegal under anti-trust law; only those mergers that would substantially reduce competition are illegal.

Statements a, b, c, and d are all true. You may wish to look at the answer to essay #2 for a detailed discussion related to statement a. Contestable markets are market structures that may populated by only one or a few firms yet the behavior of the firms is more like the industry is populated by many firms. The threat of entry is what characterizes a contestable market. A trust is a group of individuals who make the decisions for a group of companies. In this way, the same pricing decisions can be ensured across companies. This effectively works to fix prices. Predatory pricing is a very aggressive pricing strategy that put the predator's profits on the line for the ultimate goal of securing monopoly status.

10.   Correct answer: a.

Discussion. The Sherman Act was the first piece of anti-trust legislation enacted in the U.S. in 1890.

Statement b is not true. The Federal Trade Commission is the agency that enforces anti-trust laws. Statement c is not true. The Clayton Act outlawed stock-purchase mergers that would substantially reduce competition. Statement d is not true. Anti-trust legislation was initially enacted for corporations only. The Hart-Scott-Rodino Act extended it to proprietorships and partnerships. Statement e is not true. The Robinson-Patman Act discouraged firms from selling products at unreasonably low prices if the intent was to discourage competition.

11.   Correct answer: e.

Discussion: Anti-trust laws are designed to promote competition. Remember that a perfectly competitive market ensures a socially efficient outcome and that the other market structures lead to prices that would be higher than under perfect competition and output levels that would be lower than under perfect competition. Thus, consumers benefit the more competition there is. Of course, anti-trust legislation cannot create perfectly competitive markets out of other market types, but they are aimed at achieving markets in which freedom of entry is easier.

VIII.   ANSWER KEY: ESSAY QUESTIONS

1.   The duopolists' dilemma is that each firm, fearful that its profits will be undercut by its competitor, ends up charging a price lower than they would otherwise want to. Thus, each firm makes a smaller profit than they could if they each charged a higher price. Given this dilemma, there is an incentive for the duopolists to get together and agree to a higher price at which they will both sell their output. That way, they can both be guaranteed profits that are more attractive than when they don't agree to fix the price. While such explicit price-fixing schemes are illegal in the U.S, some firms still engage in price-fixing schemes because the fines and legal fees they might have to pay if they are found guilty of price fixing are less than the profits they anticipate earning over the time the price-fixing scheme is in operation.

There are a number of different types of price-fixing schemes. Firms can form a cartel and agree to all sell at a fixed price or agree that some firms can sell at price X while others sell at price Y. A price-matching scheme is another pricing strategy. It is not explicitly illegal. In this strategy, a firm announces (through the media) that it will match the prices of its competitor. It is important that the firm be credible in its policy. Since the competitor believes that any low price it tries to sell at will be matched, and, thus, that their profits will be competed for, they will choose to sell at the same high price, too. Thus, the firm announcing the price-matching policy is able to continue selling at the high price. In this way, both firms enjoy higher profits than if there was no matching policy. Price leadership is another form of price fixing although it is an implicit agreement. In this set up, the firm that is the price leader sets the price and all other firms simply follow suit. That way, there is no price competition and, implicitly, the price at which firms sell is fixed.

Price-fixing agreements, whether explicit or implicit, carry a temptation to cheat. The temptation exists because, once the price is fixed, the cheaters know that, if they sell at below the fixed price, they will get a larger share of the market and thereby reap increased profits. However, cheaters should think about the long-term consequences of cheating since the other firms that are selling at the fixed price might punish the cheaters (and, unfortunately, themselves as well) by all selling at a lower price, perhaps the one at which the cheaters were selling ("the duopoly price") or even one low enough that all firms earn zero economic profit (the grim-trigger strategy). The threat of retaliation which arises in a repeated game sequence may curtail, to some degree, the temptation to cheat.

2.   If I ran the only bakery in town and it was very profitable, I would be worried that other entrepreneurs, seeing how profitable I was, would be motivated to open up other bakeries in town. Thus, I would be, in the terms of the textbook, an "insecure monopolist." My insecurity would be that the future success (read profitability) of my bakery may be threatened by the entry of other bakeries into the town. So, what to do? I would consider lowering the price I charge for the array of baked goods I provide to my customers. Of course, I would realize that the lower price might lead to lower economic profits (if my revenue didn't increase and my costs remained the same or even if, at the lower price, my revenue increased, but my costs increased by more). The lower price and presumably lower economic profits would make it less attractive for other firms to enter the business and, thus, I may be able to secure my monopoly status and the long-term prospect of at least positive economic profits.

On the other hand, if I do nothing to deter entry and it occurs, I will likely see my profits reduced. However, if they do not fall by as much as my "low price deterrence strategy," then it would make sense for me to do nothing.

Take It to the Net

We invite you to visit the O'Sullivan/Sheffrin page on the Prentice Hall Web site at:

http://www.prenhall.com/osullivan/

for this chapter's World Wide Web exercise.

CHAPTER 14
PUBLIC GOODS, TAXES, AND PUBLIC CHOICE

I.   OVERVIEW

In this chapter, you will learn about public goods -- goods that benefit society but are so expensive to pay for that no individual can pay for it by him- or herself. You will learn that government policy, including the tax system, can be used to ensure that worthwhile public goods are provided to society.   You will also learn that sometimes the government is unable to make informed decisions about which public goods to provide. You will learn what distinguishes public goods from private goods and learn of the special challenges that public goods create in a market economy. You will revisit the spillover principle that was learned in Chapter 3 of your textbook. You will learn about a branch of economics called "public choice" which studies the way in which governments operate and how they make decisions.

II.   CHECKLIST

By the end of this chapter, you should be able to:

√   Define a public good and the characteristics of a public good.
√   Compare and contrast public and private goods.
√   List some real world examples of public goods.
√   Explain what spillover benefits (external benefits) are and give some examples.
√   Explain how in the presence of spillover benefits, the market equilibrium determined by demand and supply is not efficient.
√   Explain how a subsidy by a government might lead to a more efficient outcome in the case of spillover benefits.
√   Discuss the three reasons for government inefficiency.
√   Explain the free-rider problem and why voluntary contributions will generally not lead to the provision of a public good.
√   Discuss some ways in which organizations can increase the voluntary contributions that they receive.
√   Use supply and demand analysis to analyze the effects of taxes.
√   Explain the forward and backward shifting effects of a tax on a good.
√   Predict who will bear the bulk of the burden.
√   Explain the three views on how the government operates.
√   Explain the median-voter rule.

III.   KEY TERMS

Spillover benefit: the benefit from a good experienced by people who do not decide how much of the good to produce or consume.
Public good: a good that is available for everyone to consume, regardless of who pays and who doesn't.
Private good: a good that is consumed by the single person or household who pays for it.
Free-rider problem: each person will try to get the benefit of a public good without paying for it, trying to get a free ride at the expense of others.
External benefit: another term for spillover benefit.

Government failure: a situation in which the government fails to make an efficient choice in providing public goods or subsidies.

Deadweight loss from taxation: the difference between the total burden of a tax and the amount of revenue collected by the government.

Excess burden: the difference between the total burden of a tax and the amount of revenue collected by the government.

Median-voter rule: a rule suggesting that the choices made by government will reflect the preferences of the median voter.

Public choice: a field of economics that explores how governments actually operate.

IV.   PERFORMANCE ENHANCING TIPS

PET #1

The market demand and supply curves of goods with spillover benefits or spillover costs do not depict the efficient equilibrium outcome.

This means that, in the presence of spillover benefits or costs, the equilibrium price and quantity represented by the intersection of market demand and supply curves is not "efficient." This means that the price and quantity outcome does not take into account those consumers (or producers) that receive benefits or incur costs but are not directly using the good. Your book gives a good example using education as the good.

PET #2

A subsidy is a transfer of money from the government to private citizens; a tax is a transfer of money from private citizens to the government.

Since a subsidy is the reverse of a tax, it is sometimes referred to as a "negative tax." It should be pointed out, however, that the ability of the government to extend subsidies to certain private citizens or groups of private citizens comes from the taxes that private citizens (households and businesses) pay to the government. Thus, your tax dollars are used to pay for government subsidies. Thus, indirectly, your tax dollars are transferred to other citizens in society.

PET #3

A tax on a good or service is represented by shifting the supply curve to the left. The rise in the equilibrium price depends on how flat or steep (elastic) the demand curve is.

To see this, look at the graph below.

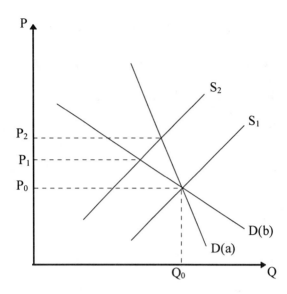

The steeper demand curve, D(a), is the less elastic demand curve; the flatter demand curve, D(b), is the more elastic demand curve. The shift in the supply curve from S_1 to S_2 is caused by a tax on the good. As you can see, the equilibrium price rises by more along the less clastic demand curve, D(a), and rises by less laong the more elastic demand curve. Thus, more of the tax is shifted forward to consumers with a less elastic demand curve than with a more elastic demand curve. Consequently, when demand is less elastic and, thus, price rises more to consumers so that more of the tax is paid for by them, less of the tax is shifted backward to input suppliers. This means that, with a less elastic demand curve, input suppliers bear less of the burden of the tax than when demand is more elastic.

PET #4

A tax on the supply of a good shifts the supply of the good to the left, reduces the equilibrium quantity sold, and, thus, reduces the demand for inputs used in producing the good and, thus, the price of inputs.

You should know from Chapter 4 of your textbook and the Practicum that a leftward shift in the supply of good X reduces the equilibrium quantity (and raises the price of the good) of good X. From this, you should be able to logically infer that, if industry X is selling fewer units of output, it will need fewer units of inputs. In economics terms, this means that the demand for inputs will decline. You should know from Chapter 4 of your textbook and the Practicum that a decrease in the demand for any good (represented by a leftward shift in demand) will reduce the equilibrium price (and reduce the equilibrium quantity) of the good. In this case, the good is an input into good X.

One input into the production of most goods is labor. Thus, a tax on good X may not only raise the price of good X, it may also reduce the demand for labor (and other inputs) used in making good X. When the demand for labor declines, the equilibrium price (in this case, wage) of labor and the equilibrium quantity will decline (that is, some workers will lose their jobs). You may want to review the Application on Luxury Taxes in Chapter 14 of your textbook.

V.   PRACTICE EXAM: MULTIPLE CHOICE QUESTIONS

1.   Which one of the following describes a public good?

a.   it is rival in consumption and excludable.
b.   it is non-rival in consumption and excludable.
c.   it is rival in consumption and non-excludable.
d.   it is non-rival in consumption and non-excludable.
e.   none of the above.

2.   Which pair of the following is an example of a private good and a public good?

a.   preservation of endangered species/space exploration.
b.   public housing/free concert in a city park.
c.   highways/ice cream.
d.   newspapers/golf courses.
e.   law enforcement/national defense.

3.   Which one of the following statements is NOT true?

a.   the government spends money only on public goods, not private goods.
b.   public and private goods can both generate spillover benefits.
c.   the interaction of market demand and supply will not necessarily lead to an efficient outcome if a good generates spillover benefits or costs.
d.   education is likely to generate a workplace spillover.
e.   a government subsidy for a good with a spillover (external) benefit can lead to a more efficient outcome.

4.   Which one of the following statements is NOT true of a subsidy?

a.   subsidies are often given in the case of private goods that carry spillover (external) benefits.
b.   subsidies internalize a spillover (external) benefit.
c.   subsidies are ultimately paid for by taxpayers.
d.   a subsidy for education might come in the form of federal grants for financial aid.
e.   all of the above are true of subsidies.

5.   Which one of the following is NOT an example of a private good with a spillover benefit?

a.   education.
b.   on-the-job training.
c.   the space program.
d.   preventative health care.
e.   research at private universities.

6.   Which one of the following explains why the government may not always make good choices about which goods to provide and which goods to subsidize?

a.   inadequate information on the true benefits and costs of a particular good.
b.   a tax system that cannot always impose higher taxes on those who would use more of a public good than others.

c.   special interest groups lobby for their own interests and policymakers often give in to them.

d.   people do not always reveal the true amount of benefits they would receive from certain government projects and programs.

e.   all of the above.

7.   Which one of the following explains why voluntary contributions typically do not work as a way of funding public goods and goods with spillover benefits?

a.   the free-rider problem.

b.   the chump problem.

c.   the anonymity problem.

d.   the no-free-lunch problem.

e.   X-gifting.

8.   Which one of the following is NOT true of voluntary contributions as a way of funding public goods and goods with spillover benefits?

a.   some citizens will not contribute at all.

b.   some citizens will contribute an amount that is small relative to the benefits they receive from the good.

c.   voluntary contributions work better than taxes at ensuring that a project is funded.

d.   voluntary contributions may increase through programs like "matching contributions" and giving coffee mugs, etc., to contributors.

e.   public radio and t.v. has been very successful at overcoming the free-rider problem.

9.   Suppose the government imposes a tax on the sale of new refrigerators. The government collects the tax from appliance centers and other outlets that sell the refrigerators. Who pays for the tax, assuming market demand is negatively sloped and supply is a horizontal?

a.   consumers.

b.   consumers and refrigerator input suppliers.

c.   appliance centers and other outlets.

d.   consumers and appliance centers.

e.   refrigerator input suppliers.

10.   Which one of the following statements is true of a tax that is collected from producers in a perfectly competitive market?

a.   it shifts the demand curve to the left.

b.   the demand for inputs will decline and so will the price of inputs.

c.   in the long run, producers' profits will decline.

d.   the price of output will decline.

e.   it shifts the supply curve to the right.

11.   Consider the market for yachts. A tax on yachts collected by the government from yacht producers will:

a.   shift more of the tax forward to consumers if demand is inelastic than if it is inelastic.

b.   put the tax burden on consumers and yacht input suppliers, including workers in the yachting industry.
c.   reduce the price of yacht inputs by more if input supply is inelastic rather than elastic.
d.   reduce the equilibrium quantity of yachts sold.
e.   all of the above.

12.   Use the graph below to determine the deadweight loss (excess burden) of a tax placed on gasoline.

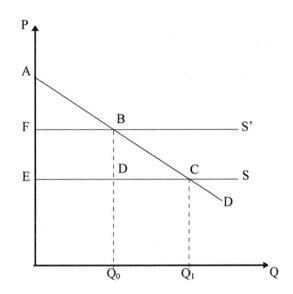

a.   area ABF.
b.   area BCD.
c.   area FBCE.
d.   area FBED.
e.   area ABC.

13.   The median-voter rule:

a.   is that people vote with their feet, i.e., move to communities where there median preferences are reflected.
b.   may not be true if people cannot vote on individual issues but must instead vote on packages.
c.   suggests that the decisions made by elected officials may not always be the most efficient.
d.   implies that candidates for office will take extreme positions.
e.   (a) and (c).

14.   Public choice economics suggests that government decisions are made based on:

a.   the government's desire to make the economy operate more efficiently.
b.   the median voter.
c.   the self-interest of politicians.
d.   people voting with their feet.
e.   all of the above.

VI.   PRACTICE EXAM: ESSAY QUESTIONS

1.   Suppose that you are the head of a government agency that oversees retraining programs for the unemployed. Discuss whether the service that your agency delivers is a public or private good. Will the private market of demand and supply lead to an efficient outcome? Why or why not? Discuss how your agency is funded. How well do you think a voluntary contribution scheme wouldwork in funding your program?

2.   Use demand and supply diagrams to discuss and illustrate the effects of a tax on peanut butter, consumers of peanut butter, and peanut growers. Be sure to discuss the extent of forward and backward shifting and the deadweight loss caused by the tax.

VII.   ANSWER KEY: MULTIPLE CHOICE

1.   Correct answer: d.

Discussion: A public good is both non-rival and non-excludable in consumption. Non-rival means that one person's consumption of the good does not rival another person's ability to consume/use the good. That is, more than one person can consume/use the good at the same time. Non-excludable means that people who do not pay for the good cannot be excluded from using and receiving the benefits of the good. Thus, even if one person were to pay for the good, others could use it without having to pay for it.

Statement a describes a private good. A private good can only be consumed and, thus, enjoyed by the consumer. That is, it is rival in consumption. A private good can also only be consumed/used by the person paying for it. That is, a private good is excludable. Reading a book, attending a movie, going to a private school, buying a house, and eating an ice cream cone are some examples.

As an aside, you should remember that a private good can have spillover benefits as can a public good.

2.   Correct answer: b.

Discussion: Public housing is both rival and excludable in consumption even though it is a government-provided good. A free concert in a city park is non-rival and non-excludable. More than one person can enjoy it and people can enjoy it regardless of whether they pay for it. Of course, citizens who live around the park who may not prefer the noise of the concert will experience a spillover (external) cost.

Statement a is an example of two public goods. Statement c is an example of a public good/private good (instead of vice-versa). Statement d is an example of two private goods. Statement e is an example of two public goods.

3.   Correct answer: a.

Discussion: Statement a is not true because a government spends money on public goods like highways, law enforcement, and space exploration as well as on education (a private good with spillover benefits), housing, and food (a private good).

Statement b is true because a public good like the space exploration program can generate spillover benefits -- high-tech companies may learn new and improved ways to do things from the space exploration program. Private goods like education, health care, and even deodorant create spillover benefits. Statement c is true because, when a private good has spillovers, not all of the benefits and costs of the good are revealed in the demand and supply curves. That is, not all of the consumers or even producers are represented in the demand and supply curves. Statement d is true -- education generates not only workplace but civic spillovers. Statement e is true because the government, by subsidizing particular goods, is attempting to achieve a more desirable (truthful) market outcome.

4.   Correct answer: e.

Discussion: All of the above are true of a subsidy. While statement a is true, it does not mean that the government provides subsidies to any and every private good that carries a spillover benefit. Statement b means that a subsidy forces an external benefit to be reflected in the market demand curve. Statement d suggests that there are many ways in which the government can give money back to citizens for the purchase of a private good. Statement c is also true, as discussed in PET #2.

5.   Correct answer: c.

Discussion: Statement c is an example of a public good, not a private good, which has spillover benefits. All of the other examples are examples of private goods with spillover benefits.

6.   Correct answer: e.

Discussion: The government does not always end up funding projects and programs that are efficient from an economic perspective. Statements a-d all provide reasons why this may happen. Statements a and d are related in that the government will have inadequate information on the true costs and benefits of a particular program if people are not truthful in revealing how much they would really benefit (and presumably pay) for a good.

7.   Correct answer: a.

Discussion: The free-rider problem is that people who benefit from a program may not be willing to pay for it because they figure that other people who benefit from it will contribute to it. Thus, the free rider will get to use the program without having to pay for it. Talk about utility maximization! The problem is that, when everyone behaves this way, the program does not receive enough funds to be funded and, thus, the program is not started up and nobody gets to use it.

8.   Correct answer: c.

Discussion: Statement c is not true; taxes work better at ensuring that a project is funded than do voluntary contributions. In effect, a tax ensures that everybody pays for the project, not just those willing to contribute.

Statements a and b reflect a common problem with voluntary contributions. Statement d suggests that there are ways (that are costly to somebody, however) to increase voluntary contributions to a specific project. Statement e is true; in fact, public radio and t.v. have used some of the tactics listed in statement d as a way of increasing voluntary contributions.

9.   Correct answer: b.

Discussion: A tax leads to "forward shifting" -- i.e., consumers pay some of the tax and "backward shifting" -- i.e., input suppliers pay some of the tax (in the form of receiving a lower price for the inputs they provide). While the appliance center may write and send the check to the government, the tax dollars paid by the appliance center are, in effect, collected from the consumers and input suppliers. As an aside, if the demand for refrigerators was vertical (perfectly inelastic), consumers would pay for the entire tax.

10.   Correct answer: b.

Discussion: A tax collected from producers is represented by shifting the supply curve to the left. Thus, statements a and e are not true. As the supply curve shifts to the left, the price of output will rise. Thus, statement d is not true. Statement c is not true because, as your textbook points out, producers' profits remain at zero in the long run.   Statement b is true because, when the supply curve shifts to the left, not only does the price rise, but the equilibrium quantity falls. Suppose the good in question is furniture. As the equilibrium quantity of furniture sold declines, the demand for inputs used in making furniture, like labor and wood, will decline. As the demand for these inputs declines, the price of the inputs declines. (See PET #4 for review.)

11.   Correct answer: e.

Discussion: A tax on yachts will shift the supply of yachts to the left. If demand for yachts is inelastic (steeper), the price paid by consumers will rise by more than if the demand for yachts was elastic (see PET #3 for review).   As just discussed in the answer to question (10), consumers and input suppliers of yachts both bear the burden of the tax. Since the demand for inputs will decline, there will be a drop in the price of yacht inputs. The price drop will be bigger the more inelastic is the supply of the inputs.

12.   Correct answer: b.

Discussion: The deadweight loss is the loss in the area of consumer surplus that is not covered by the gain in tax revenue collected by the government. In this case, the initial consumer surplus area is area ACE. After the tax, when the price goes up, the consumer surplus area is ABF. The loss in consumer surplus is thus FBCE. However, the gain in tax revenue is the amount of the tax times the equilibrium quantity. This is measured by the area FBDE. Thus, the deadweight loss is the difference between the area FBCE and FBDE which is BCD.

13.   Correct answer: e.

Discussion: The median-voter rule is that government decisions made by elected officials represent the preferences of the median voter which is the voter whose preferences are exactly midway between the preferences of all of the voters. However, the median-voter rule is best applied to government decisions that are made on an individual basis rather than as part of a package. That is, the median-voter rule may not be correct if voters vote "yes" or "no" on a package of programs rather than "yes" or "no" on each item in the package. Also, the median-voter rule means that the most efficient outcomes are not necessarily guaranteed. Since the median voter's preferences do not necessarily reflect the most efficient outcomes for society, there is no guarantee that the median-voter rule will lead to the most efficient government decisions.

Statement a is not the definition of the median-voter rule. Statement d is not true of the median-voter rule; in fact, the median-voter rule implies that candidates will come closer and closer in their positions on issues as election day approaches.

14.   Correct answer: e.

Discussion: There are many views in public choice economics on how the government actually arrives at the decisions that it makes. All of the above are possible and not necessarily mutually exclusive.

VIII.   ANSWER KEY: ESSAY QUESTIONS

1.   The worker retraining program is a private good with spillover benefits. It is a private good because only those enrolled in the retraining program are able to use it. Furthermore, only companies that pay for the program, also supported by subsidies from the government, are able to use it. However, there are spillover benefits to the retraining program. Not only do the unemployed and the companies using the program benefit, but society benefits as well. People who are employed pay taxes and are less likely to get involved in illegal activities. Since the retraining program has spillover benefits, the market demand and supply curves will not lead to an efficient outcome, i.e., not enough worker retraining will be provided by the private market on its own. This is why the government subsidizes the worker retraining programs. This gets the private market to "internalize" the external benefits. While my agency is funded through subsidies provided by the government and also through companies paying into the program for its use, the government subsidies ultimately come from tax-paying citizens. A voluntary contribution scheme would probably not lead to the level of support currently provided because of the free-rider problem. What typically happens under a voluntary contribution scheme is that some people who use the program will not contribute anything at all while others will contribute but not in accordance with the actual benefits they receive. Thus, a voluntary contribution scheme would likely lead to an underfunded program which may not be able to continue to run. Of course, I might suggest that our agency's fundraising efforts include matching contributions and free gifts. However, somebody will have to pay for these.

2.   A tax on peanut butter is represented by a leftward shift in the supply curve. The supply curve of peanut butter is drawn horizontally to reflect that, in the long run, this industry is a constant-cost industry. Thus, the leftward shift in the supply curve, drawn horizontally, appears as an upward shift showing that, at every quantity supplied the price at which suppliers would now be willing to produce would be higher. This is because part of the money they receive on the sales of peanut butter will have to be paid in taxes to the government. The leftward shift in the supply curve does two things: (1) the equilibrium price of peanut butter rises; and (2) the equilibrium quantity of peanut butter falls. The graph below shows this.

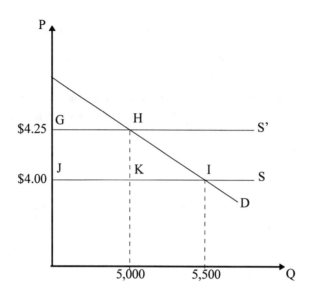

The rise in the price of peanut butter means that consumers will now pay more for peanut butter. That is, some of the tax is shifted forward to consumers. The equilibrium price rises but not by the full $0.50. The extent of the price increase to consumers depends on how elastic the demand for peanut butter is. If the demand for peanut butter is very elastic (perhaps because there are a lot of close substitutes like cream cheese, butter, jelly, etc.), the price rise will not be very great -- certainly not the full $0.50. Suppose the equilibrium price rises from $4.00 a jar to $4.25. Suppliers must still pay $0.50 per jar in taxes to the government, which means the supplier will be left with $3.75. The price that they receive per jar of peanut butter has effectively dropped from $4.00 to $3.75. Will their profits decrease? Perhaps in the short run, but in the long run the costs of peanut butter production will fall so that in the end the producer will still be earning $4.00 per jar of peanut butter. The reason the cost of peanut butter production will fall is that the equilibrium quantity of peanut butter sold drops. Peanut butter producers thus need less peanut butter to bring to the market. This, in turn, means that peanut butter producers will not need to buy as many peanuts. So, the demand for peanuts will decrease and this will bring down the price of peanuts, an input into the production of peanut butter. Thus, peanut growers in effect bear some of the burden of the tax because they receive a lower price for their output. This is the backward-shifting nature of the tax. In the long run, with a tax of $0.50, peanut growers will receive $0.25 less for their peanuts, which means that the cost of production to the peanut butter producers will decline. That's why the peanut butter producer is still, in a way, receiving $4.00 per jar of peanut butter. Or, you could say the profit per jar of peanut butter will be unchanged before and after the tax.

As for the tax revenue, the government collects $0.50 per jar of peanut butter. The new equilibrium quantity (let's say it is 5,000 jars per week) times the tax per jar gives the government $2,500 in tax revenue per week.

As for consumers, they pay a higher price for peanut butter and purchase a smaller equilibrium quantity so their consumer surplus declines. The graph shows that the decline in consumer surplus (area GHIJ) exceeds the gain in tax revenue (area GHKJ) so that on net there is a deadweight loss to society equal to area HIK.

Take It to the Net

We invite you to visit the O'Sullivan/Sheffrin page on the Prentice Hall Web site at:

http://www.prenhall.com/osullivan/

for this chapter's World Wide Web exercise.

CHAPTER 15
ENVIRONMENTAL PROBLEMS AND PUBLIC POLICY: GLOBAL WARMING, OZONE DEPLETION, ACID RAIN, AND URBAN SMOG

I.   OVERVIEW

In this chapter, you will learn about the economic consequences and policy surrounding environmental problems. You will learn how a public policy such as a tax on polluters both leads to firms taking steps to cut the pollution that they create when they produce output and reduces the amount of output that polluters produce. You will also learn that the government can use regulation to reduce the amount of pollution that producers may be generating. You will learn about the traditional form of pollution regulation, which is command and control based, and the modern form of pollution regulation which, is market-based. You will learn which policy is most efficient from an economic standpoint. You will learn about global warming, ozone depletion, acid rain, and urban smog and how public policy has been devised to reduce these problems.

II.   CHECKLIST

By the end of this chapter, you should be able to:

√   Explain the two ways in which a pollution tax reduces the level of pollution.
√   Explain the effects of a tax on pollution using demand and supply.
√   Use the marginal principle to determine how much abatement a firm would undertake in response to a pollution tax.
√   Discuss how command and control regulations work to reduce pollution.
√   Compare the efficiency of command and control regulations to a tax.
√   Explain the effects of pollution regulation using demand and supply.
√   Discuss how market-based pollution permits work to reduce pollution.
√   Compare the efficiency of pollution permits to a tax and regulations.
√   Explain when pollution permits will be traded -- who will buy and who will sell them.
√   Compare the effects of marketable versus non-marketable permits in reducing the amount of pollution.
√   Discuss some of the shortcomings of pollution permits.
√   Explain some of the economic effects of global warming on agriculture.
√   Discuss the economic effects of a carbon tax on reducing global warming.
√   Discuss the economic effects of a ban on CFCs aimed at reducing ozone depletion.
√   Discuss the type of regulation currently used to control urban smog and suggest some alternative policies.

III.   KEY TERMS

Pollution tax: a tax or charge equal to the spillover cost per unit of waste.
External cost: the part of production cost that is external to the organization that decides how much of a particular good to produce.

Command and control policy: a pollution-control policy under which the government *commands* each firm to produce no more than a certain volume of pollution and *controls* the firm's production process by forcing the firm to use a particular pollution-control technology.

System of marketable pollution permits: a system under which the government picks a target pollution level for a particular area, issues just enough pollution permits to meet the pollution target, and allows firms to buy and sell the permits.

Carbon tax: a tax based on a fuels carbon content.

IV.   PERFORMANCE ENHANCING TIPS (PETS)

PET #1

A spillover cost of production (such as pollution) is a cost that producers do not explicitly pay for unless they are forced to by the government.

Consider a firm that produces chemicals. A byproduct of the production process is that some emissions are released into the air. The emissions create pollution which creates health hazards for which people ultimately pay. The chemical producer generates a spillover cost by polluting the air and creating costs for other members of society. Because air is free, the chemical producer does not have to explicitly pay for the "use of the air." A tax on the chemical producer, in effect, forces it to pay for the cost of the air (and indirectly, assuming the tax revenues are used to help clean up the air) for the health costs that spill over to society.

PET #2

"Abatement" is the term used for "pollution clean up."

When a firm undertakes an abatement project, it is cleaning up (or at least reducing) the amount of pollution that it creates.

You should also know that the marginal cost of pollution clean up increases. That is, the cost of *reducing* pollution by one unit, and then by one more, and then by one more, increases. For example, Table 1 of Chapter 15 of your textbook shows that, as waste per ton of output is reduced from 5 gallons of waste per ton to 0 gallons of waste per ton, the production cost of one ton of output increases. This, means, in effect, that the cost of doing more and more clean up for the same one ton of output increases. Using the numbers from Table 1, the clean-up costs increase from $60 to $116. The marginal cost of eliminating a gallon of waste from 5 gallons to 4 gallons is $1 ($61-$60), and the marginal cost of eliminating a gallon of waste from 4 gallons to 3 gallons is $3 ($64-$61), and so on. Thus, the marginal cost increases.

PET #3

A tax imposed on polluters raises their cost of production and, hence, the price at which they sell their output. This is represented by a leftward shift in supply. The equilibrium quantity of output the producer sells will decline. The tax thus works to reduce the amount of pollution by (1) reducing the amount of production the firm undertakes (and consequently the pollution that results), and (2) by motivating the firm to devise abatement methods so as to avoid having to pay the tax. Thus, new and improved methods of abatement may emerge.

PET #4

A sale of a pollution permit from one firm to another will occur if two conditions are satisfied: (1) the seller receives more money from the sale of the permit than is his marginal cost of having to abate, and the buyer pays less for the permit than is his marginal cost of having to abate; and (2) the buyer is willing to pay an amount to the seller which is equal to or more than the seller is willing to sell the permit for.

Condition (1) can be explained in the following way. A seller of a permit gives up some of his right to pollute. Without the right to pollute, the seller must abate (do pollution clean up). If the seller can receive, say, $500,000 for his permit but must pay $400,000 to devise a clean-up method, the seller will sell the permit. A buyer of a permit buys the right to pollute more than he is currently polluting. With the right, the seller doesn't have to clean up as much, so the cost of abatement (pollution clean-up) declines. If the buyer can pay, say $500,000 for a permit to pollute and, thus, avoids $600,000 in abatement costs, the buyer will purchase the permit. This is just an application of the marginal principle.

Condition (2) is just a way of saying that the buyer's willingness to pay is greater than or equal to the seller's willingness to accept. To put it in more practical terms, suppose you would like to buy a used t.v. for your apartment or dorm room and the amount you would be willing to pay is $100. If the seller is willing to accept $75, then a deal could be struck. You may buy the t.v. for $85. In the example above, if the seller of the permit was willing to sell at $500,000 and the buyer was willing to pay at $600,000, a deal could be struck.

V.   PRACTICE EXAM: MULTIPLE CHOICE QUESTIONS

1.   Which one of the following is NOT a public policy for reducing pollution?

a.   a tax on polluters.
b.   marketable permits for pollution.
c.   non-marketable permits for pollution.
d.   government regulation.
e.   subsidies to polluters.

2.   In economics, pollution:

a.   is a spillover (external) cost.
b.   is a private good.
c.   generates diminishing returns.
d.   is really a cost of production.
e.   (a) and (d).

3.   Which one of the following is an effect of a pollution tax on paper production?

a.   the price of paper will decline.

b.   paper producers will have an incentive to abate.
c.   the quantity of paper produced will rise.
d.   the marginal cost of paper production will decline.
e.   none of the above.

4.   Use the table below to decide how many gallons of water per ton of output produced a firm will decide to emit.

Waste per ton	Clean-up Cost per ton	Tax Cost per ton
20 gallons	$100	$60
19 gallons	$102	$57
18	$106	$54
17	$112	$51
16	$120	$48

a.   20 gallons.
b.   19 gallons.
c.   18 gallons.
d.   17 gallons.
e.   16 gallons.

5.   Which one of the following is true of traditional pollution regulation (command and control policy)?

a.   the policy imposes that a single abatement technology (method of clean-up) be used.
b.   it creates an incentive to pollute.
c.   it encourages innovation in new and less costly methods of abatement.
d.   it is less costly than imposing a tax on polluters.
e.   all of the above are true.

6.   Which one of the following is true of a comparison between a pollution tax and traditional pollution regulation?

a.   regulation raises the price of the output of the polluter more than would a pollution tax.
b.   firms produce and sell less output under regulation than a tax.
c.   pollution is reduced by less with a regulation than with a tax.
d.   regulation does not produce any tax revenue that can be used to fund other clean-up projects.
e.   all of the above.

7.   Marketable pollution permits:

a.   make it hard to predict how much pollution abatement will actually take place.
b.   can only be bought and sold by polluters.
c.   may lead to severe pollution in some areas.
d.   lead to the high-abatement-cost firms selling the permits and the low-abatement-cost firms buying the permits.
e.   are not as effective as non-marketable permits at reducing the amount of pollution.

8.   Which one of the following would explain why a firm might not sell its marketable pollution permit?

a.   the cost to the firm of reducing pollution is greater than the price the firm will get for selling the permit.
b.   the cost to the firm of reducing pollution is less than the price the firm will get for selling the permit.
c.   the cost to the firm of increasing pollution is greater than the price the firm will get for selling the permit.
d.   the cost to the firm of increasing pollution is less than the price the firm will get for selling the permit.
e.   none of the above.

9.   Which one of the following is NOT true of global warming?

a.   it is due to an accumulation of carbon dioxide in the atmosphere.
b.   there is uncertainty about how much the earth's temperature will actually rise.
c.   total rainfall is expected to decrease.
d.   a carbon tax (a tax on the burning of fossil fuels like oil, coal, and gasoline) is one solution aimed at reducing the pace of global warming.
e.   sea levels are expected to increase.

10.   Which one of the following is NOT expected to be an effect of the ban on production of CFCs (chlorofluorocarbons)?

a.   a slower pace of ozone depletion.
b.   innovation of products that achieve the same purpose as CFCs.
c.   short-run increase in the price of refrigerators.
d.   innovation in products that have previously used CFCs.
e.   all of the above.

11.   Which one of the following statements is true?

a.   a recent study of global warming suggests that crop production may fall substantially.
b.   the state of Arizona helps pay for abatement associated with global warming effects that are produced in other countries.
c.   a ban on the production of CFCs has been in place since 1985.
d.   the government currently uses non-marketable permits to control the amount of urban smog.
e.   all of the above are true.

VI.   PRACTICE EXAM: ESSAY QUESTIONS

1.   Explain how a tax on polluters works to help reduce the amount of pollution.

2.   Explain how a system of marketable permits to pollute works to reduce the amount of pollution. Be sure to discuss who will buy and sell the permits and why some communities do not like the system.

VII.   ANSWER KEY: MULTIPLE CHOICE QUESTIONS

1.   Correct answer: e.

Discussion: A subsidy to a polluter may not discourage them from polluting. All of the other public policies are discussed in your textbook as ways in which the government attempts to reduce the amount of pollution.

2.   Correct answer: e.

Discussion: Pollution is a spillover cost of production because it imposes costs on other segments of society that bear the cost of pollution such as health costs, inability to use a river to fish or a lake to swim, etc. Pollution should also rightly be considered a cost of production because a firm that pollutes a river or the air is using the river or the air in the production process. Thus, it should be treated as a cost just like the use of labor and raw materials is considered a cost of production.

Statement b is not correct because pollution is a public good (that is, in fact, bad).   Statement c is not correct because the reduction of pollution entails increasing marginal costs.

3.   Correct answer: b.

Discussion: A tax forces the polluting firm to bear some of the cost of polluting in production. Since the tax imposes a cost on the firm, the firm has an incentive to avoid it by finding methods of abatement.

Statement a is not correct because the price of paper will rise. Statement c is not correct because the quantity of paper produced will decline. Statement d is not correct because the marginal cost of abatement will increase. Statement e cannot be correct because statement b is true.

4.   Correct answer: b.

Discussion: The marginal cost of reducing pollution from 20 gallons to 19 gallons per ton is $2 whereas, if the polluter did not clean up, the tax cost would be $3. (The government forces the polluter to pay $3 more to pollute 20 gallons instead of 19 gallons). Thus, the marginal cost of abatement is less than the tax cost, so the firm should abate.

The marginal cost of reducing pollution from 19 gallons to 18 gallons per ton is $4 whereas, if the polluter did not clean up that one more gallon of waste, the tax cost would be $3. Since the tax cost of polluting by one more gallon is less than the cost of cleaning up, the polluter will not clean up but will instead pay the tax cost. The same reasoning applies to the 17th and 16th gallons.

5.   Correct answer: a.

Discussion: A command and control pollution policy imposed by regulators forces all firms in the same industry to use the same method of abatement.

Statement b is not true; regulation does not create the incentive to pollute but rather forces the polluter not to pollute. Statement c is not true because the policy discourages innovation in pollution abatement by dictating that all firms use the same method of clean-up. Statement d is not true because command and control regulation is more costly to polluters than a tax. Statement e is not true because statement a is true.

6.   Correct answer: e.

Discussion: A pollution tax is more efficient than traditional pollution regulation. All of the statements above are reasons why it is more efficient.

7.   Correct answer: c.

Discussion: Marketable pollution permits mean that a firm that buys the permit has the right to pollute more than the target level set by the government. Thus, some firms with high costs of abatement will buy up a lot of permits and pollute a lot. If the firm resides in your community, your community will experience a lot of pollution.

Statement a is not true because marketable pollution permits make it easy to predict how much pollution will be emitted by firms, collectively. While the government cannot predict how much each firm will emit individually, the government can predict how much firms will in total (collectively) emit. Statement b is not true because marketable pollution permits can be purchased by environmental groups, as well. Statement d is not true; it is the reverse -- low-abatement-cost firms sell their permits to high-abatement-cost firms. Statement e is not true because marketable permits are more effective than non-marketable permits in reducing the amount of pollution.

8.   Correct answer: a.

Discussion: If the firm sells its permit, it will not have the right to pollute as much and, thus, will have to do more clean-up. The clean-up means that the firm will incur a cost. If the cost of clean-up is more than the firm can receive from the sale of its permit, it will choose to hold on to the permit and thereby avoid the cost of clean-up. If it chose to sell its permit, it would not receive enough money to cover the clean-up costs that it would incur as a result of not having a permit to pollute. Thus, based on the marginal principle, it makes sense not to sell the permit.

Based on the above reasoning, statements b, c, d and e cannot be true. In fact, statement b suggests that the firm would sell the permit. This is because the price the firm would receive from selling the permit is greater than the costs of clean-up it will incur without having the permit.

9.   Correct answer: c.

Discussion: Global warming is expected to increase, not decrease, the amount of rainfall. All of the other statements are true.

10.   Correct answer: e.

Discussion: The ban on CFCs has been established for the purpose of reducing the pace of ozone depletion (and, thus, the amount, too). The ban on CFCs will inspire innovation in products that previously used CFCs as well as in finding a replacement for CFCs. Because refrigerators (air conditioners, hairspray, etc.) used CFCs in the past and must now find another technology that achieves the same purpose as CFCs, the cost of producing a refrigerator will rise, at least in the short run.

11.   Correct answer: b.

Discussion: Since air circulates around the world, an oil refinery in Houston contributes to global warming just as much as an oil refinery in Bogota. Thus, firms in the U.S. have been mandated to help reduce the problem of global warming that occurs anywhere in the world. This means that they can pay for abatement in cities and countries different from where they are located.

A recent study of global warming suggests that crop production may not fall by as much as previously predicted, in part because farmers will find new ways of growing crops just as efficiently as before in a "globally-warmed" climate. The ban on CFCs has been in place since 1996. The government currently uses a traditional command and control regulatory policy to control urban smog.

VIII.   ANSWER KEY: ESSAY QUESTIONS

1.   A tax on polluters implicitly raises their cost of production as they must pay for the tax or adopt methods of abatement to avoid the tax. Abatement, of course, is a cost to the firm. However, since the tax creates the incentive to adopt methods of abatement, pollution will be reduced by the abatement actions of the firms. Secondly, a pollution tax raises the cost of output that the polluter produces. (This is represented by a leftward shift in supply). A higher cost of production is, in part, passed on to consumers through a higher consumer price. The higher price reduces the equilibrium quantity of the output demanded. Firms respond by producing less of the output, which means they, in turn, end up polluting less. It may also happen that firms invent a similar product that has a manufacturing process that does not pollute or pollutes by much less.

2.   A system of marketable permits is a new form of regulation aimed at reducing the amount of pollution. Under such a system, the government sets a target limit of pollution that they desire to achieve. They then give firms permits to pollute, but only by a specified amount. The innovation is that firms can buy and sell the permits so that they are not constrained to pollute only up to the amount allotted in the permit. However, in total, the target amount of pollution desired by the government is maintained. For example, suppose there are only two firms that pollute and the government issues permits to each of them allowing them to emit 30 tons of waste per year. The government's target level of pollution is thus 60 tons of waste per year. If one firm sells its permit to the other, the selling firm can no longer emit any waste (it must completely abate) and the buying firm is now permitted to emit up to 60 tons of waste per year. Thus, the target level of waste per year is achieved while each individual firm's emission level may vary.

A firm for which it is very expensive to abate (clean up) will be a buyer of a permit if the price they have to pay for the permit (the right to pollute) is less costly than having to clean up. A firm for which it is not very expensive to abate will be a seller of a permit if the price it can sell the permit for is greater than the cost of having to clean up. In this case, the money it receives for the permit would pay for the firm's clean-up and leave it with extra money that it could use elsewhere. For a deal to be struck, the buyer's willingness to pay must be equal to or greater than the seller's willingness to accept. For example, if the buyer was willing to pay $200,000 for a permit and the seller was willing to accept

$175,000, then the two could likely reach a price at which an exchange of the permit for money would take place.

Some citizens do not like the system of marketable permits because they may end up getting a lot more pollution in their community, especially if they have a high-cost-of-abatement firm in their town. The high-cost-of-abatement firm is much more likely to be a buyer of permits and, thus, will acquire the right to pollute more rather than less under the policy.

Take It to the Net

We invite you to visit the O'Sullivan/Sheffrin page on the Prentice Hall Web site at:

http://www.prenhall.com/osullivan/

for this chapter's World Wide Web exercise.

CHAPTER 16
IMPERFECT INFORMATION AND DISAPPEARING MARKETS

I.   OVERVIEW

In this chapter, you will learn about the effect of imperfect information on buyers and sellers and the price at which they strike deals. You will learn that markets with imperfect information are typically "mixed markets" meaning that the quality of a good sold in a particular market is not uniform and that it is difficult for buyers to know whether the good that they are purchasing is of high or low quality. That is, there is a chance that a buyer will purchase a high-quality good and a chance that a buyer will end up purchasing a low-quality version of the same good. You will learn that imperfect information arises when one side of the market (either buyers or sellers) has more information about the good in question than the other side of the market. You will learn that this situation is referred to as an information asymmetry and that it arises most commonly in the market for used goods and insurance. You will learn about the adverse-selection problem. You will also learn what a thin market is and why it occurs. You will use probabilities to compute expected amounts that uninformed buyers may be willing to pay. You will learn about some methods used to overcome the asymmetric information problem. You will also learn about applications of asymmetric information to the market for used cars, baseball pitchers, auto insurance, malpractice insurance, and health insurance.

II.   CHECKLIST

By the end of this chapter, you should be able to:

√   Define asymmetric information.
√   Explain the effects of asymmetric information on the price, quality, and volume of a good sold in a market.
√   Apply the asymmetric information problem to a market for used goods or insurance.
√   Explain why asymmetric information typically raises the cost of insurance and lowers the price of used goods.
√   Explain why the actual probability of a buyer purchasing a lemon (low-quality good) in a used market is greater than the probability that may be casually assumed.
√   Define the adverse-selection problem and explain what gives rise to it.
√   Define a thin market and explain what gives rise to it.
√   Explain the difference between community and experience ratings used by the health insurance industry.
√   Use probabilities to compute expected prices.
√   Convert ratios into probabilities.

III.   KEY TERMS

Adverse-selection problem: the uninformed side of the market must choose from an undesirable or adverse selection of goods.
Asymmetric information: one side of the market -- either buyer or seller -- has better information about the good than the other.

Thin market: a market in which some high-quality goods are sold, but fewer than would be sold in a market with perfect information.

Community rating: in a given community or metropolitan area, every firm pays the same price for medical insurance.

Experience rating: each firm pays a different price for medical insurance depending on the past medical bills of the firm's employees.

IV.   PERFORMANCE ENHANCING TIPS (PETS)

PET #1

The expected (or average) amount that a buyer is willing to pay for a good of unknown qualilty is computed using the probabilities associated with whether the good is high or low quality (we'll assume only two categories of qualities) and what the corresponding prices would be for a good of a certain quality.

Let's suppose that you are considering buying a used computer. You are aware that more lemon computers are likely to be sold in the used market than not. Suppose the probability of getting a faulty computer is 75% and the probability of buying a good computer is 25%. If the going price for a good, used computer were $1,000 and the going price for a faulty, used computer were $200, what is the expected price at which used computers will sell in the mixed market of good and faulty computers?

To answer the question, use the following formula:

(probability of high-quality good/100) X price of high-quality good + (probability of low-quality good/100) X price of low-quality good.

Thus, your answer to the question should be:

(25/100) X ($1,000) + (75/100)X($200) = 0.25 X $1,000 + 0.75 X 200 = 250 + 150 = $400.

PET #2

The probability of a low- (or high-) quality good in the market can be determined by dividing the observations of a low- (or high-) quality good by the total number of goods (i.e., sum of low- plus high-quality goods).

Suppose you have done some research on the market for used evening gowns and determined that in your town, 30 used evening gowns are typically for sale each month. Further, you've determined that typically, 20 of the used evening gowns are very high quality and that 10 of the evening gowns are low quality.   What is the probability in any given month that you or somebody that you may give advice to will buy a low-quality evening gown?

The probability of purchasing a low-quality evening gown is (10/30) X 100 = 33.3%
Thus, the probability of buying a high-quality evening gown must be 66.7% (100% - 33.3%).

V.   PRACTICE EXAM: MULTIPLE CHOICE QUESTIONS

1.   A mixed market is one in which:

a.   consumers can be buyers and sellers and producers can be sellers and buyers.
b.   there are different qualities of a good being sold in the market and there is imperfect information about the quality of each good.
c.   a seller of a good requires that the purchase of one good be tied to the purchase of another.
d.   demand is positively sloped and supply is negatively sloped.
e.   none of the above.

2.   In a market for used goods,

a.   the seller has more information than the buyer about the quality of the good.
b.   the buyer has more information than the seller about the quality of the good.
c.   there are no high-quality used goods for sale.
d.   low-quality used goods will be underpriced.
e.   the quality of used goods sold in the market will typically rise over time.

3.   Which one of the following is an example of asymmetric information?

a.   a grocery store selling cookies that are stale.
b.   a builder building a house with 2" instead of 4" studs.
c.   a company hiring an employee that has an addiction to sleeping pills.
d.   a seller at a flea market selling stolen goods.
e.   all of the above.

4.   Which one of the following is true of a used market, e.g., used market for cars?

a.   a consumer typically overestimates the probability of getting a lemon (low-quality car).
b.   the more pessimistic buyers become that their chance of buying a high-quality car is high, the lower will the price of all (low- and high-quality) used cars become.
c.   there is an adverse-information problem.
d.   the willingness to pay and the willingness to accept are equal.
e.   (b) and (d).

5.   The adverse-selection problem is that:

a.   the informed side of the market pays more for a good than the less informed side of the market.
b.   a seller does not inform a buyer of all of the add on fees that will be incurred upon the purchase of a good.
c.   product differentiation makes it difficult to decide which product to buy.
d.   the uninformed side of the market must choose from an undesirable selection of goods.
e.   all of the above.

6.   Which one of the following is an equilibrium?

a.   buyers assume a 40% chance of getting a lemon and 8 lemons and 2 plums are supplied.

b.   buyers assume a 60% chance of getting a lemon and 6 lemons and 4 plums are supplied.
c.   buyers assume a 40% chance of getting a lemon and 4 lemons and 4 plums are supplied.
d.   buyers assume an 80% chance of getting a lemon and 2 lemons and 8 plums are supplied.
e.   buyers assume an 75% chance of getting a lemon and 7 lemons and 3 plums are supplied.

7.   Which one of the following is NOT true of a thin market?

a.   it may be caused by asymmetric information.
b.   there are relatively few high-quality goods sold.
c.   in a thin market, there may be some sellers of high-quality goods because of extenuating circumstances (moving out of the country, increased family size, etc.)
d.   the price of a high=quality good will be higher than if the market was thick.
e.   all of the above.

8.   A mixed market is:

a.   dominated by low-quality goods.
b.   one in which there is asymmetric information.
c.   one where buyers encounter an adverse-selection problem.
d.   typical of used goods and insurance.
e.   all of the above.

9.   Use the following information, complete the sentence below:

> Average cost of settling a lawsuit of a careful plastic surgeon = $6,000.
> Average cost of settling a lawsuit of a reckless plastic surgeon = $36,000.
> Probability that a careful doctor will want insurance = 25%
> Probability that a reckless doctor will want insurance = 75%

Assuming insurance companies cannot distinguish between careful and reckless plastic surgeons, an insurance company will charge $____ for malpractice insurance and a careful plastic surgeon would be incline to _____ insurance.

a. $28,500; not buy.
b. $21,000; not buy.
c. $36,000; not buy.
d. $21,000; buy.
e. $42,000; not buy.

10.   The use of "experience rating" of health insurance has resulted in:

a.   lower costs of insurance for all firms.
b.   lower costs of insurance for firms with a history of lower medical bills of its employees.
c.   higher costs of insurance for all firms.
d.   firms investing in safety and health programs for their employees.
e.   (b) and (d).

VI.   PRACTICE EXAM: ESSAY QUESTIONS

1.   Suppose you are a college admissions director and every year you receive 5,000 applications for admission to your school while your school only has 1,000 slots open.   Your school is prestigious and has a reputation for producing some of the best and brightest college graduates on the national market.   What problems might you encounter as the admissions director?   How might you handle them?

2.   Explain the effects of asymmetric information on the price, quality, and volume of used computers sold in a market.

VII.   ANSWER KEY: MULTIPLE CHOICE QUESTIONS

1.   Correct answer: b.

Discussion: In a mixed market, there are different qualities of a good being sold and unfortunately the buyer or seller of the good may not know for sure (has imperfect information) what the quality of the good is.   The market for used goods is typically a mixed market as is the market for insurance.

All of the other statements are bogus.

2.   Correct answer: a.

Discussion: A used market is a market for which there is asymmetric information -- in this case, the information is asymmetric because the seller knows more about the true quality of the good than does the buyer.

Based on the above, statement b is not true.   Statement c is generally not true (only in extreme cases would no high-quality used goods be for sale) because a used market is also one that is "mixed" in that high and low-quality versions of the same good will be offered for sale.   Statement d is not true because the price of low-quality used goods is based on the price at which a high- and low-quality version of the good would be priced.   This leads to a higher price for a low-quality good than reflects its true value.   Statement e is not true because there is a tendency for the quality of goods sold in a use market will decrease over time.

3.   Correct answer: e.

Discussion: While asymmetric information typically arises in a market for used goods, it can occur elsewhere.   All of the above examples are cases in which one party (the buyer or the seller) has more information about the product than the other party.

4.   Correct answer: b.

Discussion: When buyers become more pessimistic that their chance of buying a high-quality car is high, they will attach a lower probability to the price they would be willing to pay for a high-quality car and, thus,   a higher probability to the price they would be willing to pay for a low-quality car.   This necessarily lowers the price that a buyer would be willing to pay for a car about which they have no information as to its quality.

You may wish to review PET #1 and attach different probabilities to that, as sociated with buying a good computer and a faulty one and then see what happens to the expected price of the computer.

Statement a is not true; consumers typically underestimate the probability of purchasing a lemon. Statement c is not correct because the term is "adverse selection" not "adverse information." Statement d is not true because there are typically differences in the willingness to pay and accept (which is why buyers and sellers bargain with each other). Statement e is not true because statement d is not true.

5.   Correct answer: d.

Discussion: The adverse-selection problem arises in a mixed market because the quality of every good being sold in a particular market is not known to the buyer. That is, the uninformed side of the market must choose which good to buy knowing that some of the selection is of poor quality but not knowing which of the goods are poor quality.

6.   Correct answer: b.

Discussion: An equilibrium will be reached in the market when the assumed (or perceived) chance of purchasing a lemon is equal to the actual chance. In statement b, the actual chance is $(6/10)X100 = 60\%$. (See PET #2 for review).

Statement a is not correct because the actual chance is 80%. Statement c is not true because the actual chance is 50%. Statement d is not true because the actual chance of getting a lemon is 20%. Statement e is not true because the actual chance of getting a lemon is 70%.

7.   Correct answer: d.

Discussion: A thin market is a market in which there are relatively few high-quality goods but an abundance of low-quality goods being offered for sale. This drives down, not up, the price of the good in a thin market. If the market were thicker, the price of the good would be higher than in a thin market. Thus, in a thin market, where both qualities of good are being sold at the same price, it will generally be the case that low-quality goods are overpriced (relative to their true value) and high-quality goods underpriced (relative to their true value).

A thin market, in part, exists because of asymmetric information. Asymmetric information leads to a lower price for the high-quality good and, thus, induces many of the sellers of the high-quality good not to sell. However, there will be some high-quality goods being sold perhaps because sellers find themselves in extenuating circumstances where they are forced to sell their good.

8.   Correct answer: e.

Discussion: Your book stresses that all of the above are true of a mixed market and hopefully so, too, will your instructor because then you'll be prepared for a question like this!

9.   Correct answer: c.

Discussion: In this example, insurance companies face an adverse-selection problem about plastic surgeons because they do not have as much information about how careful or reckless a plastic surgeon is while the plastic surgeon knows more about him- or herself than the insurance company.   Faced with the adverse-selection problem, insurance companies protect themselves against it by charging a price that is equal to the average settlement that the reckless plastic surgeon pays.   In this example, that price is $36,000.   However, since careful doctors know that they are careful and that their average settlement is $6,000, they find it less costly to settle than to pay for malpractice insurance.   Thus, careful doctors will not buy the insurance.

Based on the above reasoning, statements a, b, d, and e are not correct.

10.   Correct answer: e.

Discussion: Health insurance that is experience rated charges a price to its customers that is based on the history of medical bills that the insurance company must cover for its customer.   Customers with high medical bills will see the premiums that they must pay to have health insurance increase.   Thus, a firm that pays the health insurance premiums of its employees has an incentive to keep its employees healthy and safe on and off the job.   This explains why firms invest in health and safety programs for their employees.   While these programs cost the firm money, the firm expects to save more money through having lower health insurance premiums to pay.

Statements a and c are not correct because experience rating raises the cost of insurance to those firms with a history of high medical bills and lowers the cost to those firms with a history of low medical bills.

VIII.   ANSWER KEY: ESSAY QUESTIONS

1.   As the admissions director, and having read Chapter 16 of my textbook, I would recognize that I am facing an adverse-selection problem that arises because of asymmetric information.   There is asymmetric information because the students (the sellers of their talents and aptitude) have more information about themselves (the product they are selling) than I might have about their true abilities. Students vary a good deal in quality, and their high school academic record may not always be the best reflection of the quality of a student.   That is, some students may have shining academic records but, in fact, be very poor students.   In the language of the used car market, some students are "lemons."   In fact, the pool of students applying to the school represents a mixed market -- there are high-quality and low-quality students in the pool together.   As the admissions director, I would like to avoid the problem of admitting lemons, particularly because the admittance of such students could ultimately harm the prestigious reputation of the college.

So, as admissions director, I may not only use high school transcripts and SAT or ACT scores to determine who should be admitted, but I may also require a written essay, personal interviews, letters of reference, and evidence of extracurricular activity involvement.   The additional information may help reduce the probability that I will admit lemons to my college.   In a way, you could say that essays, interviews, and the like are the school's form of insurance against admitting a poor student.

2.   In a market with asymmetric information, the price of a used good is typically lower than it would otherwise be.   The reason is that a used market is a mixed market where high-and low-quality

goods are being sold without obvious information on which of the goods are high quality and which are low quality. In such a market, the seller has more information about the quality of the good being sold than the buyer has. Thus, buyers attach a probabilty to the possibility that they will end up buying (unbeknownst to them) a low-quality good rather than a high-quality good. Since buyers are not willing to pay very much for a low-quality good, the probability that they will end up buying one is factored into the price that they will offer to pay. This means that high-quality used goods will also have to be sold at a lower price. For example, a buyer may be willing to pay $1,000 for a high-quality used computer but only $200 for a low-quality used computer. Thus, the price they will be willing to offer will range between $200 and $1,000 and will depend on how likely the buyer thinks they are to end up getting a low quality computer. That is, the equilibrium price for used computers (regardless of their quality) will range between $200 and $1,000. The higher the probability that buyers attach to getting a low quality computer, the lower will be the equilibrium price at which used computers sell.

Since the equilibrium price of used computers (both high and low quality) will be lower than otherwise, the quality of used computers offered for sale will be lower than otherwise, too. This is because sellers with high-quality computers will not, unless extraordinary circumstances dictate, be willing to part with their computers for such a low price. This means that, in the used market for computers, there will be a lot more low quality computers for sale than one might expect had they not taken account of how the price feeds into determining the quality of used computers offered for sale. The market may also end up being a "thin" market in the sense that there will be fewer high-quality computers for sale in because the sellers of the high-quality computers have elected not to sell at the low price.

Take It to the Net

We invite you to visit the O'Sullivan/Sheffrin page on the Prentice Hall Web site at:

http://www.prenhall.com/osullivan/

for this chapter's World Wide Web exercise.

CHAPTER 17
THE LABOR MARKET

I.   OVERVIEW

In this chapter, you will learn about the labor market using demand and supply analysis where the price of labor is the wage rate. You will learn that demand for labor is a derived demand since the demand for labor is derived from the demand for the output that labor produces. You will learn what will cause the wage rate and employment to change. You will learn why the wage rate differs for different occupations and for different groups of people. You will analyze the effects of various public policies aimed at the labor market: a minimum wage law, comparable worth, and occupational licensing.   You will learn about labor unions. You will learn about the labor market in a setting where the employee has more information than the employer about how productive he or she will be on the job. You will learn that "efficiency wages" may be paid by an employer to reduce the problems that may arise with the information asymmetry. Finally, you will learn about monopsony power in the labor market and its effect on the wage rate.

II.   CHECKLIST

By the end of this chapter, you should be able to:

√   Explain why the supply of labor is positively sloped.
√   Explain why the demand for labor is negatively sloped.
√   Explain what will cause the demand for and supply of labor to shift and analyze the effects on the equilibrium wage and employment.
√   Explain why the short-run labor supply curve is more steeply sloped than the long-run supply curve.
√   Use the marginal principle to determine whether a firm would benefit by hiring one more worker.
√   Discuss a firm's short-run demand for labor and relate it to diminishing returns.
√   List four explanations for why wages differ across different occupations.
√   Explain why women and blacks on average earn less for an hour of work than do white males.
√   Discuss the learning and signalling effect to explain why college graduates typically earn more than high school graduates.
√   Discuss the trade-offs associated with a minimum wage law.
√   Define comparable worth policies and describe their effects on wages and employment.
√   Discuss occupational licensing and its effect on wages and employment.
√   List some examples of craft unions and labor unions.
√   Discuss the history of labor unions in the United States.
√   Discuss three ways in which a labor union attempts to raise the wage of the union members.
√   Discuss whether unions can create more productive workers.
√   Explain efficiency wages and why they may be paid by a firm.
√   Explain what monopsony power is and how it can affect wages and employment.

III.   KEY TERMS

Derived demand: the demand for an input like labor that is derived from the demand for the final product.
Marginal product of labor: the change in output per unit change in labor.

177

Marginal revenue product of labor: the extra revenue generated from one more unit of labor; equal to price of output times the marginal product of labor.

Short-run demand curve for labor: a curve showing the relationship between the wage and the quantity of labor demanded in the short run.

Market supply curve for labor: a curve showing the relationship between the wage and the quantity of labor supplied.

Output effect: the change in the quantity of labor demanded resulting from a change in the quantity of output.

Input substitution effect: the change in the quantity of labor demanded resulting from a change in the relative cost of labor.

Long-run demand curve for labor: a curve showing the relationship between the wage and the quantity of labor demanded in the long run.

Learning effect: the increase in a person's wage resulting from the learning of skills required for certain occupations.

Signaling or screening effect: the increase in a person's wage resulting from the signal of productivity provided by completing college.

Comparable worth: a policy under which the government specifies a minimum wage for some occupations.

Labor union: an organized group of workers, the main objective of which is to improve working conditions, wages, and fringe benefits.

Craft union: a labor organization that includes workers from a particular occupation, for example, plumbers, bakers, or electricians.

Industrial union: a labor organization that includes all types of workers from a single industry, for example, steel workers or auto workers.

Monopsony: a market in which there is a single buyer of an input.

IV.   PERFORMANCE ENHANCING TIPS (PETS)

PET #1

The wage rate is the price of labor.

Since the wage rate is the price of the commodity labor, demand and supply analysis can be used to examine what happens to the price of labor (wage rate) when the demand or supply of labor change.

PET #2

Factors other than a change in the wage rate that are relevant to the labor market may cause the demand and supply curves for labor to shift. Changes in the wage rate cause a movement along the demand and supply curves.

For review, you may wish to review PET #1 of Chapter 1 of the Practicum as well as PET #1-5 of Chapter 4 of the Practicum.

PET #3

A higher wage rate will cause some workers to work more (quantity of labor supplied increases) and will cause some workers to work less (quantity of labor supplied decreases).

For workers that work more hours when the wage rate rises, they are behaving according to the law of supply. That is, for these workers, the supply of labor is positively sloped. These workers will reduce the amount of leisure time they take (because the opportunity cost of leisure time has increased since the wage rate has increased) and, therefore, work more hours. We could say that these workers substitute more work for less leisure time.

For workers that work fewer hours when the wage rate rises, they are not behaving according to the law of supply since they increase the amount of leisure time they take and, thus, work fewer hours. That is, for these workers, the supply of labor is negatively sloped. Workers may choose to respond this way to a higher wage rate because they recognize that they can now work fewer hours (more leisure time) and still maintain the same income. We could say that these workers substitute more leisure time for less work.

You should be aware that Chapter 17 of the text points out some other reasons why the supply curve will be positively sloped.

PET #4

The marginal revenue product of labor is equal to the price at which a firm sells its output multiplied by the marginal product (productivity) of labor.

To see this, note that the price of output (P) is measured as $ per unit of output. The marginal product of labor is measured as the addition to output produced by one more worker (or from one more hour of work). That is, (Δ output/one unit of labor). When price is multiplied by the marginal product of labor, the result is:

$$P \ X \ (\Delta \ output/one \ unit \ of \ labor) = (P \ X \ \Delta \ output \ )/one \ unit \ of \ labor$$

where (P X Δ output) = Marginal Revenue. Thus, the marginal revenue product of labor is the addition to revenue that one more worker generates for the firm.

PET #5

Factors that cause an increase in the demand for output that labor produces will lead to an increase in the demand for labor and, thus, an increase in the equilibrium wage.

A firm's demand for labor is a derived demand for labor. It is derived from the demand for the output that labor helps to produce. An increase in the demand for *output* leads to an increase in the price of output. The increase in the price of output means that each worker's work effort (productivity) will add more to the revenue of the firm than before the price increase. That is, the marginal revenue product of labor increases. Using the marginal principle, the marginal benefit to the firm of additional workers has increased. If the wage rate (marginal cost of an additional worker) is unchanged, the firm will find it profit-maximizing to hire more workers.

PET #6

A minimum wage policy is like a minimum price (or price floor, price support).

Remember from Chapter 6 that a minimum price is a price below which the price may not fall. For a minimum price policy to be effective, it must be set above the equilibrium price. In the case of minimum wage policy, a minimum wage that is set above the equilibrium wage will create a surplus of labor (quantity of labor supplied will exceed quantity of labor demanded). If the minimum wage is set below the equilibrium wage, the policy is ineffective since there is no tendency for the equilibrium wage to fall below the minimum wage. You may want to review PET #3 from Chapter 6 of the Practicum.

PET #7

*An efficiency wage is a wage that is paid by a firm that is **above** the equilibrium wage (or going market-rate) for a particular job or occupation.*

An efficiency wage may be paid by a firm in order to attract high quality, productive workers, to reduce the worker's incentive to shirk (i.e., make them work harder), and to reduce absenteeism and turnover. The higher wages paid by the firm may not necessarily mean that the firm's profits will suffer. The workers may be more productive than their counterparts working for other firms in the same industry who are not being paid an efficiency wage. Thus, even though the firm's wage cost may be higher with efficiency wages, the cost of production may not rise because the productivity increase acts to offset the higher labor costs..

V.   PRACTICE EXAM: MULTIPLE CHOICE QUESTIONS

1.   If an increase in the wage rate causes workers to reduce the amount of hours they work and increase the amount of leisure time they take, then:

a.   the labor supply curve for these workers is positively sloped.
b.   the labor supply curve for these workers is negatively sloped.
c.   these workers are obeying the law of supply.
d.   the demand for these workers is derived.
e.   the marginal product of these workers is negative.

2.   Which one of the following would NOT be considered a possible response to a higher wage rate for computer technicians in Palo Alto?

a.   a decrease in the amount of hours worked.
b.   an increase in the amount of hours worked.
c.   an increase in the number of individuals who pick computer technician over other occupations.
d.   migration to Palo Alto.
e.   all of the above.

3.   Which one of the following is an explanation for why the long-run demand curve for labor is negatively sloped?

a.   an increase in the wage rate raises the price at which output is sold and, thus, increases the profits of firms.

b.   a decrease in the wage rate causes fewer people to be willing to work.
c.   a decrease in the wage rate lowers the cost of labor and causes firms to use more labor instead of other more expensive inputs.
d.   an increase in the wage rate reduces the productivity of workers.
e.   all of the above.

4.   In which country would labor be likely to be most expensive?

a.   India.
b.   Haiti.
c.   Mexico.
d.   Italy.
e.   the Phillipines.

5.   Consider the market for lawyers. Suppose the number of lawyers passing the Bar exam in 1998 is larger than it has ever been in the past. What effect would this have on the market for lawyers?

a.   a decrease in the wage rate (salary) paid to lawyers and an increase in the demand for lawyers.
b.   a decrease in the wage rate (salary) paid to lawyers and an increase in the supply of lawyers.
c.   an increase in the wage rate (salary) paid to lawyers and a decrease in the demand for lawyers.
d.   an increase in the wage rate (salary) paid to lawyers and an increase in the supply of lawyers.
e.   (a) and (b).

6.   Which one of the following would increase the demand for labor?

a.   an increase in the price of output that labor produces.
b.   an increase in the productivity of labor.
c.   an increase in the price of capital.
d.   a minimum wage law.
e.   (a), (b), and (c).

7.   Which one of the following is a reason for why the relative wage of certain occupations is high?

a.   few people who have the skills necessary to perform the job.
b.   high education and training costs.
c.   undesirable job features.
d.   licensing restrictions.
e.   all of the above.

8.   Which one of the following has NOT been suggested as an explanation for the gender and race gap in earnings?

a.   women and blacks have, on average, less education than white males.
b.   women and blacks have, on average, less work experience than white males.
c.   gender/race discrimination.
d.   women and blacks are only a small percentage of the total work force.
e.   all of the above.

9.   Which one of the following statements is true?

a.   In 1992, a typical college graduate earned 82% more than the typical high-school graduate.
b.   a college education provides a signal to a potential employer that the job candidate has desirable skills.
c.   the "learning effect" of a college education is that students learn new skills that enable them to work in higher-skill jobs.
d.   over the last twenty years, technological change has created a big increase in the demand for high-skilled workers
e.   all of the above.

10.   Suppose the current wage rate in the service industry is $5.00/hour. A minimum wage policy for the service industry that sets the minimum wage at $5.25 will create a _____ of jobs and a minimum wage policy for the service industry that sets the minimum wage at $4.50 will create a _____ of jobs.

a.   loss; gain
b.   gain; loss
c.   loss; no effect
d.   no effect; gain
e.   loss; loss

11.   Which one of the following statements is true?

a.   a minimum wage policy may lead to a decrease in the price of output that minimum wage workers produce.
b.   a comparable worth policy is designed to reduce the wage rate that men earn.
c.   an example of occupational licensing is a requirement that a worker complete a certain number of hours of education and retraining every three years in order to remain licensed.
d.   a labor union has monopsony power.
e.   none of the above are true.

12.   Occupational licensing schemes:

a.   restrict entry into the profession.
b.   increase wages.
c.   increase production costs.
d.   are designed to protect consumers.
e.   all of the above.

13.   Which one of the following statements is NOT true?

a.   the Wagner Act guaranteed workers the right to join unions and required each firm to bargain with a union formed by a majority of its workers.
b.   the Taft-Hartley Act gave government employees the power to strike when their health or safety was imperiled.

c.   The Landrum-Griffin Act guaranteed union members the right to fair elections, made it easier to monitor union finances, and made the theft of union funds a federal offense.

d.   Fewer than 20% of U.S. workers belong to unions.

e.   The number of government workers in unions has more than doubled in the last thirty years.

14.   Unions attempt to increase the wages of their members by:

a.   negotiating with the firm.

b.   advertisements that encourage people to buy products with the union label.

c.   featherbedding.

d.   striking.

e.   all of the above.

15.   Which one of the following statements is true?

a.   a firm that pays efficiency wages may see an increased work effort by its employees as well as a reduction in absenteeism and turnover.

b.   featherbedding may lead to lower costs of production.

c.   a firm knows more about the productivity and skill level of a potential employee than the potential employee knows about his or her own productivity and skill level.

d.   the labor market is a fixed market.

e.   a monopsonist in the labor market uses its power to increase the wage rate.

VI.   PRACTICE EXAM: ESSAY QUESTIONS

1.   Consider the market for graphic designers in Charlotte. Let the current equilibrium wage be $11/hour. Suppose that the demand for graphic designers in Charlotte increases by 10%. Discuss what will happen to the equilibrium wage in the short and long run. Be sure to explain why the results are different. Assume the elasticity of labor supply in the short run is 0.5 and in the long run is 2.

2.   Discuss the purpose of unions and their intended impact on wages and employment. What are some ways in which union membership leads to more productive workers?

VII.   ANSWER KEY: MULTIPLE CHOICE QUESTIONS

1.   Correct answer: b.

Discussion: The labor supply curve is a graph of the wage rate against the amount of labor (or labor time) supplied. An increase in the wage rate that reduces the amount of labor supplied reflects a negative or inverse relationship between the wage rate and the amount of labor supplied.

Statement a is not correct based on the above reasoning. Statement c is not correct because, if the workers were obeying the law of supply, then the labor supply curve would be positively sloped. Statement d is not correct because the relationship between the wage rate and labor supplied tells us nothing about the demand for labor.   Statement e is not correct because the marginal product of labor is a component of the demand for labor, not the supply. Furthermore, if the marginal product of workers was negative, no firm would hire them.

2.   Correct answer: e.

Discussion: A higher wage rate may induce some workers to work fewer hours (because they can maintain the same income at a higher wage but working fewer hours) and, thus, take more leisure time. Some workers may do the opposite -- they may choose to work more hours and thereby increase their earnings substantially. The choice depends on the workers' preferences for leisure time over income (and increased consumption and saving). A higher wage rate also has the effect of attracting workers to the profession. Many students choose college majors based on what they expect the wage (salary) to be for that particular job when they graduate. Higher expected wages tend to attract students into those majors. A higher wage rate also causes people to move to those places where they can earn a higher wage.

3.   Correct answer: c.

Discussion: A decrease in the wage rate creates a substitution effect -- the firm finds it less costly to use labor to help produce output than to use other relatively more expensive inputs. Thus, the firm will decide to use more labor and fewer of the other inputs (e.g., conveyor belt) as a less costly, alternative way to produce output.

Statement a is not correct because it is not an explanation for why the demand curve is negatively sloped. It is also not a correct statement because a higher wage (unless it is an efficiency wage that creates offsetting productivity gains) typically reduces a firm's profits. Statement b is not correct because it is a reference to labor supply not labor demand. Statement d is not correct because it is not an explanation for why the demand curve is negatively sloped. Since statements a, b, and d are not correct, statement e cannot be correct.

4.   Correct answer: d.

Discussion: Labor is likely to be most expensive in countries where the population is relatively small and/or where the skill level of workers is high. Conversely, labor is likely to be less expensive in countries where labor is abundant (big population) and/or the skill level of workers is low. India, Haiti, Mexico, and the Phillipines are all countries with big populations and low skilled-workers. Italy, a western European country, has relatively more skilled workers and a relatively smaller population.

5.   Correct answer: b.

Discussion: The big increase in the number of lawyers passing the Bar exam would be represented by a rightward shift in the supply of lawyers. The shift would have the effect of lowering the equilibrium wage (salary) paid to lawyers. As the wage decreased, the quantity of lawyers demanded (movement along the labor demand curve) would increase.

Statement a is not correct because the demand for lawyers does not increase (i.e., labor demand does not shift to the right); the *quantity* of lawyers demanded increases (movement along the labor demand curve). Statements c and d are not correct because the wage rate decreases, not increases. Statement e is not correct because statement a is not correct.

6.   Correct answer: e.

Discussion: Statement a will cause an increase in the demand for labor. When the price of output that labor produces increases, the marginal revenue each worker generates for the firm increases and, thus, workers become more valuable to the firm. This would lead to an increase in the demand for labor. Statement b will also cause an increase in the demand for labor. More productive (higher marginal product) workers are more beneficial to a firm (generate more output and, thus, more revenue). Thus, firms will demand more labor when workers' productivity increases. Statement c will also cause an increase in the demand for labor. When capital becomes more expensive, firms will decide to substitute labor in production for capital (since labor would be relatively less costly). Statement d will cause a decrease in the *quantity* of labor demanded. That is, a minimum wage policy causes a movement along the demand curve, but not a shift in the demand for labor (decrease in demand).

7.   Correct answer: e.

Discussion: Higher wages are paid to workers who have skills that few people have. This is why chemical engineers are paid more than a clerk at a shoe store. Doctors, professors, lawyers, veterinarians, etc., are all professions which entail more than a college education and, thus, are more costly professions to enter. Jobs with undesirable features (perhaps risky jobs like oil rig drillers) tend to be paid more because there are fewer people willing to work in dangerous situations. Thus, the supply of labor in these professions is typically not as large as in, say, retail sales, and the wages are correspondingly higher. Licensing restrictions limit the supply of workers in the licensed professions. This, too, leads to correspondingly higher wages.

8.   Correct answer: d.

Discussion: Statement d has not been used as an explanation for the gender and race gap. The gender and race gap in earnings is that women and blacks typically earn less than a white male counterpart who is doing the same job. The difference in earnings has been explained in several ways (that are not necessarily mutually exclusive). The gender gap may be due to the fact that women and blacks typically have less education and less work experience than white males. That is, these groups of workers, on average, are less valuable to a firm than a worker with more education and work experience. Gender and race discrimination have also been suggested as explanations for the earnings gaps between men and women and white males and black males.

9.   Correct answer: e.

Discussion: All of the above are true. Statement a provides evidence that workers that have more education are better paid. Statement b is an example of the "screening" or "signalling" effect that graduation from college provides to potential employers. Statement c suggests that a college education produces workers with higher skills and thereby, admission into better paid professions. Statement d suggests that workers in fields like engineering and computer technology have seen (and may continue to see) increases in wages bigger than those in other professions.

10.   Correct answer: c.

Discussion: A minimum wage is a floor below which the wage may not drop. A minimum wage law set at $5.25/hour is a policy that will not permit the wage to drop below that rate. Since the current wage is

$5.00/hour, the minimum wage policy raises the wage to $5.25/hour. The increase in the wage rate reduces the quantity of labor demanded (movement along the demand curve) and, thus, causes a loss of jobs. An increase in the wage rate also raises the quantity of labor supplied (movement along the supply curve). A minimum wage of $4.50/hour is not effective because the equilibrium wage is $5.00/hour. Since $5.00/hour is an equilibrium wage, there is no tendency for it to drop below $5.00/hour. Thus, a restriction that the wage not be permitted to fall below $4.50 is meaningless. This means that the policy will not have an effect on the quantity of labor demanded or supplied or on the equilibrium wage of $5.00/hour. Therefore, statement c is the only correct answer.

11.   Correct answer: c.

Discussion: Occupational licensing requirements typically place restrictions on workers in the profession. Workers typically must fulfill a certain set of conditions in order to become licensed or remain licensed. The conditions may be that the workers meet certain educational requirements or a specified number of hours spent on the job per year.

Statement a is not correct because a minimum wage typically raises the price of output that minimum wage workers produce. This is because a minimum wage typically raises a firm's cost of production (without leading to increased worker productivity) which is passed on to consumers in the form of higher prices. Statement b is not correct because a comparable worth policy is designed to raise the level of wages of women to that of men (not to bring the wages of men down). Statement d is not correct because a labor union is a seller of labor in the labor market. A monopsonist in the labor market is defined as a single buyer of labor (not seller). Since statement c is true, statement e cannot be correct.

12.   Correct answer: e.

Discussion: All of the above are true. However, while occupational licensing schemes are designed to protect consumers from incompetent workers, such schemes may not always be effective. To wit, there are surgeons who are licensed to practice who have amputated the wrong leg or removed the wrong kidney from a patient.

13.   Correct answer: b.

Discussion: Statement b is not true. The Taft-Hartley Act gave the government the power to break up strikes if they imperiled national health or safety.   For example, former president Ronald Reagan fired all striking airtraffic controllers and hired non-union air traffic controllers since such a strike imperiled air safety. All of the other statements are true.

14.   Correct answer: e.

Labor unions (of which the AFL-CIO is the umbrella organization) attempt to increase the wages of their members as well as to improve working conditions and enhance fringe benefits. Unions do this through (1) negotiation with the firm (which may lead to a strike as part of the negotiation tactic), (2) by creating a demand for the product they produce (remember that the demand for labor is a derived demand; the stronger the demand for output, the higher the wage paid to employees that produce the output), and/or (3) through featherbedding (dictating that a firm must hire so many workers for a particular task). That is, featherbedding is designed to increase the demand for labor and, thus, the wage. Featherbedding, however, can backfire and actually reduce the wage paid to workers. This can happen if featherbedding leads to higher production costs and, thus, a higher price for the output the workers produce. If the price of the output rises, the amount sold will decline and this will have a tendency to reduce the demand for labor and reduce the wage.

15.   Correct answer: a.

Discussion: Efficiency wages may lead workers to work harder (and not shirk), but also to reduce the frequency with which they call in sick and their desire to quit the job. When Henry Ford raised the wage he paid his workers from $3/ day to $5/day, he effectively paid them an efficiency wage since the going market rate was $3/day.

Statement b is not true because featherbedding raises costs of production. Statement c is not correct because employees know more about their own productivity and skill level than does a potential employer. Statement d is not correct; a labor market is a mixed market, meaning that both high and low-skill workers exist in the market, and it can be difficult for a firm to know which type of worker it is hiring. Statement e is not correct because a monopsonist uses its power in the market to reduce the wage rate.

VIII.   ANSWER KEY: ESSAY QUESTIONS

1.   An increase in the demand for graphic designers would be represented by a rightward shift in the demand for graphic designers. The increased demand for graphic designers would raise the wage above $11/hour. The degree to which the wage rises depends on how elastic the labor supply curve is. In the short run, the supply of labor is less elastic than in the long run. This means that the short-run supply of graphic designers will be steeper than the long-run supply of graphic designers. In the short run, the influence of migration and choice of graphic designer as an occupation cannot be felt on the labor market. That is, the short run is a time period that is not long enough to allow for individuals to migrate to Charlotte to fill the increased demand for graphic designers or for college students and others to alter their career decisions so that they can be hired as a graphic designer. Thus, the increased demand puts a lot more pressure on the wage to rise (because of the limited response on the supply side). If the short-run elasticity of supply is 0.5% and the demand for graphic designers increased by 10%, then the increase in the wage rate would be 20%. The formula to be used is analogous to the elasticity of demand formula that was covered in Chapter 5 of your textbook and is reviewed in Chapter 5 of the Practicum. The formula is:

Elasticity (E) = %ΔQ/%ΔP

where in this case, you know that the elasticity of supply is 0.5% and that the %ΔQ is 10% since that is how many more graphic designers are demanded. Since we are analyzing the labor market, the %ΔP is the %Δwage. (The wage rate is the price of labor). Thus, plugging in the numbers and solving for %ΔP yields:

%ΔP (i.e., wage) = %ΔQ/E = 10%/0.5 = 20%.

Thus, in the short run, the wage rises by 20% which, in dollar terms, is equal to (0.20 X $11/hour) = $2.20. The new wage, in the short run, is $13.20/hour.

In the long run, the higher wage and demand for graphic designers causes people to migrate to Charlotte and enter the profession of graphic design. This takes some pressure off of the wage. With a long-run elasticity of supply of 2, the equilibrium wage in the long run will change by:

$\%\Delta P = 10\%/2 = 5\%$

Thus, in the long run, the wage rises by 5% which in dollar terms is equal to (0.05 X $11/hour) = $0.55. The new wage, in the long run, is $11.55/hour.

In the long run, the wage rises by less than in the short run because the increased demand for graphic designers is matched by a bigger pool of available graphic designers. Existing firms do not have to compete as strongly with each other (by offering better wage rates) in order to attract graphic designers to work for them as they do in the short run when the pool of available graphic designers is limited.

2.   Unions (which came into being in the late 1800s) are organized groups of employees that, at tempt to negotiate with the firm for higher wages, better working conditions, and better benefits. Unions also attempt to maintain employment for the union members. Since a union is an organization within a firm, the union has more power than an individual in negotiating with the management of the firm.

While unions attempt to increase the wages of the union members, they confront a problem. A negotiation for higher wages may raise production costs and, thus, the price of the output the firm sells. If the higher price reduces the amount of output the firm is able to sell, the firm has an incentive to layoff workers. (Remember that the demand for labor is derived from how much output and at what price the output can be sold.) Naturally, unions want to avoid any loss of employment for their union members. This is why some unions try to hold membership down. A smaller membership means that a firm would have to think twice about laying off some of its workers because these employees are vital to the firm's operation. Without them, the firm may not be able to operate at all.

Unions also recognize that there are other ways to increase wages without directly asking for higher wages. Unions may promote products produced under the union label. That is, unions attempt (through advertising) to increase the demand for the product(s) that they produce. Unions may also advocate work rules that establish how many workers must be used to fulfill certain tasks. This is called "featherbedding." For example, unions may dictate that a roadside construction crew consist of 4 workers when perhaps 3 could do the job just as well. Featherbedding thus leads to an artificially increased demand for labor and supposedly would lead to a higher wage -- just what the union is after in the first place. However, featherbedding can backfire. If featherbedding leads to higher production costs and thereby a higher price for the output the workers are producing, the demand for labor could actually decline. This is because a higher price of output will reduce the amount of output sold, so fewer workers are needed.

In terms of a graph, featherbedding is designed to shift out (to the right) the demand for labor. Thus, the wage will rise and employment will increase. However, as the price of output rises, the demand for labor shifts back in (to the left). If the price increase is big enough, the demand for labor could shift back in by enough that the new wage and employment level are below what the initial wage and employment level were.

To see this, look at the graph below.

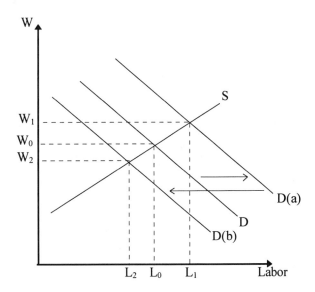

The curves labelled S and D are the initial supply and demand curves prior to featherbedding. The desired impact of featherbedding is to increase the demand for labor to D(a). However, as the price of output rises (because of production cost increases associated with the featherbedding), the demand curve may shift back to D or even worse D(b). At D(b), the new equilibrium wage and employment level is below what the starting wage and employment level were.

One of the assumptions so far has been that the higher wage that union members are paid is not offset by an increase in union member productivity. That is, the higher wage (without any corresponding rise in worker productivity) is what leads to higher production costs and a higher price for the output which, unfortunately for the union, reduces the demand for labor. However, this turn of events can be avoided if the higher wage leads to more productive workers. That is, if the higher wage is offset by employees becoming more productive, the firm's production costs may not increase and, thus, the price at which output is sold need not necessarily increase with the higher wage rate. There are two ways in which union members may have an incentive to be more productive. First, since the union promotes communication between the management of the firm and the workers, workers may be more satisfied on the job because any problems they have may be dealt with more swiftly by management. Furthermore, the more satisfied workers are, the less likely they are to quit. Thus, turnover rates of union members may be lower. This translates to more experienced workers (the longer one stays on the job the more experienced one becomes). More experienced workers are assumed to be more productive. Second, the higher wage may be viewed as an "efficiency" wage in the sense that the higher wage motivates workers to work hard (so as to keep their well-paying jobs).

Take It to the Net

We invite you to visit the O'Sullivan/Sheffrin page on the Prentice Hall Web site at:

http://www.prenhall.com/osullivan/

for this chapter's World Wide Web exercise.

CHAPTER 18
INTEREST RATES AND PRESENT VALUE

I. OVERVIEW

In this chapter, you will explore the market for loanable funds. You will explore the supply of loanable funds which are provided by savers (lenders) and the demand for loanable funds which are used by borrowers. You will learn why households and businesses save and how the interest rate influences total saving each year. You will learn why households, businesses, and the government borrow and how the interest rate influences how much, in total, is borrowed each year. You will use supply and demand analysis to examine the effects of changes in the supply and demand of loanable funds on the price of loanable funds, which is the interest rate. You will learn that more risky financial assets typically pay a higher interest rate to the lender. You will learn about stocks and how the effective interest that they pay is determined differently from savings accounts and bonds. You will revisit the problems associated with asymmetric information in a market and apply them to the market for loanable funds. You will learn about how to make wise investment decisions (financial or otherwise). This requires that you compare the present value of different options under different interest rates. You will learn how to calculate the present value of a future payment if you receive the future payment, say, at the end of ten years, versus receiving a payment once each year for ten years.

II. CHECKLIST

By the end of this chapter, you should be able to:

√ Explain the slope of the supply curve for loanable funds.
√ Explain the slope of the demand curve for loanable funds.
√ Explain what would cause the supply and demand curves of loanable funds to shift.
√ Explain what would cause the interest rate to change.
√ Explain the effect of taxes on the payments a saver actually receives.
√ Discuss the problems of asymmetric information in the loanable funds market and why lenders (e.g., banks) may credit ration.
√ Explain the importance of making present value calculations in deciding on different investment options.
√ Calculate the present value of $X paid in Y years to the present value of $X paid each year for Y years.
√ Use present value calculations to make a decision about whether or not to undertake a particular investment that carries a future payment.

III. KEY TERMS

Market for loanable funds: a market in which savers (the suppliers of funds) and borrowers (the demanders of funds) interact to determine the equilibrium interest rate (the price of loanable funds).
Interest rate: the amount of money paid for the use of a dollar for a year.
Supply curve for loanable funds: a curve that shows the relationship between the interest rate and the quantity of loanable funds supplied by savers.

Demand curve for loanable funds: a curve that shows the relationship between the interest rate and the quantity of loanable funds demanded by borrowers.

Corporation: a legal entity that is owned by people who purchase stock in the corporation.

Corporate stock: a certificate that reflects ownership in a corporation and gives the holder the right to receive a fraction of the corporation's profit.

Government or corporate bond: a promissory note issued by a corporation or a government when it borrows money.

Dividends: the part of a corporation's profit paid to stockholders.

Present value: the maximum amount a person is willing to pay today for a payment to be received in the future.

Credit rationing: the practice of limiting the amount of credit available to individual borrowers.

IV.   PERFORMANCE ENHANCING TIPS

PET #1

Factors other than a change in the interest rate that are relevant to the market for loanable funds may cause the demand and supply curves for loanable funds to shift. Changes in the interest rate cause a movement along the demand and supply curves.

For review of this concept, see PET #1 of Chapter 1 of the Practicum as well as PET #s1-5 of Chapter 4 of the Practicum.

PET #2

The suppliers of loanable funds are "savers" who can also be referred to as "lenders." The demanders of loanable funds are "borrowers."

PET #3

Present value calculations can be used to determine how much money you would have to save or put away today in order to accumulate a certain sum of money in the future.

Suppose that you would like to have $500 in one year in order to purchase a new kitchen table and chairs set. Further, suppose that the interest rate that you could earn if you put your money today into a money market account is 6% per year. How much would you have to put away today in order to have $500 in the future? That is, what is the present value of a future payment of $500 in one year?

The formula that you would use (from the book) is:

present value = future payment$/(1 + $ interest rate$/100)^i$

Here, the future payment is $500, the interest rate is 6% and $i = 1$ year. Thus, the present value is:

$500/(1+0.06)^1 = $500/1.06 = $471.70.

This means that you would have to put $471.70 in the bank today in order to amass $500 one year from today.

Suppose you were going to save for three years instead of one year. How much would you have to put away today in order to amass $500 in three years? Assume the interest rate you can earn is fixed at 6% per year.

Obviously, you will have to put away less than $471.70 since you will be accumulating interest for two additional years. Let's see how much you would have to put away:

present value = $500/(1+0.06)^3 = $500/1.191 = $419.81.

Thus, you would have to put $419.81 in a bank today in order to have $500 three years from today given that the current interest rate is 6%.

PET #4

*The present value of an investment decision which yields $X dollars in Y periods is calculated differently from an investment decision that yields $X/Y dollars **each period** for Y periods.*

There is a subtle but significant difference between the two investment plans stated above. A failure to understand or be aware of the difference could lead to poor financial decisions or, worse, incorrect answers on an exam! Let's explore the difference by using a concrete example.

Suppose you are told that you will receive a future payment of $10,000 in 5 years. This is different from receiving a payment of $2,000 each year for 5 years for a total of $10,000. To see this, calculate the present value of each payment, being sure to use the correct formula. Assume the current interest rate is 8%.

The present value of a $10,000 payment 5 years from today is:

$10,000/(1+0.08)^5 = $10,000/1.4693 = $6,805.83

In other words, if you were given $6,805.83 today and put it in the bank for 5 years at 8% interest per year, you would have $10,000 at the end of 5 years. In effect, you may be indifferent between receiving $6,805.83 today or $10,000 in the future.

In contrast, the present value of a $2,000 payment starting today (i=0) for 5 years (until i = 4) is:

$2,000/(1.08)^0 + $2,000/(1.08)^1 + $2,000/(1.08)^2 + $2,000/(1.08)^3 + $2,000/(1.08)^4 = $8,624.25

Note that $(1.08)^0$ is equal to 1.0 which means that the present value of $2,000 (i.e., $2,000/(1.08)^0) paid to you today is $2,000. (As an algebra point, any number raised to the zeroth power is equal to 1.0).

Notice that the present value of receiving payments of $2,000 every year for 5 years starting today for a total of $10,000 is greater than the present value of a $10,000 payment 5 years from today. The reason is that, when you are paid a stream of money each year, you can invest it at the current interest rate and make money on it. If you are paid $2,000 once each year for 5 years starting today, you could put the $2,000 into the bank and earn an 8% interest rate on the first $2,000 for 5 years; the next year when you receive another

$2,000, you will earn an 8% interest rate on that $2,000 for the remaining 4 years and so on for the remaining payments of $2,000. In effect, you accumulate more interest earnings by getting $2,000 every year for 5 years compared to receiving $10,000 at the end of 5 years. That is why the present value of a stream of $2,000 payments received every year for 5 years is greater than the present value of receiving $10,000 in 5 years.

PET #5

You should compare the present value of future payment(s) to the current (today) cost of a project or investment in order to decide whether it is worthwhile to undertake a project. Do NOT compare the anticipated value of the future payment(s) to the current (today) cost.

For example, suppose your firm is considering opening a new factory. The cost is $1,000,000. However, the factory will be in operation one year from now at which time you anticipate earning profits of $200,000 every year for 10 years. Should your firm undertake the project of opening a new factory?

It is NOT correct to compute the benefits by simply multiplying the $200,000 in profits earned every year by 10 years. That is, it would not be correct to say that the benefit of opening the factory is $2,000,000. Nor is it correct to then compare this figure to the $1,000,000 start-up cost and conclude that the factory should be opened because the benefit exceeds the cost.

The correct way to decide whether it is worthwhile to pay $1,000,000 to open up a factory that will produce a stream of "future payments" (benefits) of $200,000 each year starting one year from now is to compare the start-up cost to the *present value* of the payments of $200,000. In order to make a present value calculation, you must know what the current interest rate is. Suppose the interest rate is 10%. What is the present value of receiving future payments of $200,000 for 10 years starting one year from today (year = 1).

Present value = $200,000/(1.10)^1 + $200,000/(1.10)^2 + ...+ $200,000/(1.10)^{10} = $1,228,913.40

Since the present value of the future benefits is greater than the start-up cost , the project is worthwhile to undertake. If the present value had been less than the start-up cost of $1,000,000 it would not be wise for your firm to open the new factory. It would be wiser for your firm to put the $1,000,000 into a financial asset that will earn 10% interest each year for 10 years.

PET #6

Taxes reduce the effective interest rate that a saver earns on invested funds.

Suppose that you invest $1,000 in a certificate of deposit that has a 7% annual interest rate. At the end of one year, you will have $1,000 X (1.07) = $1,070. You earned $70 in interest on your $1,000 investment. However, suppose that your income is taxed at a rate of 25%. You will have to pay the government 25% of your interest earnings. What are your effective (or after-tax) interest earnings and the effective (or after-tax) interest rate?

Since you earned $70 in interest, you must pay 25% to the government. 25% of $70 = 0.25 X $70 = $17.50. Thus, you are left with $70 - $17.50 = $52.50. These are your effective interest earnings. Your effective interest rate is the percent of $1,000 that you earned. This would be calculated by taking $52.50 and dividing it by $1,000 and then multiplying that number by 100. Thus, the effective interest rate would be [$52.50/$1,000] X 100 = 5.25%.

Another formula that you can use to calculate the effective interest rate (or after-tax interest rate) is:

interest rate X [1 - tax rate/100]. Thus, you would have:

7% X [1 - 25%/100] = 7% X [1-0.25] = 7% X [0.75] = 5.25%

V.   PRACTICE EXAM: MULTIPLE CHOICE QUESTIONS

1.   The supply curve for loanable funds:

a.   shows how much borrowers, in total, would be willing to borrow at various interest rates.
b.   shows how much savers, in total, would be willing to save at various interest rates.
c.   is negatively sloped.
d.   does not depend on the interest rate.
e.   (b) and (c).

2.   The demand curve for loanable funds:

a.   is negatively sloped.
b.   shows that, at higher interest rates, total saving rises.
c.   shows that, at higher interest rates, total borrowing decreases.
d.   (a) and (b).
e.   (a) and (c).

3.   Which one of the following statements is true?

a.   governments may cover the difference between their tax revenues and their expenditures by borrowing (issuing government bonds).
b.   taxes increase the net benefit from saving.
c.   an increase in the interest rate will cause firms to borrow more money.
d.   the demand for loanable funds is provided by savers.
e.   none of the above statements are true.

4.   If firms decide to expand their production facilities because the economy is booming:

a.   the supply of loanable funds will decrease.
b.   the demand for loanable funds will decrease.
c.   the interest rate will rise.
d.   borrowing will decline.
e.   (a) and (c).

5.   Suppose that the government increases its spending to fund health care. At the same time, the government cuts taxes on households. What will be the combined effect of these two policies?

a.   the interest rate will rise and the equilibrium quantity of loanable funds will rise.
b.   the interest rate will fall and the equilibrium quantity of loanable funds will rise.
c.   the interest rate will rise and the equilibrium quantity of loanable funds will decline.
d.   the effect on the interest rate is ambiguous but the equilibrium quantity of loanable funds will rise.
e.   the interest rate will rise but the effect on the equilibrium quantity of loanable funds is ambiguous.

6.   According to the graph below, which one of the following statements is true?

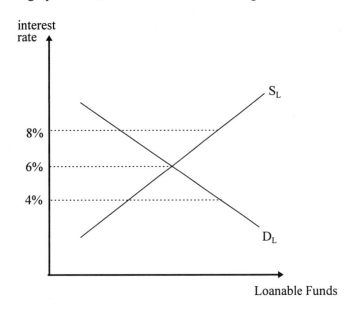

a.   if households decide to consume less today, the interest rate will rise.
b.   if the government fixes the interest rate at 4%, there will be a shortage of loanable funds.
c.   if the government fixes the interest rate at 8%, there will be a shortage of loanable funds.
d.   a decline in the equilibrium interest rate will reduce the amount of borrowing.
e.   an increase in the supply of loanable funds and a decrease in the demand for loanable funds will have an ambiguous effect on the interest rate.

7.   Which one of the following statements is true?

a.   savings accounts are insured by the federal government for $1 million dollars.
b.   government bonds are more risky than corporate bonds.
c.   different financial assets pay different interest rates because of differences in their riskiness.
d.   a purchase of stock in a corporation entitles you to receive a fixed dividend payment every quarter.
e.   a capital gain is an increase in the profits of a firm

8.   Which one of the following statements is NOT true?

a.   at higher interest rates, a lender faces a higher risk (probability) of lending to individuals who will default on their loans.
b.   the adverse-selection problem faced by lenders arises because the pool of borrowers at higher interest rates is composed of a greater percentage of borrowers that will default than at lower interest rates.

c.   credit rationing is the practice of limiting the amount of credit (loan) available to individual borrowers.

d.   the market for loanable funds is a mixed market because there are high-quality borrowers (those not likely to default on their loans) and low-quality borrowers (those likely to default on their loans) and lenders do not know with perfect certainty which borrower type they are lending to.

e.   the market for loanable funds is characterized by adverse information.

9.   Suppose you are working for a non-profit organization and one of your donors has bequeathed $25,000 to your organization. However, the $25,000 will not be paid to your organization until 3 years from today. What is the present value of the future payment of $25,000? Assume the current interest rate is 7.5%.

a. $25,000.
b. $20,124.
c. $4,664.72
d. $31,057.42
e. $5,925.93

10.   Which one of the following statements is correct?

a.   Produce a new line of fad products that will cost $10,000 to produce but will generate a 3-year stream of profits of $4,000 starting one year from today. The current interest rate is 10%.

b.   The present value of $5,000 to be paid 5 years from today is $4,796.37 assuming the interest rate is 3%.

c.   The present value of $25,000 paid every year for 4 years starting today is greater than the present value of $100,000 paid in 4 years, assuming the current interest rate is 8%.

d.   The present value of $10,000 paid in 1 year assuming an interest rate of 10% is less than the present value of $10,000 paid in 2 years assuming an interest rate of 6%.

e.   none of the above.

VI.   PRACTICE EXAM: ESSAY QUESTIONS

1.   Explain the effects of an increase in government borrowing on the loanable funds market. What will happen to total saving? Will every saver choose to save more?

2.   Suppose you work as a financial advisor for a corporation. The corporation is considering two options. The first option is to open up a glass factory in Knoxville. The cost of start up is $100,000 and it is expected that, one year after the factory is opened, $40,000 a year in profits will be made for 5 years. The interest rate is 10% per year. The second option is invest the $100,000 in a government bond that pays 10% per year for 5 years. What would you advise your company to do?

VII.   ANSWER KEY: MULTIPLE CHOICE QUESTIONS

1.   Correct answer: b.

Discussion: The supply of loanable funds comes from savers -- that is, savers lend funds to borrowers. The price of loanable funds is the interest rate. You know from Chapter 4 that, as the price of a good rises, the quantity supplied increases, i.e., the supply curve is positively sloped. The same is true for the supply curve for loanable funds. It, too, is positively sloped. Thus, statement c is not correct, nor is statement e. Statement a is not correct; borrowers are demanders of loanable funds. Statement d is not correct because the supply of loanable funds does depend on the interest rate.

2.   Correct answer: e.

Discussion: The demand curve for loanable funds represents, at various interest rates, how much borrowers would be willing to borrow. At higher interest rates, it becomes more costly to borrow (i.e., the price of borrowing increases), so total borrowing declines. This means that there is a negative relationship between the interest rate and borrowing. Thus, statements a and c are correct. The demand curve for loanable funds does not tell us anything about the behavior of savers, so statement b is not correct.

3.   Correct answer: a.

Discussion: The government can be a borrower, just like an individual, household, or firm can be. The government borrows when its tax revenues are not enough to cover its expenditures. (The government is said to run a budget deficit). In order to cover its expenditures, the government borrows funds from the private sector by issuing bonds (promissory notes).

Statement b is not true because taxes decrease the net benefit from saving. Statement c is not true because an increase in the interest rate will cause firms to borrow less money. Statement d is not correct because the demand for loanable funds comes from borrowers, not savers.

4.   Correct answer: c.

Discussion: When firms decide to expand their production facilities (build new factories, enlarge and renovate existing ones), they typically must borrow the funds necessary for the expansion. Thus, the demand for loanable funds will increase. As the demand for loanable funds increases, the price of loanable funds, the interest rate, rises. For this reason, statement c is correct and statement b and d are incorrect. Statement a is not correct because the supply of loanable funds does not decrease, nor does it increase (i.e., there is no shift in the supply curve).

5.   Correct answer: d.

Discussion: The government increase in spending on health care is financed through government borrowing. This raises the demand for loanable funds (demand for loanable funds shifts right) and by itself increases the equilibrium interest rate and the equilibrium quantity of loanable funds. The tax cut raises the benefit to savers of saving and, thus, increases the supply of loanable funds. This increases the supply of loanable funds (supply of loanable funds shifts right) and by itself, lowers the equilibrium interest rate and increases the equilibrium quantity of loanable funds. Since the two shifts have opposite effects on the interest rate, the change in the interest rate is ambiguous. However, both shifts raise the equilibrium quantity of loanable funds. Thus, statement d is the only correct option.

6.   Correct answer: b.

Discussion: Statement b is an example of a "maximum price" that you learned about in Chapter 6. If the government fixes the interest rate at 4% and the current equilibrium interest rate is 6%, then the government is not permitting the interest rate to rise to what would be its equilibrium value. At an interest rate of 4%, the quantity of loanable funds demanded exceeds the quantity of loanable funds supplied and so there will be a shortage of loanable funds.

Statement a is not correct because a decrease in consumption today is the flip side of increased saving today which would be represented by an increase in the supply of loanable funds (supply shifts right). Statement c is not correct; if the government fixed the interest rate at 8%, there would be a surplus of loanable funds. Statement d is not correct because a decline in the equilibrium interest rate will increase the amount of borrowing (movement along the demand curve). Statement e is not correct. An increase in the supply of loanable funds (supply shifts right) reduces the interest rate. A decrease in the demand for loanable funds (demand shifts left) reduces the interest rate. Both actions reduce the interest rate so that there is no ambiguity about what will happen to it.

7.   Correct answer: c.

Discussion: There are many different interest rates in the financial market. Higher interest rates are typically paid on financial assets that are more risky in order to entice lenders (savers) into lending their funds to the borrowers. If two bonds were both paying an 8% interest rate but one was riskier than another, which bond would you invest in? Naturally, you would want the lower-risk bond. However, if the riskier bond was paying 15% interest, you may be willing to invest in it despite the fact that it is riskier.

Statement a is not correct; savings accounts are insured by the federal government for up to $100,000. Statement b is not correct because government bonds are less risky than corporate bonds. The view is that the government is less likely to default on its bonds than is a corporation. Statement d is not correct because a dividend payment is not fixed. It may vary from quarter to quarter depending on the financial health (profitability) of the firm. For example, one quarter, a corporation may $0.25 in dividends on each stock and another quarter only $0.10 in dividends. Statement e is not correct because a capital gain is defined as an increase in the price of a stock. (The price of the stock may rise because the firm's profits increase but there are numerous other reasons why a firm's stock price may increase.)

8.   Correct answer: e.

Discussion: The market for loanable funds is characterized by asymmetric information, not adverse information. All of the other statements are true.

9.   Correct answer: b.

Discussion: The present value of a $25,000 payment 3 years from today is calculated by dividing $25,000 by $(1.075)^3$. That is, $25,000/1.2423 = $20,124.

Statement a cannot be correct. The present value of a future sum of money is always less than the future sum (unless the interest rate is zero). For the same reason, statement d cannot be correct (unless the interest rate was negative). Based on the calculations above, statements c and e are also not correct.

10.   Correct answer: c.

Discussion: The present value of $25,000 paid every year for 4 years starting today at an interest rate of 8% is $25,000 + $25,000/1.08 + $25,000/(1.08)^2 + $25,000/(1.08)^3 = $89,427.43. The present value of $100,000 paid in 4 years is $100,000/(1.08)^4 = $73,502.99.

Statement a is not correct. The cost is $10,000 and the present value of the future payments (benefits) is $4,000/(1.10)^1 + $4,000/(1.10)^2 + $4,000/(1.10)^3 = $9,947.41. Since the cost exceeds the present value of the benefits, the project should not be undertaken. Statement b is not correct because the present value of $5,000 paid in 5 years assuming the interest rate is 3% is = $5,000/(1.03)^5 = $4,313.04. Statement d is not correct because the present value of $10,000 paid in one year at an interest rate of 10% is $10,000/1.10 = $9,090.91 and is greater than the present value of $10,000 paid in 2 years at an interest rate of 6% is $10,000/(1.06)^2 = $8899.96.

VIII.   ANSWER KEY: ESSAY QUESTIONS

1.   An increase in government borrowing, which the government undertakes by issuing government bonds that savers purchase (thereby lending their funds to the government), represents an increase in the demand for loanable funds. An increase in the demand for loanable funds raises the price of loanable funds like an increase in the demand for a good raises the price of the good. The price of loanable funds is the interest rate, so the interest rate rises. As the interest rate rises, the quantity of loanable funds supplied by savers rises. This is represented as a movement along the supply of loanable funds curve. Thus, the equilibrium quantity of total saving rises to meet the increased demand for loanable funds. However, even though the interest rate is higher and the quantity of total saving is higher, not every saver may have decided to save more in response to the higher interest rate. Some may have chosen to save less since the higher interest rate means that their savings are earning more interest. (These savers are the "party hearty" crowd your book refers to). Some savers may not change the amount they save; they're just happy that they are making more money each year in interest than before the interest rate had gone up. Since total saving rises, however, the people who do decide to save more as the interest rate goes up collectively bring enough saving into the market for loanable funds to more than offset the reduction in saving coming from the "party hearty" crowd. Thus, on net, the total level of saving rises as the interest rate rises.

2.   I would start by computing the present value of the project and compare it to the cost. The present value is calculated as:

$40,000/(1.10) + $40,000/(1.10^1) + $40,000/(1.10)^2 + $40,000/(1.10)^3 + $40,000/(1.10)^4 + $40,000/(1.10)^5 = $151,631.50

Since the cost of the project is less than the present value, it appears that the project would be worthwhile. The company comes out ahead by $51,631.50 since it spends (costs) $100,000 today and gets back (in present value terms) $151,631.50. That is, the benefit in today's term is $51,631.50. However, the company could just hold onto the $100,000 today. The benefit of $100,000 in today's terms is $100,000 which exceeds the benefit from the project. Thus, it would make more sense for the company to hold on to the $100,000. In fact, if the company invests the $100,000 into an account earning 10% for five years, the $100,000 will be worth $161,051 in 5 years [= $100,000 X (1.10)^5]. Therefore, while the firm makes $61,051 in interest, it also keeps the $100,000 investment. Thus, it would be even better for the company to simply invest the money into an account earning 10% per year for the next five years since it will have $161,051 compared to netting $51,631.50 in five years.

Take It to the Net

We invite you to visit the O'Sullivan/Sheffrin page on the Prentice Hall Web site at:

http://www.prenhall.com/osullivan/

for this chapter's World Wide Web exercise.

CHAPTER 19
ECONOMIC CHALLENGES FOR THE TWENTY-FIRST CENTURY

I.   OVERVIEW

As the title to this chapter suggests, you will learn about some of the major economic challenges confronting the U.S. in the twenty-first century. You will learn about poverty, how it is measured, how it has changed, what may cause it, and some public policies aimed at reducing poverty. You will learn about the distribution of income and how it is measured, how it has changed, and what may cause it to have changed. You will also learn about some public policies that may be viewed as worthwhile if a more even distribution of income is desired. You will learn about the aging of the U.S. society and the implications the change in our demographics has for a number of government programs and their funding. You will also learn about some policy reform proposals designed to confront the economic problems presented by our aging society. You will also learn about government-funded health care programs and the costs and benefits associated with them. You will learn about the challenges of reforming the health care system.

II.   CHECKLIST

By the end of this chapter, you should be able to:

√   Explain what the four major economic challenges facing the U.S. are as outlined in your textbook.
√   Describe how the government defines who is considered to be "poor" or living in poverty.
√   Discuss some of the characteristics of the poor.
√   Offer some explanations for what causes poverty.
√   Discuss some of the major anti-poverty programs and the advantages and disadvantages of them.
√   Discuss some of the key changes to welfare programs that have commenced in 1997.
√   Define what an income distribution is.
√   Describe some characteristics about the U.S. distribution of income.
√   Offer some explanations for why the U.S. distribution of income has changed.
√   Discuss some public policies that might lead to a more equal distribution of income.
√   Discuss the problems the U.S. may confront as our society ages.
√   Explain how the social security system works and why it may not be sustainable.
√   Discuss some of the reform proposals that have been advanced for improving the future viability of the social security system.
√   Discuss two major problems with the U.S. health care system and what their proximate cause is.
√   Discuss the reform proposals that have been advanced for improving the health care system.

III.   KEY TERMS

family: a group of two or more individuals related by birth, marriage, or adoption who live in the same housing unit.
household: a group of related family members and unrelated individuals who live in the same housing unit.
poverty budget: the minimum amount the government estimates that a family needs to avoid being in poverty.
Aid for Family With Dependent Children (AFDC): a government poverty program that provides assistance to families with children under the age of 18.

201

Supplemental Security Income (SSI): a special program for the aged, the blind, and the permanently disabled.

Medicaid: a program that provides medical services to the poor.

Earned Income Tax Credit (EITC): a tax subsidy given to low-wage workers with children.

Social Security: a government program that provides retirement, survivor, and disability benefits

Medicare: the government program that provides health benefits to those over 65 years of age.

dependency ratio: the ratio of the population over 65 years of age to the population between 20 and 65.

social insurance: a system which compensates individuals for bad luck, low skills, or misfortune.

pay-as-you-go: retirement system that pays benefits to the old with taxes currently levied on the young.

managed competition: a health system in which organizations such as HMOs compete for patients.

IV.   PERFORMANCE ENHANCING TIPS (PETS)

PET #1

Debate over an economic problem may have three sources: (1) how the problem is defined; (2) how the problem is interpreted; and (3) solutions presented for dealing with the problem.

It is particularly important for you to consider the first two potential sources of debate before you argue for or against a solution to a problem. For example, you have learned that poverty is based on what a family's total income is relative to a government estimate of the "minimum" amount needed. For a two-person family, the government determined the minimum to be $9,414 in 1993. If you disagree with the government's figure (perhaps because of how they calculated it) and instead believe the figure is $7,000, you may end up concluding that poverty isn't as big a problem as that reported by the government. Secondly, even if you agree with the government's definition of who is classified as living in poverty, you may not agree with the interpretation of the problem. For example, suppose the government reports that 15.1% of the population lives below the poverty line. The government (or President of the U.S.) may deem this to be a major problem. You may disagree. You may think that 15.1% is a fairly small proportion of the overall population and, thus, may feel that there are other more pressing problems that the government should focus on. Thirdly, even if you agree with the government's method for measuring a problem and their interpretation of it, you may disagree with the current public policy for dealing with the problem or over the reforms that have been suggested.

As you can see, there are several points at which you and your classmates may debate. An understanding of at what points your views differ from those of your classmates will help clarify your discussion.

PET #2

Interpret statistics with care.

The best way to understand this PET is to look in your textbook at Table 1. The first column of Table 1 shows the number of people (in millions) who live in poverty across different categories for 1993. The second column of Table 1 shows the poverty rates for different categories of people for 1993. For example, for the entire U.S. population, 39.3 million lived below the poverty line in 1993. That is, 15.1% of the total U.S. population lived below the poverty line.

The table also shows that the poverty rate for blacks was 33.3%. What this means is that 33.3% *of the black population* (not of the population living below the poverty level) lived below the poverty line in 1993. In other words, it is not correct to say 33.3% of the 39.3 million people living in poverty were black. In fact, as the table shows, with 39.3 million living in poverty and 10.9 black, we could say that 27.7% [= (10.9/39.3) X 100] *of those living in poverty* were black. Likewise, the table shows that 10.4% of people with only a high school degree lived in poverty in 1993. It is not correct to say that 10.4% of the 39.3 million living in poverty had only completed a high school education. However, you could conclude that 15.3% [= (6.0/39.3) X 100] of those living in poverty have only a high school degree.

PET #3

The median and the average are not necessarily the same number.

Consider the following five observations on income:

Obs. #1; Obs. #2; Obs. #3; Obs. #4; Obs. #5
$20,000; $30,000; $10,000; $100,000; $40,000.

The average is computed as the sum of the numbers divided by the sample size. In this case, the sum is $200,000 and the sample size is 5. Thus, the average is $200,000/5 = $40,000. In this example, there is one observation with an income above the average; the remaining four observations are for incomes below the average.

The median is the number corresponding to the midpoint observation number in the sample (when the sample is ranked from lowest to highest or vice-versa).

First, the sample above must be ranked from lowest to highest income. Thus, we would have:

Obs. #1; Obs. #2; Obs. #3; Obs. #4; Obs. #5
$10,000; $20,000; $30,000; $40,000; $100,000.

In this case, the midpoint observation number is 3 (2 observations below it, 2 observations above it). The number corresponding to the midpoint observation number is $30,000. Thus, the median income is $30,000. In this sample, there are an equal number of incomes below $30,000 as there are above $30,000.

The example shows that an average is influenced by extreme high (or low) numbers whereas a median is not.

V.   PRACTICE EXAM: MULTIPLE CHOICE QUESTIONS

1.   According to the U.S. government, a poor family is one:

a.   whose total income plus wealth is less than the amount required to satisfy the family's "minimum needs."
b.   whose debts exceed the value of their assets.
c.   who has four or more dependents and only one working family member.
d.   whose total income is less than the amount required to satisfy the family's "minimum needs."

e.   who has no shelter, food, or clothing.

2.   Which one of the following is NOT true based on the numbers given:
        Persons in poverty = 40 million
        Total population = 240 million
        Persons under age 18 living in poverty = 16 million
        Persons with no high school diploma living in poverty = 8 million
        Total population under age 18 = 80 million
        Total population of persons with no high school diploma = 32 million

a.   16.7% of the population lives in poverty.
b.   40% of those living in poverty are under age 18.
c.   13.3% of the population does not have a high school diploma.
d.   33.3% of those under age 18 live in poverty.
e.   25% of those without a high school degree live in poverty.

3.   Which one of the following statements is NOT true based on statistics for the U.S. in 1993?

a.   the poverty rates for blacks and hispanics are over three times the white race.
b.   the poverty rate for single-parent families headed by women is over five times the rate of two-parent families.
c.   the poverty rate for the elderly has steadily increased since the 1960s.
d.   the poverty rate for high school dropouts is over eight times the rate of college graduates.
e.   about two thirds of poor households have at least one part-time worker.

4.   Which one of the following has NOT been offered as an explanation for poverty in the U.S.?

a.   technological innovation that has decreased the demand for low-skill workers.
b.   globalization has forced U.S. workers to compete with foreign workers for jobs.
c.   health problems.
d.   disabilities.
e.   all of the above.

5.   Which one of the following statements is true?

a.   AFDC payments are a fixed sum that do not decrease as the income of a poor family increases.
b.   the government spends more on non-cash programs for the poor than on cash assistance.
c.   Medicaid is a cash-assistance program provided to families with children.
d.   About three-quarters (75%) of AFDC recipients who are women spend 10 or more years in the program.
e.   The U.S. income redistribution system is more effective at reducing poverty than a number of other European nations.

6.   Which one of the following statements is NOT true of the U.S. welfare system?

a.   it tends to discourage able-bodied individuals from working.
b.   there is a lack of child support from absent fathers.
c.   the government provides one type of assistance in dealing with a range of problems.

d.   under the bill signed by President Clinton, lifetime welfare benefits would be limited to five years (with some exemptions).

e.   all of the above are true.

7.   Which one of the following statements is true? Assume statistics are for 1992.

a.   the average family income in the U.S. was $39,000.
b.   50% of the U.S. population earns $39,000.
c.   50% of the U.S. population earns less than $39,000.
d.   almost half of all of the income earned in the U.S. comes from those workers earning $39,000 or less.
e.   a family of four earning $39,000 income is defined as "poor."

8.   Which one of the following statements is true?

a.   technological change has increased the demand for college graduates and those with advanced degrees.
b.   the U.S. has a comparative advantage in production requiring high-skill labor.
c.   the wealthiest 1% of U.S. households own 40% of the nation's total wealth.
d.   the share of the nation's income earned by the top 20% of income earners has increased but has decreased for every other income-earning group.
e.   all of the above are correct.

9.   Which one of the following statements is NOT true?

a.   dependency ratios around the world have risen.
b.   the rise in the dependency ratio for the U.S. presents a potential problem for Social Security.
c.   Social Security is a save-as-you-go system.
d.   social security payments may be considered an "anti-poverty" program.
e.   the social security system is funded through a tax on employers and a tax on employees.

10.   Which one of the following statements is true of Social Security?

a.   it was put into place in 1945, at the end of World War II, to provide benefits to widows and orphans.
b.   100% of the civilian work force is covered by Social Security.
c.   Medicare is not part of the Social Security system.
d.   employers and employees contribute an equal dollar amount of taxes to the Social Security system.
e.   low-wage earners receive a lower percentage of their average lifetime wages than do high-wage earners.

11.   Which one of the following is offered as a method for funding social security in the future?

a.   higher taxes.
b.   cut benefits.
c.   privatize the social security system.
d.   invest payroll taxes in the stock market.
e.   all of the above.

12.   Which one of the following statements is true of the U.S. health care system?

a.   the share of GDP that the U.S. spends on health care has decreased dramatically since 1960.
b.   the marginal principle is typically violated in the health care industry because doctors base decisions on healing people, not on maximizing the profits of their practice.
c.   all individuals are covered by health insurance.
d.   traditional health insurance policies (not HMOs), because of their reimbursement features, do not create an incentive for patients and doctors to keep costs down.
e.   (b) and (d).

VI.   PRACTICE EXAM: ESSAY QUESTIONS

1.   Define poverty. Explain some causes of poverty. Discuss some of the U.S. programs that help reduce poverty.

2.   Discuss the problems with the U.S. system of health care and policy reform proposals that have been suggested. How does the aging of society play a role in the problems.

VII.   ANSWER KEY: MULTIPLE CHOICE QUESTIONS

1.   Correct answer: d.

Discussion: The U.S. government defines a family to be poor based on their income earnings (from working and from interest earned on financial investments) relative to an income level that is deemed necessary to must meet a family's "minimum needs." These minimum needs include, but are not limited to, food, shelter, and clothing.

Statement a is not correct because the wealth of a family is not (at least directly) considered. It is indirectly considered in that income earned from financial investment would obviously be larger for wealthier families. Statement b is not correct because income, not assets minus debts (or net worth), is considered. Statement c is not correct because the poor are not defined by how many dependents relative to working members there are in a family. Statement e is not correct although it may describe whom we consider to be poor.

2.   Correct answer: d.

Discussion: Statement d is not correct. There are 80 million people under the age of 18. Of that 80 million, 16 million of those live in poverty. The calculation is (16/80) X 100 = 20%. Thus, the correct answer is 20%.

Statement a is correct. The total population is 240 million, and 40 million of those live in poverty. The calculation is (40/240) X 100 = 16.7%. Statement b is correct. The number of people living in poverty is 40 million. Of those 40 million, 16 million are under the age of 18. The calculation is (16/40) X 100 = 40%. Statement c is correct. The total population is 240 million, and 32 million of this population do not have a high school diploma. The calculation is (32/240) X 100 = 13.3%. Statement e is correct. There are

32 million people without a high school degree. Of that 32 million, 8 million live in poverty. The calculation is (8/32) X 100 = 25%.

3.   Correct answer: c.

Discussion: The poverty rate for the elderly has actually decreased, not increased, since the 1960s. It has declined from 35% in 1959 to 12.2% in 1993.

4.   Correct answer: e.

Discussion: All of the above explain why some people live in poverty. Statements a and b have also been offered as explanations for the change in the income distribution in the U.S. since the early 1980s.

5.   Correct answer: b.

Discussion: Statement b is the only correct answer. The government spends more on non-cash programs like foodstamps, medicaid, and housing assistance. Medicaid, is by far, the biggest source of government spending on a non-cash program. You may wish to look at Table 2 of Chapter 19 of your text for reference.

Statement a is not true. In fact, AFDC payments to the poor decrease as the income of the poor increases. Statement c is not true. Medicaid is a **non**-cash assistance program. Statement d is not true. The correct figure is 25%. Statement e is not true. European nations are more effective at reducing poverty through their income redistribution schemes than the U.S. is.

6.   Correct answer: e.

Discussion: Statements a, b, and c refer to some of the problems encountered under the current U.S. welfare system. The payment schemes (except for, perhaps, the earned income tax credit) tend to make it more costly to work than to stay at home (perhaps with children) and receive government assistance. The inability to collect child support from absent fathers is also a problem. The cost of the program could be reduced if collection rates increased. Also, the government has a number of different programs but they are not designed to deal with different types of problems that cause families to be in poverty. Some people live in poverty only temporarily and need short-term assistance; some people live in poverty because of a lack of skills or education and, thus, would benefit from education and training programs. Some people live in poverty because of disabilities or poor physical or mental health. This group of people may require longer-term assistance from the government.

The new welfare bill signed by President Clinton imposes lifetime limit of 5 years of welfare benefits. In addition, much of the control over welfare is given back to the states who will receive block grants (sums of money) from the federal government to spend on the welfare programs of their choice.

7.   Correct answer: a.

Discussion: The average family income in the U.S. was $39,000. This statistic, however, tells you nothing about the "distribution of income." That is, many people earn substantially more than $39,000 and many people earn substantially less than $39,000.

Statement b is not correct. The fact that the average income is $39,000 does not mean that 50% of the population earns $39,000. Statements c and d are not correct. Table 3 (which shows income ranges for groupings of 20% of the population) reveals that 40% of the working population (2 X 20%) earns collectively 14.3% (4.2% + 10.1%) of all of the income generated by the working population. Statement e is not correct. A family of four earning $14,763 (as your book states) would be considered "poor."

8.   Correct answer: e.

Discussion: Statement a can be used to explain not only the change in the income distribution but also why the percentage of college graduates living in poverty is very low compared to hose with a high school degree or those who do not have a high school diploma. The comparative advantage the U.S. has in production requiring high-skill labor means that low-skill labor may face increased competition for jobs from workers around the globe. The U.S. stratification of wealth ownership is very extreme compared to other industrialized nations. Statement d is a comment about how the income distribution has changed in the U.S.

9.   Correct answer: c.

Discussion: Statement c is incorrect; the social security system is a "pay-as-you-go" system. This means that people who pay into it now, while they are working, will receive retirement benefits not based on what they have put into the system, but on what workers in the future will pay into the system.

Statement a is correct. The dependency ratio is the ratio of the population over 65 years of age to the population between 20 and 65. These ratios have risen around the world. Statement b is correct because the rise in dependency ratios means that there will be a higher proportion of people collecting social security benefits relative to those of working age than in the past. Since the social security system is a pay-as-you-go system, the ability to fund retirees at the rate they are currently being funded may be impaired. Statement d is correct since social security benefits are paid to retirees (thereby helping to alleviate poverty of the elderly), as well as to families of a deceased worker and those with disabilities. It also redistributes income in the sense that the benefits paid to low-income earning retirees are proportionately higher than to high-income earning retirees. Statement e is correct. Both employers and employees contribute in equal amount to the social security system through a payroll tax.

10.   Correct answer: d.

Discussion: Statement d is the only correct answer. Statement a is not correct; social security was put into effect in 1935 after the Great Depression. Statement b is not correct. There are some workers who are not covered by social security (about 8% are not covered). Statement c is not correct. Medicare is actually part of the social security system. It is health coverage for the elderly. Statement e is not correct; the social security system is redistributive which means that, upon retirement, low-wage earners receive a higher percentage of their average life-time wages in social security than do high-wage earners.

11.   Correct answer: e.

Discussion: All of the above have been discussed. Of course, different proposals are favored and opposed by different groups of people. Current workers today would probably not be in favor of higher taxes since they would have to pay them. They may prefer cutting benefits instead. The reverse would be true for those receiving benefits. Some feel that privatization of the social security system is the best option since social security is a form of saving; each worker should decide for him- or herself how much to save for their future. Some feel that investing payroll taxes in the stock market is risky since the value of stocks are so volatile. For example, suppose you retire in a year when the price of stocks has dropped considerably. The social security benefit that you receive could then be adversely affected.

12.   Correct answer: e.

Discussion: Statement b is true and is one reason why the cost of health care has risen dramatically. Statement d is also correct. If patients know that their insurance policies will pay for any procedures that they themselves cannot pay for, they have no incentive to avoid costly (potentially unnecessary) procedures. Since doctors know that they will be reimbursed by insurance companies for any procedures they may do, they too, have an incentive to order the most expensive, but sometimes unnecessary procedures.

Statement a is not correct; the share of U.S. GDP that is attributed to health care has increased dramatically, not decreased. Statement c is not correct. One of the problems with the current health care system is that not all persons are covered. One proposal has been to provide government mandated "universal" coverage so that everybody in the U.S. is covered by a health insurance policy. This would mean, in effect, that insurance companies could not deny coverage to "high risk" (and, therefore, potentially costly) individuals.

VIII. ANSWER KEY: ESSAY QUESTIONS

1.   Poverty is defined with respect to family size and income earnings relative to a minimum income level established by the government. The minimum income level is based on an income that would satisfy a family's "minimum needs." The income level is actually estimated by computing what a family's minimum food budget would be. This figure is then multiplied by 3 to arrive at an income level used to define who is and who is not living in poverty. For example, for a four-person family, the "poverty budget" is $14,763. Four-person families with an income above $14,763 are not considered to be poor while those four-person families with income at or below $14,763 are defined as "poor."

Poverty has many causes. An obvious answer to what causes poverty would simply be to say that it is caused by not working (or not working enough). Without a job, and therefore, without an income, an individual cannot provide for him- or herself (or their family) which is what leads to poverty. However, a deeper answer needs to examine what causes individuals to be out of work or to lack the earning power necessary to keep them out of poverty. Thus, some explain poverty as a result of a lack of education (and, therefore, skills). A minimum wage earner, who typically has little education and low skills, that is providing for a family of four, may not be able to produce an income above the poverty line. Some explain poverty based on poor health (physical or mental) or disabilities. These workers have difficulty finding or maintaining employment and consequently end up without a reasonable and stable source of income. Another explanation for poverty is that some people are limited in their ability to work because of family commitments -- raising children or caring for a sick or disabled family member.

There are numerous government programs that help to reduce poverty, either explicitly through cash or non-cash assistance, or through education and training. The social security system, of which Medicare is a part, can be thought of as an anti-poverty program, particularly for the elderly, as it guarantees a certain dollar-benefit every month. Aid to Families with Dependent Children (AFDC) is a cash-assistance program that is explicitly aimed at the poor. The earned-income-tax-credit is a redistributive arm of the U.S. tax system aimed at giving generous tax refunds to the working poor. The government also provides health coverage (through Medicaid), housing assistance and food stamps (non-cash programs) to the poor. In addition to these programs that are explicitly aimed at the poor, there are worker retraining programs, unemployment compensation plans, financial assistance for education (student loans), etc., which may indirectly help to alleviate the sources of poverty.

2.   The U.S. system of health care is considered to be problematic largely because of the rising costs of health care -- increases in the price of health care outpace price increases in just about every other industrial sector. And, there seems to be no slowing down. Also, as the price of health care and health insurance rise, it will be more difficult for individuals to pay for their own health care needs and health insurance policies. This means that a rising proportion of the population may not be able to pay for health insurance. However, when individuals can't pay for health insurance, the government typically ends up footing the bill. In general, doctors do not deny access to health care because an individual cannot pay. Doctors provide their services and then attempt to collect their fee from the government. Thus, health care may be a potentially costly component of government spending. Indeed, government spending for health coverage for the poor (Medicaid) was $118 billion in 1994 as Table 2 of Chapter 19 of your textbook shows. This spending is nearly 5 times the total spent on food stamps and housing assistance combined. The aging of the U.S. society also elevates the potential cost of funding government health care. As more and more citizens reach the age of 65, they have access to Medicare. However, as more and more people become eligible for Medicare, government spending for it will likely rise. Given that Medicare benefits are part of the social security system and the fact that dependency ratios are rising, the ability to fund Medicare in the future may be severely strained.

There is an opportunity cost to the rising level of government spending on health care. For a given source of tax revenue, the government will be forced to cut other government programs in order to fund health care. Alternatively, and still an opportunity cost to consider, the government may increase taxes so that it has more revenue to spend on health care and yet be able to maintain the current level of funding of other programs.

There are several reform measures that have been suggested. Some of the reform measures are aimed at controlling the costs of health care (which will in turn, help reduce the government funding needs of it in the future). The emergence of health maintenance organizations has been one reform. HMOs are set up with an objective of providing quality care while at the same time containing health care costs. Another proposal has been to introduce HMOs to Medicare. Currently, Medicare operates under the traditional doctor-patient-insurance billing system. The introduction of HMOs may help contain health care costs for the elderly. Mandated universal health coverage has also been proposed as a way of reducing government's ultimate responsibility for providing health care for those who cannot pay. Another reform proposal has been to establish an institute that assesses whether the marginal benefit of a new medical technology is greater than the cost of it. This reform proposal is aimed at reducing health care costs by introducing medical technologies that create a net benefit (marginal benefit > marginal cost) to society.

Take It to the Net

We invite you to visit the O'Sullivan/Sheffrin page on the Prentice Hall Web site at:

http://www.prenhall.com/osullivan/

for this chapter's World Wide Web exercise.

CHAPTER 20
THE BIG IDEAS IN MACROECONOMICS

I.   OVERVIEW

In this chapter, you will be introduced to a branch of economics called "macroeconomics." You will learn about many of the national statistics used in reporting on the state of the U.S. economy. You will learn how these statistics are constructed and what they mean. You will learn about Gross Domestic Product (GDP), inflation, unemployment, labor productivity, and economic fluctuations (or the business cycle). You will learn what a recession and depression are and how frequently the U.S. has suffered them. You will learn about different types of unemployment and the problems they present for the economy. You will learn how economic growth is measured. You will learn about two schools of thought in macroeconomics -- Classical Thought and Keynesianism.

II.   CHECKLIST

By the end of this chapter, you should be able to:

√   Explain what the study of macroeconomics is.
√   Define gross domestic product (GDP).
√   Explain what types of goods and services would be included in the computation of GDP and which would not.
√   Explain the difference between real and nominal GDP and which measure is used for assessing economic growth.
√   Calculate a growth rate.
√   Use a growth rate to compute the value of GDP after X number of years.
√   Use the Rule of 70 to calculate the time it takes for some variable to double.
√   Define labor productivity and describe what has happened to it since the 1970s.
√   Define a recession and a depression.
√   Explain how the unemployment rate is calculated.
√   Define the labor force.
√   Explain who would be considered unemployed.
√   Describe the different types of unemployment and their causes.
√   Define the natural rate of unemployment and "full employment."
√   Define inflation and deflation.
√   Explain the focus of Classical economics and Keynesian economics.

III.   KEY TERMS

Macroeconomics: the branch of economics that looks at the economy as a whole.
Gross Domestic Product: the total market value of all the final goods and services produced within an economy in a given year.
Intermediate goods: goods used in the production process that are not final goods or services.
Real GDP: a measure of GDP that controls for changes in prices.
Nominal GDP: the value of GDP in current dollars.
Economic growth: sustained increases in the real production of an economy over a period of time.

Growth rate: the percentage rate of change of a variable.
Labor productivity: the amount of output produced per worker.
Recession: six consecutive months of negative economic growth.
Peak: the time at which a recession begins.
Trough: the time at which output stops falling in a recession.
Depression: the common name for a severe recession.
Unemployed: individuals who are looking for work but do not have jobs.
Labor force: the employed plus the unemployed.
Unemployment rate: the fraction of the labor force that is unemployed.
Cyclical unemployment: the component of unemployment that accompanies fluctuations in real GDP.
Frictional unemployment: the part of unemployment associated with the normal workings of the economy such as searching for jobs.
Structural unemployment: the part of unemployment that results from the mismatch of skills and jobs.
Natural rate of unemployment: the level of unemployment at which there is no cyclical unemployment.
Full employment: the level of employment that occurs when the unemployment rate is at the natural rate.
Price level: an average of all the prices in the economy
Chain-type price index for GDP: a measure of the average level of prices of the goods and services contained in GDP.
Inflation: the rate of change of the price level in the economy.
Classical Economics: the study of the economy when it operates at or near full employment.
Keynesian Economics: the study of business cycles and economic fluctuations.

IV.   PERFORMANCE ENHANCING TIPS

PET #1

Nominal GDP will increase because of an increase in the price level and/or because of an increase in output (production). Real GDP will increase because of an increase in output (production).

Nominal GDP is the "market value" or "current-dollar" (today's prices) measure of the amount of output an economy in total produced over a given time period (usually a year). If prices rise, without any increase in the amount of output produced, nominal GDP will increase. Such an increase, however, should in no way be construed as economic growth since output did not grow at all.

To make an analogy, suppose you are the financial analyst for a particular firm and you observe that its revenue has increased. The firm's revenue may have increased either because (1) the price at which the firm sells its output has increased; (2) the firm sold more output (while there was no increase in price); or (3) some combination of the two.

The same is true of nominal GDP. However, economic analysts and policymakers are interested in what has happened to output exclusively. This is because an increase in output typically means that more people were employed and/or that labor was more productive and this is good news for the economy. Nominal GDP unfortunately isn't an accurate picture of what has happened to output because a change in nominal GDP is influenced by what has happened to prices as well as production. Real GDP, which takes out the effects of price changes on nominal GDP, gives a more accurate picture of what has happened to production.

PET #2

Economic growth is measured by the percentage change in real GDP, not by the percentage change in nominal GDP.

Suppose you calculate the growth rate of real GDP to be 3.2% and the growth rate of nominal GDP to be 6%. Which measure is appropriate to evaluate economic growth, and what can you infer about inflation?

The appropriate measure of economic growth is the rate of change in real GDP. In this case, we would say that the economy grew by 3.2%. Since nominal GDP increased by 6%, we could infer that the inflation rate was roughly 2.8% (= 6% - 3.2%). We should not say that the economy grew by 6%.

PET #3

To be considered unemployed, an individual must be 16 years or older, have actively sought paid employment in the last four weeks, and must not be employed in a part-time job.

The government's definition about who is considered unemployed is very specific. Several pre-conditions must be satisfied before the government identifies an individual as unemployed. First, the individual must be 16 years or older. Second, the individual must have *actively* sought *paid* employment in the last *four* weeks. That is, if an individual does nothing but read the newspaper want ads in search of a job, the government would not consider this person unemployed. The individual would be classified as "not part of the labor force." In other words, the individual may not have a job but his or her actions signal they don't care to work. An individual must also have sought paid employment. For example, an individual that does not have a job and applies for a position as a volunteer at a hospital would not be considered unemployed (nor as part of the labor force). Finally, an individual must have looked for a job in the last four weeks. That is, if it's been two months since an individual has actively searched for a job, that individual would not be classified as "unemployed" by the government. The government would classify that individual as not part of the labor force. Finally, if an individual has a part-time job, even if it is a job the individual doesn't want to be doing or is planning on leaving, the government would, in this case, classify the individual as "employed."

PET #4

To be considered part of the labor force, an individual must either have a paying job (full-time or part-time) or have actively sought paid employment in the last four weeks.

This PET tells you that the labor force consists of those individuals with jobs (the employed) and those individuals who do not have a job but who would like to work if they could (the "unemployed").

PET #5

The Rule of 70 can be used to determine either the time periods it will take for a variable to double or the growth rate necessary for a variable to double in X time periods.

Your book uses the Rule of 70 in discussing economic growth, but it has many other applications as well. Suppose you decide that you would like to see your salary double in 10 years. What percentage raise must you get each year in order to achieve your goal? Using the Rule of 70, you would divide 70 by the number of years over which you have set your goal. The growth rate necessary for you to realize your goal is 7% (70/10) **each** year. Let's look at another example. Suppose that you invest $1,000 into a certificate of deposit that carries an interest rate (growth rate of your money) of 5% a year. How many years will it take for your investment's value to double? Using the Rule of 70, you would divide 70 by the growth rate. Thus, you would find that it would take 14 years (70/5) = 14 years for your investment to double, i.e., increase to $2,000.

One word of caution: if the growth rate is stated on a monthly or quarterly basis, the time period to double should be stated in monthly or quarterly terms (instead of yearly) as well. For example, suppose the government reported that they expected real GDP to grow at 2% each quarter. Using the Rule of 70, at that growth rate, it would take 70/2 = 35 quarters for real GDP to double. Thirty-five quarters is 8.75 years.

V.   PRACTICE EXAM: MULTIPLE CHOICE QUESTIONS

1.   Which one of the following would NOT be considered a macroeconomic issue?

a.   inflation.
b.   economic growth.
c.   international trade.
d.   national unemployment.
e.   consumer behavior.

2.   The author of *The General Theory of Employment, Interest, and Money* was:

a.   John Maynard Keynes.
b.   Leon Walras.
c.   Adam Smith.
d.   Milton Friedman.
e.   David Ricardo.

3.   The output of an economy is called:

a.   market goods.
b.   gross domestic product.
c.   national volume.
d.   the net balance.
e.   national product.

4.   GDP is the total market value of:

a.   all final goods and services exchanged in an economy in a given year.
b.   all goods and services purchased by households in a given year.
c.   all final goods and services produced within an economy since 1900.
d.   all final goods and services produced by an economy in a given year.
e.   intermediate and final goods produced in a given year.

5.   Which one of the following would NOT be included in current GDP?

a.   the purchase of a new jetski.
b.   services rendered by a financial planner.
c.   a trip to Hilton Head.
d.   the purchase of a two-year-old used set of Ping golf clubs.
e.   the purchase of flour by a househusband or housewife.

6.   The most common measure of economic growth is:

a.   changes in real GDP because only changes in output are measured.
b.   changes in nominal GDP because it considers changes in both output and prices.
c.   changes in the consumer price index because it measures changes in the income of a typical family of four.
d.   changes in the chain-type price index because it measures the ability of the economy to respond to higher costs of production.
e.   changes in labor productivity since it measures whether workers' standard of living is changing.

7.   Suppose the economy was expected to grow at 4% a year for the next five years. If GDP this year is $100 billion, what will it be at the end of five years?

a. $120 billion.
b. $121.67 billion.
c. $104 billion.
d. $537.82 billion.
e. $305.18 billion.

8.   Suppose that you would like to see your salary double in ten years. What must the growth rate of your salary be each year in order for you to achieve your goal?

a.   7%.
b.   1.7%.
c.   1.4%.
d.   10%.
e.   14%.

9.   Labor productivity depends on the amount of _____ an economy has.

a.   machines
b.   buildings (or factories)
c.   equipment
d.   technology
e.   all of the above.

10.   Which one of the following defines a "recession"?

a.   a one-year decline in real GDP.
b.   a protracted period of low economic growth.
c.   a two-quarter decline in real GDP.

d.   a growth rate of real GDP that is negative.
e.   the movement of real GDP from trough to peak.

11.   Which one of the following statements is true?

a.   during the Great Depression, the unemployment rate reached 25%.
b.   the unemployment rate is calculated as the number of unemployed individuals/labor force.
c.   the labor force is equal to a country's population.
d.   (a) and (b).
e.   (a), (b), and (c).

12.   Which one of the following is an example of a frictionally unemployed individual?

a.   J. Martin, who lacks the skills necessary to be employed.
b.   Lee, who lost his job as an art director because of a recession.
c.   Jan, who has a Ph.D. in economics but is a bus driver.
d.   Helena, who has just graduated from college and is searching for a job as an architect.
e.   none of the above.

13.   Which one of the following statements is NOT correct?

a.   the natural rate of unemployment is estimated to be 5 - 6.5% in the U.S.
b.   the term "full employment" means that 100% of the labor force is employed.
c.   an inflation rate of 5% may arise even if some prices are falling.
d.   inflation is the percentage change in the price level.
e.   deflation occurs when the price level declines.

14.   Keynesian economics is concerned with:

a.   business cycles or economic fluctuations.
b.   the behavior of the economy when it operates at full employment.
c.   long run economic growth.
d.   hyperinflation.
e.   real analysis.

VI.   PRACTICE EXAM: ESSAY QUESTIONS

1.   Suppose you are an economic advisor to a tiny island country that produces only volleyballs. As part of your job, you must help the president of the island prepare the "State of the Island" address. In the first quarter of 1997, you find that island produced a market value (or current dollar value) of $1,000,000 volleyballs. In the second quarter of 1997, the island produced a market value of $1,200,000 of volleyballs. Furthermore, your statistics tell you that **annual** inflation for the tiny island country from the first quarter to the second quarter of 1997 was 80%. What would you tell your president to report in her "State of the Island" address?

2.   Describe the different types of unemployment and discuss which type may be most problematic for a country.

VII.   ANSWER KEY: MULTIPLE CHOICE QUESTIONS

1.   Correct answer: e.

Discussion: Consumer behavior is an issue studied in microeconomics.   Statements a-d are all macroeconomic issues.

2.   Correct answer: a.

Discussion: John Maynard Keynes is also considered the father of Keynesian economics. He wrote during a period when Britain and the U.S. were suffering severe economic downturns.

Leon Walras is known for "general equilibrium analysis." Adam Smith is known for his book *The Wealth of Nations* and for espousing the "invisible hand." Milton Friedman is an economist who won the Nobel Prize in Economics in 1976. He is best known for "monetarism." David Ricardo is best known for his theory of comparative advantage as a basis for mutually beneficial free trade.

3.   Correct answer: b.

Discussion: No discussion necessary.

4.   Correct answer: d.

Discussion: GDP is the total market value of all **final** goods **and** services **produced** within an economy **in a given year**. The terms that are bolded in the sentence are important to the definition.

Statement a is not correct because GDP is a measure of what is produced, not what is sold, in a given year. There may be goods sold in a given year, that were produced in a prior year. These goods would be "used goods" and should not be part of current year GDP. Statement b is not correct because GDP is the purchase of final (for end use) goods and services. Households and businesses purchase goods and services for end use. For example, a business may use an airline for business travel. Statement c is not correct because GDP is the value of what is produced in a particular (or given) year. It is not the sum of the value of production since the turn of the century. Statement e is not correct because GDP does not include the market value of intermediate goods (such as plastics used in auto production or wood used in furniture).

5.   Correct answer: d.

Discussion: GDP is measure of the value of goods and services produced in a given year. Since the golf clubs are used, they were produced two years ago and hence should not be included in current GDP.

Statements a, b, c, and e are all examples of either goods or services purchased for "end use." In other words, they are "final" goods or services.

6.   Correct answer: a.

Discussion: Economic growth is measured as the percentage change in **real** GDP, typically reported on an annualized basis. Real GDP takes out the effects of price changes on nominal GDP. (See PET #1 of this chapter for review.)

Statement b is not correct because nominal GDP is influenced by not only changes in output (production) but changes in prices as well. Changes in prices do not reflect economic growth and so should not be considered. This last sentence also means that statements c and d are not correct. Statement e is not correct although labor productivity and economic growth are related.

7.   Correct answer: b.

Discussion. The formula to use is GDP in year n = current GDP X $(1 + \text{growth rate})^n$. Thus, GDP after five years will be $100 billion X $(1.04)^5$ = $100 billion X 1.2167 = $121.67 billion. Based on this, none of the other statements are correct.

If you used $100 billion X (1.40), you would incorrectly get $537.82 billion.

8.   Correct answer: a.

Discussion: You must use the Rule of 70 to arrive at the answer. The Rule of 70 is: Number of years to Double = 70/growth rate. Since you know the number of years to double is ten years, you have 10 = 70/growth rate. Thus, the growth rate must be 7% in order for your goal to be achieved.

9.   Correct answer: e.

Discussion: The productivity of labor (how much output each worker is able to produce over a given time period) is affected by the amount (including quality and age) of machines that the workers use; by the building or factory (including quality and age) that workers work in; by the equipment they have to work with (tools, computers, fax machines, etc); and by the state of technology.

10.   Correct answer: c.

Discussion: A recession is a two-quarter (or six month) decline in real GDP. This also means that economic growth would be negative for two quarters.

Statement a is not correct because a recession is a two-quarter decline in real GDP, not a one-year decline. Statement b is not correct. Low (but positive) economic growth does not define a recession. Statement d is not correct because it needs a qualifier on how many quarters there was negative growth. For example, a one-quarter negative growth rate would not constitute a recession. Statement e is not correct because a movement from trough to peak would define an economic expansion.

11.   Correct answer: d.

Discussion: Unbelievable as it may seem, the unemployment rate was 25% meaning that one-fourth of the nation's labor force was unemployed during the Great Depression. That statistic is very high by historical standards and fortunately, the U.S. has not experienced unemployment like that since the Great Depression. It should be mentioned that by 1940 (11 years after the Great Depression commenced), the unemployment rate was 17% which is still rather high by post-World War II standards. Statement b is the calculation used by the government to measure the unemployment rate.

Statement c (and therefore statement e) is not correct. A nation's labor force is not equal to its population. If it were, infants would be considered unemployed!

12.   Correct answer: d.

Discussion: A frictionally unemployed individual is someone who has either newly entered the labor market in search of a job, re-entered the labor market after an absence (perhaps to raise a child) in search of a job, or left their job in search of another job. Thus, Helena would be considered a new entrant into the labor market. She is frictionally unemployed because she has yet to find a job.

Statement a is an example of a structurally unemployed individual. Statement b is an example of a cyclically unemployed individual. Statement c is an example of an individual who has a job, albeit a job for which her skills are above those necessary to perform the job.

13.   Correct answer: b.

Discussion: The term "full employment" allows for there to be frictional and structural unemployment. Some unemployment is always to be expected in the natural functioning of an economy. Thus, 100% of the labor force will not typically be employed. This is a way of saying that there will always be some "natural unemployment" in an economy. The current estimate of the natural unemployment rate for the U.S. is 5 - 6.5%.

Statement c is a correct statement because inflation measures what happens to the average level of prices. Since the price level is an average of prices of all different types of goods and services, it may turn out that some prices have actually fallen while other have risen in such a way that, on average, the price level may rise by 5%. Statement d is correct. A decline in the price level is referred to as "deflation."

14.   Correct answer: a.

Discussion: Keynesian economics is concerned not only with business cycles or economic fluctuations, but with the behavior of the economy when it operates at a level well below full employment. Since Keynesian economics is the study of economic fluctuations, it focuses on short run changes in real GDP and not long run economic growth.

VIII.   ANSWER KEY: ESSAY QUESTIONS

1.   First of all, the figures on the market value of output are in current dollars and thus are measures of the island's **nominal** GDP. The growth rate in nominal GDP between the first and second quarter is [($200,000)/$1,000,000] X 100 = 20%. The 20% figure, if annualized as is common for reporting of GDP growth rates, would be 20% X 4 = 80%. So, on an annualized basis, nominal GDP has increased by 80%. However, nominal GDP can increase because (1) output (production of volleyballs) has increased, (2) the price of volleyballs has increased, or (3) some combination of the two. Since inflation (increase in prices) does not constitute economic growth, the growth rate in nominal GDP should not be used to assess whether or not the economy has grown. The effects of higher prices on the nominal GDP growth rate must be taken

out. Since you also know that inflation, on an annualized basis, for your country was 80% between the first and second quarter of 1997, you can infer what has happened to the growth rate of output (real GDP). The growth rate of real GDP can be roughly measured as the difference between the growth rate of nominal GDP and the inflation rate. Thus, you would report that the growth rate in real GDP for the island was 0%. So, you would tell the president to sadly report that the economy did not grow. Moreover, the economy suffered double-digit inflation on the order of 80% on an annualized basis (or 20% = (80%/4) on a quarterly basis.)

2.   The three types of unemployment are cyclical, frictional, and structural. The sum of the three is the unemployment rate. The sum of the frictional and structural unemployment rates is called the "natural rate of unemployment." Cyclical unemployment is caused by the ups and downs of the economy. Sometimes the economy booms and sometimes it goes into a recession. People who lose their jobs because the economy goes into a recession are categorized as cyclically unemployed. It is presumed that once the economy comes out of the recession, these people will be re-employed. Cyclical unemployment is of a fairly short-term nature, particularly in comparison to structural unemployment. Frictional unemployment occurs as people re-enter the labor force or enter the labor force for the first time (say, upon graduation from high school or college). These people may be unemployed for a time as they search for a job to which their skills are matched. Frictional unemployment also arises because people leave their jobs in search of another job -- perhaps a better paying one or one that is more satisfying. Frictional unemployment is also of a fairly short-term nature, particularly in comparison to structural unemployment. New entrants, re-entrants, and job switchers are part of a natural functioning economy. There will always be, at any point in time, these types of people looking for jobs. In other words, we should not expect that the frictional unemployment rate could be pushed to 0%. The third type of unemployment is structural unemployment. Structural unemployment occurs because of a mismatch between the skills a worker possesses and the skills necessary to obtain a job. Structural unemployment is of a longer-term nature. The structurally unemployed tend to have a more difficult time finding work and may even require retraining or new skills in order to find work. Structural unemployment is also a natural part of the economy in the sense that the structure of the economy changes over time and so, too, the demand for different types of workers. For example, the U.S. economy has become a more high-tech economy and the service industry has grown as an employer relative to the manufacturing industry. This structural change in the economy leads to unemployment in pockets of industry across the nation that are outmoded.

Take It to the Net

We invite you to visit the O'Sullivan/Sheffrin page on the Prentice Hall Web site at:

http://www.prenhall.com/osullivan/

for this chapter's World Wide Web exercise.

CHAPTER 21
BEHIND THE ECONOMIC STATISTICS

I.   OVERVIEW

In this chapter, you will learn about how the statistics discussed in the previous chapter -- GDP, the unemployment rate, and the inflation rate are measured. You will see that these statistics may not always portray the most accurate picture of the state of the economy. You will learn that limitations to these statistics are caused by the difficulties in accurately measuring national output, prices around the country, and who exactly is unemployed. You will be re-introduced to the circular flow diagram which shows how the product market is related to the factor market. You will see that gross domestic product (GDP) and national income are closely related measures.   You will learn how the government calculates real GDP and the chain-type price index. You will learn how the government compiles information on the unemployed. You will learn about "discouraged workers" and the "underemployed." You will learn how the government compiles information on the consumer price index (CPI) and how this measure of the price level differs from the chain-type price index. You will learn why the percentage change in the CPI may overstate inflation You will learn how to compute a growth factor and see it used in real GDP and chain-type price construction.

II.   CHECKLIST

By the end of this chapter, you should be able to:

√   Describe the four main categories of purchasers of GDP.
√   Discuss the subcategories of consumption expenditures, private investment expenditures, government expenditures, and net exports.
√   Define depreciation.
√   Define transfer payments and explain why they are not considered a government purchase of GDP.
√   Explain why imports are subtracted from purchases of GDP and exports are added to purchases of GDP.
√   Define a trade deficit and explain how it relates to foreigners purchases of U.S. assets.
√   Explain the relationship between GDP and GNP.
√   Describe the five main categories of national income.
√   Define personal income and personal disposable income.
√   Explain the limitations of GDP (what it does not measure) and explain whether or not these limitations lead to an over or underestimate of GDP.
√   Define the labor force participation rate and distinguish it from the unemployment rate.
√   Define a discouraged worker and address whether or not a discouraged worker is considered unemployed.
√   Define an underemployed worker and address whether or not an underemployed worker is considered unemployed.
√   Compute a growth factor for real GDP or the chain-type price index.
√   Define the consumer price index and compare it to the chain-type price index.
√   Explain why and by how much it is believed that the percentage change in the CPI overstates inflation.
√   Explain some consequences of overstating the rate of inflation.

III.   KEY TERMS

Capital: the buildings, machines, and equipment used in production.

Factors of Production: labor and capital used to produce output.

Consumption expenditures: purchases of newly produced goods and services by households.

Non-Durable goods: goods that last for short periods of time, such as food.

Durable goods: goods that last for a long period of time, such as household appliances.

Services: reflect work done in which individuals play a prominent role in delivery and range from haircutting to health care.

Investment expenditures: purchases of newly produced goods and services by firms.

Depreciation: the wear and tear of capital as it is used in production.

Gross investment: actual investment purchases.

Net investment is gross investment minus depreciation.

Government purchases: purchases of final goods and services by all levels of government.

Net exports: exports minus imports.

Trade surplus: another name for net exports or exports minus imports.

Trade deficit: negative net exports or imports minus exports.

Transfer payments: payments to individuals from governments that do not correspond to the production of goods and services.

Gross National Product (GNP): GDP plus net income earned abroad.

Net National Product: GNP less depreciation.

Indirect taxes : sales and excise taxes.

National Income: Net National Product less indirect taxes.

Value-added: the sum of all the income (wages, interest, profits, rent) generated by an organization.

Personal income: income (including transfer payments) that is received by households.

Personal disposable income is personal income after taxes.

Underground economy : economic activity that should be in the GDP accounts but does not show up because the activity is either illegal or unreported.

Discouraged workers : workers who left the labor force because they could not find jobs.

Underemployed: workers who hold a part-time job but prefer to work full time or hold jobs that are far below their own capabilities.

Labor force participation rate: the fraction of the population over sixteen years of age that is in the labor force.

Growth Factor: one plus the growth rate

Consumer Price Index (CPI): a price index that measures the cost of a fixed basket of goods chosen to represent the consumption pattern of individuals.

Chain index: a method for calculating the growth in real GDP or the chain-type price index for GDP that uses data from neighboring years.

Cost of living adjustments: automatic increases in wages or other payments that are tied to a price index.

IV.   PERFORMANCE ENHANCING TIPS

PET #1

The expenditure approach to measuring U.S. GDP is to sum up the purchases, whether purchases of U.S.- or foreign-produced goods and services, by U.S. consumers (or "households"), businesses and the government, add expenditures by foreign residents on goods and services produced in the U.S (exports of the U.S.) and subtract expenditures by U.S. consumers, businesses, and the government on foreign-produced goods and services (imports of the U.S.).

Your professor may write it as:

GDP = C + I + G + EX - IM

where:

C = consumption expenditures by households on goods and services whether produced domestically or abroad.

I = gross investment expenditures by firms. This is primarily spending on plant and equipment, whether produced domestically or abroad.

G = government expenditures on goods and services, whether produced domestically or abroad.

EX = exports.

IM = imports.

PET #2

An increase in businesses' inventories reflects production that took place in the current year and should be added to GDP, even though the output was not purchased. A decrease in businesses inventories reflects purchases of output that was produced in a prior year and should be subtracted from GDP.

PET #3

Net investment that is positive is the addition to a nation's stock of capital above and beyond its current level. Net investment that is zero means that a nation's stock of capital is neither increasing nor decreasing beyond its current level. Net investment that is negative means that a nation is not investing enough to replace capital that is being worn out.

To illustrate the difference between gross investment and net investment, consider the stock of shoes that you currently have. Suppose you have 10 pairs of shoes. Over the course of the year, 3 of the pairs wear out (depreciate) and are no longer any good. If you buy 7 more pairs of shoes that year, your gross investment in shoes is 7 pairs. However, because you are replacing 3 pairs that have worn out, your net investment in shoes is 4 pairs. That is, at the end of the year, you will now have 14 pairs of shoes. You have, on net, added 4 (7-3) pairs to the stock of 10 pairs of shoes that you started out with.

Suppose instead that you bought 3 pairs of shoes that year. While three pairs would be your gross investment, your net investment would be zero. You have only replaced what you have worn out. Thus, you are no better off at the end of the year since your stock of shoes remains at 10 pairs.

Now, suppose that you bought 1 pair of shoes that year. While three pairs would be your gross investment, your net investment would be -2 (1-3). You have not invested enough to replace the 3 pairs of shoes worn out. Thus, your stock of shoes will decline from 10 pairs to 8 pairs.

The same is true for a country. A country whose net investment is zero will not be adding to its capital stock; a country that is not replacing its worn-out capital will see its capital stock shrink. As you will see in later chapters, this can have implications for the rate of growth an economy will be able to achieve.

PET #4

Government purchases of GDP is government spending on goods and services for which there was productive effort. Thus, government spending on transfer payments (e.g., social security, unemployment compensation) and interest on the national debt are not part of the government purchases included in GDP.

While your textbook makes this PET quite clear, it is worth repeating.

PET #5

A country that runs a trade deficit (the value of imports is greater than the value of exports) is on net borrowing from foreigners. A country that runs a trade surplus (the value of exports is greater than the value of imports) is on net lending to foreigners.

For example, suppose the U.S. has a trade deficit of $100 billion. This means that the U.S. is not earning enough foreign currency on its exports to cover payments in foreign currency on its imports. Where can the U.S. get the extra $100 billion in foreign currency to cover the trade deficit? The U.S. must borrow the funds from foreigners (i.e., foreigners lend foreign currency to the U.S). Since residents of the U.S. can also lend to foreigners, we say that the trade deficit implies that the U.S. is borrowing $100 billion more from foreigners than it is lending to them. In other words, on net the U.S. is borrowing from foreigners.

Another way of saying that the U.S. is on net borrowing from foreigners is to say that foreigners are on net lending to the U.S. They are lending to the U.S. by taking their savings and using them to buy U.S. assets (e.g.,, U.S. stocks and bonds). As an analogy, if you buy a bond from a company, you are in effect, lending your savings to the company and the company is borrowing from you.

PET #6

GDP per capita (per person) is not necessarily the best measure of the standard of living of a country's residents.

GDP per capita is often used as a measure of comparing the standards of living across countries; high GDP per capita countries are presumed to have higher standards of living than low GDP per capita countries. However, the use of GDP per capita to compare living standards does not take into account quality of life issues like crime, pollution, traffic congestion, access to health care, status of the educational system, etc. Thus, the country with the highest GDP per capita may not necessarily offer the highest "quality of life."

PET#7

Discouraged workers are not considered as unemployed because they are not actively seeking paid employment. Hence, they are also not considered part of the labor force. Underemployed workers hold jobs and are thus considered employed and, therefore, part of the labor force but not part of the unemployed.

PET #8

(The growth factor minus 1) X 100 equals the growth rate.

Suppose that you are told that real GDP in 2000 is $150 billion and real GDP in 2001 is $165 billion. The growth factor is $165/$150 = 1.10. The growth rate is thus (1.10 - 1) X 100 = 10%.

Alternatively, as your book points out, the growth factor is 1 plus (the growth rate/100). That is, if the growth rate is 10%, the growth factor is 1 + 10/100 = 1.10.

V.   PRACTICE EXAM: MULTIPLE CHOICE QUESTIONS

1.   Which one of the following would NOT be considered a component of GDP?

a.   spending by a household on a used t.v. set.
b.   spending by the government on social security benefits.
c.   a decline in the level of businesses' inventories over last year.
d.   spending by a firm on a foreign-made piece of equipment.
e.   all of the above would not be considered in GDP.

2.   Which one of the following sectors purchases the largest share of GDP?

a.   consumers.
b.   firms.
c.   the government.
d.   foreigners.
e.   proprietors.

3.   Which one of the following statements is true?

a.   durable goods are those that last for a short period of time.
b.   an example of a non-durable good is a dishwasher.
c.   services are the fastest growing component of consumption spending.
d.   net investment = gross investment + depreciation.
e.   an example of investment in economics would be the purchase of a stock.

4.   Which one of the following would give a correct measure of GDP?

Let C = consumption expenditures, I = gross investment expenditures, G = government expenditures; EX = exports, and IM = imports.

a.   GDP = C + I + G + EX + IM.
b.   GDP = C + I + G + EX - IM.
c.   GDP = C + I + G.

d. $GDP = C + I + G - EX - IM$.
e. $GDP = C + I - G + EX + IM$.

5.   If the U.S. runs a trade surplus,

a.   U.S. exports are greater than U.S. imports.
b.   U.S. imports are greater than U.S. exports.
c.   the U.S. is a net lender to foreign countries.
d.   U.S. sales of assets to foreigners are greater than U.S. purchases of assets from foreigners.
e.   (a) and (c).

6.   Which one of the following is NOT included in national income?

a.   wages.
b.   savings by households.
c.   corporate profits.
d.   net interest earnings.
e.   rental income.

7.   Which one of the following statements is true?

a.   GDP calculations include the value of services performed by a homemaker such as cleaning or
          cooking.
b.   under-the-table transactions lead to an overestimate of GDP.
c.   the labor force participation rate is the percentage of the labor force that is employed.
d.   all individuals over 16 years of age that do not have a job are considered unemployed.
e.   married men and women tend to have the lowest unemployment rates.

8.   The government considers a discouraged worker as:

a.   someone who does not have a job but is actively seeking paid employment.
b.   someone who is working at a job that is below their skill level.
c.   not part of the labor force.
d.   someone who has a part-time job but seeks full-time employment.
e.   a postal employee.

9.   Which one of the following is the correct growth factor assuming real GDP in 1998 is $5,000
          trillion and real GDP in 1999 is $6,000 trillion?

a.   0.56.
b.   1.20.
c.   0.65.
d.   1.83.
e.   1.44.

10.   Which price index is the most widely used by the government and the private sector.

a.   producer price index.

b.   consumer price index.
c.   the GDP deflator.
d.   the chain-type price index.
e.   the core index.

11.   Which one of the following statements is true of the Consumer Price Index?

a.   it does not take account of the price of imported goods and services.
b.   the goods used to construct the index do not change from month to month.
c.   it does not take into account the price of used goods.
d.   it understates the true rate of inflation.
e.   all of the above are true.

VI.   PRACTICE EXAM: ESSAY QUESTIONS

1.   Discuss the four components of spending on GDP and explain why intermediate goods purchased by businesses are not included in GDP.

2.   Explain why the CPI overstates the true rate of inflation. What impact does this have for cost-of-living adjustments and social security payments?

VII.   ANSWER KEY: MULTIPLE CHOICE

1.   Correct answer: e.

Discussion: Only spending for goods and services produced domestically, this year, is a component of GDP. Spending on a used t.v. set constitutes spending this year on a prior year's production. Spending by the government on social security benefits is spending on a good or service for which there is no underlying productive effort and thus does not constitute spending on this year's GDP. A decline in businesses' inventories over last year means that businesses sold goods this year that were produced in a prior year. (Likewise, an addition to businesses' inventories means that there were goods produced this year that did not get sold this year -- an addition to inventories thus is included in GDP.) Spending by a firm (or individual) on a foreign-made good or service (imports) constitutes spending on good or service not produced in the domestic (home) country. Thus, such spending does not reflect spending on domestically produced GDP.

2.   Correct answer: a.

Discussion: Consumers are, by far, the largest spending sector in the U.S. economy. The government is a larger spending sector than are firms.

3.   Correct answer: c.

Discussion: Services are the fastest growing component of consumption spending. This is partly driven by demographic changes.

Statement a is not correct; durable goods are goods that last a long time. Statement b is not correct. In fact, a dishwasher is an example of a durable good. Most households will keep a new dishwasher at least three years. Statement d is not correct. Net investment = gross investment minus depreciation. Statement e is not correct. In economics, investment is defined as the purchase of plant, machinery, and equipment. Investment, in economics, is not "financial investment."

4.   Correct answer: b.

Discussion: Remember that GDP is the total dollar value of the goods and services an economy produces in a given year. That production is purchased by consumers, businesses, the government and foreigners. Thus, it must be a truism that the total dollar value of production equals the total dollar value of spending on that production. However, since consumers, businesses, and the government can also purchase foreign-made goods and services (termed "imports"), we must subtract these out of C, I, and G in order to have a measure of spending by consumers, businesses, and the government on only domestically produced goods and services (which constitute GDP). We add spending by foreigners on domestically produced goods and services (termed "exports") to spending by the other sectors of the economy to arrive at the total amount of spending for the goods and services our economy has produced in a given year.

5.   Correct answer: c.

Discussion: A trade surplus is defined as an excess of exports over imports. Thus, statement a is correct and means that the U.S. is selling more goods and services to foreigners than it is in total purchasing from foreign countries. Alternatively, this means that foreigners are purchasing more goods and services from the U.S. than they are selling to us. This means that through trade, foreigners are not earning enough dollars on their sales of goods and services to the U.S. to pay for their purchases of goods and services from the U.S. The way in which foreign countries can finance their trade deficits is for them to borrow dollars from the U.S. In other words, the U.S. (the trade surplus country in this example) is on net lending dollars to foreign countries. Thus, statements a and c are correct.

Statement b is not correct; it would imply a trade deficit.   Statement d is not correct. Statement d is a way of saying that the U.S. would be on net borrowing from foreign countries (i.e., issuing bonds, etc. -- assets -- that foreigners are, in turn, buying). If foreigners were buying U.S. assets, they would be, in effect, lending to the U.S. (This would imply that the U.S. had a trade deficit.)

You may wish to review PET #5 of this chapter.

6.   Correct answer: b.

Discussion: National income is the sum of wages and benefits, corporate profits, proprietors' income, interest earnings, and rental income. Saving does not make up national income. It, however, comes from national income. That is, a country can save from its national income.

7.   Correct answer: e.

Discussion: Whereas married men and women tend to have the lowest unemployment rates, teenagers tend to have the highest unemployment rates.

Statement a is not correct. GDP calculations do not consider the value of services provided by a homemaker. If the value of services (such as laundry service, cleaning service, chauffeur, etc.) provided by homemakers were considered, the GDP figures would be higher. In fact, it is estimated that a homemaker's services should be valued at roughly $40,000. Statement b is not correct because under the table transactions are unrecorded. They escape government calculations and hence government statistics. It is believed that, if the value of these transactions were recorded they would add an additional 7% to GDP (since they do constitute production of a good or service). Statement c is not correct; the labor force participation rate is calculated as the labor force (sum of employed plus unemployed individuals) divided by the population. Statement d is not correct because only individuals over 16 years of age that have actively sought paid employment in the last four weeks are considered unemployed.

8.   Correct answer: c.

Discussion: Discouraged workers are individuals that have stopped searching for employment (because they are so discouraged about their prospects of actually finding work). Since these workers are not actively seeking employment, they are not considered unemployed and thus are not part of the labor force, either.

Statement a is not correct based on the discussion above. Statement b defines an individual who is "underemployed." Statement d does not define a discouraged worker. In fact, someone who has a part-time job is considered employed and part of the labor force. Statement e is included for a laugh.

9.   Correct answer: b.

The growth factor is calculated by dividing the most recent number by the more distant number. Thus, the growth factor is $6,000/$5,000 = 1.20. The growth factor implies a 20% growth rate of real GDP between 1998 and 1999.

10.   Correct answer: b.

Discussion: The Consumer Price Index (CPI) is the price index that is most widely used by the government. The government uses the CPI to make cost-of-living adjustments to social security benefits it pays out to retirees. Such cost-of-living adjustments are given so as to keep the "real" or "purchasing power" value of the benefit the same from year to year. The private sector also uses the CPI to make cost-of-living adjustments to wages, particularly to union wages.

The producer price index (not discussed in your textbook) is a price index of goods and services used by producers. It is sometimes referred to as the "wholesale price index." The GDP deflator and the chain-type price index are price indices that are constructed from the prices of the goods and services in GDP. The core index is (not discussed in your textbook) is a price index that subtracts food and energy prices out of the CPI. Food and energy prices tend to be the most volatile (fluctuating) prices in the index.

11.   Correct answer: b.

Discussion: The Consumer Price Index is based on a basket of goods and services that a typical household buys. The goods and services included in the basket do not change from month-to-month when the government collects the price data. Thus, the CPI is based on a fixed basket of goods and services.

Statement a is not correct because the CPI can include the price of imported goods and services. The chain-type price index and GDP deflator do not include the price of imported goods and services. Statement c is not correct because the CPI may include the price of used goods. Statement d is not correct; it is currently estimated that the percentage change in the CPI overstates the true rate of inflation by 0.5% - 1.5%. Thus, if the government reports a rate of inflation of 4%, the true rate of inflation is likely to be 2.5 - 3.5%.

VIII.   ANSWER KEY: ESSAY QUESTIONS

1.   The four components of spending on GDP (I will consider U.S. GDP) are:

(1)   Consumption expenditures. This is spending by U.S. households on final goods and services, whether the goods and services are produced in the U.S. or abroad. That is, some consumption expenditures by U.S. households are for foreign-produced goods and services. For example, suppose that consumption expenditures in the U.S. totalled $5 trillion; further if $1 trillion of the spending was on foreign-produced goods and services, then we could say that households purchased $4 trillion worth of U.S. produced goods and services.

(2) Investment expenditures. Investment expenditures has several components. The main component of investment spending is spending by businesses on plant and equipment. Businesses, of course, can purchase U.S.-produced equipment or foreign-made equipment. A second component of investment expenditures is residential housing. Purchases of new housing are considered investment expenditures even though households, not businesses, are typically the buyers. A third component of investment expenditures is "inventory investment." When businesses decide to add to their inventories from last year, they are investing in their inventory. Businesses may choose to build up their inventories in anticipation of a strong sales year.

(3)   Government expenditures. This is spending by the government on goods and services for which there was productive effort. The government buys legal services from lawyers, paper from paper manufacturers, computers from computer manufacturers, guns from gun manufacturers, and so on. The government, too, can buy from U.S. manufacturers or from foreign manufacturers.

(4)   Net Exports. This is spending by foreigners on U.S.-made goods and services minus spending by U.S. entities on foreign-made goods and services. Since items (1), (2), and (3) above contain spending by households, businesses, and the government on foreign-made goods and services, these must be subtracted out to arrive at an estimate of how much spending was undertaken by U.S. households, businesses, and the government on only U.S.-produced goods and services (i.e., U.S. GDP). However, since foreigners can purchase U.S. output just as U.S. residents purchase U.S. output, we must also include export spending in constructing a measure of GDP.

In sum, U.S. GDP is equal to consumption expenditures plus investment expenditures plus government expenditures plus exports minus imports.

The purchase of intermediate goods by businesses is not a component of GDP. To do so would lead to double-counting (which would lead to an overestimate of GDP). Here's why. Suppose you buy a computer system and pay $2,000 for it. The $2,000 price tag reflects the value of all of the production that went into producing the computer and making it available to a retail store where it can be sold to you. Thus, the $2,000 price tag is a measure of all of the production that has taken place. This number is used in computing GDP.

Suppose that of the $2,000 price tag on the computer system, $1,300 was due to the components used in the computer system. (We'll assume the components were produced in the U.S.) If we included the $1,300 in addition to the $2,000 in computing U.S. GDP, we would be double-counting the value of production that has actually taken place. The $2,000 already reflects $1,300 worth of production.

2.   The CPI overstates the true rate of inflation because the basket of goods and services that are priced from month-to-month do not change. Implicitly, this means that consumers do not change their consumption spending patterns, either. However, consumers are able to alter and do alter their spending patterns in response to price changes. For example, suppose the price of a name-brand medicine goes up and that this brand is one of the goods in the basket used to construct the CPI. Consumers may switch to a generic brand of the medicine, thus avoiding the higher price for the name brand. However, the CPI will not register this switch to a lower priced brand because it is constructed based on a fixed basket of goods and services. In fact, the CPI will increase because the price of the name-brand medicine which is included in the CPI has increased, even though consumers have been able to avoid the price increase. Thus, percentage changes in the CPI may overstate the actual rate of inflation to consumers.

The CPI may also overstate the rate of inflation because any increases in the prices of goods and services in the CPI are all considered to be inflationary. However, some prices increase because the good or service being purchased has improved. For example, suppose the new safety features of automobiles cause automobile prices to rise. An automobile today is now a different product from what it was in the past. It is a safer vehicle. The higher price tag should thus not be considered as inflationary because consumers are paying a higher price but getting more for their money.

For both of these reasons, it is estimated that percentage changes in the CPI overstate the true rate of inflation by 0.5% - 1.5%.

Cost-of-living adjustments and social security benefits are tied to the rate of change in the CPI. This means that they will be adjusted upward by the percentage increase in the CPI. For example, if the CPI inflation rate for 1996 was 2%, then social security benefits will automatically increase by 2%. This means that, if a retiree was receiving a $1,000 per month social security payment, the payment would increase by 2% to $1,020. The same would be true for any worker or individual who has a payment tied to the CPI.

If the CPI currently overstates the true rate of inflation, then, in effect, too much in social security benefits are being paid out. In the example above, if the true rate of inflation is actually 1%, then the retiree's benefit would only rise to $1,010 and the government would save $10 per month. While this may seem like a small saving for the government, multiply it by 12 months and the number of people receiving social security benefits. As you can imagine, the savings to the government (and ultimately the taxpayers) could end up being quite large.

However, retirees may argue that the CPI rate of inflation isn't relevant to compute their purchasing power. That is, the basket of goods and services used to construct the CPI is not the basket that they typically purchase. Since retirees are older, they may argue that they spend more of their income on medical services than that reflected in the CPI. Since medical fees are increasing at a much faster pace than, say entertainment or transportation prices, retirees may feel that the government should continue to make cost-of-living adjustments based on a number that overstates the true rate of inflation.

Take It to the Net

We invite you to visit the O'Sullivan/Sheffrin page on the Prentice Hall Web site at:

http://www.prenhall.com/osullivan/

for this chapter's World Wide Web exercise.

CHAPTER 22
CLASSICAL ECONOMICS: THE ECONOMY AT
FULL EMPLOYMENT

I. OVERVIEW

In this chapter, you will learn about Classical Economics which is the study of the factors that enable an economy that is already operating at full employment to produce more output (GDP). You will learn that, in the Classical model, employment together with a given capital stock determines how much output an economy can produce. You will learn how changes to employment and/or the capital stock affect the level of output. The tools you will use to study the relationship between employment, the capital stock and output are the aggregate production function and a supply and demand model of the labor market. You will be introduced to supply-side economics and learn that many of the tenets of supply-side economics can be analyzed in the framework of the Classical model. You will analyze policies aimed at moving the economy to a higher level of output. You will see that some government spending policies can lead to "crowding out" and/or "crowding in." That is, you will see how changes in government spending can lead to changes in consumption, investment, and net exports. You will see that such government spending policies come at an opportunity cost when the economy is operating at its full-employment level.

II. CHECKLIST

By the end of this chapter you should be able to:

√   Explain, in the context of a Classical model, what factors determine the level of output an economy is capable of producing.

√   Define and graph a production function.

√   Explain the shape of the production function.

√   Discuss how changes in the capital stock affect the production function.

√   Discuss labor demand and explain why it is negatively sloped when graphed against the real wage rate.

√   Discuss labor supply and explain the substitution and income effects on the slope of the labor supply curve.

√   Relate changes in the capital stock and employment to the level of output an economy can produce. Illustrate such changes with a production function and the demand and supply model of the labor market.

√   Discuss the effects of a change in the capital stock on the labor market and the real wage rate.

√   Discuss the effects of a tax on labor on employment, the real wage, and output.

√   Define the full-employment level of output (potential output).

√   Discuss the Laffer curve.

√   Define crowding out and crowding in.

√   Explain what causes crowding out and crowding in and which sectors of the economy may be crowded out or in as a result of an increase in government spending.

III. KEY TERMS

Supply-side economics: the school of thought that emphasizes the importance of taxation for influencing economic activity.

Classical economics: the study of the economy as it operates at full employment.

Aggregate production function: shows how much output is produced from capital and labor.

Stock of Capital: the total of all the machines, equipment, and buildings in the entire economy.

Labor: the total effort of all workers in an economy

Short run production function: shows how much output is produced from varying amounts of labor, holding the capital stock constant.

Real wage rate: the wage rate paid to workers adjusted for inflation.

Substitution effect: an increase in the wage rate increases the opportunity cost of leisure and leads workers to supply more labor.

Income effect: an increase in the wage rate raises a worker's income at the current levels of hours of work and may lead to more leisure and a decreased supply of labor.

Full-employment output or **potential output:** the level of output that results when the labor market is in equilibrium.

Laffer curve: a relationship between tax rates and tax revenues that illustrates that high tax rates may not always lead to high tax revenues if high tax rates discourage economic activity.

Supply-siders: economists who believe that taxes have strong adverse affects on the economy.

Crowding out: reductions in consumption, investment, or net exports caused by an increase in government purchases.

Closed economy: an economy without international trade.

Open economy: an economy with international trade.

IV.   PERFORMANCE ENHANCING TIPS (PETS)

PET #1

The production function is a graph relating output to the input labor. The capital stock is held fixed. Thus, changes in the capital stock will cause the production function to shift and changes in labor will cause movements along the production function.

You may wish to review PET #1 from Chapter 1 of the Practicum.

An increase in the capital stock will shift the production function up (and to the left). The shift shows that, for every amount of labor as before, more output is able to be produced. A decrease in the capital stock works in reverse.

An increase in the amount of labor that an economy uses will cause a movement out along the production function to higher levels of output. A decrease in the amount of labor will cause a movement down along the production function to lower levels of output.

PET #2

The shorthand notation for a production function, $Y = F(K,L)$, is also a shorthand notation for an equation that relates the amount of output to the amount of capital and labor an economy uses.

For example, Y = F(K,L) means that the amount of output an economy produces depends in some specific way on the amount of capital and labor used. A specific equation for Y = F(K,L) may be:

$$Y = 0.7 \cdot L + 0.3 \cdot K$$

Thus, if you are told that the amount of labor an economy has available is 1,000,000 units and the amount of capital an economy has available is 200,000, then you could determine how many units of output an economy could produce. You would plug in the numbers to get Y = 0.7•(1,000,000) + 0.3•(200,000) = 700,000 + 60,000 = 760,000 units of output.

PET #3

Crowding out occurs at the full-employment level of output because any increase in government purchases of output necessarily requires a reduction in purchases by some other sector(s) of the economy (consumers, businesses, foreign).

First of all, you may wish to replace the term "crowding out" with "reduction in" if it makes it easier for you to understand what crowding out is about. That is, when government spending increases, spending by other sectors of the economy will be reduced.

Let's look at some examples of crowding out. Suppose Country A is operating at the full-employment level of output and at this level is producing $2 trillion worth of goods and services. Further, suppose that consumers purchase total $1.2 trillion; businesses purchases total $0.4 trillion; and government purchases total $0.6 trillion. Thus, total purchases equal $2.2 trillion which is more than the $2 trillion produced by Country A. Thus, it must be that the foreign sector, i.e., exports minus imports, purchases total -$0.2. That is, $0.2 trillion of the $2.2 trillion purchased by consumers, businesses, and the government of Country A is satisfied through foreign supply.

Now, suppose the government increases its spending from $0.6 trillion to $1.0 trillion. With the economy operating at full employment, only $2 trillion worth of output can be produced by Country A even though total spending by Country A's consumers, businesses, and government now totals $2.6 trillion. Something has to give -- consumer, business, and foreign-sector spending will have to be rearranged to accomodate the increase in government spending.

Let's look at one example of crowding out. Suppose Country A's consumers and businesses do not change their spending behavior (so they continue to purchase 1.2 + 0.4 = $1.6 trillion) while government spending has increased to $1 trillion. Thus, Country A's consumers, businesses, and government in total purchase $2.6 trillion worth of output. The $2.6 trillion worth of purchases by consumers, businesses, and the government must be satisfied through $2 trillion worth of production by Country A supplemented with $0.6 trillion worth of (net) production from abroad. That is, Country A must import $0.6 trillion more than it will export. Thus, Country A's trade balance declines to -$0.6 trillion. That is, the trade deficit gets worse. In this sense, we would say that net exports are crowded out (reduced) by $0.4 billion because the trade balance worsens from -$0.2 trillion to -$0.6 trillion.

Let's look at another example of crowding out. Suppose that consumers and businesses both cut back their purchases by $0.2 trillion but that the trade deficit remains at -$0.2 trillion. Here, we would say that consumption and investment spending are crowded out (reduced) by a total of $0.4 billion (0.2 + 0.2). The crowding out of spending by the private sector accomodates the increased government spending. Thus, purchases by Country A's consumers, businesses, and government would total $2.2 trillion (1.0 + 0.2 + 1.0). Since the country can only produce $2 trillion worth of output, the foreign sector brings in an additional $0.2 trillion (i.e., Country A imports $0.2 trillion more than it exports) to satisfy the purchases of Country A's residents.

V.   PRACTICE EXAM: MULTIPLE CHOICE QUESTIONS

1.   Classical economics assumes:

a.   that wages and prices are completely flexible.
b.   shocks to an economy are not long lasting.
c.   an economy has a natural tendency to return to a state of full employment.
d.   the potential or full-employment level of output is determined by the amount of capital and labor an economy has available.
e.   all of the above.

2.   An economy that operates at its full employment or potential output level experiences:

a.   cyclical unemployment only.
b.   frictional unemployment only.
c.   structural unemployment only.
d.   frictional plus structural unemployment.
e.   cyclical plus frictional unemployment.

3.   The short-run aggregate production function:

a.   is negatively sloped.
b.   shows that output increases but at a decreasing rate.
c.   will shift down (to the right) as the stock of capital increases.
d.   reflects increasing marginal returns.
e.   shows how the level of output changes as more capital is employed, holding the stock of labor fixed.

4.   Which one of the following would shift the demand for labor to the right (increase the demand for labor)?

a.   an increased tax on workers that employers must pay.
b.   a decrease in the real wage rate.
c.   an increase in the capital stock.
d.   an increase in the supply of workers.
e.   a minimum wage.

5.   Which one of the following statements is true of labor supply?

a.   if the income effect dominates the substitution effect, the labor supply curve will be positively sloped.

b.   if the income effect dominates the substitution effect, the labor supply curve will be negatively sloped.
c.   a higher real wage rate may induce some workers to take on more leisure time and work less.
d.   empirical estimates suggest that the labor supply curve is nearly horizontal.
e.   (b) and (c).

6.   In the Classical model, an increase in the capital stock will _____ the real wage rate and _____ the full-employment level of output.

a.   increase/increase
b.   increase/decrease
c.   decrease/decrease
d.   decrease/increase
e.   have an uncertain effect on/increase

7.   In the Classical model, immigration may:

a.   increase labor supply.
b.   reduce the equilibrium real wage rate.
c.   raise the full-employment level of output.
d.   cause a temporary rise in the unemployment rate.
e.   all of the above.

8.   A supply-side economist believes all but which one of the following?

a.   a cut in the tax rate could increase tax revenues collected by the government.
b.   a very high tax rate might discourage people from working.
c.   very high tax rates may reduce the level of economic activity.
d.   a tax on labor may lead to higher employment.
e.   all of the above.

9.   Assuming a country is operating at the full-employment level of output, a government that increases its share of purchases of its country's GDP:

a.   incurs an opportunity cost.
b.   may find that its exports decline and its imports increase.
c.   may find that investment spending declines.
d.   may find that consumer spending declines.
e.   all of the above.

10.   Suppose you are given the following information on GDP and shares (percentages) of GDP purchased by consumers, businesses, the government, and the foreign sector:

GDP = $3 trillion
Share of consumption expenditures = 50%
Share of investment expenditures = 15%
Share of government expenditures = 15%
Share of net exports = 20%

Based on these numbers, which one of the following statements is true?

a.   an example of crowding out would be if the share of consumption expenditures increased to 60% and the share of investment expenditures decreased to 5%.

b.   an example of crowding out would be if the share of consumption expenditures increased to 75% and the share of net exports declined to -5%.

c.   an example of crowding out would be if the share of government expenditures increased to 25% and consumption expenditures fell by 7% and investment expenditures fell by 3%.

d.   an example of crowding out would be if all of the shares fell by, say, 5%.

e.   if the share of government expenditures increased to 30% and investment expenditures increased to 20% but consumption expenditures decreased to 30%, we would conclude that the private sector, on net, had been crowded in.

VI.   PRACTICE EXAM: ESSAY QUESTIONS

1.   In the U.S. during the 1980s, the capital stock increased as did the supply of labor. Europe experienced similar events. What effects would these changes have on employment and GDP and what might explain why the U.S. experienced lower real wages whereas Europe experienced higher real wages?

2.   Compare and contrast the effects of an increase in the stock of capital on the real wage rate, employment, and output (GDP) for a labor supply curve that is vertical and one that is positively sloped. What does it mean for a labor supply curve to be vertical?

VII.   ANSWER KEY: MULTIPLE CHOICE QUESTIONS

1.   Correct answer: e.

Discussion: Statement a is a Classical economist's way of saying that markets (labor, capital, goods) will move to equilibrium quickly. Statement b means that shocks to an economy are not long lasting which is a way of saying that the economy adjusts quickly to negative circumstances and thus returns quickly to the full-employment level of output. That is, recessions should not be long lasting. Statement c means that the economy, without government intervention, will cure itself (quickly) of any economic downturns. Statement d means that the supply-side of the economy (supply of factors of production, resources) determines how much output can be produced at full employment.

2.   Correct answer: d.

Discussion: An economy that operates at its full-employment level of output does NOT have a zero rate of unemployment. There will, at any point in time, be some unemployment that is part of a natural-functioning, healthy economy. The unemployment rate that presides when the economy operates at the full-employment level of output is referred to as the "natural rate of unemployment." The natural rate of unemployment consists of frictional plus structural unemployment. Remember that frictional unemployment is due to new entrants, re-entrants, and job leavers searching for work. Structural unemployment is due to the mismatch of skills between workers and the needs of industry. These types of unemployment will occur even when the economy is operating at its potential level of output.

3.   Correct answer: b.

Discussion: Statement b implies two things: (1) the aggregate production function is positively sloped, and (2) the slope flattens out as the level of output produced increases. That is, the aggregate production function exhibits diminishing returns.

Statement a is not correct because the aggregate production function is positively sloped. Statement c is not correct; an increase in the stock of capital will be represented by an upward shift (to the left) in the aggregate production function. The shift shows that, with more capital, more output can be produced for any level of labor employed than before. Statement d is not correct; the aggregate production function exhibits diminishing marginal returns. Statement e is not correct; the aggregate production function shows how output changes as the amount of labor employed changes, holding the capital stock fixed.

4.   Correct answer: c.

Discussion: An increase in the capital stock will raise the productivity of workers and thus increase the benefit to firms of hiring workers. That is, firms would be willing to hire more workers at every wage rate than before. Alternatively, a rightward shift in demand also shows that firms would be willing to pay a higher real wage rate than before for every amount of labor. (You may wish to review PET #4 of Chapter 4 for insight.)

Statement a is not correct; a tax on labor paid by employers will shift the demand for labor to the left. Statement b is not correct. A decrease in the real wage rate will cause a movement along the labor demand curve (not a shift of it). The decrease in the real wage rate will raise the **quantity** of labor demanded. Statement d is not correct. An increase in the supply of workers would be represented by a rightward shift in the labor supply curve, not a rightward shift in the labor demand curve. Statement e is not correct. A minimum wage will cause a movement along the labor demand curve, not a shift in it.

5.   Correct answer: e.

Discussion: The income effect is that, at higher real wage rates, workers earn more per hour and therefore need not work as many hours to maintain the same level of real income as at lower real wages. In this case, higher real wage rates would be associated with lower employment, not higher employment. Thus, the labor supply curve would be negatively sloped. You also learned in this chapter that a higher real wage rate may induce some workers to work more (not less). That is, these workers substitute more work effort for less leisure time. If the substitution effect dominated, then the labor supply curve would be positively sloped.

Statement a is not correct based on the discussion above. Statement d is not correct; empirical estimates suggest that the labor supply curve is nearly vertical.

6.   Correct answer: a.

Discussion: An increase in the capital stock will shift the demand for labor to the right (see multiple choice question 3 for review). An increase in the demand for labor, as for any good, will increase the price of labor, i.e., the real wage rate. Thus, the real wage rate will rise. The rightward shift in the demand for labor will also raise the amount of labor employed. With more labor employed and more capital available for production, the full-employment level of output must necessarily increase.

7.   Correct answer: e.

Discussion: Immigration adds to an economy's available pool of workers, i.e., labor supply increases. As labor supply increases (rightward shift in labor supply), the real wage rate will decline and thus more workers will become employed. With more workers employed, the full-employment level of output will rise. However, it should be noted that immigration may cause a temporary increase in the unemployment rate as the immigrants search for jobs. In the classical model, the increase in the unemployment rate should be short-lived.

8.   Correct answer: d.

Discussion: A supply-side economist does NOT believe that a tax on labor may lead to higher employment. A supply-side economist would be concerned that a tax on labor would lead to lower employment by making workers more costly to firms.

Supply-side economists do believe that it is possible for a cut in the tax rate to generate more tax revenues for the government, not less, because economic activity by workers and firms will increase, generating more income. Thus, the income base on which tax revenues are collected will rise and could potentially lead to more tax revenues for the government despite the tax rate cut. Supply-siders also believe that cuts in tax rates may encourage people to work more (not less). That is, supply-siders believe the substitiution effect on labor supply dominates the income effect.

9.   Correct answer: e.

Discussion: An increase in government spending incurs an opportunity cost because it crowds out spending by other sectors of the economy. Thus, an increase in government spending may incur an opportunity cost (giving up something) of decreased spending by consumers. That is, the economy, as a whole must give up some spending by consumers. The increased government spending also leads to crowding out of net exports (i.e., exports will decline but imports will rise) and investment spending. This is not to say that some groups of consumers or businesses will not be crowded in. For example, your book mentions that an increase in government spending on highways may crowd in (increase) some types of investment spending.

10.   Correct answer: c.

Discussion: Crowding out is caused by an **increase** in **government** expenditures. Crowding out means that an increase in government spending causes a reduction in spending by consumers and/or businesses and/or through net exports. Thus, statements a and b cannot be correct because there is no basis for crowding out. Government spending has not changed. Statement d cannot be correct because government expenditures along with consumption and investment expenditures decline. Statement e is not correct because the share of government expenditures increased by 10% but investment expenditures increased by 5% while consumption expenditures declined by 20% so that, in total, private-sector spending was crowded out (reduced) by -15% = (+5% - 20%), not crowded in, on net. Statement d is the only statement that reflects crowding out. In this case, while government expenditures rise by 10%, consumption expenditures are reduced by 7% and investment expenditures by 3% for a total of a 10% reduction in private-sector spending. That is, private-sector spending is crowded out by the increase in government spending.

VIII.   ANSWER KEY: ESSAY QUESTIONS

1.   The increased capital stock makes labor more productive. As such, the marginal benefit to the firm of workers increase. An increase in the marginal benefit of workers is represented by a rightward shift in the demand for labor curve. As the demand for labor shifts to the right, the real wage rate increases and the level of employment increases as well.

The increased supply of labor would be represented by a rightward shift in the labor supply curve. The increased supply of labor leads to a lower real wage rate (which induces firms to hire more workers) and a higher level of employment.

The two effects together suggest that unambiguously the level of employment will increase. However, the net effect on the real wage depends on the magnitude of the shift rightward in the demand for labor relative to the shift rightward in the supply of labor. A first case is that the increase in the demand for labor is larger than the labor supply increase. Here, the real wage rate will rise. A second case is that the increase in the demand for labor is smaller than the increase in the supply of labor. Here, the real wage will fall. Since the U.S. experienced an increase in employment alongside a decrease in the real wage, the second case must be applicable. In Europe, the level of employment increased as did the real wage. These combined effects would indicate that the first case is applicable.

2.   If the labor supply curve is vertical, it means that a higher real wage rate does not induce more people to enter the labor force. That is, the real wage rate simply does not influence, in the aggregate, the labor force's choice between leisure and working. It has no effect in the aggregate. Some people may choose to enter the labor force whereas others might work fewer hours (part-time), but the combined effect of everybody's decision leaves no net increase in employment as the real wage rate rises. What may be happening is that the income effect and the substitution effect are working to offset each other. Remember that the income effect would, by itself, make the labor supply curve negatively sloped. However, the substitution effect would make it positively sloped. If the two effects "cancel" then a vertical labor supply curve may result. While a vertical labor supply curve indicates that changes in the real wage do not have an impact on the aggregate amount of labor supplied, it does not rule out the possibility of other factors (e.g.,, taxes) influencing labor supply.

If labor supply is vertical and the capital stock increases, which would translate into an increased demand for labor, the increased demand for labor would have no effect on the level of employment. To see this, look at the graph below.

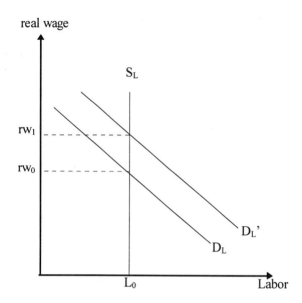

Notice that employment does not change but the real wage does. It rises. As for the effects on the level of output, the increased capital stock would shift the production function up, to the left, as shown below.

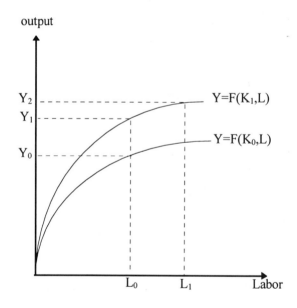

Suppose the economy was initially using L_0 amount of labor. Given L_0 and the initial capital stock, K_0, the economy would produce an output level of Y_0. After the capital stock increases to K_1, the production function would shift up, to the left. At the same time, the demand for labor increases but because labor supply is vertical, there is no change in employment. Thus, L_0 remains the amount of labor available in the economy. But, with the larger capital stock, the new production function shows that Y_1 can be produced instead of Y_0.

If the labor supply curve is positively sloped, the increase in the capital stock will increase the demand for labor and thus increase employment. In this case, the increased capital stock has two effects: (1) the production function shifts up, and (2) the level of employment increases (from L_0 to L_1). The combination of these events enables the economy to produce at output level Y_2 (see above) which is greater than output level Y_1.

Take It to the Net

We invite you to visit the O'Sullivan/Sheffrin page on the Prentice Hall Web site at:

http://www.prenhall.com/osullivan/

for this chapter's World Wide Web exercise.

CHAPTER 23
WHY DO ECONOMIES GROW?

I.   OVERVIEW

In this chapter, you will learn how capital deepening and technological progress can affect a country's ability to grow. You will learn how savings and investment play a role in capital deepening as well as what determines technological progress. You will also learn how international trade and public policy ultimately affect economic growth through their effects on savings and investment. You will learn how research and development and investment in education may affect the growth rate a country is able to achieve. You will also see how population growth affects economic growth and real wages. You will use a production function to illustrate how capital deepening and technological progress alter the level of output a country is able to produce. You will be re-introduced to the difference between gross investment and net investment and will see why it is important in understanding the basis for economic growth. You will learn about growth accounting which is an attempt to estimate the contributions of capital deepening, labor growth, and technological progress to economic growth. You will learn about productivity and how capital deepening and technological progress affect productivity and real wages. You will learn about the sources of technological progress and how policy can be directed at enhancing technological progress. You will also learn about real GDP per capita as a basis for comparing living standards across countries.

II.   CHECKLIST

By the end of this chapter, you should be able to:

√   Define economic growth.
√   Discuss how a country's standard of living can be measured and some problems with making direct comparisons to another country's standard of living.
√   Use the Rule of 70 to analyze how long it will take a country to double its standard of living if it grows at X% per year.
√   Use the Rule of 70 to analyze what growth rate it would have to achieve in order for its standard of living to double in X years.
√   Define capital deepening and illustrate its effects on real wages, the production function, and the level of output.
√   Explain how savings and investment are related.
√   Explain the distinction between gross and net investment. Explain which type of investment is important to economic growth.
√   Explain the effect of population growth on output per worker and discuss ways in which policy can be used to mitigate the effect.
√   Explain how government spending and a trade deficit can be used to enhance capital deepening.
√   Define technological progress.
√   Discuss growth accounting.
√   Define labor productivity.
√   Discuss what has happened to U.S. labor productivity since the 1970s and offer possible explanations.
√   Discuss some causes of technological progress.
√   Define creative destruction.
√   Give some examples of government policy that would raise the rate of technological progress.

III. KEY TERMS

Capital deepening: increases in the stock of capital per worker.

Technological progress: an increase in output without any increases in inputs.

Real GDP per capita: inflation-adjusted gross domestic product per person. It is the usual measure of living standards across time and between countries.

Exchange Rate: the rate at which one currency trades for another

Convergence: the process by which poorer countries "catch up" with richer countries in terms of real GDP per capita.

Saving: total output minus consumption.

Growth Accounting: a method to determine the contribution to economic growth from increased capital, labor, and technological progress.

Labor productivity: output per hour of work.

Creative destruction: the process by which competition for monopoly profits leads to technological progress.

Human capital: investments in education and skills.

IV. PERFORMANCE ENHANCING TIPS (PETS)

PET #1

Real GDP per capita is a country's real GDP level divided by its population. It is not an appropriate measure of what a typical individual's before- or after-tax real income is.

Real GDP per capita is not a useful measure of average income for a working individual or household. The reason is that the calculation for real GDP per capita assumes that the dollar figure for real GDP is a measure of the income that accrues to every individual in the population, whatever his or her age, and whether they are working. Also, real GDP, while an approximate measure of national income, is not a good measure of personal income (i.e., before-tax household income) or of disposable income (i.e., after-tax household income) -- income that accrues to working individuals. In fact, real GDP exceeds aggregate real personal and aggregate real disposable income by a substantial amount. Thus, when your textbook reports that real GDP per capita in the U.S. was $24,750 in 1993, it does not imply that on average, every working individual earns $24,750. It also does not imply that on average, a family of four's before or after-tax real income is $99,000 ($24,750 X 4).

PET #2

The pool of savings available to fund investment in Country A can come from the savings of Country A's residents or from the savings of foreign countries' residents who lend their savings to Country A.

Suppose that U.S. residents in total save $500 billion a year, $450 billion of which is placed in the U.S. and the remaining $50 billion which is lent to other countries. Further, suppose that foreigners save $1 trillion a year, $100 billion of which is lent to the U.S. On net, the U.S. pool of private savings will be $450 billion + $100 billion = $550 billion. This pool of savings will be available to fund private and/or government investment projects.

PET #3

Net investment is the change in a country's capital stock after taking account of depreciation. Thus:
*   net investment = gross investment - depreciation.*

You can also rearrange the equation above as:
        gross investment = net investment + depreciation.
        depreciation = gross investment - net investment.

PET #4

Net investment that is positive is the addition to a nation's stock of capital above and beyond its current level. Net investment that is zero means that a nation's stock of capital is neither increasing nor decreasing beyond its current level. Net investment that is negative means that a nation is not investing enough to replace capital that is being worn out.

PET #3 of Chapter 6 of the Practicum covered this principle and used an illustration that is worth repeating here. To illustrate the difference between gross investment and net investment, consider the stock of shoes that you currently have. Suppose you have 10 pairs of shoes. Over the course of the year, 3 of the pairs wear out (depreciate) and are no longer any good. If you buy 7 more pairs of shoes that year, your gross investment in shoes is 7 pairs. However, because you are replacing 3 pairs that have worn out, your net investment in shoes is 4 pairs. That is, at the end of the year, you will now have 14 pairs of shoes. You have, on net, added 4 (7-3) pairs to the stock of 10 pairs of shoes that you started out with.

Suppose instead that you bought 3 pairs of shoes that year. While three pairs would be your gross investment, your net investment would be zero. You have only replaced what you have worn out. Thus, you are no better off at the end of the year since your stock of shoes remains at 10 pairs.

Now, suppose that you bought 1 pair of shoes that year. While three pairs would be your gross investment, your net investment would be -2 (1-3). You have not invested enough to replace the 3 pairs of shoes worn-out. Thus, your stock of shoes will decline from 10 pairs to 8 pairs.

The same is true for a country. A country whose net investment is zero will not be adding to its capital stock and so will not experience the benefits of capital deepening; a country that is not replacing its worn out capital will see its capital stock shrink and will not experience the benefits of capital deepening.

PET #5

In order for a country to grow through capital deepening, its savings must be greater than the depreciation of the capital stock.

This PET is just an application of PET #3 and #4. That is, a country must save enough to ensure that its level of net investment is positive (greater than zero).

PET #6

The Rule of 70 can be used to determine either the time periods it will take for a variable to double or the growth rate necessary for a variable to double in X time periods.

This is a repeat of PET #5 from Chapter 5. However, you will use it again in this chapter, especially in making cross-country comparisons of growth. For example, suppose you are told that the U.S. growth rate is 3% per year and that the Japanese growth rate is 5% per year. Which country's real GDP will double more quickly? Using the Rule of 70, it will take the U.S. approximately 23 years (70/3) to double its real GDP whereas Japan's real GDP will double in 14 years (70/5). For another example, suppose you are told that Canada has undertaken an ambitious economic plan. One goal is for real GDP to double in 10 years. What growth rate must Canada sustain each year for 10 years in order to achieve the goal? Using the Rule of 70, the answer would be 7% per year (70/10 years).

One word of caution: if the growth rate is stated on a monthly or quarterly basis, the time period to double should be stated in monthly or quarterly terms (instead of yearly) as well. For example, suppose the government reported that they expected real GDP to grow at 2% each quarter. Using the Rule of 70, at that growth rate, it would take 70/2 = 35 quarters for real GDP to double. Thirty-five quarters is 8.75 years.

V.   PRACTICE EXAM: MULTIPLE CHOICE QUESTIONS

1.   Which one of the following statements is NOT true of real GDP per capita?

a.   if a country's real GDP per capita grows at 2% per year, it will take 35 years for real GDP per capita to double.
b.   it is difficult to compare real GDP per capita across countries because of differences in consumption patterns.
c.   it is difficult to compare real GDP per capita across countries because of differences in currencies.
d.   if U.S. real GDP per capita is $25,000, German real GDP per capita is 60,000 marks and the exchange rate is 2 marks per U.S. dollar, then we can be sure that Germany has a higher real GDP per capita than the U.S.
e.   all of the above are true.

2.   Which one of the following statements is NOT true?

a.   there has been a convergence of real GDP per capita among the developed (industrialized) countries.
b.   there is strong evidence that less developed countries grow at faster rates than developed countries.
c.   real GDP per capita may decline if the growth rate in real GDP is less than the population growth rate.
d.   the average growth rate in real GDP per capita between 1960-93 for Japan was about 5% per year.
e.   the level of real GDP per capita amongst countries will eventually converge if the low real GDP per capita countries grow at rates faster than the high real GDP per capita countries.

3.   In an economy with no government or foreign sector:

a.   savings must equal gross investment.
b.   savings must equal net investment.
c.   savings must equal depreciation.

d.   savings will be less than investment.

e.   savings will be greater than investment.

4.   A change in a country's capital stock is equal to:

a.   the level of gross investment.

b.   the level of net investment.

c.   the rate of depreciation of a country's capital stock.

d.   the level of savings.

e.   (a) and (d).

5.   Which one of the following statements is true of capital deepening?

a.   for a fixed amount of capital, increases in a country's work force will lead to increases in the amount of output per worker.

b.   a government that uses its tax revenues to fund the construction of new highways and bridges is not engaging in capital deepening because the government creates a budget deficit.

c.   trade deficits always hurt the ability of a country to deepen its capital stock.

d.   capital deepening will stop when depreciation is zero.

e.   capital deepening is a source of economic growth.

6.   Which one of the following would NOT be an example of technological progress?

a.   discovery of a new tax loophole which enables companies to reduce the amount of taxes they pay to the government.

b.   the invention of the computer.

c.   the invention of a conveyor belt.

d.   the discovery of converting steam to energy.

e.   the invention of the washing machine.

7.   Which Nobel-prize-winning economist developed a method for measuring technological progress?

a.   Franco Modigliani.

b.   Milton Friedman.

c.   Robert Solow.

d.   Sir Charles Godfrey.

e.   Gerard Debreu.

8.   Which one of the following statements is true of growth accounting?

a.   technological progress has accounted for roughly 1% of the growth rate in U.S. output.

b.   growth accounting determines how much of a country's growth in output is due to growth in worker productivity and to growth in prices (inflation).

c.   a country whose main source of growth in output is through technological progress will typically be able to enjoy a higher level of consumption than a country whose main source of growth is through increases in the capital stock.

d.   the slowdown in U.S. labor productivity has been explained by a reduced rate of capital deepening.

e.   the effect of advances in information technology on labor productivity is easily measured.

9.   Which one of the following has NOT been considered a potential source of technological progress?

a.   research and development in fundamental sciences.
b.   monopolies that spur innovation.
c.   inventions designed to reduce costs.
d.   the scale of the market.
e.   all of the above have been considered potential sources of technological progress.

10.   Which one of the following statements is NOT true?

a.   technological progress enables a country to produce more output with the same amount of labor and capital.
b.   education can promote technological progress.
c.   creative destruction is the process of replacing plant and equipment before it has fully depreciated.
d.   patents may promote technological progress.
e.   the protection of intellectual property rights may promote technological progress.

11.   Suppose Country A's real GDP per capita is $10,000 and Country B's real GDP per capita is $20,000. If Country A's real GDP per capita is growing at 7% per year while Country B's real GDP per capita is growing at 3.5% per year, after how many years will Country A's real GDP per capita exceed Country B's real GDP per capita?

a.   10 years.
b.   60 years.
c.   80 years.
d.   7 years.
e.   20 years.

VI.   PRACTICE EXAM: ESSAY QUESTIONS

1.   Explain why the citizens of a country that experiences economic growth through only technological progress may enjoy a better standard of living than a country that experiences economic growth only through an increase in the capital stock.

2.   Discuss the different sources of technological progress.

VII.   ANSWER KEY: MULTIPLE CHOICE QUESTIONS

1.   Correct answer: d.

Discussion: Statement d is not true. It is not appropriate to compare real GDP per capita across countries by using the going exchange rate to convert the real GDP per capita of one country to another country's currency. Thus, even though using the exchange rate, Germany's real GDP per capita would equal $30,000 (60,000 marks / 2 marks per dollar) and thus exceed U.S. real GDP per capita, it is not correct to infer that Germany's real GDP per capita and thus the standard of living is better than in the U.S.

Differences in consumption patterns and the prices of goods across countries must be evaluated in arriving at a correct comparison of real GDP per capita. Thus, statements b and c are true. Statement a is an application of the Rule of 70. With a growth rate of 2% per year, it will take 35 years (70/2) for a country's real GDP per capita to double.

2.   Correct answer: b.

Discussion: Statement b is not true. Economists have found only weak evidence that less developed countries have grown at a rate faster than developed countries.

Statement a is true for developed countries. Statement c is necessarily true. Since real GDP per capita is equal to a country's real GDP divided by its population, then an increase in the population growth rate that exceeds the growth rate in real GDP will necessarily lead to a decline in real GDP per capita. Statement d is true. Statement e is true. (For a numerical example of the principle, see the answer to question 11.)

3.   Correct answer: a.

Discussion: A country's savings (in the absence of a government or foreign sector) is used by (lent to) businesses who in turn purchase plant and equipment, i.e., invest or add to the capital stock. The investment by businesses may be undertaken to replace worn out capital (depreciation) or to purchase new capital. Gross investment is the sum of these two activities and saving provides the funds necessary for both.

Statements d and e cannot be true of an economy that does not have a government or a foreign sector. It is necessarily true that savings must equal (gross) investment.

4.   Correct answer: b.

Discussion: A country's capital stock will change when its net investment changes. If net investment is positive, a country's capital stock will increase. This is because the country will not only be replacing worn out capital, it will be adding more new plant and equipment to its capital stock. If net investment is negative, a country's capital stock will decrease. This is because the country will not even be totally replacing its worn out capital. Remember that net investment is gross investment minus depreciation. You may wish to review PET #4 of this chapter for more detail.

5.   Correct answer: e.

Discussion: Capital deepening is an increase in the amount of capital available per worker. Since capital deepening enables workers to produce more output per day, capital deepening leads to economic growth (increases in output).

Statement a is not true. For a fixed amount of capital, increases in a country's work force will lead to a decline in capital per worker (i.e., total capital/number of workers), not an increase. Statement b is not true. When a government spends your tax dollars on such things as highway and bridge construction (or research and development, or education for that matter), it is adding to the stock of capital (physical or human) and thereby engaging in capital deepening. Statement c is not true. A country that runs a trade deficit may incur the trade deficit because it is importing a lot of plant and equipment (capital). Thus, a trade deficit is not necessarily a bad thing for a country since it can promote capital deepening. This, of course, assumes that the country is deficit spending on capital goods not on consumption goods. Statement d is not true. Capital deepening will stop when net investment is zero (i.e., when gross investment equals depreciation).

6.   Correct answer: a.

Discussion: Technological progress is defined as progress that enables a country to produce more output with the same amount of capital and labor. The discovery of a new tax loophole does not add to the amount of output a country can produce with the same amount of capital and labor. It simply keeps dollars in the hands of businesses and out of the hands of the government.

7.   Correct answer: c.

8.   Correct answer: c.

Discussion: Your book discusses a comparison of the growth rates achieved by Hong Kong and Singapore. The discussion points out that technological progress enables the citizens of a country to consume more than a country that grows through increases in the capital stock. This is because increases in the capital stock are funded from saving. That is, in order to increase the capital stock, a country must save more. This means that a country must consume less. Thus, a country that experiences growth because of increases in the capital stock is probably a country where the level of consumption is not very high. In contrast, if growth occurs through technological progress (which presumably is not being funded from savings), then a country does not have to reduce its consumption level in order for growth to occur.
Statement a is not true. Technological progress has accounted for roughly 35% of the growth rate in U.S. output. That is, with a U.S. growth rate in output of 3% a year, 1% of that 3% is attributed to technological progress, i.e., 1/3 = 33% of the growth rate is attributed to technological progress. Statement b is not true. Growth accounting determines how much of a country's growth in output is due to growth in the capital stock, the labor force, and technological progress. Statement d is not true. The slowdown in U.S. labor productivity has not been explained by a reduction in the capital stock. A number of explanations (discussed in your text) have been offered but none seem to do a good job of explaining why U.S. labor productivity has declined since the 1970s. Statement e is not true. The effect of advances in information technology on labor productivity have been very difficult to quantify. This, in part, is due to the fact that the information technology advances primarily affected the service sector where output per worker is much harder to quantify than, say, for the manufacturing sector.

9.   Correct answer: e.

Discussion: Research and development, either private or government funded, leads to technological advances not only within the industry conducting the research and development but for other related industries. Monopolies, particularly those granted through patents, can spur innovation. Monopoly status confers the possibility of long-term profits to a firm which in turn spurs a firm to innovate. Secondly, as other firms try to break the monopoly status by producing a similar product (a process called "creative destruction"), other innovations are generated. Inventions that are designed to reduce costs are another source of technological progress. Here again, the profit-maximizing motive of the firm can promote innovation. A firm that reduces its costs through innovation will see bigger profits. The scale of the market also spurs innovation. The possibility that a product, once developed, will be mass marketed (e.g., disposable diapers) also creates an incentive to innovate. That is, if firms see a huge profit potential in an innovative product, they will produce it.

10.   Correct answer: c.

Discussion: Creative destruction is a process whereby firms compete with an innovating monopolist by introducing a new, better, version of the product which, in turn, generates more innovation.

Statement a is true and means that technological progress can increase the productivity of labor, as well as capital. Statement b is true. Your book discusses a case in which education (investment in human capital) is thought to be the key to technological progress. A more educated society is a more intelligent society and a more intelligent society is more likely to innovate than one that is not as well educated. Statement d is true. Successful patents guarantee an innovator profits for a long period of time. The incentive to reap profits thus leads to innovation and technological progress. Statement e is true. If property rights are not protected, neither are profits from innovations. Thus, without property rights, there is a reduced incentive to innovate and technological progress is likely to be shunted.

11.   Correct answer: e.

Discussion: Country A's real GDP per capita will double to $20,000 in 10 years (70/7). In another 10 years, it will double from $20,000 to $40,000. Country B's real GDP per capita will double in 20 years (70/3.5). Thus, Country B's real GDP per capita will be $40,000 in 20 years. After the 20th year, assuming Country A will continue to grow at 7% a year while Country B grows at 3.5% a year, it must be true that Country A's real GDP per capita will surpass Country B's real GDP per capita after the 20th year.

VIII.   ANSWER KEY: ESSAY QUESTIONS

1.   Technological progress enables a country to produce more output with the same amount of capital and labor as before. Because more output can be produced without any increase in the capital stock, a country's citizens do not have to reduce their consumption spending (i.e., increase the level of their savings today) in order to fund additions to the capital stock. Thus, citizens can consume a higher share (percentage) of output than citizens of a country that grows through additions to its capital stock. In this way, we might say that the citizens are able to enjoy a better standard of living. When a country experiences economic growth through additions to its capital stock, its citizens are, in effect, sacrificing current consumption (i.e., they are saving more today) so that businesses can purchase new plant and equipment with the savings. The purchases of new plant and equipment benefit society as a whole in the future by enabling the country to grow at a faster rate than it would have if its citizens had not been willing to reduce consumption spending today. However, there is a cost to the citizens in that their standard of living may not be as enjoyable because of reduced consumption. So, technological progress permits economic growth without the sacrifice of reduced consumption in the present whereas economic growth through additions to the capital stock comes at a cost.

This, of course, assumes that technological progress is not funded through savings. Some types of technological progress (innovations) may arise without any necessary increase in savings required. If they did, then what is true of economic growth through additions to the capital stock would be true of economic growth through technological progress.

A good example of the sacrifices that a country's citizens must make in terms of reduced consumption spending is present-day Russia. The country is trying to rebuild itself and requires a lot of new, updated plant and equipment. The funds to pay for the new plant and equipment must come from somewhere. They must come from the savings of Russian citizens who lend their savings to businesses (i.e., business borrow from the citizens). Another way to look at the problem is to apply the principle of crowding out. If a country can only produce $X of output, it must be divided up between consumers and businesses (assuming no government). Thus, if a country wants to add to its capital stock, businesses must be able to increase their spending on plant and equipment which means consumers must reduce their spending on consumption goods since the Country As a whole can only produce a limited amount of output.

2.   Technological progress has many sources. Technological progress can occur through the research and development efforts of government or privately-funded channels.   Sometimes the research and development has spillover benefits for other industries which can, in turn, promote further technological progress. Technological progress also arises through the creative, educated, and talented minds of a nation's workforce.   Thus, education (particularly in engineering and the sciences) can promote technological progress. The granting of patents to firms that innovate (which gives the firm a monopoly status) also promotes technological progress. A firm's desire to innovate is affected by the potential profit reward. A firm that is awarded a patent has more assurance that the profits it will earn on its innovation will not, at least for a time, be reduced by other firms competing with it. A legal framework for the protection of intellectual property rights also promotes technological progress through assuring innovative firms that profits they make from new ideas will be justly protected. This also helps to ensure that innovative firms will have a continued desire to innovate. Without such protection, firms may decide that the payoff from innovating is not enough and so technological progress is held back. Technological progress can also be influenced by the market potential. A bigger market presents a bigger potential profit opportunity. This is why free trade, which is a way of broadening a firm's market potential, may also encourage technological progress. Just think of the profit opportunities if U.S. firms were able to freely export to China, the world's biggest market and almost 30 times the size of the U.S. market! Now, there's an incentive to come up with new and improved products! Technological progress also occurs through a firm's desire to reduce its costs (and thereby increase its profits).

A careful look at the list above suggests that innovation and therefore technological progress is fundamentally prompted by two things: an educated society and a profit motive.

Take It to the Net

We invite you to visit the O'Sullivan/Sheffrin page on the Prentice Hall Web site at:

http://www.prenhall.com/osullivan/

for this chapter's World Wide Web exercise.

CHAPTER 23: APPENDIX

I.   OVERVIEW

In the appendix, you will use a simple model of an economy along with a graphic representation of it that develops the explicit relationship between savings, gross investment and depreciation, and capital deepening. In the simple model, the population will be held constant (zero growth rate) and there is assumed to be no government (and, therefore, no government spending, taxing, or policy) and no foreign sector (and, therefore, no exports or imports). You will learn that a country that saves more today increases its capital stock, capital per worker (i.e., capital deepening), real wages, and also its potential for future growth. You will learn that a higher rate of savings today comes at a sacrifice -- decreased consumption today. You will learn that the difference between the level of savings and the amount of depreciation determines the change in a country's capital stock. If the level of savings are just equal to the amount of depreciation, a country's net investment is zero. When this occurs, a country's economic growth through additions to the capital stock and capital per worker (capital deepening) will stop. You will learn that an increase in the saving rate of a country will lead to a higher capital stock and ultimately more output. You will learn that technological progress through raising output can increase the level of savings and thus lead to increases in the capital stock.

II.   CHECKLIST

By the end of this appendix, you should be able to:

√   Depict the process of economic with a Solow diagram.
√   Explain how capital deepening is affected by savings relative to depreciation.
√   Explain how a higher level of savings can lead to higher real wages and more output.
√   Explain how technological progress enhances capital deepening.

III.   KEY TERMS

Please see the key terms to Chapter 8.

IV.   PERFORMANCE ENHANCING TIPS (PETS)

Please see the PETS to Chapter 8.

V.   PRACTICE EXAM: MULTIPLE CHOICE QUESTIONS

1.   Capital deepening will stop when a country's:

a.   saving rate is equal to the rate of depreciation of the capital stock.
b.   level of savings are equal to the amount depreciation of the capital stock.

c.   gross investment is 1%.
d.   consumption equals savings.
e.   diminishing returns occur.

2.   If depreciation is greater than the level of savings:

a.   technological progress will not occur.
b.   real wages will rise.
c.   output per worker (labor productivity) will decrease (assuming the size of the workforce does not change).
d.   the capital stock will decline.
e.   (c) and (d).

3.   Technological progress leads to:

a.   increases in output per worker.
b.   increases in gross investment.
c.   increases in the level of savings.
d.   increases in real wages.
e.   all of the above.

4.   Which one of the following statements is NOT true of the Solow model?

a.   an economy grows, the level of savings increase at an increasing rate.
b.   capital per worker increases if the level of savings are greater than the amount of depreciation of a country's capital stock.
c.   output increases but at a decreasing rate.
d.   it may take decades for the process of capital deepening to come to an end.
e.   all of the above are true.

VI.   PRACTICE EXAM: ESSAY QUESTION

1.   Explain how technological progress can enhance capital deepening.

VII.   ANSWER KEY: MULTIPLE CHOICE QUESTIONS

1.   Correct answer: b.

Discussion: Capital deepening arises when a country's capital stock is increased (relative to its workforce) so that the amount of capital per worker increases. Thus, one way in which capital deepening will stop is when a country stops adding to its capital stock. Statement b means that a country is saving just enough to fund replacement of worn out capital (depreciation) and no more. That is, a country's capital stock will not be increasing; it will remain at the same level (say $1 billion).

Statement a is not correct. It is the **level** of savings and **amount** of depreciation, not the saving rate (which is a percentage of income) or the depreciation rate (which is a percentage of the capital stock), which ultimately determine what will happen to a country's capital stock. Statement c is not true. Just because gross investment is equal to 1% does not mean that a country's capital stock will increase. Remember, it is net investment that matters in determining whether the capital stock will grow or not. Statement d is meaningless. The relationship between consumption and savings does not imply anything about what happens to a country's capital stock. Statement e is not correct. Diminishing returns has nothing to do with whether a country's capital stock will increase.

2.   Correct answer: e.

Discussion: If depreciation is greater than the level of savings, a country's net investment will be negative which also means that a country's capital stock will decline. This has two implications. As a country's capital stock declines, and assuming the size of the workforce does not change, the amount of capital per worker will decline. With less capital per worker, workers will be less productive and so output per worker (labor productivity) will decline. Thus, statements c and d are true.

Statement b is not true because real wages would fall, not rise. This is because with less capital per worker, workers are less productive. If workers are paid based on how productive they are, their real wages will fall, not rise. Statement a is not true. Technological progress can occur independently of what is happening to the capital stock (and thus the relationship of depreciation to savings).

3.   Correct answer: e.

Discussion: Technological progress increases the amount of output a country can produce with a given amount of labor and capital. Thus, output per worker will increase. With more output and, therefore, more income, the level of savings will rise. As the level of savings rises, a country is able to fund more gross investment. Since technological progress increases the amount of output per worker, workers' real wages will rise. (They are more productive and so will be paid accordingly.)

4.   Correct answer: a.

Discussion: Statement a is not true because, as an economy grows, the level of savings increase but at a decreasing rate. This is because, as an economy grows, output (and hence income) increases but at a decreasing rate. With a saving rate constant at, say, 10% of income, the level of savings will also increase as an economy grows, but at a decreasing rate.

Statement b is true. See the answer to question (2) for more detail. Statement c is true; it is another way of saying that there are diminishing returns to the aggregate production function. Statement d is true. Your book emphasizes that the process of capital deepening will eventually come to an end when the amount of depreciation is equal to the amount of savings of the country. However, it may take a long time for this equality to be fulfilled.

VI.   PRACTICE EXAM: ESSAY QUESTION

1.   Technological progress increases the amount of output a country can produce with a given amount of labor and capital. With more output and, therefore, more income, the level of savings will rise. As the level of savings rises, a country is able to fund more gross investment. As long as the increased level of savings exceeds that amount needed to replace worn-out capital, the capital stock will increase. Thus,

technological progress not only promotes economic growth on its own but also fosters the potential for more growth through capital accumulation.

Take It to the Net

We invite you to visit the O'Sullivan/Sheffrin page on the Prentice Hall Web site at:

http://www.prenhall.com/osullivan/

for this chapter's World Wide Web exercise.

CHAPTER 24
COORDINATING ECONOMIC ACTIVITY:
AGGREGATE DEMAND AND SUPPLY

I.   OVERVIEW

In this chapter, you will use a model of aggregate demand and aggregate supply to study the short and long-run effects of changes in aggregate demand and supply on the price level and output. You will learn what causes aggregate demand and aggregate supply to shift and what determines the slope of each curve. You will learn about "shocks" that can move an economy in one direction or another. You will also learn how changes in government and central bank policy can move the economy in one direction or another. You will learn how, in a market-based economy, the price system can act to coordinate economic activities. You will also learn about those circumstances which may impair the ability of the price system to coordinate economic activities efficiently.

II.   CHECKLIST

By the end of this chapter, you should be able to:

√   Give some examples of economic shocks and discuss their impact on output and the price level.
√   Explain the Real Business Cycle view of an economy.
√   Explain how a free-market price system can coordinate economic activity.
√   Explain what the "invisible hand" is.
√   List and discuss the limits of coordinating economic activity through the price system.
√   Define a futures market.
√   Define a "real" price and explain its role in the price system.
√   Discuss some methods used to overcome the economic coordination problem when prices are sticky.
√   Describe the "short run" and the "long run" in macroeconomics.
√   Explain why the aggregate demand curve is negatively sloped.
√   List factors that would cause the aggregate demand curve to shift and in which direction.
√   Explain why the aggregate supply curve is drawn horizontally for the short run and vertically for the long run.
√   Compare and contrast the effects of shifts in aggregate demand on output and the price level in the short run and the long run.
√   Describe the effects of shifts in aggregate supply on output and the price level.

III.   KEY TERMS

Economic fluctuations: movements of GDP above or below normal trends.
Business cycles: another name for economic fluctuations.
Short run in macroeconomics: the period of time that prices are fixed.
Real business cycle theory: the economic theory that emphasizes the role of technology shocks as a cause of economic fluctuations.
The Invisible Hand: the term that economists use to describe how the price system can efficiently coordinate economic activity without central government intervention.

258

Focal points: obvious points of agreement in bargaining situations.
Keynesian economics: models in which demand determines output in the short run.
Demand side economics: another name for Keynesian economics.
Real price : the nominal price of a product adjusted for inflation.
Aggregate demand: the relationship between the level of prices and the quantity of real GDP demanded.
Wealth effect: the increase in spending that occurs because the real value of money increases when the price level falls.
Aggregate Supply: the relationship between the level of prices and the quantity of output supplied.
Classical Aggregate Supply: a vertical aggregate supply curve. It reflects the idea that in the long run, output is determined solely by the factors of production.
Keynesian aggregate supply curve: a horizontal aggregate supply curve. It reflects the idea that prices are sticky in the short run and firms adjust production to meet demand.
Supply shocks: external events that shift the aggregate supply curve.

IV.   PERFORMANCE ENHANCING TIPS (PETS)

PET #1

Changes in output in the Keynesian economic model (short-run model) are associated with changes in employment.

For example, if an economy produces more output (i.e., real GDP increases), employment is expected to have increased. If an economy produces less output (i.e., real GDP decreases), employment is expected to have decreased.

PET #2

Economic fluctuations are defined as changes in the level of output (real GDP) over time.

Economic fluctuations are also referred to as "the business cycle."

PET #3

Shifts in aggregate demand are caused by factors that lead to changes in spending other than changes in the price level.

This is just an application of PETs #1 and #6 from Chapter 4 of the Practicum which you may want to review. Since aggregate demand is composed of spending by households (consumers), businesses (firms), the government, and the foreign sector, any change in these spending components not caused by a change in the price level will be represented by a shift in aggregate demand. These spending components may change for a variety of reasons (change in taxes, interest rates, money supply, exchange rate, etc).

For example, suppose the interest rate increases. A rise in the interest rate makes it more costly for households and businesses to borrow money to fund their purchases. Thus, a rise in the interest rate will reduce consumption and business spending. This would be represented by a leftward shift in the aggregate demand curve.

PET #4

Shifts in the aggregate supply curve are caused by factors that lead to changes in an economy's capacity to produce output.

An economy's capacity to produce depends on a number of factors: the size and productivity of its labor force, the age and amount of the capital stock, and the state of technology. Changes in these factors will be represented by a shift in the aggregate supply curve.

For example, suppose the government increases spending on research and development. The spending fuels technological advancement. An advance in the state of technology means that an economy will be able to produce more output with its given set of resources than before the technological advance. The advance in the state of technology would then be represented by a rightward shift in the aggregate supply curve.

V.   PRACTICE EXAM: MULTIPLE CHOICE QUESTIONS

1.   According to Keynes, the main cause of the Great Depression in the U.S. was:

a.   insufficient demand for goods and services.
b.   excess capacity in production.
c.   the stock market crash.
d.   unemployment.
e.   low real wages.

2.   The real business cycle view of the economy is that:

a.   the business cycles is caused by changes in real wages.
b.   changes in investment spending drive the business cycle.
c.   changes in technology causes changes in the potential level of output.
d.   economic fluctuations are viewed as changes in potential output, not as movements away or toward it.
e.   (c) and (d).

3.   Which one of the following statements is true?

a.   Keynesian economic thought deals with the behavior of the economy in the long run.
b.   in the short run, the aggregate demand curve is horizontal.
c.   a criticism of the real business cycle theory is that it cannot explain recessions very well.
d.   the invisible arm is the price system that coordinaties economic activity.
e.   all of the above are true.

4.   Which one of the following statements is NOT an explanation for economic fluctuations?

a.   transportation costs.
b.   lack of focal points.
c.   sticky prices.
d.   insufficient information contained in prices.

e.   (a) and (b).

5.   Futures contracts:

a.   set a price to be paid in the future for delivery of a commodity today.
b.   can help reduce the problem associated with too few prices.
c.   exist for goods like computers and cars.
d.   eliminate the problem of sticky prices.
e.   (a) and (c).

6.   If all prices, including input prices, are rising by 10%, then:

a.   real prices are increasing by 10%.
b.   the demand for all goods and services must be increasing by 10%.
c.   firms may be unsure of whether to produce more in response to the increased price of their good.
d.   firms' profits will decline by 10%.
e.   inflation will be zero.

7.   In which market would the price be least likely to be "sticky"?

a.   wages of union teachers.
b.   steel rods.
c.   fresh fruit.
d.   trucks.
e.   wages of government workers.

8.   A consequence of sticky prices in the aircraft industry would be:

a.   a shortage or surplus of airplanes.
b.   a shortage or surplus of labor in the aircraft industry.
c.   a shortage or surplus of aircraft parts.
d.   a vertical production function.
e.   (a), (b), and (c).

9.   Which one of the following is a reason for why the aggregate demand curve is negatively sloped?

a.   a decrease in the price level raises the purchasing power of money and wealth.
b.   a decrease in the price level raises interest rates which reduces spending.
c.   an increase in the price level raises exports.
d.   an increase in the price level reduces the amount of output produced.
e.   a decrease in income causes people to save more.

10.   Which one of the following would shift the aggregate demand curve to the left (decrease aggregate demand)?

a.   an increase in the money supply.
b.   an increase in government spending.
c.   an increase in exports.

d.   an increase in taxes.
e.   a decline in the capital stock.

11.   In the short run, an increase in aggregate demand will increase _____ (the price level; output; the price level and output) and in the long run will increase _____ (the price level; output; the price level and output).

a.   the price level and output/the price level
b.   the price level and output/output
c.   output/the price level
d.   the price level/the price level
e.   output/the price level and output

12.   Which one of the following statements is true?

a.   In the Keynesian model, the level of output is determined by demand.
b.   In the Classical model, the level of output is determined by demand.
c.   In the Classical model, the aggregate supply curve is horizontal.
d.   where aggregate demand and aggregate supply intersect is the full-employment level of output.
e.   (b) and (c).

13.   In the short run, a drop in oil prices will lead to:

a.   a lower price level with no change in output.
b.   a lower price level and a higher output level.
c.   a lower price level and a lower output level.
d.   a higher price level and a higher output level.
e.   a higher price level and a lower output level.

VI.   PRACTICE EXAM: ESSAY QUESTIONS

1.   Explain the short and long-run effects of an increase in the money supply on the price level and output. Be sure to address why the results are different.

2.   There are two parts to this question. Briefly answer each. (a) Discuss what would happen to U.S. output and the U.S. price level in the short run if foreign goods and services became more expensive. (b) Discuss what would happen to U.S. output and the U.S. price level in the short run if the capital stock declined.

VII.   ANSWER KEY: MULTIPLE CHOICE QUESTIONS

1.   Correct answer: a.

Discussion: Keynes thought that the Great Depression was caused by too little spending taking place in the U.S. economy. This insufficient demand for goods and services lead to a reduced demand for workers which consequently led to a very high unemployment rate.

Statements b, c, and e may be consequences (not causes) of the Great Depression. While the stock market crash may have been partly responsible for the Great Depression, it is not the reason that Keynes stressed.

2.   Correct answer: e.

Discussion: Real business cycle economists do not make a distinction between the current level of output an economy is producing and the potential level of output that could be produced. They argue that whatever the level of output an economy is producing, that is the potential level. Thus, fluctuations in the level of output are referred to as fluctuations in the potential level of output and not as movements away or toward it. Real business cycle economists also believe the reason for the fluctuations in output is technological changes.

Statement a is not correct although a real business cycle economist might agree that real wages can change with fluctuations (changes) in output (i.e., the business cycle). Statement b is not applicable to real business cycle economists.

3.   Correct answer: c.

Discussion: Real business cycle theory has been criticized on the grounds that it cannot explain recessions, particularly deep and lasting recessions, very well. A real business cycle economist would have to argue that there had been a technological decline in order for a recession to occur. However, since technology seems to advance and rarely ever declines, at least in modern, industrialized countries, the real business cycle theory cannot explain recessions very well.

Statement a is not correct; Keynesian economic thought deals with the behavior of the economy in the short run, defined as a period of time during which prices are fixed. Statement b is not correct; in the short run, the aggregate supply curve is horizontal. Statement d is not correct; the invisible hand (Adam Smith's term) is the price system which coordinates economic activity.

4.   Correct answer: e.

Discussion: Sticky prices, insufficient information, and too few prices are explanations your textbook offers for explaining economic fluctuations. Transportation costs have not been offered as an explanation, nor is it discussed in your textbook. Focal points are obvious points of aggreement and to an economist can help coordinate, to a degree, economic activity even in the absence of prices.

5.   Correct answer: b.

Discussion: Futures contracts are contracts that set a price today between buyer and seller that will be paid at some point in the future when delivery of the commodity takes place. Thus, futures contracts help eliminate uncertainty about what price a buyer will have to pay (and a seller will receive) when the commodity is sold at a later date. Thus, statement a is not correct. Futures contracts can help reduce the problem of too few prices. An example of "too few prices" is the absence of a known price today for what a commodity purchased in the future will cost. Your book gives the example of a person who is saving today so that they can purchase a car in the future. The problem is that it is not known to the buyer or seller today what that price will be.

Statement c is not correct; in fact, futures contracts exist for only a limited number of commodities. These commodities are things like foreign currency, gold, silver, oil, pork bellies, tin, etc. Statement d is not correct; futures contracts do not have any impact on the stickiness of prices.

6.   Correct answer: c.

Discussion: If all prices are rising by 10%, firms may not know whether the increase in the price of the good it sells is due to an increase in the demand for it or not. If the price increase is due to general inflation in the economy, then the firm should not conclude that the price increase reflects an increased demand for their product. In this case, the firm should not produce more output. However, if the firm is wrong and the increased price is due to an increased demand, then the firm will not have produced enough to meet the new demand. This could hurt customer relationships. The point is that inflation creates uncertainty for firms about demand conditions for their product.

Statement a is not correct; if all prices were rising by 10%, then real prices (inflation-adjusted prices) would not be changing at all. The percentage change in real prices would be 0%. Statement b is not correct because there may be other reasons why prices rise besides an increase in the demand for the product. Statement d is not correct. In this case, firm's profits will not change. This happens because the price at which they sell their output is rising by the same percentage as the cost of producing the output is rising. Thus, the percentage change in profits will be zero. Statement e is not correct. If all prices are rising by 10%, it necessarily follows that inflation will rise by 10%. However, the converse is not true. If inflation is reported to be 10%, it does not necessarily mean that **all** prices are rising by 10%; some may be rising by more, some by less (and some could actually be falling).

7.   Correct answer: c.

Discussion: When prices are "sticky," it means that prices don't move up or down immediately in response to changes in demand or supply. Such price stickiness may be due to contracts that have been set that fix the price at which a good or service sells for a period of time. Thus, wages of union and government workers (and most workers in general) are considered sticky. The price for durable goods like steel rods, trucks, etc. are also typically set by a contract. Even prices on pre-printed brochures and menus may be sticky since businesses may not be able to quickly change the price for their output when there is a shift in demand or supply. Fresh fruit, however, is a good that is much less likely to be sticky.

8.   Correct answer: a.

Discussion: The consequence of sticky prices is that, when demand and/or supply shift, the price does not immediately change. Consequently, an excess demand or supply can be created. If a shortage or surplus of airplanes emerges, then the amount of labor and aircraft parts used in producing airplanes will also be affected. If wages in the aircraft industry and prices in the aircraft parts industry are not sticky, then a shortage or surplus may not arise. A production function shows the relationship between output and labor for a given capital stock and state of technology. It has nothing to do with sticky prices.

9.   Correct answer: a.

Discussion: When the price level drops, the average level of prices of goods and services declines. This means goods and services are less costly to consumers. This, in turn, means that the purchasing power of consumers' money and wealth (how many goods and services they can buy) will have increased. Since the real value of consumers' money and wealth has increased, they will be inclined to buy more when the price level drops. This is a way of saying that aggregate demand is negatively sloped. As the price level drops, the amount of total output desired to be purchased will increase.

Statement b is incorrect because a decline in the price level lowers interest rates, not raises them. Statement c is incorrect because an increase in the price level implies that exports are becoming more expensive to foreign residents. Thus, an increase in the price level would reduce exports, not raise them. Statement d is incorrect; the relationship between the price level and the amount of output produced is an aggregate supply concept, not an aggregate demand concept. Statement e is incorrect; aggregate demand shows the relationship between the price level and the amount of output in total demanded by an economy. It does not show the relationship between income and savings.

10.   Correct answer: d.

Discussion: A leftward shift in the aggregate demand curve means that aggregate demand for goods and services has declined. An increase in taxes would reduce the amount of spending in the economy and thus translate to a decrease in aggregate demand for goods and services.

Statements (a), (b), and (c) are all events that would raise the amount of spending in an economy and thus would be represented with a rightward shift in the aggregate demand curve. Statement e is an aggregate supply concept. A decline in the capital stock (a factor of production) would be represented by an upward shift in the short-run aggregate supply curve and a leftward shift in the long-run aggregate supply curve.

11.   Correct answer: c.

Discussion: To see this, look at the graphs below. Your text represents the short run with a horizontal aggregate supply curve and the long run with a vertical aggregate supply curve. Compare what happens to the price level and output (real GDP) in the short and long run when aggregate demand increases.

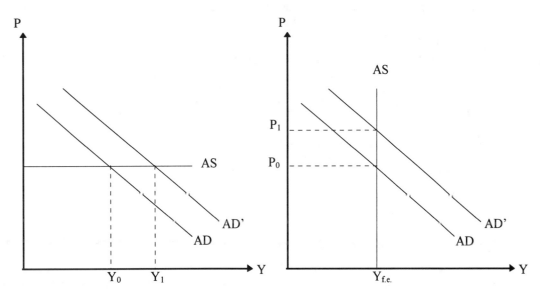

As you can see, in the short run, output increases without any change in the price level. This is because of sticky prices. Thus, any desired increased in spending is fully matched by an increase in production. In the long run, the economy is assumed to be producing at full capacity (full employment, or potential). This means that, physically, the economy does not have the resources to produce any more. Thus, when aggregate demand increases, businesses cannot respond by, in the aggregate, producing any more output. However, with buyers wanting to purchase more output, they will compete with each other for the limited output by offering to pay a higher price for it (much like at an auction). Ultimately, the price level rises. It rises by enough to keep aggregate demand equal to the amount the economy is able to produce. Thus, the price level rises in the long run with no change in the level of output produced.

Given the discussion above, statements a, b, d, and e cannot be correct.

12.   Correct answer: a.

Discussion: The Keynesian model is a "demand-driven" model meaning that the level of output an economy produces is determined by the demand for the goods and services it produces. Low demand will mean a low output level.

Statement b is not true; in the Classical model, the level of output is determined by the factors of production an economy has. Statement c is not true; in the Classical model, aggregate supply is represented as a vertical line. Statement d is not true; the intersection of aggregate demand and supply produce an "equilibrium" output level but the equilibrium output level may not be the full employment output level. For example, the full employment output level may be $1.5 trillion worth of goods and services whereas the intersection of aggregate demand and supply produce an output level of $1 trillion.

13.   Correct answer: b.

Discussion: A drop in oil prices is an example of a supply shock. Oil is a key input into production and, when its price changes, it affects the aggregate supply curve. In effect, the lower price of oil makes production less costly. This would be represented by a downward shift in the short-run aggregate supply curve (i.e., the same amount of output can be produced as before, but now at a lower price level). As the short-run aggregate supply curve shifts down along the aggregate demand curve, you will see that the equilibrium price level will drop and the equilibrium output level will rise. Output rises because the lower price level creates a real wealth, interest rate, and trade effect which all lead to increased spending. Since the cause of the increased spending is a drop in the price level (which is graphed on the axis), the increased spending is represented by a movement along the aggreagate demand curve (not a rightward shift in it). With increased spending, businesses respond by producing more which is why output rises.

Given the discussion above, none of the other statements are correct.

VIII. ANSWER KEY: ESSAY QUESTIONS

1.   In the short run, prices are sticky and output is demand determined. Thus, the increase in the money supply which raises spending by households and businesses leads to an increase in aggregate demand. As aggregate demand shifts out to the right, with prices sticky, there is no change in the price level. However, in the short run, businesses respond to the increased demand by producing more output and so the level of output produced rises. In the long run, prices (including input prices) are flexible and the economy is assumed to operate at its full-employment level of output. The full-employment level of output is determined by supply conditions -- labor, capital, and technology. If the economy is operating at full

employment, an increase in the money supply which fuels spending, will lead to an increase in aggregate demand for output. However, since the economy is at full employment, it is not physically able to produce any more output in response to the increased demand for it. Thus, the level of output cannot/does not change. The consequence of an increase in aggregate demand with no corresponding increase in production creates upward pressure on the prices of goods and services and so, in the long run, the price level rises.

2(a).   If foreign goods and services become more expensive, U.S. consumers will be less likely to buy foreign-produced goods and services. They may, in turn, buy U.S.-made equivalent goods and services as a substitute (e.g., instead of buying a car produced in Japan, buy a car produced in the U.S). From a foreigner's perspective, if their goods and services become more expensive, they may look to buy the same goods and services produced in the U.S. since they may be less expensive here. Thus, there will be an increase in demand for U.S. goods and services. This is represented by a rightward shift in the aggregate demand curve. In the short run, with prices sticky, the aggregate supply curve is horizontal. The increase in aggregate demand will not cause any change in the price level but the level of output the economy produced will increase.

2(b).   The capital stock is what helps a country produce output. If the capital stock declined, the output level a country produces will decline. This is an example of a negative supply shock. In the short run, a reduction in a country's ability to produce output is represented by an upward shift in the horizontal aggregate supply curve (i.e., every level of output able to be produced becomes more expensive to produce). As the horizontal aggregate supply curve shifts up along the aggregate demand curve, the price level rises and the level of output produced declines. Thus, the economy suffers a higher price level (inflation) and a lower output level. This outcome is sometimes referred to as "stagflation."

Take It to the Net

We invite you to visit the O'Sullivan/Sheffrin page on the Prentice Hall Web site at:

http://www.prenhall.com/osullivan/

for this chapter's World Wide Web exercise.

CHAPTER 25
KEYNESIAN ECONOMICS AND FISCAL POLICY

I.   OVERVIEW

In this chapter, you will learn about a short-run model of the economy referred to as a Keynesian economic model. You will learn that the model emphasizes how changes in spending, particularly government spending, can influence the level of output in the short run. You should remember that the model is simple in the sense that it holds a number of factors like prices, interest rates, exchange rates, and wages constant in order to highlight the affect of spending on output. You will see how spending by households, businesses, the government, and the foreign sector determines how much is in total produced in an economy. You will be introduced to multiplier analysis and see how some initial change in spending can lead to a multiple change in the level of output. You will learn about fiscal policy which is the use of government spending and changes in taxes to influence the level of output produced by an economy. You will learn a little of the history of Keynesian economic policy in the U.S. You will learn about the automatic stabilizer properties of a tax and transfer payments system.

II.   CHECKLIST

By the end of this chapter, you should be able to:

√   Discuss the key features of a Keynesian economic model.
√   Discuss Keynesian economic policy.
√   Explain autonomous spending.
√   Use the Keynesian cross diagram to show how changes in spending create changes in output.
√   Discuss macroequilibrium and situations of disequilibrium using the Keynesian cross diagram.
√   Discuss the role of inventories in situations of disequilibrium.
√   Explain the consumption function and the equation for the consumption function.
√   Define the marginal propensity to consume, save, and import.
√   Define the multiplier.
√   Describe how the multiplier works in an economy.
√   Compare the effects on output of an increase (or decrease) in government spending of $X to a cut in taxes of $X.
√   Define the government spending multiplier, the tax multiplier, and the balanced budget multiplier.
√   Give a brief history of the application of Keynesian economic ideas to the U.S. economy.
√   Define automatic stabilizers and explain what they do.

III.   KEY TERMS

Equilibrium output: the level of GDP where the demand for output equals the amount that is produced.
Consumption function: the relationship between the level of income and consumption spending.
Autonomous consumption: the part of consumption that does not depend on income.
Marginal propensity to consume (mpc): the fraction of additional income that is spent.
Marginal propensity to save: fraction of additional income that is saved.

Multiplier: the ratio of changes in output to changes in spending. It measures the degree to which changes in spending are "multiplied" into changes in output.

Keynesian fiscal policy: the use of taxes and government spending to affect the level of GDP in the short run.

Disposable personal income: the income that ultimately flows back to households, taking into account transfers and taxes.

Expansionary policies: policy actions that lead to increases in output

Contractionary policies: policy actions that lead to decreases in output.

Budget deficit: the difference between a government's spending and its taxation.

Permanent income: an estimate of a household's average level of income.

Automatic stabilizers: economic institutions that reduce economic fluctuations without any explicit action being taken.

Marginal propensity to import: the fraction of additional income that is spent on imports.

IV.   PERFORMANCE ENHANCING TIPS (PETS)

PET #1

In the Keynesian model with prices and the price level fixed, output is also a measure of income. Thus, the two terms "output" and "income" may be used interchangeably.

PET #2

In the Keynesian cross diagram, the purpose of the 45-degree line is to permit you to read output (income) off of the vertical axis to more easily compare it to the level of total spending that occurs at that income level.

To understand this, look at the graph below.

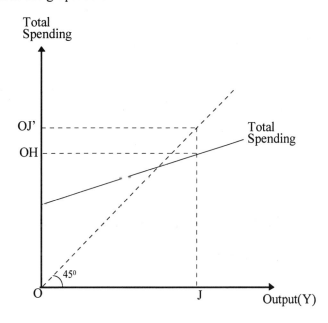

A comparison of total spending to income (output) at income (output) level OJ may at first appear difficult to do since spending is measured on the vertical axis but income is measured on the horizontal axis. However, you can measure income on the vertical axis by drawing a line from income level OJ up to the 45-degree line and over to the vertical axis. Mark this as OJ'. This is a measure of income read off of the vertical axis. Since total spending at income level OJ is read by taking that income level up to the spending graph and over to the vertical axis (marked as OH), you can see that income and output exceed total spending. Thus, you could conclude that businesses inventories will be building up since too much has been produced relative to how much is in total being purchased by the economy.

PET #3

The difference between consumption spending (C) and imports (M) is defined to be spending by households on domestic goods and services.

In a model with exports and imports, consumption spending is defined as spending by households on domestic **and** foreign-produced goods and services. If consumption figures reported for the U.S. are $45 billion, part of that $45 billion is spending on U.S.-made goods and services and part on foreign-made goods and services. If imports are reported to be $5 billion, then the difference between consumption and imports will define the amount of spending by U.S. households on U.S.-made goods and services only. In this case, the amount would be $40 billion.

PET #4

The relationship between changes in spending, output, and the multiplier is given by the formula:

$$\Delta y = \textbf{multiplier} \cdot \textbf{initial } \Delta \textbf{ in spending}$$

Given any two of these three pieces of the formula, you should be able to figure out the third.

For example, suppose you are told that the multiplier is 2.5 and that income and output have decreased by $100 billion. What might be the cause? A change in spending of $100/2.5 = $40 billion might be the cause. It may be that government spending declined by $40 billion or that investment spending declined by $40 billion, etc.

Suppose you are told that the marginal propensity to consume is 0.9 and the marginal propensity to import is 0.3. Further, you are told that investment spending has increased by $20 billion. What will be the effect on income and output? Since you know the marginal propensity to consume and the marginal propensity to import, you can compute the multiplier as $1/1-(0.9-0.3) = 1/0.4 = 2.5$. With the increase in investment spending of $20 billion, you can compute the change in income and output as $2.5 \cdot $20 billion = $50 billion.

Suppose you are told that government spending has increased by $10 billion and that income and output increased by $20 billion. What must the multiplier's value be? Using the formula in bold above, the multiplier would be $20 billion/$10 billion = 2.

PET #5

Autonomous consumption, investment spending, government spending, exports, and autonomous imports are components of total spending in an economy that do not depend on the level of income. This means that changes in income (output) will not cause changes in these spending components. However, changes in these spending components can cause changes in income (output).

For example, suppose you are given the following information:
$C = 100 + 0.9 \cdot (y - T)$
$I = 150$
$G = 200$
$X = 20$
$M = 50 + 0.1 \cdot y$

Based on this information, the multiplier for the economy is $1/1-(0.9-0.1) = 1/0.2 = 5$. Suppose you are told that government spending increases by $20 billion. Based on multiplier analysis, income and output will rise by 5 X $20 billion = $100 billion. While the increase in government spending leads to an increase in income and output, the increase in income will not affect the C_a, I, G, X or M_a (which is autonomous imports that your textbook has set to zero by writing $M = m \cdot y$). However, overall consumption (C) and overall imports (M) will be affected because they depend on the level of income. The extent to which they depend on the level of income is given by the marginal propensity to consume (0.9) and the marginal propensity to import (0.1). If income increases by $100 billion, since the marginal propensity to consume is 0.9, consumption spending will increase by $0.9 \cdot 100 = \$90$ billion. Also, since the marginal propensity to import is 0.1, imports will increase by $0.1 \cdot 100 = \$10$ billion. The $90 billion increase in consumption spending is spending by households on domestic **and** foreign goods. Since imports (spending on foreign goods) have increased by $10 billion, the increase in spending on domestic goods is $80 billion ($90 - $10).

PET #6

There are several formulas for the multiplier. Each formula depends on the variables assumed to depend on income.

The simplest formula that your book introduces is a multiplier formula of $1/(1-b)$ where b is the marginal propensity to consume. This formula applies to a model in which there are either no taxes and no import or taxes and imports are autonomous (i.e., do no depend on the level of income). For example, if b = 0.8, then the multiplier is $1/0.2 = 5$.

The next multiplier formula your book introduces is one in which taxes depend on the level of income so $T = t \cdot y$. In this case, the multiplier's formula is $1/[1-b \cdot (1-t)]$. For example, if b = 0.8 and the tax rate is 0.1, the multiplier is $1/1-0.72 = 1/0.38 = 2.63$.

Then, your book introduces a multiplier formula where taxes are autonomous (i.e., do not depend on the level of income) but there are imports which do depend on the level of income so $M = m \cdot y$. In this case, the multiplier's formula is $1/1-(b-m)$. For example, if b = 0.85 and m = 0.10, the multiplier is $1/1-0.75 = 1/0.25 = 4$.

PET #7

The magnitude of the multiplier depends on the marginal propensity to consume (b), the marginal propensity to import (m), and the tax rate.

A bigger marginal propensity to consume will increase the magnitude of the multiplier and vice-versa. A bigger marginal propensity to import will decrease the magnitude of the multiplier and vice-versa. A bigger tax rate will decrease the magnitude of the multiplier and vice-versa.

For example, suppose b = 0.9 and m = 0.1, and that the tax rate is zero. The multiplier will be 1/1-(0.9-0.1) = 1/0.2 = 5. Now, suppose marginal propensity to consume decreases to 0.85. What will the multiplier's value be? The multiplier will be 1/1-(0.85-0.1)= 1/0.25 = 4.

Now, suppose that the marginal propensity to import decreases to 0.05 while the marginal propensity to consume remains at 0.9. The multiplier will be 1/1-(0.9-0.05) = 1/0.15 = 6.67.

Now, suppose that the tax rate is no longer zero but 10% (i.e., t = 0.10). Also, for simplicity, assume that the marginal propensity to import is zero. When taxes do not depend on income, the multiplier would be 1/1-0.8 = 1/0.2 = 5. When taxes depend on income, the multiplier will be 1/1-0.8•(1-0.1) = 1/1-0.72 = 1/0.38 = 2.63.

PET #8

A change in government spending of $X will have a bigger impact on income and output than a change in taxes of $X because government spending works directly on total spending whereas taxes work indirectly on total spending through consumption spending.

Remember, that in the Keynesian model, the level of output an economy produces depends on total spending. An increase in government spending will thus increase the level of output. The amount that output will increase depends on the size of the multiplier.

For example, suppose the marginal propensity to consume is 0.75 and the marginal propensity to import is 0. The multiplier is 1/1-(b-m) = 1/1-(0.75-0) = 1/0.25 = 4. Now, suppose government spending increases by $25 billion. The increase in income and output will be 4 X 25 = $100.

Compare this increase in income and output to a cut in taxes of $25 billion (the same amount by which government spending has increased). You know that the cut in taxes will increase consumption spending. The amount by which consumption spending will increase is NOT $25 billion. The reason is that the marginal propensity to consume is 0.75. In this case, consumption spending will increase by 0.75•$25 billion = $18.75 billion. The remainder of the tax cut will be saved (25 - 18.75 = 6.25). Income and output will increase by the multiplier times the change in consumer spending. Thus, income and output will increase by 4 X $18.75 = $75 billion. As you can see, the cut in taxes is not as expansionary on spending and thus on output as is an equivalent increase in government spending.

V.   PRACTICE EXAM: MULTIPLE CHOICE QUESTIONS

1.   Which one of the following statements is true of the graph below?

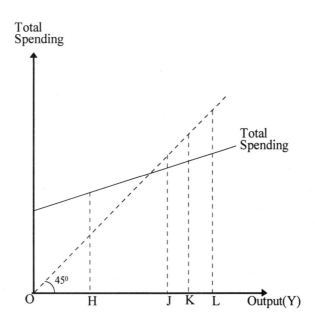

a.   at output level OH, inventories are accumulating.
b.   at output level OK, total spending exceeds output.
c.   output level OJ is the equilibrium level of output.
d.   at output level OL, inventories are accumulating.
e.   at output level OH, consumption equals savings.

2.   Which one of the following statements is true about the consumption function below?

C = 20 + 0.75•(y-T)

a.   the marginal propensity to save must be 1.75.
b.   if income is 250 and taxes are 50, then consumption is 150.
c.   if income is 400 and taxes are 120, then savings must be 50.
d.   the slope of the consumption function is 0.25.
e.   the autonomous level of consumption cannot be determined without information on income and taxes.

3.   Which one of the following would cause the consumption function to shift down?

a   an increase in stock prices.
b.   a decrease in income.
c.   a decrease in wealth.
d.   a fall in interest rates.
e.   (b) and (c).

4.   Which one of the following is true of equilibrium in an economy in which there is no government and no foreign sector?

a.   I = S.

b.   C = S.
c.   C = I.
d.   Y = C.
e.   Y = I.

5.   Which one of the following statements is NOT true of the multiplier?

a.   it is greater than 1.0.
b.   it will increase with an increase in the marginal propensity to consume.
c.   it will increase with a decrease in the marginal propensity to import.
d.   it gives the multiple by which output will change in response to a change in, e.g., investment spending.
e.   all of the above are true.

6.   Given a multiplier of 2, a decrease in investment spending of $40 billion will:

a.   increase equilibrium output by $80 billion.
b.   decrease equilibrium output by $80 billion.
c.   increase equilibrium output by $20 billion.
d.   decrease equilibrium output by $20 billion.
e.   decrease equilibrium output by $40 billion.

7.   Suppose the President would like to increase the level of output an economy produces by $100 billion, no more and no less. Further, suppose the multiplier is 3. Which one of the following policy options would work?

a.   increase government spending by $33.33 billion.
b.   increase taxes by $33.33 billion.
c.   increase government spending by $300 billion.
d.   increase government spending by $100 billion.
e.   increase government spending by $33.33 billion and reduces taxes by $33.33 billion.

8.   A fiscal policy of increasing government spending by $50 billion and increasing taxes by $50 billion will (assuming the marginal propensity to consume is 0.5 and the marginal propensity to import is 0):

a.   decrease autonomous consumption by $25 billion.
b.   raise output by $100 billion.
c.   create a budget deficit.
d.   raise output by $50 billion.
e.   (a) and (d).

9.   Which one of the following statements is true?

a.   Keynesian fiscal policy was actively used during the Great Depression.
b.   President Kennedy applied Keynesian economics to the U.S. economy through a tax cut.
c.   a tax surcharge was imposed during the late 1960s to combat high unemployment.

d.   the tax cuts introduced by President Reagan in the early 1980s were proposed as part of a Keynesian fiscal policy prescription.

e.   all of the above are true.

10.   A temporary tax cut is:

a.   expected to be very expansionary.

b.   not expected to have much affect on spending and output.

c.   will raise permanent income.

d.   an example of an automatic stabilizer.

e.   none of the above.

11.   Automatic stabilizers:

a.   are part of the tax and transfer payment system.

b.   work without enacting any laws.

c.   help stabilize the business cycle.

d.   tend to reduce spending during economic expansions and raise spending during economic contractions.

e.   all of the above.

12.   Which one of the following statements is true?

a.   an increase in income will reduce imports.

b.   if the multiplier is 2 and exports increase by $10 billion, output will increase by $20 billion.

c.   an increase in the marginal propensity to import will increase the multiplier.

d.   a cut in tax rates will reduce the slope of the consumption function.

e.   (b) and (c).

VI.   PRACTICE EXAM: ESSAY QUESTIONS

1.   Explain why an initial increase in spending leads to a multiple expansion in output. What role does the magnitude of the marginal propensity play? Use a simple model with a government but no foreign sector.

2.   Suppose that you are chair of the Council of Economic Advisors and must make a recommendation to the President about what policy actions may need to be taken given that the economy is suffering a severe recession. What might you recommend and why?

VII.   ANSWER KEY: MULTIPLE CHOICE QUESTIONS

1.   Correct answer: d.

Discussion: At output (income) level OL, the amount the economy produces, OL, is greater than the amount of output in total purchased at that income level. Total spending at income level OL is read off the vertical axis and is OM, as shown below.

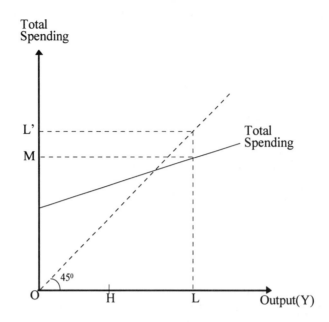

To compare this spending level to the output level, use the 45-degree line to measure the OL output level on the horizontal axis off of the vertical axis. The output level read off of the vertical axis is OL'. Since OL' is greater than OM, output exceeds total spending which means that businesses inventories will be piling up (accumulating).

Statement a is not correct because, at output level OH, spending exceeds current output and so inventories are being depleted. Statement b is not correct because output is greater than total spending. Statement c is not correct. The equilibrium level of output occurs where the 45-degree line and the total spending line intersect. Statement e is not correct. There is not enough information in the graph provided to say anything about the relationship between consumption and savings.

2.   Correct answer: c.

Discussion: If income is $400 and taxes are $120, then disposable income is $280. The consumption function shows that the marginal propensity to consume is 0.75. Thus, 0.75 X $280 of disposable income will be used by households to buy goods and services (consume). This amount is $210. Since autonomous consumption is $20, then total consumption based on a before-tax income level of $400 is $230. Since income is $400 and $230 is spent on goods and services and $120 is spent on taxes, the remainder is saved. Thus savings are ($400 - $230 - $120) = $50.

Statement a is not correct. The marginal propensity to save (mps) is 1 minus the marginal propensity to consume. Thus, the mps is 0.25. Statement b is not correct based on the discussion above. Statement d is not correct. The slope of the consumption function is 0.75 as is given in the equation for consumption. Statement e is not correct because the autonomous level of consumption is given in the equation. It is equal to the value of consumption that would occur even if income were zero and in this case is $20.

3.   Correct answer: c.

Discussion: A shift down in the consumption function means that, for every level of income, consumer spending is now lower. That is, autonomous consumption spending has declined. A decrease in wealth could cause consumers to be more frugal and thus spend less at every level of income than they had been willing to spend before.

Statement a is not correct. An increase in stock prices would increase wealth and thus lead to an increase in autonomous consumption which would shift the consumption function up. Statement b is not correct because a decrease in income would be represented by a movement down along the consumption function, not by a shift in it. Remember that since income is graphed on the axis, changes it will cause movements along the consumption function but not shifts in it. You may wish to review PET #1 of Chapter 1 of the Practicum. Statement d is not correct. A fall in interest rates makes it less costly for households to borrow in order to buy a new car or a new home. Thus, lower interest rates will lead to an increase in autonomous consumption which would be represented by an upward shift in the consumption function. Statement e is not correct because statement b is not correct.

4.   Correct answer: a.

Discussion: macroequilibrium occurs where total output (y) is equal to total spending. Total spending in an economy where there is no government and no foreign sector is just the sum of spending by households (C) and businesses (I). Thus, $y = C + I$. Furthermore, since output equals income and since there is no government, there are also no taxes. Thus, income can be either spent (C) or saved (S). Thus, $y = C + S$. By substitution in the equilibrium condition, $C + S = C + I$ which means $S = I$.

5.   Correct answer: e.

Discussion: The multiplier is greater than 1.0. This means that some initial change in spending will have a bigger impact on output than the initial change in spending. For example, if spending increases by $20 billion, output and income will increase in the first round by $20 billion but will then continue to increase as more spending and hence more production and income are generated. Thus, output will increase by more than the initial $20 billion increase in spending. The multiplier's value depends on the marginal propensity to consume and import (and on the tax rate). A bigger marginal propensity to consume means that after the first-round increase in income of $20 billion, more consumption will occur than with a lower marginal propensity to consume. With more consumption occurring, more output and income will be generated in the second, third, fourth....spending rounds. This can be described by saying that the multiplier will be bigger for a bigger marginal propensity to consume. A bigger marginal propensity to consume means that after the first round increase in income of $20 billion, more imports will be purchased than with a lower marginal propensity to import. With more income being used to buy foreign-made goods and services, less income is left available to buy domestic-made goods and services. Thus, with less spending on domestic goods and services, less domestic production and income will be generated. That is, the multiplier will decrease as the marginal propensity to import increases.

6.   Correct answer: b.

Discussion: First, you should be able to rule out answers a and c since a decrease in investment spending will lead to a decrease in output, not an increase. Next, you should be able to rule out answer e since the multiplier is a number that is not equal to 1. Given that the multiplier is 2, the $40 billion reduction in investment spending will circulate through the economy with multiplier effects leading to a reduction in output and income of $80 billion. You may wish to review PET #4 of this chapter to see how to use the formula.

7.   Correct answer: a.

Discussion: Since you are given the multiplier and the desired change in output, all you need to do is to apply the formula reviewed in PET #4. With a multiplier of 3, any spending increase of $33.33 billion will lead to an increase in output of $100 billion.

Statement b cannot be correct because an increase in taxes would reduce spending and thus would decrease output, not increase it. Statement c is not correct because an increase in government spending of $300 billion will lead to an increase in output of $900 billion. Statement d is not correct because an increase in government spending of $100 billion will lead to an increase in output of $300 billion. Statement e is not correct. The increase in government spending of $33.33 billion will increase output by $100 billion and the cut in taxes of $33.33 billion will raise consumption spending by the mpc times $33.33 billion. In total, output would rise by more than $100 billion since more than $33.33 billion worth of initial spending will take place.

8.   Correct answer: e.

Discussion: The increase in taxes of $50 billion will cause consumers to cut back on their spending. Thus, autonomous consumption will decline. By how much? Since the marginal propensity to consume is 0.5, autonomous consumption spending will decline by 0.5 X $50 billion = $25 billion. This reduction in consumption will have a multiplier effect on output. Since the mpc is 0.5 (and the marginal propensity to import and the tax rate is zero), the multiplier is $1/(1-0.5) = 2$. Thus, the fall in consumption spending of $25 billion will lead to a $50 billion fall in output. However, government spending has increased at the same time that taxes have been increased. The increase in government spending will work to raise output. By how much? Since the multiplier is 2, the increase in government spending of $50 billion will lead to an increase in output of $100 billion. On net, with output rising by $100 billion but declining by $50 billion (via the tax increase), output will increase by $50 billion. This is an example of the balanced budget multiplier. The balanced budget multiplier is 1 which means that any increase in spending of $X will lead to an $X increase in output.

Since taxes and government spending increase by the same amount, the budget will not go to a deficit (or surplus, either) but will remain in balance.

9.   Correct answer: b.

Discussion: President Kennedy applied a tax cut to the U.S. economy on the advice of Walter Heller, then chair of the Council of Economic Advisors. The belief was that the U.S. economy could be doing better than it currently was and that a tax cut would help get the economy to grow and thus bring the unemployment rate down.

Statement a is not correct. While Keynes wrote during the Great Depression, his views were not put into practice in the U.S. until the 1960s. Statement c is not correct. A tax surcharge (increase) was imposed by President Nixon to combat inflation. The objective of the tax increase was to reduce spending and thus the demand for goods and services in an effort to take the pressure off of prices. Statement d is not correct. The tax cuts introduced by President Reagan were billed as part of the "supply-side" prescription for the U.S. economy. Undeniably, they would carry demand-side effects. But, the view was that the tax cuts would promote work effort and additions to the capital stock which would thereby enhance the growth of the U.S. economy.

10.   Correct answer: b.

Discussion: A temporary tax cut is recognized by people to be temporary and thus is not expected to have a lasting impact on their income. Thus, people do not alter their spending behavior much in response to the tax cut. In fact, some studies suggest that people tend to save most of a temporary tax cut. Thus, the temporary tax cut has little effect on spending and consequently little effect (through the multiplier) on output.

Statement a is not correct because the policy is not likely to be very expansionary as discussed above. Statement c is not correct; a temporary tax cut raises temporary income. Statement d is not correct; an automatic stabilizer does not require legislative action as a temporary tax cut would.

11.   Correct answer: e.

12.   Correct answer: b.

Discussion: Exports are an autonomous component of spending and constitute spending by foreigners on goods produced by another country. Thus, if our exports increase by $10 billion, that means there is more spending on our goods. With a multiplier of 2, output will increase by $20 billion.

Statement a is not correct. Imports depend on income. Since the marginal propensity to import is positive, it means that increases in income will lead to increases in imports and decreases in income will lead to decreases in imports. Statement c is not correct; an increase in the marginal propensity to import will reduce the multiplier, not raise it. (See the answer to question 5 for more detail.) Statement d is not correct. A cut in tax rates raises the slope of the consumption function. A lower tax rate means that, effectively, there is more income available for consumers to spend.

VI.   PRACTICE EXAM: ESSAY QUESTIONS

1.   An initial increase in spending of, say, $30 billion, will **initially** lead to an increase in output and income of $30 billion. (With more output being produced, more income is generated.) This is not the end of the effects on the economy of the initial increase in spending. Since income has now increased by $30 billion, consumers (households) will go out and spend more. Just how much more they spend depends on the magnitude of the marginal propensity to consume (mpc). If the mpc is 0.9, households will spend an additional 0.9 X 30 = $27 billion. Their spending, of course, generates production and income in an amount equal to $27 billion. At this point, output has now increased by $57 billion which is more than the initial $30 billion increase in spending. The multiplier effect continues because the additional $27 billion worth of income propels more spending in an amount equal to 0.9 X 27 = $24.3 billion which further activates production and income by $24.3 billion. At this point, output has now increased by $81.3 billion in total. This is the multiplier effect in action and is dependent on how much consumers like to spend of additional income they receive. In the end, the multiplier formula dictates that the initial $30 billion increase in spending, given an mpc of 0.9, will lead to a $300 billion increase in output. This is because the multiplier is 1/1-0.9 = 1/0.1 = 10. If the mpc had been 0.6, then less

spending would occur for each increase in income. For example, after the initial increase in output and income of $30 billion, only 0.6 X 30 = $18 billion in spending and hence output and income would be generated. This is $9 billion less (27-18) than is generated when the mpc is 0.9. Thus, a smaller mpc creates a smaller multiplier effect which shows up in a smaller multiplier. In this case, with an mpc of 0.6, the multiplier would be 1/1-0.6 = 1/0.4 = 2.5. For an extreme, if the mpc was 0 (which means that, when consumers receive additional income they do not spend any of it), the multiplier would be 1 and the total increase in output coming from the initial $30 billion increase in spending would be $30 billion. There would be no multiplier effect.

2.   As chair of the Council of Economic Advisors and having a knowledge of economics confined to material that I've learned up through this chapter, I would be inclined to advise expansionary fiscal policy. Expansionary fiscal policy can be carried out in two ways -- through increases in government spending and/or permanent cuts in taxes. An increase in government spending works directly on spending and in comparison to an equal dollar tax cut is more stimulative to output. For example, a $50 billion increase in government spending will raise output by more than a $50 billion cut in taxes. This is because the $50 billion tax cut does not generate $50 billion worth of spending; it generates less than $50 billion worth of spending. If the marginal propensity to consume is 0.8, a $50 billion tax cut will increase spending by $40 billion which is $10 billion less than if government spending is used instead. Thus, the initial spending stimulus to the economy is smaller and for a given multiplier, its effects on output will also be smaller.

However, this is not to say that a tax cut is inferior to government spending as a tool of policymakers. If my council deems it necessary to unleash $50 billion worth of spending into the economy, we could cut taxes by more than $50 billion. In fact, if we cut taxes by $62.5 billion, we will generate the desired $50 billion increase in spending (0.8 X $62.5). One difference with the tax cut policy compared to an increase in government spending is that it is the private sector that is doing the spending and not the government. Some people may find this preferable. On the other hand, a tax cut (holding government spending constant) will increase the budget deficit by $62.5 billion whereas an increase in government spending (without cutting taxes) will increase the budget deficit by $50 billion. In any case, I'd let the President make the choice -- that's what he's been elected to do anyway.

I would warn the President that the effects of the expansionary fiscal policy may not turn out to be what my staff and I have estimated. The reason is that the budget deficit that is created in an effort to get the economy out of the recession may have some bad side effects on the economy that are not considered in the simple Keynesian model that I am using to formulate policy. For example, if the budget deficit makes people more worried about the economy and, therefore, more cautious about spending, then the multiplier may not be as big as assumed.

Take It to the Net

We invite you to visit the O'Sullivan/Sheffrin page on the Prentice Hall Web site at:

http://www.prenhall.com/osullivan/

for this chapter's World Wide Web exercise.

CHAPTER 26
INVESTMENT AND FINANCIAL INTERMEDIATION

I. OVERVIEW

In this chapter, you will learn about the factors that affect investment in an economy. You will be given a broader definition of investment than that used in GDP accounts. You will see how the interest rate, the inflation rate, taxes, a firm's stock price, and the current state of the economy can affect how much investment an individual or business may be willing to undertake. You will re-encounter the reality principle and see how it affects the costs of borrowing and lending. You will see how investment spending moves with the business cycle. You will learn why higher interest rates tend to reduce the level of investment spending in an economy, how tax incentives can be used to influence investment spending, and how stock prices influence the level of investment spending. You will learn what financial intermediation is and how it can facilitate investment in an economy by overcoming a coordination problem. You will learn that financial intermediaries pool the saving funds from individuals and households and lend them to borrowers. You will also learn that financial intermediaries help reduce the risk of lending and borrowing because of diversification.

II. CHECKLIST

By the end of this chapter, you should be able to:

√ Explain why investment is volatile.
√ Discuss what percentage of GDP is investment spending.
√ Explain the multiplier-accelerator model of investment spending.
√ Explain the difference between nominal and real interest rates/returns.
√ Calculate nominal and real interest rates.
√ Explain why savers may be hurt by inflation and why borrowers may benefit by inflation.
√ Define the expected real interest rate/return.
√ Explain why investment spending and the interest rate are negatively related.
√ Describe the neo-classical theory of investment and the Q-theory of investment.
√ Define a financial intermediary and describe its function.
√ Define liquidity and why it is important.
√ Define diversification and explain its affects on risk.
√ Give some situations in which financial intermediaries failed to function and what role the government can play in preventing such malfunctions.

III. KEY TERMS

Nominal interest rates: interest rates that are quoted in the market.
Real interest rate: the nominal interest rate minus the actual inflation rate.
Expected real interest rate: the nominal interest rate minus the expected inflation rate.
Financial intermediaries: organizations that receive funds from savers and channel them to investors.
Accelerator theory: the theory of investment that emphasizes that current investment spending depends positively on the expected future growth of real GDP.
Pro-cyclical: a component of GDP is pro-cyclical if it rises and falls with the overall level of GDP.

Multiplier-accelerator model: a model in which a downturn in real GDP leads to a sharp fall in investment which, in turn, triggers further reductions in GDP through the multiplier.

Neo-classical theory of investment: a theory of investment that emphasizes the role of real interest rates and taxes.

Q-theory of investment: the theory of investment that links investment spending to stock prices.

Bond: a promise or IOU to pay money in the future in exchange for money now.

Liquid: an asset is liquid if it can easily be converted to money on short notice.

IV.   PERFORMANCE ENHANCING TIPS (PETS)

PET #1

Remember that, in economics, investment spending is largely spending on plant and equipment. It is NOT the purchase of stocks and bonds and other financial assets (which economists would refer to as savingss).

PET #2

The investment schedule will shift when factors other than the interest rate that are relevant to investment spending change. Changes in the interest rate will cause movements along the investment schedule.

For example, consider the investment schedule below:

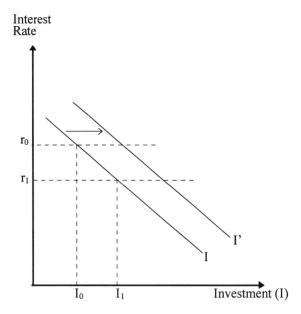

Suppose that the government enacts a tax credit for investment spending on plant and equipment. The tax credit makes it less costly for businesses to purchase plant and equipment. The tax credit will increase the level of investment spending at every interest rate as before. We would represent this by shifting the investment schedule out, to the right to I'. However, since the investment schedule is negatively sloped when graphed against the interest rate, an increase in the interest rate will reduce the quantity of investment spending and a decrease in the interest rate will increase the quantity of investment spending. Thus, changes in the interest rate cause movements along the investment schedule, not shifts in it.

This is just an application of PET #1 from Chapter 1 of the Practicum.

PET #3

Investors are borrowers.

An investor is an individual or business who borrows funds from savers (either directly or indirectly). The investor uses the borrowed funds to undertake an investment project for which the borrower expects the payoff from the project to be large enough to not only pay back the saver but to also have made a profit.

PET #4

The real interest rate is equal to the nominal interest rate minus the rate of inflation. You can equivalently say that the nominal interest rate is equal to the real interest rate plus the rate of inflation.

For example, suppose you are told that the nominal interest rate is 7% and that the inflation rate is 3%. The real interest rate is 4%. Likewise, if you are told that the real interest rate is 4% and the inflation rate is 3%, the nominal interest rate must be 7%.

PET #5

The real interest rate determines the level of investment spending, not the nominal interest rate.

For example, compare two cases: (1) a nominal interest rate of 15% when the inflation rate is 10%; and (2) a nominal interest rate of 8% when inflation is 2%. In case (1), the real interest rate is 5% and, in case (2), the real interest rate is 6%. Thus, even though, in case (1), the nominal interest rate is higher, the real cost of borrowing is lower. Thus, the real interest rate is a better indicator of the true cost of borrowing funds for investment spending.

PET #6

The accelerator model of investment spending assumes that investment spending depends on expected output (income), much like the consumption spending is assumed to depend on income.

An accelerator model of investment spending could be represented by writing out an investment function:

$$I = g + h \cdot Ey$$

where $h > 0$, g is autonomous Investment and Ey Is expected output. Since h is greater than zero, It means that expected increases in output and income (y) lead to increases in investment spending. The amount by which a $1 increase in expected output changes investment spending is given by h. You should recognize that "h" plays the same role that "b" plays in the consumption function of Chapter 10. You could say that "h" is the marginal propensity to invest. For example, if h = 0.25, every $1 increase in expected output (income) will generate $0.25 worth of investment spending.

V.   PRACTICE EXAM: MULTIPLE CHOICE QUESTIONS

1.   Which one of the following statements is NOT true of investment?

a.   the payoff is typically uncertain or unknown.
b.   an increase in the real interest rate raises investment spending.
c.   according to the accelerator model, expected growth and investment spending are positively related.
d.   investment spending is procyclical.
e.   investment spending is a volatile component of GDP.

2.   The multiplier-accelerator model:

a.   emphasizes how increases in investment spending can plunge the economy into a recession.
b.   is that acceleration in the growth of the economy can trigger increases in interest rates which lead to reductions in investment spending.
c.   is that investment spending is a function of "animal spirits."
d.   explains how a downturn in real GDP can lead to a sharp fall in investment which will, in turn, trigger further reductions in GDP.
e.   none of the above.

3.   Interest rates quoted by banks and that appear in the newspaper are:

a.   nominal interest rates.
b.   real interest rates.
c.   inflation-adjusted interest rates.
d.   official interest rates.
e.   federal funds rates.

4.   Which interest rate would be likely to be the highest?

a.   a six-month interest rate on a U.S. government treasury security.
b.   a one-year certificate of deposit rate offered by a bank.
c.   a ten-year interest rate on the bond of a very stable, healthy corporation.
d.   a ten-year interest rate on a loan to a start-up business.
e.   a ten-year interest rate on a U.S. government treasury security.

5.   If you put $1,000 of your savings into a one-year certificate of deposit that offers a nominal interest rate of 5.31%, then:

a.   your real return will be 7.31% if the inflation rate was -2% that year.
b.   your real return will be 3.31% if the inflation rate was -2% that year.
c.   your real return will be -10.62% if the inflation rate was -2% that year.
d.   your real return will be 10.62% if the inflation rate was -2% that year.
e.   your real return will be 2.655% if the inflation rate was -2% that year.

6.   Which one of the following statements is correct?

a.   nominal interest rate = real interest rate + inflation rate.
b.   nominal interest rate = real interest rate - inflation rate.

c. real interest rate = nominal interest rate + inflation rate.

d. real interest rate = nominal interest rate/inflation rate.

e. inflation rate = real interest rate - nominal interest rate.

7. Based on the investment schedule below, how many of the projects would be undertaken assuming an interest rate of 6%?

Investment	Cost	Return
A	$1,000	$1,030
B	$2,000	$2,100
C	$500	$550
D	$5,000	$5,250
E	$300	$306

a. one project would be undertaken.

b. two projects would be undertaken.

c. three projects would be undertaken.

d. four projects would be undertaken.

e. five projects would be undertaken.

8. The Q-theory of investment is that:

a. real interest rates and taxes play a key role in determining investment spending.

b. investment spending increases when stock prices are high.

c. the quantity of output a firm sells will determine its investment spending.

d. the GDP of a nation will determine the overall level of investment spending.

e. changes in investment spending are both quick and typically made quarterly.

9. Which asset would be most liquid?

a. real estate.

b. an antique car.

c. money in a bank account.

d. money in an individual retirement account.

e. money in a pension fund.

10. Which one of the following is NOT a function of a financial intermediary?

a. channels funds from savers to borrowers (investors).

b. poollng of funds from savers.

c. reduce the risk of placing savings in financial assets.

d. providing liquidity to households at reduced cost.

e. all of the above.

11. Which one of the following statements is true?

a. the savings and loan crisis of the 1990s was due to the big U.S. budget deficit.

b. deposit insurance guarantees savings up to $1,000,000.

c.   savings and loan institutions were very profitable during the 1970s when there was high inflation.
d.   deposit insurance was created to prevent bank runs from recurring.
e.   banks keep 100% of the funds provided by savers on hand.

VI.   PRACTICE EXAM: ESSAY QUESTIONS

1.   Explain why real interest rates are more closely related to investment spending than nominal interest rates are. Also, explay how high real interest rates affect investment spending and output.

2.   Explain how banks, by funding diverse investment projects, can reduce the risk of losing money on the total amount funded.

VII.   ANSWER KEY: MULTIPLE CHOICE QUESTIONS

1.   Correct answer: b.

Discussion: Statement b is incorrect because an increase in real interest rates reduces, not raises, investment spending.

Statements a is correct and means that investment spending is risky. It also means that, when savers lend their funds to investors (borrowers), their savings are subject to risk, as well. Statement c is correct. The accelerator model suggests that, when businesses expect the economy to boom, investment spending will increase now and when they expect the economy to go into a recession, they will reduce investment spending now. Statement d means that, when output (real GDP) increases, investment spending increases and vice-versa. Statement e means that investment spending fluctuates a lot more than some of the other spending components of GDP.

2.   Correct answer: d.

Discussion: The multiplier-accelerator model links investment spending to changes in output through the multiplier (as discussed in the previous chapter) and further adds that, when output changes, investment spending, in turn, changes again setting off further changes in output.

Statement a is not correct; increases in investment spending would help to push the economy up, i.e., to do better. Statement b is not correct because the multiplier-accelerator model does not address the role of interest rates. Statement c is not correct. Keynes coined the term "animal spirits" which meant that sharp swings in the moods of investors could trigger sharp swings in investment spending. Statement e is not correct because statement d is correct.

3.   Correct answer: a.

Discussion: Nominal interest rates are often referred to as quoted or stated rates. Real interest rates are inflation-adjusted interest rates.

4.   Correct answer: d.

Discussion: The interest rate that would be likely to be the highest would be the one corresponding to the financial instrument that is most risky. In order to induce savers to provide funds to borrower for risky projects, borrowers must be willing to pay a higher interest rate in order to compensate the savers for their willingness to share the risk. A loan to a start-up business is obviously more risky than any of the other financial instruments listed in statements a, b, c, or e.

5.   Correct answer: a.

Discussion: The real interest rate or real return is the nominal interest rate (what is actually paid) minus the inflation rate. In this case, the inflation rate is negative meaning that the economy is experiencing deflation -- the price level is declining. Thus, the real interest rate (the purchasing power of the interest proceeds) will be greater than 5.31% because, at the end of the year, prices will be, on average, 2% lower and so the saver will find that the interest proceeds stretch farther in terms of what they can be used to purchase. Thus, the real return is 7.31% = (5.31% - (-2%)).

6.   Correct answer: a.

Discussion: The nominal interest rate is the sum of the real interest rate plus the inflation rate. Statement a can also be rewritten to say that the real interest rate is equal to the nominal interest rate minus the rate of inflation (as discussed in the answer to #5). All of the other statements are thus incorrect.

7.   Correct answer: a.

Discussion: Since the interest rate is 6%, only those investment projects earning a return greater than 6% will be worthwhile. Otherwise, an individual could just put money in the bank and earn 6%. Investment project A's return is 3% [($1,030-$1,000)/$1,000] X 100. Investment project B's return is 5% [($2,100 - $2,000)/$2,000] X 100. Investment project C's return is 10% [($550-$500)/$500]X100. Investment project D's return is 5% [($5,250-$5,000)/$5,000] X 100. Investment project E's return is 2% [($306-$300)/$300] X 100. Thus, since only investment project C has a return greater than 6%, it will be the only project that is worthwhile to invest in. All of the other projects earn a return less than 6%.

8.   Correct answer: b.

Discussion: The Q-theory of investment, originated by James Tobin, a Nobel-prize-winning economist, relates investment spending to stock prices. Statement a is a description of the neo-classical theory of investment. None of the other statements define the Q-theory of investment.

9.   Correct answer: c.

Discussion: The asset that is most liquid would be the one that is most quickly and easily convertible to cash. Money in a bank account satisfies this condition relative to the other options. Real estate and an antique car would have to be posted for sale and finding a buyer may take time. Money in an individual retirement account and in a pension fund will require some paper work for withdrawal and may involve penalties for early withdrawal.

10.   Correct answer: e.

Discussion: Financial intermediaries provide all of the functions listed above. Examples of financial intermediaries are: commercial banks, savings and loans, investment banks, insurance companies, mutual fund companies, etc.

11.   Correct answer: d.

Discussion: Bank runs occurred in the early 1930s (and even before then). A bank run is when a bank's customers (depositors) run to the bank and ask to withdrawal all of their money. Since banks do not, by law, have to keep all of a depositors' money on hand, customers found that they could not retrieve all of their money. This, of course, caused people to panic. Sometimes, bank runs are referred to as bank panics. Bank runs can reak financial havoc on depositors and an economy in general. Thus, the government established deposit insurance so that customers could be sure that up to $100,000 worth of their money was protected (would be there if they needed it).

Statement a is not correct; the savings and loan crisis of the 1990s was, in part, due to the deregulation of the savings and loan industry coupled with the deposit insurance scheme provided by the government. Statement b is not correct; deposits are insured up to $100,000. Statement c is not correct; savings and loan institutions were unprofitable and many went bankrupt during the inflationary era of the 1970s. Statement e is not correct; banks are legally permitted to keep less than 100% of depositor's money on hand.

VIII.   ANSWER KEY: ESSAY QUESTIONS

1.   First of all, it is the real interest rate that influences investment spending and not necessarily the nominal interest rate. For example, compare two cases: (1) a nominal interest rate of 15% when the inflation rate is 10%, and (2) a nominal interest rate of 8% when inflation is 2%. In case (1), the real interest rate is 5%, and in case (2), the real interest rate is 6%. Thus, even though, in case (1), the nominal interest rate is higher, the real cost of borrowing is lower. Thus, the real interest rate is a better indicator of the true cost of borrowing funds for investment spending.

At higher real interest rates, the opportunity cost of funding an investment project increases. In other words, the real rate of return necessary to be earned by the investment project must pass a higher hurdle in order for it to be considered more worthwhile than taking those funds and placing them in a bank or other interest-bearing asset. For example, a firm may consider opening up a new factory or developing a new line of products. However, if the expected real payoff from funding such an investment is not as high as what could be earned by the firm simply investing those funds into an interest-bearing financial asset, then the firm may be inclined not to fund the investment project. Thus, higher real interest rates are typically associated with lower levels of investment spending. If higher real interest rates lead to lower levels of investment spending and lower levels of investment spending, through the multiplier, lead to lower levels of output (at least in the short run), then higher interest rates may be associated with lower levels of output (i.e., a stagnating economy). From the previous chapter, a reduction in investment spending of, say, $10 billion, caused by higher real interest rates, would lead to a reduction in output of say $20 billion if the multiplier is 2. Now, if the $20 billion decline in output influences investment spending as well, then investment spending may decline further (even without a change in real interest rates). That is, investment spending may decline by $2 billion more, and thus lead to a further drop in output of $4 billion (2 X $2 billion). This is an example of the multiplier-accelerator model at work.

2.   A basic principle of finance is that diversification reduces risk. For example, suppose you have $5,000 to invest. It may be less risky for you to invest $1,000 in five different financial assets than to invest all $5,000 into one financial asset. The reason why is that you spread out the risk of losing money (downside risk) on your $5,000, particularly if the returns on the $1,000 investments that you make are negatively correlated. Negative correlation means that, when one return is low, the other is likely to be high. (If the returns were positively correlated, when one return is low, the other would be low as well. Of course, the reverse is true -- if one return is high, the other would be likely to be high.) Since you can eliminate the downside risk of having both assets give low returns when they are positively correlated, it may make more sense to place your money into assets that are negatively correlated. The same is true of banks who profit by making loans to different customers. They can reduce the risk of losing money by lending to a variety of different investment projects with different risk/return levels. If the bank is able to reduce the risk of losing money on loans it makes, it also reduces risk to its depositors of being able to pay them their money should they wish to withdrawal it.

Take It to the Net

We invite you to visit the O'Sullivan/Sheffrin page on the Prentice Hall Web site at:

http://www.prenhall.com/osullivan/

for this chapter's World Wide Web exercise.

CHAPTER 27
MONEY, THE BANKING SYSTEM, AND THE
FEDERAL RESERVE

I.   OVERVIEW

In this chapter, you will learn what money is, what the functions of money are, and how the money supply can be influenced by a central bank and the banking system. You will learn about different measures of money. You will learn how the banking system works and how it can influence the money supply through making loans to businesses and households. You will learn that the U.S. banking system operates under a fractional reserve system and it is this system that enables banks, through loan creation, to influence the money supply. You will learn how the U.S. central bank (the Federal Reserve) can act to control the banking system's ability to extend loans to businesses and households. You will be introduced to another multiplier concept -- the money multiplier. You will also learn about the structure of the Federal Reserve system and what its primary functions are.

II.   CHECKLIST

By the end of this chapter, you should be able to:

√   Define money.
√   Explain the three properties of money.
√   Describe a barter system.
√   Explain how money solves the problem of a "double coincidence of wants."
√   Compare and contrast M1 and M2.
√   Define assets, liabilities, and net worth.
√   List some items that would be considered an asset of a bank; list some items that would be considered a liability of a bank.
√   Define required reserves and excess reserves.
√   Discuss how banks make loans, i.e., discuss the process of money creation.
√   Explain how the creation of a loan by one bank can lead to a multiple expansion in the money supply.
√   Define the money multiplier and use it to compute changes in the money supply.
√   Explain why the money multiplier may be smaller than the simple formula suggests.
√   Describe how open market operations work and how they may influence the money supply.
√   Describe how changes in the required reserve ratio can affect the money supply.
√   Define the discount rate and the federal funds rate.
√   Describe how changes in the discount rate can affect the money supply.
√   Discuss the primary functions of the Federal Reserve.
√   Define the Board of Governors and the Federal Open Market Committee.
√   Discuss the role of the Chairman of the Federal Reserve System.

III.   KEY TERMS

Money: anything that is regularly used in exchange.
Barter: trading goods directly for goods.

Double coincidence of wants: the problem in a system of barter that one individual may not have what the other desires.

Medium of exchange: the property of money that exchanges are made using money.

Unit of account: the property of money that prices are quoted in terms of money.

Store of value: the property of money that value is preserved between transactions.

M1: the sum of currency in the hands of the public, demand deposits, and other checkable deposits.

M2: M1 plus other assets including deposits in savings and loans and money market mutual funds.

Balance sheet: an account for a bank which shows the sources of its funds (liabilities) as well as the uses for the funds (assets).

Assets: the uses of the funds of a financial institution.

Liabilities: the sources of external funds of a financial intermediary.

Net worth: the difference between assets and liabilities.

Reserves: the fraction of their deposits that banks set aside in either vault cash or as deposits at the Federal Reserve.

Required reserves: the reserves that banks are required to hold by law against their deposits.

Excess reserves: any additional reserves that a bank holds above required reserves.

Reserve ratio: the ratio of reserves to deposits.

Money multiplier: an initial deposit leads to a multiple expansion of deposits. In the simplified case:
increase in deposits = [initial deposit]/[1/reserve ratio].

Open market purchases: the purchase of government bonds by the Fed which increases the money supply.

Open market sales: sales of government bonds to the public which decreases the money supply.

Discount rate: the interest rate at which banks can borrow from the Fed.

Federal funds market: the market in which banks borrow and lend reserves to one another.

Central bank: a banker's bank; an official bank which controls the supply of money in a country.

Lender of last resort: a name give to policies of central banks that provide loans to banks in emergency situations.

Federal Reserve Banks: one of twelve regional banks that are an official part of the Federal Reserve System.

Board of Governors of the Federal Reserve: the seven person governing body of the Federal Reserve system in Washington, DC.

Federal Open Market Committee: the group that decides on monetary policy and consists of the seven members of the Board of Governors plus five of twelve regional bank presidents on a rotating basis.

IV.   PERFORMANCE ENHANCING TIPS (PETS)

<u>PET #1</u>

When you withdraw money from your checking account to hold as cash, you have not increased the money supply. You have simply converted one form of money into another form.

Remember that the most liquid components of money are coin and currency and demand deposits (checking account balances). That is, both are components of the money supply. Thus, when you withdraw money from your checking account as cash, you have simply exchanged one form of money for another. The reverse also holds. If you deposit $100 in cash into your checking account, you have not decreased the money supply.

PET #2

Money and income do not measure the same thing in economics. Money is what you hold as cash and in your checking account and income is what you earn.

For example, you may earn $1,000 a week and keep $700 a week in your checking account and $100 as cash. The remaining $200 you may put into, e.g.,, a mutual fund or stock fund. The cash money and that in your checking account is "money" and is what you primarily use to make payments with. At any given point in time, the amount of money you have may not correspond to the amount of income you earn.

PET #3

*The required reserve ratio is the ratio (or fraction or percentage) of **demand deposits** that a bank must legally hold on reserve, either in its vault or with the Federal Reserve Bank.*

PET #4

The required reserve ratio applies to a bank's demand deposits and not to its total reserves.

Suppose a bank has $250,000 in reserves and $1,000,000 in demand deposits. If the required reserve ratio is 10%, then the bank must by law hold $100,000 as required reserves. Since the bank is currently holding $250,000 in reserves, the other $150,000 are referred to as "excess reserves." Do not make the mistake of applying the required reserve ratio to the bank's total reserves. That is, it is not correct to conclude that the bank's required reserves are 10% of $250,000 or $25,000.

PET #5

When a bank makes a loan, it effectively gives the borrower a check or checking account for the amount of the loan. Thus, loans add to the money supply.

V.   PRACTICE EXAM: MULTIPLE CHOICE QUESTIONS

1.   The defining property of money is that:

a.   it is accepted as a means of payment.
b.   it is easy to carry around.
c.   its value depends on gold.
d.   it can be saved.
e.   it is countable.

2.   Which one of the following is NOT true of money?

a.   it serves as a store of value.
b.   it serves as a unit of account.
c.   it serves as a medium of exchange.
d.   it is equal to income.

e.   all of the above are true.

3.   Suppose you take a trip to the Bahamas after the semester ends. Upon arriving at the island, you make a stop at one of the markets and notice that everyone is carrying around jars full of little turtles. And, you notice the person in line in front of you just paid for a bottle of rum with 6 turtles. Someone else just bought a straw hat for two turtles. Thinking back to your economics class (as painful as that may be), you would conclude that:

a.   this is a barter economy.
b.   Egad, those little turtles are serving the function of money!
c.   turtles are valueless.
d.   turtle soup is a delicacy.
e.   there is a problem of double coincidence of wants.

4.   Mr. Potatohead has recently obtained a bank card from Idaho National Bank. Excited about the concept of using a little plastic card to get money from a machine, he quickly runs down to the nearest Automatic Teller Machine and withdraws $1,000. This action has:

a.   increased the money supply by $1,000.
b.   reduced the money supply by $1,000.
c.   reduced the bank's required reserves by $100 assuming the required reserve ratio is 10%.
d.   not changed the money supply.
e.   (c) and (d).

5.   Which one of the following would lead to a change in the total money supply?

a.   a customer's cash withdrawal from an ATM.
b.   a bank loan to a customer.
c.   interest payments by the Treasury on its debt.
d.   depositing a paycheck in a bank.
e.   none of the above.

6.   Which one of the following statements is true?

a.   approximately one fourth of M1 is checking account balances (demand deposits plus other checkable deposits).
b.   M2 is a narrower definition of money than M1.
c.   M2 is used by economists to measure the amount of money that is regularly used in transactions.
d.   a country for which cash bribes are an everyday part of business will have a higher cash (currency) holding per capita than countries where bribes are not standard practice.
e.   the citizens of Argentina use only Argentinian currency to make economic exchanges.

7.   Which one of the following would NOT be considered an asset of a bank?

a.   a loan to a corporation.
b.   required reserves.
c.   holdings of treasury securities.
d.   deposits of its customers.

e.   all of the above.

8.   Which one of the following statements is true?

a.   demand deposits are assets of a bank.
b.   assets + liabilities = net worth.
c.   a bank's reserves can either be kept in a bank's vault or held on deposit with a Federal Reserve bank.
d.   if a bank is holding $500 as required reserves and has $2,000 in deposits, then the required reserve ratio must be 40%.
e.   liabilities generate income for a bank.

9.   By law, banks are required:

a.   to hold 100% of customer deposits on reserve.
b.   to hold a fraction of their reserves at the Federal Reserve bank.
c.   to hold a fraction of demand deposits on reserve.
d.   to lend out no more than the amount of their required reserves.
e.   keep their discount rate at 5% or less.

10.   The money multiplier is:

a.   1/required reserve ratio.
b.   1/(1-required reserve ratio).
c.   1/marginal propensity to save.
d.   1/excess reserves.
e.   required reserves/demand deposits.

11.   Suppose that, while vacationing in Monaco, you won 25,000 French francs which is the equivalent of $5,000. When you return to the U.S., you deposit the $5,000 into your checking account. The effect is to (assuming the required reserve ratio is 20%):

a.   increase your bank's liabilities by $5,000.
b.   increase your bank's excess reserves by $4,000.
c.   lead to a multiple expansion in the money supply (checking account balances) by $25,000.
d.   increase your bank's required reserves by $1,000.
e.   all of the above.

12.   The money multiplier will be **smaller** when:

a.   bank customers prefer to hold a bigger amount of their money as cash (instead of in their checking account).
b.   banks prefer to lend out 95% of their excess reserves instead of 100%.
c.   when the marginal propensity to save declines.
d.   when the marginal propensity to consume increases.
e.   (a) and (b).

13.   The most commonly used tool in monetary policy is:

a.   changes in required reserve ratios.
b.   changes in the discount rate.
c.   open market operations.
d.   express lending transactions.
e.   loan extension.

14.   The federal funds rate is the interest rate that:

a.   banks charge on loans to each other.
b.   the Federal Reserve charges on loans to banks.
c.   banks charge their most creditworthy customers.
d.   banks pay on demand deposits.
e.   the U.S. government pays it on 30-year treasury bonds.

15.   Which set of actions could the Fed use to **increase** the money supply?

a.   discount rate cut and an open market sale.
b.   reduction in the required reserve ratio and an open market purchase.
c.   a tax cut and a reduction in the required reserve ratio.
d.   an open market purchase and a tax cut.
e.   an open market sale and a reduction in the required reserve ratio.

16.   The group responsible for deciding on monetary policy is:

a.   the Federal Open Market Committee.
b.   the Board of Governors.
c.   the Federal Advisory Council.
d.   the group of 12 Federal Reserve Bank presidents.
e.   the Federal Monetary Control committee.

17.   The purpose of having governors of the Federal Reserve serve fourteen-year terms is to:

a.   ensure that the governors become well-experienced at policymaking.
b.   insulate the governors' policy decisions from the influence of presidential elections and politics.
c.   promote unity of opinion from shared time together.
d.   establish long-standing ties with high-level officials of other nations' central banks.
e.   ensure that price stability is achieved.

VI.   PRACTICE EXAM: ESSAY QUESTIONS

1.   Suppose the banking system's required reserve ratio is 25% and that an elderly customer who has kept all of their savings, totalling $8,000, under a mattress has finally decided to deposit it in the bank. Explain the effects this action has on the bank's balance sheet and the money supply.

2.   Explain how an open market purchase of $2 million will affect the money supply assuming the required reserve ratio is 10%. How does a country's preference for holding cash (as opposed to checking accounts) affect the size of the money multiplier?

VII.   ANSWER KEY: MULTIPLE CHOICE QUESTIONS

1.   Correct answer: a.

Discussion: Money is anything that is generally accepted as a means of payment. In other words, it is used to carry out transactions or economic exchanges. At one time, gold served as money since it was accepted as a means of payment. In some foreign countries, U.S. dollars fulfill the role of "money" since they are accepted as a means of payment.

While money is typically easy to carry around, it is not the defining property of money. Today, money's value does not depend on gold -- our money is thus referred to as "fiat" money. While money can be saved (the store of value function), that is not the defining characteristic of it. Also, while money is countable, it is not the defining characteristic of it.

2.   Correct answer: d.

Discussion: See PET #2 above.

Statement a means that money can be saved (stored) and used to make future transactions (i.e., paying for college education, etc). Statement b means that money serves as a measuring rod for the value of goods and services. That is, if we had to compare the value of an apple to an orange, we could compare their values by expressing them in terms of a common denominator -- money or the dollar. Suppose an apple costs $0.35 and an orange costs $0.50, money has thus served as a unit of account. We would say that an orange is more valuable than an apple. Statement c means that money is used to pay for transactions -- buying food, paying rent, going to the movies, etc.

3.   Correct answer: b.

Discussion: This is an example where turtles are serving as the medium of exchange. That is, they are accepted by the seller as a method of payment and used by the buyer as a method of payment.

A   barter economy is one in which there is no "money." That is, there is no commodity that is universally accepted as a means of payment. In a barter economy, a double coincidence of wants problem exists. Money would help to eliminate the problem. The fact that turtles are used as a means of payment means that turtles must be valuable, not valueless. In this case, turtle soup may be a delicacy since eating turtle soup would be like eating money. However, statement d is more of a "for fun" answer than the correct answer.

4.   Correct answer: e.

Discussion: Mr. Potatohead has simply converted one form of money (demand deposits) to another form (cash). Since both demand deposits and cash are part of the money supply, the money supply has not changed. (See PET #1 for review.) However, since Mr. Potatohead as withdrawn $1,000 from the bank, the bank finds that its demand deposits decline by $1,000. With a required reserve ratio of 10%, the bank is now permitted to hold $100 less as required reserves (10% of $1,000).

5.   Correct answer: b.

Discussion: When a bank makes a loan to a customer, it effectively gives the customer a check or checking account for the amount of the loan. This action increases the money supply.

Statement a is incorrect because a customer's cash withdrawal from an ATM simply converts one form of money (demand deposits) to another (cash). There is not change in the money supply from this action. Statement c is not correct. Interest payments by the Treasury on its debt simply transfer money from government bank accounts to the bank accounts of holders of the Treasury's debt (households, businesses, etc). Statement d is not correct. If you deposit a paycheck into your bank account, your "money supply" will increase but the "money supply" in the bank account of the business that pays you will decrease by the same amount. On net, there is no change in the money supply, just a transfer of ownership.

6.   Correct answer: d.

Discussion: In a country where cash (or currency) is used in everyday business, the people of the country must carry a lot of cash around with them to get anything done -- as simple as getting a taxi, getting into a restaurant, or getting a haircut. India is a good example of a country where bribes are prevalent.

Statement a is not true; two-thirds of M1 is checking account balances (demand deposits plus other checkable deposits). Statement b is not true; M2 is a broader definition of money than M1. Statement c is not true; M1 is used by economists to measure the amount of money that is regularly used in transactions. Remember that M2 includes money held in money market mutual funds and other investments that may be used to pay for transactions, but typically not regular transactions. Statement e is not true; in developing countries like Argentina, the U.S. dollar is commonly accepted as a means of payment and often used as a store of value, too.

7.   Correct answer: d.

Discussion: Demand deposits are liabilities of a bank. They are owed to customers (on demand). That is, demand deposits (checking accounts) are an item that a bank doesn't own. Assets are items of value that a bank owns -- just like assets are items of value that we own. Thus, loans to households and businesses are an asset of a bank since the loans are items that are owed to the bank (by its customers). A bank's reserves are also an asset since they are owned by the bank (not owed by the bank). A bank's reserves are like a checking account for the bank. A bank's holdings of treasury securities (or even stock) is an asset since they are owned by the bank (not owed by the bank).

8.   Correct answer: c.

Discussion: A bank's reserves can be kept either in a bank's vault or held on deposit with a Federal Reserve bank (which is referred to as a reserve account with the Fed).

Statement a is not correct. Demand deposits are a liability of a bank. Statement b is not correct. Assets minus liabilities equal net worth. Statement d is not correct. If the bank is holding $500 as required reserves and has $2,000 in demand deposits, the required reserve ratio must be 25% ($500/$2,000). Statement e is not correct. Assets generate income for a bank. Liabilities are items that a bank owes.

9.   Correct answer: c.

Discussion: The required reserve ratio is the fraction or percentage of demand deposits that the bank is legally obligated to hold on reserve. (See PET #3 and #4 for review.)

Statement a is not correct. The U.S. banking system operates under a fractional reserve system which means that banks are legally permitted to hold only a fraction (i.e., less than 100%) of their deposits as reserves. Statement b is not correct; by law, banks must hold a fraction of their demand deposits as required reserves, not a fraction of their reserves. Statement d is not correct; banks can lend out the maximum amount of their excess reserves (an amount which typically exceeds their required reserves). By law, they cannot lend out any of their required reserves. Statement e is not correct; there is no stipulation on what interest rate banks are permitted to charge on loans to customers.

10.   Correct answer: a.

Discussion: None necessary.

11.   Correct answer: e.

Discussion: Your deposit of $5,000 into the bank increases the liabilities of the bank. That is, your checking account balance has increased by $5,000, which means that the bank is responsible to pay you, on demand, your $5,000 should you wish to withdraw it. Since the required reserve ratio is 20%, the bank is legally obligated to hold 20% of $5,000 as required reserves, i.e., $1,000. The remaining $4,000 of your deposits, the bank is permitted to lend out (or use in other ways). The $4,000 is referred to as excess reserves. If the bank lends out the $4,000 in excess reserves, the money supply will increase by $4,000 which will in turn end up in some other bank whose excess reserves will increase by $3,600. This bank will in turn lend out the $3,600. This process continues until the money supply will ultimately expand by [1/0.20] X $5,000 = $25,000. If you add the $5,000 you brought into the country to the money supply, the money supply will have in total increased by $30,000.

12.   Correct answer: e.

Discussion: The money multiplier process assumes that banks lend out all of their excess reserves and that customers do not choose to hold any of the newly created money as cash (currency) but prefer to keep it in their checking accounts. If customers prefer to hold a larger amount of their money as cash instead of in their checking accounts, banks will have fewer demand deposits and thus fewer reserves and thus a reduced ability to extend loans to customers. Remember that a bank's excess reserves serve as the base from which it is able to make loans. Thus, the money multiplier process will not go as far. Furthermore, if banks prefer to lend out a smaller amount of their excess reserves, then they will not be creating as many loans and thereby not allowing the money multiplier process to go as far.

The marginal propensities to save and consume have not been related to the money multiplier process.

13.   Correct answer: c.

Discussion: None necessary.

14.   Correct answer: a.

Discussion: Banks can borrow money from each other. The interest rate that they charge each other for the loans is called the federal funds rate. Statement b is a definition of the discount rate. Statement c is a definition of the prime rate. Statement d is a definition of the interest rate paid on checking account. Statement e is a definition of the 30-year treasury bond rate.

15.   Correct answer: b.

Discussion: The Fed has three tools that it can use to influence the money supply: open market operations, changes in the required reserve ratio, and changes in the discount rate. An open market purchase of government treasury securities from individuals and businesses that hold the treasury securities is an exchange of securities for money. In this case, individuals and businesses receive checks from the Fed and give up their securities to the Fed (which is what the Fed is purchasing). The money supply directly increases from this action. Also, since individuals and businesses will be likely to deposit at least some, if not all, of their checks into banks, banks demand deposits and thus reserves will increase. With an increase in reserves, banks will find that they are able to make more loans. The enhanced ability of banks to make loans further adds to the money supply. A reduction in the required reserve ratio frees up some of a bank's required reserves from which banks can then lend. For example, if the required reserve ratio is 20% and a bank's deposits are $1 million, the bank must hold $200,000 as required reserves. The remaining $800,000 in excess it is permitted to lend out. Now, if the required reserve ratio is reduced to 10%, the bank must now legally hold only $100,000 which means it has $900,000 to lend out. The reduction in the required reserve ratio thus enhances a bank's ability to extend loans (and thereby increase the money supply). Open market sales and increases in the required reserve ratio work in the opposite direction.

Statement a is only partially correct. A discount rate cut makes it less costly for banks to borrow money from the Fed which they can in turn lend out. Thus, a discount rate cut may increase the money supply (and vice-versa). However, an open market sale acts to reduce the money supply. Statement e is also only partially correct. A reduction in the required reserve ratio acts to increase the money supply but again, an open market sale acts to reduce the money supply.

Statements c and d cannot be correct because a tax cut simply transfers money from government bank accounts back to households and businesses. Thus, a tax cut does not affect the money supply but it does affect who is holding the money. (The same is true of a tax increase.)

16.   Correct answer: a.

Discussion: The Federal Open Market Committee (FOMC) consists of the seven governors of the Board of the Federal Reserve and five Federal Reserve Bank presidents. Four of the Federal Reserve bank presidents spend two-year rotating positions on the FOMC while the president of the New York Fed has a permanent seat on the FOMC.

17.   Correct answer: b.

Discussion: The central bank of the U.S. was designed to be independent of the government so that it would not conduct policy in a way that was driven by politics or who was running for president of the U.S. Some research shows that central banks that have greater independence from their governments and their presidents are able to achieve lower rates of inflation.

VIII.   ANSWER KEY: ESSAY QUESTIONS

1.   When the elderly customer deposits the $8,000 cash into the bank, the bank will find that it now has $8,000 more in demand deposits and $8,000 more in reserves. However, the $8,000 in reserves must be broken up into two components -- required reserves and excess reserves. Since the required reserve ratio is 25%, the bank must by law hold 25% of $8,000 as required reserves. Thus, the bank must hold $2,000 as required reserves. The remaining $6,000 are referred to as "excess reserves" and are what the bank is permitted to lend out (or use in other ways). Since the money multiplier is 1/required reserve ratio, the value of it is 1/0.25 = 4. Thus, the potential maximum increase in the checking account balance money supply is 4 X $8,000 = $32,000. Since $8,000 of the $32,000 was simply the transfer of cash to a checking account, the banking system will, in effect, be able to generate $24,000 ($32,000 - $8,000) in loans. Another way to calculate the loan expansion part of the money multiplier process is to use the formula [1/required reserve ratio] X (initial change in excess reserves) which in this case would be 4 X $6,000 = $24,000.

2.   An open market purchase is when the Fed purchases U.S. government treasury securities from individuals and businesses who currently own them. If the Fed purchases a total of $2 million in government treasury securities, it effectively writes a check totalling $2 million which it gives to individuals and businesses. For example, if the Fed purchases 200,000 treasury securities and paid $1,000 for each one, then the total open market purchase is $2,000,000. If each seller of the treasury security deposits his check for $1,000 into a bank, the banking system will find that it has $2 million more in demand deposits and consequently $2 million more in reserves. With a required reserve ratio of 10%, the banking system must hold $200,000 (0.10 X $2,000,000) as required reserves. The banking system can then lend out the remaining $1,800,000. Thus, the money supply increases directly through the open market purchase and then indirectly through influencing the banking systems ability to make loans. The money multiplier process dictates that the potential maximum increase in the money supply is (1/0.10) X $2,000,000 = 10 X $2,000,000 = $20,000,000. Of the $20 million, $2 million is a direct result of the open market purchase and $18 million is a result of banks making loans. (To figure out the effect of the loan expansion process, use (1/required reserve ratio) X (initial change in excess reserves) = 1/0.10 X $1,800,000 = $18,000,000 i.e., $18 million).

The simple money multiplier used above assumes that all of the money generated is redeposited in other banks. Nobody holds any of it as cash. If the public preferred to hold some of the money as cash, then the money multiplier would be smaller than 10. The public's preference for holding money as cash instead of in checking accounts reduces the reserves of the banking system and thereby reduces their reserves and their ability to make loans.

Take It to the Net

We invite you to visit the O'Sullivan/Sheffrin page on the Prentice Hall Web site at:

http://www.prenhall.com/osullivan/

for this chapter's World Wide Web exercise.

CHAPTER 28
MONETARY POLICY IN THE SHORT RUN

I.   OVERVIEW

In this chapter, you will learn how the Fed, through monetary policy, is able to influence interest rates and thus aggregate spending and output (GDP). The context in which you will examine monetary policy is the short run in which prices are fixed. In this setting, monetary policy actions are not directed at inflation nor do monetary policy actions affect inflation. You will learn that monetary policy works through its effects on interest rates which in turn determines spending in an economy. You will use a supply and demand model of the money market to see how changes in money supply and money demand influence the price of money, i.e., the interest rate. You will learn how monetary policy affects the price of bonds. You will also learn about the relationship between interest rates and the price of bonds. You will be re-introduced to the Keynesian cross diagram where you will see graphically how monetary policy influences the level of spending and output. You will analyze monetary policy not only in a closed economy setting but in an open economy setting as well. In the open economy setting, you will learn that monetary policy can affect not only the interest rate but the exchange rate as well. You will learn about the limits to monetary policy and the problems associated with ensuring that monetary policy has its desired effects.

II.   CHECKLIST

By the end of this chapter, you should be able to:

√   Explain how lower (higher) interest rates affect investment spending and output.
√   Discuss actions that could be taken by the Fed to lower (raise) interest rates. Use a money supply/money demand model to illustrate the effects.
√   Give several reasons for why people hold money.
√   Explain why money demand is negatively sloped when graphed against the interest rate.
√   Explain why higher interest rates reduce the price of bonds and vice-versa.
√   Use the Keynesian cross diagram to illustrate how increases in the money supply affect spending and output (and vice-versa). Be sure to discuss the Keynesian multiplier.
√   Explain the relationship between interest rates and exchange rates.
√   Discuss the effects of monetary policy on the exchange rate and net exports and explain whether the effects work to enhance or offset the interest rate and investment spending effects.
√   Give examples of expansionary and contractionary monetary policy.
√   Discuss the causes of inside lags.
√   Give some examples of inside lags as related to monetary policy.
√   Discuss the causes of outside lags.
√   Give some examples of outside lags as related to monetary policy.
√   Explain why uncertainty in forecasting interferes with good policymaking.

III.   KEY TERMS

Fixed rate mortgage: a housing loan with a constant rate over the life of the loan.
Variable rate mortgage: a housing loan in which the interest rate is adjusted for changes in market interest rates.

Transactions demand for money: the demand for money based on the desire to facilitate transactions.

Liquidity demand for money: the demand for money that arises so that individuals or firms can make purchases on short notice without incurring excessive costs.

Speculative demand for money: the demand for money that arises because holding money over short periods is less risky than holdings stocks or bonds.

Monetary policy: the range of actions taken by the Federal Reserve actions to influence the level of GDP or inflation.

Exchange rate: the rate at which one currency trades for another in the market.

Depreciation: a fall in the exchange rate or a decrease in the value of a currency.

Appreciation: a rise in the exchange rate or an increase in the value of a currency.

Inside lags: the lags in implementing policy.

Outside lag: the time it takes for policies to actually work.

Expansionary policies: policies that aim to increase the level of GDP.

Contractionary policies: policies that aim to decrease the level of GDP.

Stabilization policy: policy actions taken to move the economy closer to full employment or potential output.

Econometric models: statistical-based computer models that economists build to capture the actual dynamics of the economy.

IV.   PERFORMANCE ENHANCING TIPS (PETS)

<u>PET #1</u>

As real income (or real GDP) increases, the demand for money increases. As real income (or real GDP) decreases, the demand for money decreases.

Sometimes this point is confusing to students who will state "If I make more money (i.e., earn more income), I won't demand as much of it. Thus, the PET #1 seems backwards." The proper way to think about the relationship between money and income is this: at higher income levels, people typically make more transactions and thus need to have more money on hand (as cash or in checking accounts). That is, at higher income levels, people typically demand more money, not less (and vice-versa).

For example, consider what your average checking account balance is right now and how much you hold in your wallet. Also, consider what your income level is right now. Given that you are a student, your income is probably pretty low. Since your income is low, you probably don't buy steak and lobster every week, or go out to expensive restaurants very frequently, or take trips very frequently, or buy expensive clothing. Thus, your checking account balance plus what you hold as cash is probably low, too. However, after you graduate and start earning the big bucks, you will probably begin to undertake more transactions (money is fun to spend when you have it!). You may start buying more expensive clothing and buying it more frequently. You may decide to take some weekend visits to the beach or to some far away island. Maybe you'll even start taking tennis lessons and buying expensive art to decorate your apartment. This just means that you will need to hold more money in your checking account and in your wallet. So, we'd say that your demand for money has increased as your income has gone up.

<u>PET #2</u>

Factors relevant to the demand for money will cause the demand for money to shift. Changes in the interest rate will cause a movement along the money demand curve.

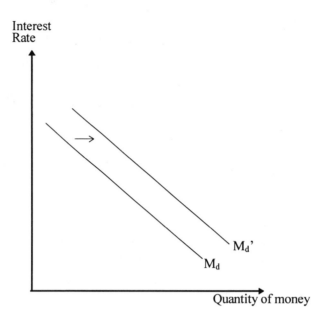

Your book suggests several other factors besides the interest rate that affect the demand for money. They are the price level and income. As the price level rises, the demand for money increases since economic transactions become more expensive and people need more money to carry out those transactions (vice-versa for a decrease in the price level). This would be represented by a rightward shift in the demand curve as shown above. Secondly, as PET #1 above suggests, changes in income also affect the demand for money. An increase in real income will increase the demand for money (shift right) and vice-versa.

Changes in the interest rate are represented as movements along the money demand curve. Higher interest rates reduce the quantity of money demanded and lower interest rates raise the quantity of money demanded.

This is just an application of PET #1 from Chapter 1 of the Practicum.

PET #3

*Bonds are sold with a **fixed** promised payment that determines, together with the price of the bond, the effective interest rate on the bond. The promised payment relative to the price of the bond (minus 1) is the effective interest rate.*

For example, suppose a bond has a promised payment of $1,100 next year. The promised payment is fixed (will not change) although the price at which the bond sells may. Suppose you buy the bond today for $1,000 and receive $1,100 next year, your return will be 10% = [($1,100/$1,000) - 1]. Now, suppose interest rates are currently 5% and the bond continues to pay $1,100 next year. You should be willing to pay $1,100/1.05 = $1,048 for the bond. In other words, if you pay $1,048 for the bond and get back $1,100 in a year, you will be earning a return of 5% [($1,100/$1,048) - 1] which is comparable to what you could earn if you put your $1,048 into some other interest-bearing asset. As you can see, lower interest rates increase the price of bonds. The price of the bond increases by enough to produce a rate of return comparable to the going interest rate given the amount of the promised payment attached to the bond.

The reverse is also true. Suppose that the interest rate increases to 20%. Now, if you wanted to buy a bond with a promised payment of $1,100 next year, you should be willing to buy it for $917 ($1,100/1.20). This is because when you pay $917 for the bond and get back $1,100 next year, you will earn a 20% [($1,100/$917) - 1] return on your investment which is comparable to what you could earn if you put your money into another interest-bearing asset today for one year (since the interest rate is now 20%). As you can see, when interest rates rise, the price of a bond decreases. The price of the bond falls by enough to produce a rate of return comparable to the going interest rate given the amount of the promised payment attached to the bond.

PET #4

An increase in the money supply (expansionary monetary policy) can occur through:

- *an open market purchase of government securities*
- *a reduction in the required reserve ratio*
- *a cut in the discount rate*

A decrease in the money supply (contractionary monetary policy) can occur through:

- *an open market sale of government securities*
- *an increase in the required reserve ratio*
- *an increase in the discount rate*

This PET is a review of material you should be familiar with from the previous chapter.

PET #5

Investment spending is spending by businesses on plant and equipment. Investment spending declines when interest rates increase (because the cost of borrowing increases) and increases when interest rates decline (because the cost of borrowing decreases).

You may wish to review PET #1 and #2 from Chapter 11 of the Practicum.

V.   PRACTICE EXAM: MULTIPLE CHOICE QUESTIONS

1.   Which one of the following statements is NOT true of money?

a.   it is a component of wealth.
b.   people hold money primarily to conduct transactions.
c.   the opportunity cost of holding money is foregone interest earnings on other financial assets.
d.   as interest rates rise, the quantity of money demanded increases.
e.   all of the above are true.

2.   Which one of the following would explain the liquidity motive for holding money?

a.   stock prices are very variable and their rate of return risky compared to money.
b.   bond prices are very variable and their rate of return risky compared to money.

c.   a need to pay for an unexpected, big expense -- like when your car breaks down.
d.   a need to pay for daily transactions like lunch.
e.   it takes time to go to the bank and withdrawal cash from your checking account.

3.   Which one of the following statements is correct?

a.   an increase in the price level will increase money demand and lower interest rates.
b.   a decrease in the price level will increase money demand and lower interest rates.
c.   an increase in real income (GDP) will increase money demand and raise interest rates.
d.   a decrease in real income (GDP) will increase money demand and raise interest rates.
e.   an increase in real income (GDP) will decrease money demand and lower interest rates.

4.   Which one of the following statements is correct?

a.   an increase in the money supply will shift the money supply curve to the right, lower interest rates, and reduce investment spending.
b.   an increase in the money supply will shift the money supply curve to the right, lower interest rates, and raise output.
c.   a decrease in the money supply will shift the money supply curve to the left, lower interest rates, and raise output.
d.   a decrease in money demand will lower interest rates and raise investment spending.
e.   (b) and (d).

5.   Which one of the following statements is correct?

a.   an open market purchase will raise interest rates.
b.   a reduction in the required reserve ratio will lower interest rates.
c.   a reduction in the discount rate will raise interest rates.
d.   a cut in the tax rate will lower interest rates.
e.   (a) and (b).

6.   If the Fed decreases the money supply, in the short run:

a.   investment spending and output (GDP) will fall.
b.   investment spending and output (GDP) will rise.
c.   investment spending will fall and output (GDP) will rise.
b.   investment spending will rise and output (GDP) will fall.
e.   investment spending will not respond to changes in the money supply.

7.   Which one of the following statements is true?

a.   as interest rates increase, the price of bonds drop.
b.   a bond priced at $100 with a promised payment of $105 next year implies an interest rate of 20% per year.
c.   if the interest rate is 7.5% and a bond has a promised payment of $1,150 next year, the price of the bond must be $1,070.
d.   as interest rates drop, the price of bonds drop.
e.   (a) and (c).

8.   An open market sale by the Fed will, in the short run:

a.   raise interest rates and increase (appreciate) the value of the U.S. dollar against foreign currencies.
b.   raise interest rates and decrease (depreciate) the value of the U.S. dollar against foreign currencies.
c.   decrease interest rates and increase (appreciate) the value of the U.S. dollar against foreign currencies.
d.   decrease interest rates and decrease (depreciate) the value of the U.S. dollar against foreign currencies.
e.   raise interest rates but have no effect on the value of the U.S. dollar against foreign currencies.

9.   Which one of the following statements is true?

a.   a cut in the discount rate will increase investment spending and net exports in the short run.
b.   an open market sale will increase investment spending and net exports in the short run.
c.   an increase in the required reserve ratio will increase investment spending and reduce net exports in the short run.
d.   contractionary monetary policy will reduce investment spending but raise exports and leave an undetermined affect on output.
e.   none of the above.

10.   Which one of the following statements is NOT true?

a.   stabilization policies are aimed at maintaining an output (GDP) level at potential (or full employment).
b.   contractionary monetary policy is used when inflation is a threat.
c.   good policymaking depends on good forecasts.
d.   difficulty with recognizing what state the economy is in is an example of an inside lag in policymaking.
e.   lags in implementing policy are referred to as outside lags.

11.   Which one of the following statements is true?

a.   outside lags mean that a policy may take effect after the economy has recovered from its problems.
b.   a depreciation of the dollar will decrease U.S. exports and increase U.S. imports.
c.   monetary policy has a longer inside lag than fiscal policy.
d.   the Fed relies only on econometric models to decide on the direction of monetary policy.
e.   none of the above are true.

VI.   PRACTICE EXAM: ESSAY QUESTIONS

1.   Use the money supply/money demand model to demonstrate how an upturn in the business cycle might affect interest rates and investment spending. If the Fed wanted to keep interest rates at the level they were at before the upturn in the business cycle, what could the Fed do?

2.   Suppose the Fed increases the money supply at the same time that the government reduces government spending. Use the Keynesian cross diagram to demonstrate the effects on spending

and output. Be sure to discuss the international channel through which monetary policy works as well.

VII.   ANSWER KEY: MULTIPLE CHOICE QUESTIONS

1.   Correct answer: d.

Discussion: Statement d is incorrect because as interest rates rise, the quantity of money demand decreases. That is, there is a negative relationship between the quantity of money demanded and the interest rate. This is reflected in a money demand curve that is negatively sloped when graphed against the interest rate. While there are other reasons that people hold money (for liquidity and speculative reasons), the transactions motive is the primary motive for holding money. The opportunity cost of holding money is foregone interest earnings on other financial assets. Money held as cash earns no interest whereas money held in a checking account may earn some interest but the interest rate is very low compared to other financial assets in which money could be placed.

Money is one component of wealth. An individual's holdings of stock, bonds, real estate, art, gold, etc., are other components of wealth.

2.   Correct answer: c.

Discussion: Money is the most liquid component of wealth. You can easily convert it to cash to pay for things or can write a check to pay for things. Obviously, money is held to pay for daily transactions (the transactions motive as implied in Statement d), but some money is held in order to cover unexpected expenses. In other words, you never know when you may need to pay for something quickly. This is the liquidity (or "precautionary") motive for holding money.

Statements a and b are examples of the speculative motive for holding money. Statement e is not an explanation of the liquidity motive.

3.   Correct answer: c.

Discussion: An increase in real income is a shift factor of money demand. At higher income levels, people undertake more transactions and thus demand more money. As the demand for money increases (shifts right) the interest rate rises, holding fixed the money supply.

Statement a is not correct; while an increase in the price level will increase money demand, interest rates will go up, not down. Statement b is not correct because a decrease in the price level will reduce money demand and reduce interest rates. Statement d is not correct because a decrease in real income will reduce money demand and reduce interest rates. Statement e is not correct because and increase in real income will increase money demand and raise interest rates.

4.   Correct answer: e.

Discussion: An increase in money supply is represented by a rightward shift in the money supply curve. As the supply of money increases, the price of money (the interest rate) drops. As the interest rate drops, investment spending increases which leads to a multiple expansion in output. Thus, statement b is correct.

A decrease in money demand will lower the price of money (the interest rate). At lower interest rates, investment spending (and consequently output) will increase. Thus, statement d is correct.

Statement a is not correct because investment spending will increase, not decrease. Statement c is not correct because a decrease in the money supply will raise, not lower, interest rates and thereby reduce investment spending and thus output.

5.   Correct answer: b.

Discussion: A reduction in the required reserve ratio is one arm of monetary policy that can lead to an increase in the money supply. Since the reduction in the required reserve ratio increases the money supply, interest rates will decrease.

Statement a is incorrect because an open market purchase is an increase in the money supply which leads to lower interest rates, not higher interest rates. Statement c is not correct because a cut in the discount rate acts to increase the money supply and thereby lower interest rates, not raise them. Statement d is not correct because a tax cut is an example of fiscal policy and, at this point, is not assumed to have any effect on interest rates. Statement e cannot be correct because statement a is not correct.

6.   Correct answer: a.

Discussion: A decrease in the money supply raises interest rates. The increase in interest rates raises the cost of borrowing and thus reduces investment spending (spending by businesses on plant and equipment). As investment spending declines, output (GDP) declines because there is less spending taking place in the economy.

Based on the answer above, none of the other statements are correct.

7.   Correct answer: e.

Discussion: Interest rates and the price of bonds are negatively related. This means that, as interest rates increase, the price of bonds drop and as interest rates drop, the price of bonds increase. Thus, statement a is correct. Statement c is also correct. Using the formula:

Price of bond = promised payment next year/(1+interest rate)

yields:

Price of bond = $1,150/1.075 = $1,070.

Statement b is not correct. Rearranging the formula above to determine the interest rate would give 5% [($105/$100) - 1], not 20%. Statement d is not correct because statement a is.

8.   Correct answer: a.

Discussion: An open market sale is a decrease in the money supply. As the money supply decreases, the price of money, the interest rate, increases. As the interest rate increases, foreigners demand more of U.S. financial assets since they offer a better rate of return. In order to buy U.S. assets, foreigners must give up their own currency for U.S. dollars. That is, the demand for dollars increases (and the supply of foreign currency increases). As the demand for dollars increases, the price of a dollar relative to foreign currency rises. In other words, the U.S. dollar appreciates against other currencies.

For this reason, statement b is not correct. Statements c and d cannot be correct since an open market sale increases interest rates, not decreases them. Statement e is not correct because monetary policy can influence the exchange rate.

9.   Correct answer: a.

Discussion: A cut in the discount rate leads to an increase in the money supply. An increase in the money supply reduces interest rates and raises investment spending. Also, the reduction in interest rates ultimately leads to a depreciation of the dollar. As the dollar depreciates, exports increase (because they become less expensive) and imports decrease (because they become more expensive). Thus, net exports increase as the dollar depreciates.

Statement b is not correct. An open market sale raises interest rates and reduces investment spending. Furthermore, an open market sale will appreciate the U.S. dollar and reduce net exports. Statement c is not correct. An increase in the required reserve ratio will reduce the money supply and raise interest rates, thereby reducing investment spending. The dollar will appreciate and net exports will decline. Statement d is not correct because contractionary monetary policy will appreciate the dollar and make U.S. exports more expensive. Thus, U.S. exports will decline (not increase).

10.   Correct answer: e.

Discussion: Lags in implementing policy (fiscal or monetary) are referred to as inside lags. (Lags in recognizing what state the economy is in are also referred to as inside lags.) Lags in policy implementation occur because it takes time for policymakers to meet and decide on what to do. The inside lag in monetary policy is much shorter than in fiscal policy.

11.   Correct answer: a.

Discussion: An outside lag is the lag or time it takes for the effects of a policy to be felt on the economy. Sometimes the outside lag is so long that the economy has recovered from its economic problems before the policy effects are felt. This is not good. If the economy has already recovered and the policy begins to take effect, the policy may now produce some undesirable and unintended consequences. For example, suppose the Fed enacted an expansionary monetary policy today because the economy was in a recession. Suppose that the effects on investment spending and GDP are not transmitted to the economy until a year later. By that time, however, the economy may be out of a recession and perhaps is growing rapidly by itself. The expansionary monetary policy might further the growth but exacerbate (increase) inflation. In this way, the policy has created some undesirable and unintended effects.

Statement b is not correct. A dollar depreciation will raise U.S. exports and reduce U.S. imports, not the other way around. Statement c is not correct. Monetary policymakers meet every six weeks and thus the inside lag is much shorter than for fiscal policy (where Congress has to meet and decide on fiscal policy). Statement d is not correct. The Fed uses both econometric models of the U.S. economy and anecdotal evidence in deciding what course of action to take.

VIII.   ANSWER KEY: ESSAY QUESTIONS

1.   An upturn in the business cycle means that output and income have increased. Money demand increases when income increases (primarily through the transactions motive). The increase in money demand is represented by a rightward shift in money demand as shown below.

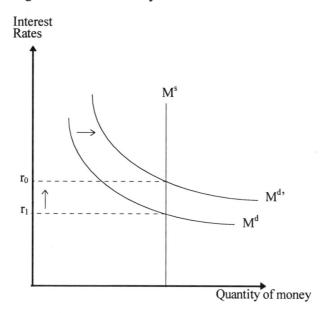

As money demand increases along a fixed supply of money, the price of money or the interest rate rises. The increase in the interest rate has a negative effect on spending. An increase in the interest rate raises the cost of borrowing and so businesses cut back on their purchases of plant and equipment (investment spending declines) and consumers, too, may cut back on their purchases of durable goods like automobiles and appliances. This translates into reduced aggregate spending which in turn reduces production and GDP. Thus, the upturn in the business cycle and output will be dampened to a degree because of rising interest rates.

If the Fed wanted to prevent the increase in interest rates, it could increase the money supply through an open market purchase, reduction in the required reserve ratio, and/or cut in the discount rate. This would serve to increase the money supply in response to the increased demand for money. This would be represented by a rightward shift in the money supply curve above (which you can draw in). Consequently, the interest rate could be prevented from rising and the dampening of the business cycle upturn curtailed.

2.   An increase in the money supply is an expansionary monetary policy because, in the short run, the policy leads to an increase in spending and thus an expansion of production, output, and income. (In the short run, prices are fixed and so the inflationary consequences of the policy are not felt.) An increase in the money supply reduces interest rates and raises investment spending. Consumer spending on durable goods may also increase. In the Keynesian cross diagram below, this is represented by an upward shift in the C+I+G+NX line.

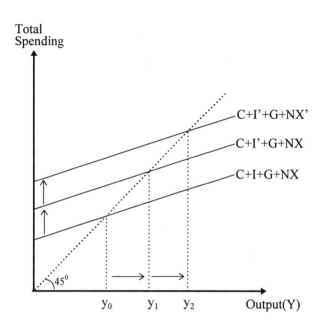

The increase in spending leads to a multiple expansion in GDP as businesses respond to the increased demand by producing more goods and services. Thus, production, output, and income increase. Furthermore, the lower interest rates lead to a depreciation of the U.S. dollar which in turn makes U.S-produced goods less expensive to foreigners who will then buy more of our goods. Thus, U.S. exports increase. On the other hand, the dollar depreciation makes foreign-produced goods more expensive to U.S. citizens who will then cut back their purchases of them and instead buy U.S.-made equivalents. Thus, U.S. imports decrease. The increase in exports and decrease in imports means that there is more spending on U.S.-made goods. That is, net exports increase. The increase in net exports is represented by an upward shift in the C+I+G+NX line above which adds to investment spending's effect on output. The interest and exchange rate effects of the expansionary monetary policy, in the short run, reinforce each other and ultimately lead to an increase in output.

A decrease in government spending is a contractionary fiscal policy. A reduction in government spending on goods and services reduces production, output, and income, in the short run. (In the short run, prices are fixed and so the deflationary consequences of the policy are not felt.) This would be represented by a downward shift in the C+I+G+NX line below.

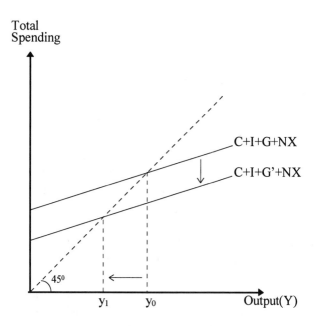

The graph shows that, as spending declines, output declines, too.

The discussion above reveals that the policies work in opposite directions. Expansionary monetary policy works to raise output (GDP) whereas contractionary fiscal policy works to reduce output (GDP), in the short run. Without knowing the magnitudes of the policy actions, it is difficult to predict whether on balance, output will rise or fall.

Take It to the Net

We invite you to visit the O'Sullivan/Sheffrin page on the Prentice Hall Web site at:

http://www.prenhall.com/osullivan/

for this chapter's World Wide Web exercise.

CHAPTER 29
FROM THE SHORT RUN TO THE LONG RUN

I.   OVERVIEW

In this chapter, you will reconsider the short- and long-run effects of monetary and fiscal policy. You will see that the short- and long-run effects can be quite different and is one reason why economists and others often debate the proper course of policy. You will learn about wage and price adjustment in the transition from the short to the long run. You will see how the adjustment process influences the long-run effectiveness of monetary and fiscal policy in controlling the level of output. You will use aggregate demand with short-run (Keynesian) and long-run (Classical) aggregate supply curves to understand the wage-price spiral as well as why policy effects differ in the short run compared to the long run. You will learn about the speed of adjustment of the economy in response to policy changes. You will also learn how changes in wages and prices affect the demand for money, interest rates, investment spending, and GDP. You will learn about a proposition referred to as the "long-run neutrality of money." You will see why some economists believe that monetary policy should not be aimed at influencing short run movements in output. You will re-encounter the concept of crowding out and see why expansionary fiscal policy may be ineffective at increasing the level of output in the long run. You will also see how contractionary fiscal policy can create crowding in and thus lead to increases in a country's capital stock and its standard of living. You will also learn about political business cycles and explore the relationship between economic policymaking and presidential politics.

II.   CHECKLIST

By the end of this chapter, you should be able to:

√   Explain what differentiates the short run from the long run in macroeconomics.
√   Explain the relationship between wages and prices (the wage-price spiral).
√   Explain why when output is above potential (and the unemployment rate below the natural rate), wages and prices increase (and vice-versa).
√   Use short- and long-run aggregate supply curves with aggregate demand to show what happens when an economy is operating above or below its potential or full-employment level of output.
√   Use aggregate demand and aggregate supply curves to discuss how monetary and fiscal policy might be used in cases where the economy is operating above or below its potential or full-employment level of output and is not expected to recover quickly on its own.
√   Use money supply and money demand, the investment schedule, and the Keynesian cross to illustrate how price adjustment can move the economy to its full-employment level of output without any policy action.
√   Define the long-run neutrality of money proposition.
√   Explain why some economists and others believe that monetary and fiscal policy have no effect on the level of output in the long run.
√   Explain why crowding out and crowding in occur and consider the implications for investment spending, total (aggregate) spending (demand), and the capital stock.
√   Discuss the long-run effects of an increase (decrease) in the money supply using the money supply and money demand graph, the investment schedule, and the C+I+G+NX line.
√   Discuss the long-run effects of an increase (decrease) in government spending using the money supply and money demand graph, the investment schedule, and the C+I+G+NX line.

√   Explain what causes a political business cycle.

III.   KEY TERMS

Wage-price spiral: the process by which changes in wages and prices reinforce each other. It occurs when output is not at full employment or potential output.

Aggregate demand curve: the relationship between the price level and the quantity of real GDP demanded.

Keynesian aggregate supply curve: the horizontal aggregate supply at the current level of prices.

Classical aggregate supply curve: the vertical aggregate supply curve at full employment.

Long-run neutrality of money: an increase in the supply of money has no effect on real interest rates, investment, or output in the long run.

Crowding out: the reduction of investment (or other component of GDP) in the long run caused by an increase in government spending.

Crowding in: the increase of investment (or other component of GDP) in the long run caused by a decrease in government spending.

Political business cycle: the effects on the economy of using monetary or fiscal policy to stimulate the economy before an election in order to improve re-election prospects.

IV.   PERFORMANCE ENHANCING TIPS (PETS)

PET #1

The short-run (Keynesian) aggregate supply curve is horizontal and shifts up when wages (or other input prices) increase and shifts down when wages (or other input prices) decrease.

PET #2

The long-run (Classical) aggregate supply curve is vertical and is positioned at the potential (or full employment) level of output. Increases in the capital stock, labor force, productivity of the labor force, and technology will cause the long-run aggregate supply curve to shift to the right. Decreases in the capital stock, labor force, productivity of the labor force, and technology will cause the long-run aggregate supply curve to shift to the left.

PET #3

Monetary and fiscal policy are policy tools that influence spending and thus aggregate demand. Changes in monetary and fiscal policy will thus, in the short run, cause aggregate demand to shift (without any change in aggregate supply).

PET #4

In the short run, increases in the money supply raise the level of output. In the long run, increases in the money supply raise only the price level, with no effect on output.

PET #5

*In the short run, increases in government spending raise the level of output. In the long run, increases in government spending raise only the price level and crowd out investment with no **demand-side** effect on output. However, since investment is crowded out, the capital stock will be reduced and aggregate supply will eventually shift to the left.*

V.   PRACTICE EXAM: MULTIPLE CHOICE QUESTIONS

1.   Which one of the following statements is NOT true?

a.   short-run or Keynesian economics refers to a time period over which wages and prices do not adjust.
b.   the Classical aggregate supply curve is vertical at the full employment (or potential) level of output.
c.   when the economy is operating below the full employment (or potential) level of output, wages and prices will in the long run decline.
d.   wage and price controls are an effective way to bring down the inflation rate.
e.   all of the above are true.

2.   Suppose an economy is currently operating above its potential level of output. One consequence would be:

a.   an increase in wages and an upward shift in the short-run aggregate supply curve.
b.   a reduction in the price level.
c.   an increase in investment spending.
d.   a leftward shift in aggregate demand as the price level rises.
e.   an unemployment rate above the natural rate of unemployment.

3.   Consider an economy that is currently operating below its potential level of output. Which one of the following statements is correct?

a.   the economy will eventually return to the potential level of output and a lower price level without an policy intervention.
b.   an open market sale may help to push the economy to the potential level of output more quickly than letting the economy adjust by itself.
c.   wages and prices will spiral upward.
d.   interest rates will decline and investment spending will increase.
e.   (a) and (d).

4.   The speed of adjustment of the economy to its potential level of output:

a.   is believed to take two - six months.
b.   influences whether policymakers decide to intervene or do nothing.
c.   was believed by President Bush's economic advisors to be fairly slow.
d.   was believed by Keynes to be fairly rapid.
e.   in Japan during the early 1990s, was believed by policymakers to be fairly slow.

5.   Which one of the following statements is true of the adjustment process?

a.   when output is above its potential level, wages will fall.
b.   when output is above its potential level, interest rates will fall.
c.   when output is below its potential level, investment spending will rise.
d.   when output is below its potential level, the demand for money will increase.
e.   (c) and (d).

6.   If output is above its potential level, then:

a.   money demand will shift to the left and the C+I+G+NX line will shift down.
b.   money demand will shift to the right and the C+I+G+NX line will shift down.
c.   money demand will shift to the left and the C+I+G+NX line will shift up.
d.   money demand will shift to the right and the C+I+G+NX line will shift up.
e.   none of the above.

7.   If output is above its potential level, then:

a.   prices will rise and money demand will shift to the left.
b.   investment spending and the level of output will decline.
c.   interest rates will increase and money demand will shift to the left.
d.   wages will rise and interest rates will decrease.
e.   money demand will shift to the right and wages will fall.

8.   The long-run neutrality of money means that changes in the money supply:

a.   have no long-run effect on real interest rates, investment, or output.
b.   have no long-run effect on prices.
c.   cause crowding out.
d.   do not shift aggregate demand.
e.   shift aggregate demand and aggregate supply by equal and offsetting amounts.

9.   In the long run, an open market sale will:

a.   increase prices and increase output.
b.   increase output and increase prices.
c.   decrease prices and increase output.
d.   decrease output and decrease prices.
e.   decrease prices and have no effect on output.

10.   In the long run, crowding out occurs because:

a.   decreases in the money supply raise interest rates and reduce investment spending.
b.   increases in government spending raise the price level and interest rates and reduce investment spending.
c.   when the economy is at the potential level of output, increases in government spending necessarily require reductions in other spending in the economy.
d.   increases in the money supply raise the price level and reduce spending by households and businesses.
e.   (b) and (c).

11.   Which one of the following statements is true of the political business cycle?

a.   politicians have an incentive to decrease the money supply about a year or so before an election.
b.   incumbent presidents have an incentive to enact contractionary policies prior to the election and expansionary policies after the election.
c.   President Carter attempted to stimulate the economy prior to his election in an effort to make voters feel good so that he would be re-elected.
d.   the political business cycle implies that the unemployment rate will decline prior to an election and rise after an election.
e.   expansionary monetary and fiscal policies are always favored by politicians.

VI.   PRACTICE EXAM: ESSAY QUESTIONS

1a.   Suppose that the price of oil increases. Use short-run aggregate supply and aggregate demand to explain the short-run **and** long-run effects of this event. Assume the economy is currently operating at the potential level of output.

1b.   Now, considering your answer to part (a), what policy or policies would you advocate? Or, would you advocate any policy intervention at all? Explain. Be sure to relate your answer to the speed of adjustment of the economy.

2.   The long-run neutrality of money proposition implies that activist monetary policy has no lasting effects on the level of output. If this is true, is there any role for the Fed in the economy?

VII.   ANSWER KEY: MULTIPLE CHOICE QUESTIONS

1.   Correct answer: d.

Discussion: Wage and price controls interfere with the natural forces of demand and supply in determining efficient outcomes and in resolving shortages or surpluses, be it in the goods, labor, or capital market. Thus, wage and price controls are not effective at bringing the rate of inflation down. Typically, once the wage and price controls are removed, there is a big upward spike in wages and prices. President Nixon found out in 1971 just how unsuccessful wage and price controls are.

Statement a is correct; Keynesian economics refers to the short run which is a period of time during which wages and prices are sticky, not flexible, and therefore do not have time to adjust to market demand or supply conditions. Statement b is correct. The Classical aggregate supply curve is used to represent the behavior of the supply-side of the economy in the long run when wages and prices are flexible and have had time to adjust to economic disturbances. In the long run, the potential level of output is determined by supply-side factors like the size (and age) of the capital stock, the size and productivity of the labor force, and the state of technology. The potential level of output is not determined or influenced by the price level. A vertical aggregate supply curve represents this independence of potential output from the price level. Statement c is correct; when the economy is operating below the potential level of output, there is an excess supply of labor (unemployment above the natural rate). The excess supply of labor exerts downward pressure on wages. As wages drop, the cost of production drops, and thus the prices at which output sells drop.

2.   Correct answer: a.

Discussion: An economy that is operating above its potential level of output is operating beyond its capacity. That is, there will be shortages of labor (and capital). The shortage of labor means that wages will rise. Since wages are an input cost of production and they have increased, the short-run aggregate supply curve will shift upward.

Given the answer above, statement b is not correct. The price level will rise in the short run, since wage costs have increased. Statement c is not correct. The increase in the price level will increase the demand for money which will, in turn, raise interest rates. The increase in interest rates will reduce investment spending, not increase it. Statement d is not correct. As the price level rises, there will be a leftward movement along the aggregate demand curve, not a shift in it. Statement e is not correct. If the economy is operating above potential, the unemployment rate must be below the natural rate of unemployment.

3.   Correct answer: e.

Discussion: If the economy is operating below the potential level of output, wages and prices will decline. As prices decline, the demand for money will decline (shift left) and the interest rate will fall. As the interest rate falls, the level of investment spending (and perhaps consumer spending on durables) will rise. The increased spending will, in turn, lead to increased production which will move the economy back up to its potential level of output. Thus, statements a and d are both correct.

Statement b is not correct. An economy that is operating below potential, if anything, needs a stimulative or expansionary policy action, not a contractionary one. An open market sale is a contractionary monetary policy since it decreases the money supply. This would move the economy further away from the potential level of output. Statement c is not correct. As mentioned above, wages and prices will spiral downward, not upward.

4.   Correct answer: b.

Discussion: Policymakers that believe the speed of adjustment is slow tend to advocate activist, stabilization policies, i.e., the use of monetary and fiscal policy to move the economy toward the potential level of output. Policymakers that believe the speed of adjustment is rapid tend to advocate non-intervention, i.e., let the economy recover on its own.

Statement a is not correct. The speed of adjustment is believed to take two to six years. Statement c is not correct. President Bush's economic advisors believed the speed of adjustment of the economy to be fairly rapid and thus took a pretty "hands off" approach regarding the use of policy to move the economy. Statement c is not correct. Keynes believed the speed of adjustment of economies to be fairly slow, not rapid. Thus, Keynes was in favor of stabilization or interventionist policies. Statement e is not correct. In the early 1990s, Japanese policymakers did not use monetary and fiscal policy despite the economic problems the country was suffering. The policymakers believed that the economy would recover quickly by itself.

5.   Correct answer: c.

Discussion: When output is below its potential level, wages and prices spiral downward. As prices drop, the price level drops as well. As the price level drops, the demand for money declines (shifts left). As the demand for money declines, the interest rate drops. As the interest rate drops, investment spending increases. Thus, statement c is correct.

Statement a is not correct. When output is above potential, wages will rise (due to labor shortages). Statement b is not correct. When output is above potential, prices will rise which will in turn increase the demand for money causing interest rates to rise, not fall. Statement d is not correct. The discussion above indicates that money demand will decrease, not increase.

6.   Correct answer: b.

Discussion: When output is above its potential level, wages and therefore prices rise. As the price level rises, the demand for money increases. This is represented by a rightward shift in the money demand curve. The increased demand for money raises interest rates and reduces investment spending. Thus, I in C+I+G+NX declines causing the C+I+G+NX line to shift down.

Based on the above discussion, none of the other answers can be correct.

7.   Correct answer: b.

Discussion: This question is an application of question (6) above. If output is above its potential level, wages and prices will rise. The increase in the price level will lead to an increase in the demand for money which will, in turn, cause interest rates to rise. As interest rates rise, investment spending declines. As investment spending declines, the economy responds by producing less output. Thus, output declines as well.

Statements a and c are not correct because money demand will shift to the right. Statement d is not correct because interest rates will increase, not decrease. Statement e is not correct because wages will rise, not fall.

8.   Correct answer: a.

Discussion: The long-run neutrality of money proposition means that monetary policy is, in the long run, ineffective at altering "real variables" which are variables like the real interest rate (nominal interest rate minus inflation rate), investment, output, and even employment. However, this is not to say that monetary policy can't affect the price level in the long run. It can and does.

9.   Correct answer: e.

Discussion: An open market sale is contractionary monetary policy, i.e., a decrease in the money supply. The decrease in the money supply shifts the aggregate demand curve to the left. As the aggregate demand curve shifts left along the long-run aggregate supply curve, the price level drops but there is no final change in the level of output the economy produces. This is an example of the long-run neutrality of money proposition.

Statements a, b, and c can be ruled out because contractionary policy in either the short or long run does not increase the level of output. Statement d is not correct because in the long run, the level of output is unaffected by monetary policy.

10.   Correct answer: e.

Discussion: Crowding out refers to what happens to private sector spending (most notably investment spending, but consumption as well) when the government increases its spending on goods and services. Increases in government spending, in the long run, move the economy above potential and thus lead to higher wages and prices. As prices rise, the price level increases and the demand for money increases. As the demand for money increases, interest rates rise and thus investment (and consumer spending on durables) declines. This is the crowding out effect. On net, government spending crowds out investment and consumer spending by an amount equal to the increase in government spending leaving no change on total spending and thus on output.   Thus, statement b is correct. Statement c is also correct. When the economy is at potential, it is physically unable to produce any more output in response to increased spending. Thus, the increase in government spending comes at the expense of a reduction in spending by businesses (investment spending) and by households (consumption spending).

Statements a and d are not correct because crowding out is not used in reference to changes in the money supply.

11.   Correct answer: d.

Discussion: The political business cycle means that incumbent politicians have an incentive to enact expansionary policies prior to the election and contractionary policies after the election. This is because the unemployment rate will tend to go down prior to an election (causing people to vote for the incumbent) and rise after an election (when they can't do anything about it).

Based on the reasoning above, statements a and b are not correct. Statement c is not correct because President Carter enacted contractionary policies prior to re-election. Statement e is not correct. Politicians do not always favor expansionary policies -- incumbents may prefer them prior to an election -- but contractionary policies may be favored in cases where inflation is high.

VIII.   ANSWER KEY: ESSAY QUESTIONS

1a.   Oil is indirectly an input into the production of most goods and services. Thus, when the price of oil increases, the cost of production rises. This is represented by an upward shift in the short-run aggregate supply curve as drawn below.

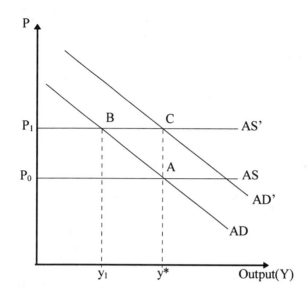

In the short run, the effect of the oil price increase is to raise the price level (create inflation) and reduce output below its potential level as indicated at point B. This combination of outcomes is sometimes referred to as "stagflation" since not only does inflation occur but the economy (output and income) stagnate. In this situation, the economy is likely to experience a surplus of labor since unemployment will increase and there will be some unused production capacity. Thus, wages and prices will begin to fall.

The decline in wages and prices will enable the economy, in the long run, to return to the potential level of output. The fall in prices will reduce the price level which will in turn reduce the demand for money. As the demand for money declines, the interest rate will fall which will in turn stimulate investment spending (and spending on consumer durables). Businesses will respond to the increased level of spending by producing more output and hiring more workers. (The spending stimulus and consequent increase in output would be shown as a movement along the AD curve from point B back to point A.)

1b.   If I believed that the speed of adjustment, i.e., the length of time it took the economy to move from point B to back to point A was relatively short, say, under one year, I would be inclined to argue that no policy intervention should take place to assist the economy's return to the potential level of output. I would argue that the economy will naturally, and rather quickly, readjust. Moreover, if the lags in policy (either fiscal or monetary) are long and/or I have my doubts about the forecasting accuracy on which the policy is based, I'd argue even more ardently in favor of a "do nothing" approach. Also, if the oil price increase reduced output (compare output levels at point A to point B) by a "trivial" amount (say 0.5%), I would be inclined to argue that the reduction in output is not significant enough to warrant policy intervention.

On the other hand, if the speed of adjustment from point B back to point A was relatively slow, I would argue that perhaps some expansionary policy intervention is warranted. I would prefer monetary policy over fiscal policy because the lags in monetary policy are shorter than for fiscal policy. In this case, the Fed could increase the money supply so as to stimulate spending (investment and consumer durables) and thus production and output. This would be represented by a rightward shift in aggregate demand along the AS' curve, as shown above. The result would be that output would return to its potential level. However, the price level would remain at its post-oil-price increase level. (Compare the price level at point C to that at point A.) Thus, there is a cost to acting now: the price level will remain higher than if we had let the economy self-adjust.

2.	There are several arguments that can be made in favor of a role for activist monetary policy. The long-run neutrality of money proposition does not imply that monetary policy is ineffective in the short run (as discussed in essay 1 above) nor does it imply that monetary policy is ineffective at influencing inflation. The long-run neutrality of money proposition only says that output cannot be influenced by monetary policy in the long run. Money, (i.e., monetary policy) can, in the short run, influence output, and money can, in the long run, influence the price level.

If the aim of the Fed is to keep the price level stable, it may need to actively use monetary policy. For example, if the economy is operating above potential, the price level will rise. To prevent this, the Fed could step in with contractionary monetary policy and thereby remove the price (and wage) pressures from the economy. On the other hand, if the economy is operating below potential, the price level will drop. If the Fed is satisfied with the current rate of inflation and doesn't see any reason for the economy to suffer (i.e., unemployment would, in this case, be above the natural rate), the Fed could step in with expansionary monetary policy (as in the example given in the answer to 1b above). Output would return to its potential level (which assumes that the Fed can influence output in the short run) without any increase in the price level relative to its starting point.

After you read the next chapter, your answer may be different.

Take It to the Net

We invite you to visit the O'Sullivan/Sheffrin page on the Prentice Hall Web site at:

http://www.prenhall.com/osullivan/

for this chapter's World Wide Web exercise.

CHAPTER 30
THE DYNAMICS OF INFLATION AND UNEMPLOYMENT

I.   OVERVIEW

In this chapter, you will learn about the role which expectations of future inflation play in preferences for holding money, wage setting, real interest rates, and the determination of inflation and unemployment. You will learn how expectations of future inflation can be influenced by the stance of monetary policy and the commitment of central bankers to maintaining low inflation. You will learn that central banks that are credibly committed to low inflation often have an easier time securing low inflation. You will use an expectations Phillips curve to explore the relationship between the change in the rate of inflation and the unemployment rate in reference to the natural rate of unemployment. You will also be introduced to the concept of the velocity of money using the equation of exchange. You will learn what role the rate of money growth, velocity growth, and growth in real GDP have in determining the rate of inflation. You will learn what role the budget deficit and how it is financed play in determining inflation. You will learn that countries that experience hyperinflation are typically countries that run large budget deficits which are financed by printing money. You will consider the costs of unemployment as well as the costs of inflation -- anticipated and unanticipated inflation. You will use the reality principle throughout the chapter.

II.   CHECKLIST

By the end of this chapter, you should be able to:

√   Discuss how expectations of inflation affect individual and business decisionmaking.

√   Explain why countries with higher money growth rates typically have higher nominal interest rates.

√   Recite the reality principle and explain money illusion.

√   Explain how money growth that exceeds the public's expected rate of inflation will increase money demand and the real interest rate, and vice-versa.

√   Define the expectations Phillips curve.

√   Discuss what happens to inflation when the unemployment rate is above the natural rate and when it is below the natural rate.

√   Use the expectations Phillips curve to predict the inflation rate (given the unemployment rate) or the unemployment rate (given the inflation rate).

√   Explain how central bankers can influence expectations of inflation.

√   Explain how a central bank that is committed to fighting inflation may deter rational wage setters from demanding excessive wage increases.

√   Discuss the empirical evidence regarding the relationship between central bank independence and the rate of inflation.

√   Define the velocity of money.

√   Set out the equation of exchange (or the quantity equation). Also, express it in terms of growth rates (i.e., percentage changes).

√   Use the equation of exchange to predict inflation or velocity given information on the other variables in the equation.

√   Define hyperinflation.

√   Discuss the major cause of hyperinflation.

√   Discuss the behavior of money demand and velocity during hyperinflation.

√   Define monetarism or what it means to be a monetarist.

√   Discuss the costs of unemployment.
√   Discuss the costs of anticipated inflation and explain how the tax system introduces a cost.
√   Discuss the costs of unanticipated inflation and some of the ways of reducing the costs.

III.   KEY TERMS

Prime rate of interest: the rate of interest that large banks charge to their best customers on short-term loans.

Real wages: nominal or dollar wages adjusted for inflation.

Money illusion: confusion of real and nominal magnitudes.

Expectations of inflation: the beliefs held by the public about the likely path of inflation for the future.

Expected real rate of interest: the nominal rate of interest minus expected inflation

Expectations Phillips curve: the relationship that describes the relationship between inflation and unemployment taking into account expectations of inflation.

Rational expectations: the economic theory that analyzes how people form expectations in such a manner that, on average, they correctly forecast the future.

Velocity of money: nominal GDP divided by the money supply. It is also the rate at which money turns over during the year.

The quantity equation: the equation that links money, velocity, prices and real output. In symbols, we have: $M \cdot V = P \cdot y$

Growth version of the quantity equation: an equation that links the growth rates of money, velocity, prices and real output:

$$
\begin{array}{c}
\text{Growth Rate} + \text{Growth Rate} = \text{Growth Rate} + \text{Growth Rate} \\
\text{of Money} \qquad \text{of Velocity} \qquad \text{of Prices} \qquad \text{of Real Output}
\end{array}
$$

Hyperinflation: an inflation exceeding 50% per month.

Monetarists: economists who emphasized the role of money in determining nominal income and inflation.

Unemployment insurance: payments received from the government upon becoming unemployed.

Anticipated inflation: inflation that is expected.

Unanticipated inflation: inflation that is not expected.

Menu costs: costs of inflation that arise from having to change printed prices.

Shoe leather costs: costs of inflation that arise from trying to reduce holdings of cash.

Usury laws: laws that do not allow interest rates to exceed specified ceilings.

IV.   PERFORMANCE ENHANCING TIPS (PETS)

PET #1

Given any three values for the variables in the equation of exchange (quantity equation), the fourth variable's value can be determined.

The growth version of the equation of exchange is:

$$\%\Delta \text{ Money} + \%\Delta \text{ Velocity} = \%\Delta \text{ price level} + \%\Delta \text{ real GDP}$$

Suppose you are told that the inflation rate is currently 3% per year and the Fed is happy to maintain this rate of inflation but would like to achieve a 4% growth rate in real GDP per year. Furthermore, you are told that the percentage change in velocity is 1% per year. What money growth rate would be consistent with the Fed's commitment to 3% inflation and 4% growth in output?

The equation above can be solved for %Δ Money as:

$$%\Delta \text{ Money} = %\Delta \text{ price level} + %\Delta \text{ real GDP} - %\Delta \text{ Velocity}$$
$$= 3\% + 4\% - 1\%$$
$$= 6\%$$

PET #2

In the long run, the rate of inflation will equal the growth rate of money, holding other factors constant.

This is just a special case of PET #1 above where "other factors constant" means that velocity and real GDP are not growing (percentage change = 0). So, if the money supply is growing at 3% a year, other factors constant, the rate of inflation will also be 3% per year.

PET #3

When expected inflation exceeds the rate of growth of the money supply, money demand will be increasing by more than money supply will be increasing. Thus, nominal and real interest rates will rise. When expected inflation is less than the rate of growth of the money supply, money demand will be increasing by less than money supply will be increasing. Thus, nominal and real interest rates will fall.

Remember from the previous chapter that increases in the price level act to increase the demand for money (and vice-versa). Similarly, when the price level is expected to increase (i.e., expected inflation is greater than zero), the demand for money will increase and at a rate equal to the expected inflation rate. Using a money supply/money demand diagram, you would represent this with a rightward shift in money demand. If expected inflation exceeds the rate of growth of the money supply, then the rightward shift in money demand will be greater than the rightward shift in money supply. As a consequence, the nominal interest rate will increase. With expectations of inflation unchanged, the real interest rate rises, too. The reverse is true when the expected rate of inflation is less than the growth rate of the money supply.

PET #4

Central banks that are credibly committed to maintaining a stable price level and low inflation reduce the expected rate of inflation held by the private sector.

The consequences of a central bank commitment to price level stability and low inflation are that workers and unions are less likely to press for excessive wage demands, long-term real interest rates are likely to be lower (which is good news for people who must borrow to purchase a new home, car, appliances, etc., and for businesses who must borrow to finance investment), and businesses are less likely to raise their price in anticipation that all prices will be going up in the future.

PET #5

If the price level is increasing by a factor of X every month, then over a year, the price level will have increased by a factor of X^{12}.

For example, if a candy bar and soda cost $1 today and the price level is increasing three-fold every month (300%), then, at the end of the month, the candy bar and soda will cost $1 X 3 = $3. At the end of the next month, the candy bar and soda will cost $3 X 3 = $9, and so on. Thus, at the end of the year, the candy bar and soda will cost $1 X 3^{12} = $1 X 531,441 = $531,441!

Alternatively, if you had $1 today and prices were increasing three-fold every month (300%), then your $1 would be worth $1/3 = $0.33 at the end of the month. At the end of the next month, the $1 would be worth $0.33/3 = $(1/3)/3 = $0.11, and so on. Thus, at the end of the year, the $1 would be worth $1/3^{12}$ = 1/531,441 = $0.0000018!

V.   PRACTICE EXAM: MULTIPLE CHOICE QUESTIONS

1.   Which one of the following statements is true?

a.   the expected real rate of interest = nominal rate + expected rate of inflation.
b.   money illusion is the confusion of nominal and real magnitudes.
c.   if two countries had the same real rate of interest but one had a higher inflation rate, it would have a lower nominal interest rate.
d.   if money demand and money supply each grow by 3% per year, the real interest rate will rise by 3% per year.
e.   Milton Friedman is the father of the rational expectations school of thought.

2.   If the public currently expected the inflation rate to be 8% and the Fed increased the money supply by 5%, then:

a.   real interest rates would increase in the short run.
b.   money demand would decline by 8%.
c.   money demand would decline by 5%.
d.   money demand would increase by 8%.
e.   (a) and (d).

3.   If the Fed increased the money supply by 10% and the public expected inflation to be 6%, then:

a.   the nominal and real interest rates will drop in the short run.
b.   in the long run, inflation will be 10%, other factors constant.
c.   real GDP will rise and unemployment will fall in the short run.
d.   in the long run, the real interest rate will remain constant.
e.   all of the above.

4.   The expectations Phillips curve shows:

a.   that, if the actual unemployment rate is below the natural rate of unemployment, inflation will rise above last year's level.
b.   the relationship between the inflation rate and the unemployment rate.

c. can be used to calculate the misery index.
d. that the natural rate of unemployment can be defined as the unemployment rate associated with a zero percent inflation rate.
e. that, if the natural rate of unemployment increases, the expectations Phillips curve will shift to the left.

5. Which one of the following statements is NOT true?

a. central bankers, through monetary policy, can influence expectations of inflation.
b. a central bank that is committed to fighting inflation will be more likely to do nothing when the unemployment rate rises above the natural rate (i.e., economy goes into a recession).
c. if people believe the Fed prefers to use expansionary monetary policy during economic downturns, they will be more inclined to push for higher nominal wages.
d. a central bank that whose sole goal is to keep the inflation rate low is more likely to use monetary policy to help stabilize output.
e. none of the above are true.

6. Empirical evidence shows that:

a. since the 1980s, unemployment rates have been lower in Europe than in the U.S.
b. countries with hyperinflation typically have very slow money growth rates.
c. countries in which central banks are more independent (autonomous) tend to have lower rates of inflation.
d. countries in which central banks are more independent (autonomous) tend to have higher GDP growth rates.
e. (c) and (d).

7. The velocity of money:

a. is equal to the supply of money divided by nominal GDP.
b. will be high when people hold onto money for a long period of time.
c. has ranged between 14 and 19 since the late 1950s for the U.S. using the M2 money supply.
d. is equal to the (price level X real GDP)/ money supply.
e. is the cause of hyperinflation.

8. Which one of the following statements is true?

a. if the growth rate in velocity is 3%, the inflation rate is 9%, and the money growth rate is 4%, then output must be growing at -2%.
b. if the monthly inflation rate is 14%, purchasing power will be cut in half in 5 months.
c. if prices are rising by a factor of 5 each month, then $1 today will be worth $0.20 at the end of the month.
d. if prices are rising by a factor of 2 each month, then something that costs $5 today will cost $20,480 at the end of the year.
e. all of the above are true.

9. Which one of the following statements is NOT true?

a.   unemployment insurance covers 100% of wages lost by unemployed workers.
b.   menu costs are the costs of having to reprint brochures, pamphlets, and other price lists as prices change.
c.   shoe leather costs are the time and inconvenience costs associated with having to withdraw cash from the bank frequently, especially during periods of hyperinflation.
d.   indexed bonds are a way of preserving the real value of the interest paid to the holder of the bond.
e.   in times of high inflation, usury laws prompt depositors to seek other outlets besides banks as a place to put their funds.

10.   Which one of the following statements is NOT true?

a.   tax brackets have been indexed for inflation since 1986.
b.   individuals who sell stocks at a profit during the year must pay taxes on the nominal gain in the value of stock.
c.   homeowners are permitted to deduct the real value of interest paid on their mortgage.
d.   considering taxes, an individual in the 28% tax bracket who earns a 10% nominal rate of interest effectively earns a 7.2% nominal return.
e.   all of the above are true.

11.   Consider two tax brackets: 15% on the first $50,000 earned and 25% on any amount earned above $50,000. An individual earning $60,000 a year will pay _____ % of his income in taxes this year. If his income rises to $70,000, he will pay _____ % next year.

a.   25%; 25%.
b.   16.7%; 17.9%.
c.   44.2%; 45.8%.
d.   15%; 25%.
e.   12.5%; 35%.

VI.   PRACTICE EXAM: ESSAY QUESTIONS

1.   Suppose the Fed conducted an open market sale in order to contain inflationary pressures in the economy. How does the policy work on short- and long-term interest rates and how might the credibility of the Fed's commitment to fighting inflation affect long-term interest rates?

2.   Explain what causes hyperinflation and what happens during episodes of hyperinflation.

VII.   ANSWER KEY: MULTIPLE CHOICE QUESTIONS

1.   Correct answer: b.

Discussion: Money illusion occurs when an increase in, e.g., the nominal wage rate, is perceived as an increase in the real wage. In fact, an increase in the nominal wage rate only makes a worker better off if the nominal wage increase is bigger in percentage terms than the inflation rate. In this case, the real wage rate would rise. However, if the percentage increase in the nominal wage is equal to the inflation rate, then there is no change in the purchasing power of the worker's wage and thus the worker is no better off than before, despite the increased nominal wage. (The same is true for savers. They should consider their real return, not their nominal return.)

Statement a is not correct. The expected real interest rate = nominal interest rate minus the expected rate of inflation. Statement c is not correct. If two countries had the same real rate of interest but one had a higher inflation rate, it would have a higher, not lower nominal interest rate. For example, if both countries had a real rate of interest of 5% and inflation was 5% in Country A and 20% in Country B, the nominal interest rate in Country A would be 10% and that in Country B would be 25%. Statement d is not correct. If money demand and money supply each grow by 3% per year, the real interest rate will not change. Statement e is not correct. Milton Friedman is the "father" of monetarism and Robert Lucas is the "father" of rational expectations.

2.   Correct answer: e.

Discussion: If the public expected the inflation rate to be 8%, they would want to hold 8% in cash and/or checking account balances. That is, money demand would increase by 8%. But, money supply is not growing as fast as money demand. This would be represented by a bigger shift rightward in money demand than the rightward shift in money supply. Thus, the nominal (and real) interest rate would increase in the short run. (See PET #3 for review.)

Statements b and c cannot be correct because money demand will increase, not decrease.

3.   Correct answer: e.

Discussion: This question is the reverse of question (2). In this case, the money supply will shift rightward by more than money demand will shift rightward (compare 10% to 6%). Thus, the nominal and real interest rates will drop in the short run. As the real interest rate drops, spending by businesses on plant and equipment (investment) will increase and lead to an increase in real GDP. As real GDP rises, the unemployment rate will fall. This all happens in the short run. In the long run, money is neutral and so the real interest rate will return to its initial level, i.e., it remains constant in the long run. However, the 10% increase in the money supply, other factors constant, will create a 10% inflation rate.

4.   Correct answer: a.

Discussion: The expectations Phillips curve shows the relationship between the unemployment rate (relative to the natural rate of unemployment) and the change in the inflation rate. The relationship is negative, i.e., if the unemployment rate is below the natural rate, say 4.7% compared to 6%), then the change in the inflation rate will increase say from 2% to 2.65%. Thus, the inflation rate will rise above last year's level.

Statement b is not true of the **expectations** Phillips curve but is true of the Phillips curve. Statement c is not correct. Moreover, you have not been introduced to the misery index (sum of inflation plus unemployment). Statement d is not correct. The expectations Phillips curve shows the natural rate of unemployment is defined where the **change** in the inflation rate is zero. Statement e is not correct. The expectations Phillips curve will shift to the right when the natural rate of unemployment increases.

5.   Correct answer: d.

Discussion: Statement d is not true. A central bank whose sole goal is to keep the inflation rate low is less likely, not more likely, to use monetary policy to help stabilize output. That is, the central bank will be more likely to "do nothing" even if output fell below its potential level.

6.   Correct answer: c.

Discussion: Empirical evidence has found a negative relationship between central bank independence and inflation rates. That is, countries with higher degrees of central bank independence typically have lower rates of inflation. Germany, Switzerland, and even the U.S. are good cases in point.

Empirical evidence does not suggest that a higher degree of central bank independence is associated with higher GDP growth rates. Thus, statement d is not true. Statement a is not true. In fact, the U.S. has had notably lower unemployment rates than Europe has had since the 1980s. Statement b is not true. Countries with excessively high money growth rates (typically countries with big budget deficits that must be financed by "printing money") have hyperinflation. Bolivia and Argentina have provided some good, recent cases in point.

7.   Correct answer: d.

Discussion: The velocity of money is defined as nominal GDP (which is equal to the price level X real GDP) divided by the money supply. Thus, statement d is correct and statement a is not correct. Statement b is not correct because the velocity of money is low, not high, when people hold onto money for a long period of time. Statement c is not correct. For the U.S., the M2 velocity of money has ranged between 1.4 and 1.9, not 14 and 19. Velocity numbers in the double digits are typically indications of hyperinflation. Statement e is not correct. The velocity of money does not cause hyperinflation. However, hyperinflation may cause the velocity of money to increase significantly.

8.   Correct answer: e.

Discussion: Statement a requires that you apply the growth version of the equation of exchange (see PET #1 for review). In this case, output growth is equal to money growth (4%) + velocity growth (3%) minus the inflation rate (9%) = -2%. Statement b requires that you apply the Rule of 70 (from previous chapters). In this case, since inflation is stated on a monthly basis, the Rule of 70 implies that purchasing power will be cut in half (inflation will double) in 70/14 = 5 months. Statement c is correct. If prices are rising by a factor of 5 each month, then $1 today will be worth 1/5 = $0.20 at the end of the month. Statement d is also correct. If prices are rising by a factor of 2 each month, then over the course of the year, prices will have increased by a factor of 2^{12} = 4,096. If something costs $5 today, then it will cost $5 X 4,096 = $20,480 at the end of the year! That shows the power of compounding!

9.   Correct answer: a.

Discussion: Statement a is not true. Unemployment insurance covers less than 100% of wages lost by unemployed workers. For example, a worker earning $2,000 a month may receive only $1,300 a month in unemployment insurance upon the loss of his or her job. Furthermore, unemployment insurance is typically provided for up to 26 weeks (39 weeks in extenuating circumstances).

10.   Correct answer: c.

Discussion: Homeowners are permitted to deduct the nominal, not real, value of interest paid on their mortgage. In times of inflation, the real value of the interest payments would be lower. Thus, if interest on mortgage payments were indexed to the rate of inflation, homeowners would not get as big a deduction as they currently are able to claim. Thus, the current provision for mortgage interest benefits homeowners.

Statements a, b, and d are all true. As for statement b, suppose you bought $1,000 worth of stock at the beginning of the year and sold it at the end of the year for $1,500. You made $500 in profit and a return of 50% ($500/$1000) X 100]. You must pay taxes on the $500 in earnings. However, if inflation was 10% that year, then the real value of the earnings are $455 = ($500/1.10). In this case, you end up paying more to the government than you would have if the rate you paid on stock gains was indexed to inflation. As for statement d, suppose you invest $1,000 into a mutual fund and earned a 10% return, i.e., $100. Since you are in the 28% tax bracket, you must pay 28% of the $100 of interest earnings to the government. Thus, you pay $28 and after taxes, make $72. Thus, your after-tax rate of return is [$72/$1,000]X100 = 7.2%

11.   Correct answer: b.

Discussion: Since the tax rate is 15% on the first $50,000 earned and the individual earns $60,000, he must pay a rate of 15% on $50,000 and then 25% on the remaining $10,000 (above the $50,000). Thus, the percentage of income paid as taxes is: 0.15 X $50,000 + 0.25 X $10,000 = 16.7%. Now, if the individual's income rises to $70,000, he must now pay 25% on $20,000 (the amount over $50,000) but continues to pay 15% on the first $50,000. Thus, the percentage of income paid as taxes is: 0.15 X $50,000 + 0.25 X $20,000 = 17.9%.

Based on the above reasoning, none of the other answers can be correct.

VIII.   ANSWER KEY: ESSAY QUESTIONS

1.   When the Fed conducts an open market sale, it sells off its holdings of (previous issues) of government bonds. The private sector (households and businesses) buy the bonds and pay for them with a check written to the Fed. Thus, bank deposits of the private sector are reduced and the money supply declines. The decline in the money supply is aimed at reducing spending in the economy and thereby taking pressure off of prices throughout the economy and thus at reducing the inflation rate. The way it works is that the contraction in the money supply temporarily causes the nominal interest rate to rise (while inflation remains at its current level). Consequently, the real interest rate rises, too. Short-term interest rates (nominal and real) will rise.

What happens to long-term interest rates depends on how the Fed's actions influences the expectations of the private sector. This is because long-term interest rates carry a premium (are higher) for higher expected rates of inflation. If the private sector believes that the Fed will bring down the inflation rate into the future (and keep it down), expectations of future inflation will be reduced and nominal long-term interest rates may not rise by as much as nominal short-term interest rates rise following the open market sale. In fact, it is possible that nominal long-term interest rates could decline even though nominal short-term interest rates rise. However, if the private sector does not believe that the Fed is commited to securing and maintaining a low rate of inflation for the economy, expectations of future inflation may not change at all and thus nominal long-term interest rate may rise (and possibly even more than nominal short-term interest rates rise).

2.   The most common cause of hyperinflation is a government budget deficit that is financed by the government printing money to pay for it. Most industrialized countries finance their government budget through tax revenues. Any shortfall between government expenditures and tax revenues (budget deficit) is financed by selling government bonds (IOUs) to households and businesses and not by printing money. The problem with financing a government budget deficit by printing money is that the money supply expands (by a multiple) of the amount of money printed. The equation of exchange (quantity equation) in growth rates shows the link between the growth rate of the money supply and the inflation rate which is one for one, assuming that the growth rate in velocity is zero and the growth rate in output is zero. That is, a country whose money supply grows by 25% per year will have an inflation rate of 25% per year. When a country continually runs a budget deficit and finances it by printing money, the private sector begins to expect higher inflation which they in turn build into their negotiations for wages. This wage pressure also adds to inflation. Before too long, the rate of inflation begins to spiral up. This is a situation of hyperinflation.

During hyperinflationary episodes, money loses its value (its purchasing power) very rapidly. For example, if inflation were 20% per month, $1 today would be worth $0.11 at the end of the year $[1/(1.20^{12})]$. Alternatively, an item that cost $1 today would cost $8.92 at the end of the year. With hyperinflation, because prices are rising so rapidly, people tend to spend it just as rapidly (before prices rise even more). Thus, during hyperinflation the velocity of money is typically very high (double digits). Shoeleather and menu costs can also become quite high during episodes of hyperinflation.

Take It to the Net

We invite you to visit the O'Sullivan/Sheffrin page on the Prentice Hall Web site at:

http://www.prenhall.com/osullivan/

for this chapter's World Wide Web exercise.

CHAPTER 31
TEN QUESTIONS (AND ANSWERS) ABOUT GOVERNMENT DEBT AND DEFICITS

I.   OVERVIEW

In this chapter, you will learn about government deficits and government debt and their impact on the economy. You will explore the relationship between government deficits and inflation, government deficits and trade deficits, and government deficits and economic growth. You will learn how the federal government calculates its budget and discover that it is different from the way state and local governments report their budgets. You will learn how government deficits are financed. You will examine the history of U.S. budget deficits and U.S. debt. You will re-encounter automatic stabilizers and assess their role in the measured budget balance of a country. You will also re-encounter the full-employment budget deficit and compare and contrast it to the actual budget position. You will learn why debt is said to impose a "burden on future generations" and that some economists disagree with this notion. You will also learn about the balanced budget amendment, the history behind it, and what proponents and critics of it have to say.

II.   CHECKLIST

By the end of this chapter, you should be able to:

√   Define a government deficit/surplus and relate it to government debt.
√   Discuss U.S historical figures on the U.S. government budget balance.
√   Define government debt and discuss U.S. historical figures on it.
√   Explain baseline budgeting and what politicians means when they say they favor "a cut" in the deficit.
√   Explain the two methods of financing a government deficit.
√   Explain monetization of the debt and the conditions underwhich a country would be likely to monetize its debt.
√   Discuss how monetizing the debt can create hyperinflation.
√   Explain what happens to the government's budget position when a country goes to war and when it goes into a recession.
√   Define the full-employment (or structural) deficit and explain its relationship to the actual deficit.
√   Discuss the burdens that national debt may impose on future generations.
√   Define "debt service."
√   Explain Ricardian equivalence and the implications it carries for savings and investment in economies that run government deficits.
√   Discuss the relationship between government deficits, savings, and investment.
√   Explain why high-saving countries are not as apt to suffer negative economic consequences when their government runs a big budget deficit.
√   Explain generational accounting.
√   Explain the difference between operating budgets and capital budgets.
√   Discuss why it may be easier for states to balance their budgets than it is for the federal government to balance its budget.
√   Discuss the pros and cons of a balanced budget amendment.
√   Explain how a budget deficit might lead to a trade deficit.

III.   KEY TERMS

Deficit: the excess of total expenditures over total revenues.

Surplus: the excess of total revenues over total expenditures.

Balanced budget: the situation when total expenditures equals total revenues.

Government expenditure: spending on goods and services plus transfer payments.

Government debt: the total of all past deficits.

Fiscal year: the calendar on which the federal government conducts its business which runs from October 1 to September 30. Fiscal year 1997 begins on October 1, 1996.

Monetizing the deficit: purchases by a central bank of newly issued government bonds.

Automatic stabilizers: the changes in taxes and transfer payments that automatically occur as economic activity changes. These changes in taxes and transfers dampen economic fluctuations.

Full-employment deficit: an estimate of what the federal budget deficit would be if the economy were operating at full employment.

Structural deficit: another term for the full-employment deficit.

Servicing the debt: paying interest on existing debt.

Ricardian equivalence: the proposition that it does not matter whether government expenditure is financed by taxes or by debt.

Generational accounting: methods that, as sign the tax burden of government debt and other programs to different generations.

Operating budgets: budgets for day-to-day expenditures.

Capital budgets: budgets for long-erm investments.

Mandate: a requirement imposed by government on lower levels of government or on the private sector.

Twin deficits: the association between increases in the federal budget deficit and the trade deficit.

IV.   PERFORMANCE ENHANCING TIPS (PETS)

PET #1

A government's budget balance is the difference between the tax revenues it collects and the expenditures on goods, services, transfer payments, and interest on the national debt it makes. A budget deficit adds to the national debt whereas a budget surplus reduces the national debt.

When tax revenues are greater than government expenditures, the government's budget is in a surplus and the stock of national debt will decline. When tax revenues are less than government expenditures, the government's budget is in a deficit and the stock of national debt will rise. When tax revenues equal goverment expenditures, the government's budget is in balance and the stock of national debt will not change.

For example, if the government runs a budget deficit of $25 billion this year and last year's debt level was $100 billion, this year's debt level will rise to $125 billion. If the government runs a budget surplus of $25 billion this year and last year's debt was $100 billion, this year's debt level will drop to $75 billion.

PET #2

When a government is unable to finance its budget deficit by selling bonds to businesses, households, and foreign citizens because nobody is willing to buy the bonds, the central bank is forced to buy the bonds. When the central bank purchases government securities issued directly by the Treasury, the money supply increases. This is sometimes simply stated as "the government prints money to pay for its budget deficit."
Notice the similarity of the effects of a central bank purchase of government securities directly from the government and an open market purchase of government securities from the private sector. The central bank purchase is similar to an open market purchase except that the central bank is purchasing bonds, not from the private sector, but from the government. The central bank pays for the bonds by issuing a check to the government. Thus, the government's checking account balance rises which also means that the nation's money supply increases.

PET #3

The deficit and debt as a percentage of GDP are calculated as:

>   *(Deficit/GDP) X 100*
>   *(Debt/GDP) X 100*

Sometimes, the deficit and debt are stated as a percentage of GDP in order to remove the "shock value" of the sheer numbers (and perhaps lead to a more balanced discussion of the potential economic problems attributed to the deficit). For example, a government deficit of $200,000,000,000 ($200 billion) doesn't seem nearly as shocking as, say, a government deficit that is, e.g., 2.3% of GDP. The same is true for the national debt.

PET #4

The full-employment or structural deficit is a measure of what the budget deficit would be if the economy were operating at full employment. It presents a better measure of the long-term fiscal stance of an economy than the actual deficit.

For example, suppose an economy, operating at full employment, initially has a budget deficit of $50 billion and then enters into a recession that lasts for a year. The recession reduces tax revenues and raises government spending on transfer payments (automatic stabilizers kick in). The government's budget deficit may rise from $50 billion to $75 billion. As the economy comes out of a recession and returns to full employment, the government's budget deficit may return to $50 billion. The causes of the $50 billion deficit that the government sustains even at full employment may be worth investigating, especially if over the past several years, the full-employment budget deficit was only $18 billion. The change in the full-employment deficit may indicate a change in the fiscal stance of the country that needs attention.

PET #5

Interest payments on the national debt (debt service) are an expenditure of the government and are paid for through tax revenues collected by the government from households and businesses. As such, interest payments carry an opportunity cost in the sense that, had debt service been lower, more tax revenues would be available to fund other government programs (or to offer a tax refund to households and businesses).

PET #6

Ricardian equivalence implies that consumption expenditures (i.e., household spending) will be crowded out (reduced) by an amount equal to the increase in government budget deficit.   Thus, investment expenditures are not crowded out.

The reduction in consumption expenditures concomittantly means that households increase their savingss by an amount equal to the increase in the government budget deficit. The rise in savings is what prevents business spending (investment) from being crowded out. In other words, the pool of savings available to fund government and business borrowing rises so that business borrowing to finance investment is not crowded out (reduced) by the amount of government borrowing.

PET #7

When a country runs a trade deficit (imports are greater than exports), it borrows the savings of foreign countries to pay for the deficit.

Countries that have trade deficits are able to pay for their deficits by borrowing from foreigners. In effect, foreigners lend their savings to the deficit country. Thus, the pool of savings available to countries that run trade deficits is supplemented by foreign savings. You may wish to review PET #5 from Chapter 6 of the Practicum.

The ability to borrow savings from abroad also means that a country that runs a **budget deficit** does not necessarily experience any crowding out. Remember that crowding out is the reduction in investment that occurs when a government borrows to pay for its deficit. The crowding out occurs because a portion of household and business savings will now be used to buy government instead of corporate bonds. When corporations cannot sell as many of their bonds as they would like, their investment spending (spending on plant and equipment) is reduced. However, when a country is able to borrow the savings of foreign countries, corporations can sell their bonds to foreigners. In effect, foreign savings helps to fund another country's investment.

PET #8

The link between budget deficits and trade deficits depends on the relationship of investment to saving. The following equation gives the relationship:

$$(S - I) + (T - G) = (EX - IM)$$

where S = private savings, I = investment spending by businesses, T = tax revenues, G = government spending, EX = exports, and IM = imports.   (T-G) is the government budget balance and (EX-IM) is the trade balance.

For example, suppose that savings are $40 billion, investment spending is $60 billion, and the budget balance is -$100 billion (i.e., budget deficit = $100 billion). By plugging the numbers into the equation above, you will see that the country's trade balance is -$120 billion. That is, the country will have a trade deficit of $120 billion.

V.   PRACTICE EXAM: MULTIPLE CHOICE QUESTIONS

1.   Monetization of the budget deficit:

a.   leads to increases in the money supply.
b.   creates a full-employment deficit that exceeds the actual deficit.
c.   occurs when the Treasury sells bonds to businesses.
d.   helps stabilize the economy.
e.   requires approval by Congress.

2.   Automatic stabilizers:

a.   lead to increases in the budget deficit as the unemployment rate increases and vice-versa.
b.   lead to increases in the full-employment budget deficit during a recession.
c.   provide a quantitative measure of expansionary fiscal policy.
d.   are government tax and spending programs that require approval by Congress.
e.   all of the above.

3.   A decrease in the national debt (total government debt):

a.   may lead to crowding in.
b.   may lead to capital deepening.
c.   may reduce the debt service.
d.   may reduce the tax burden on future generations.
e.   all of the above.

4.   If a government, for the first time ever, runs a budget deficit of $222 billion and finances part of $100 billion by selling government bonds to the central bank:

a.   investment spending will decline by $222 billion and government debt will equal $222 billion.
b.   investment spending will decline by $112 billion and government debt will equal $222 billion.
c.   investment spending will decline by $112 billion and government debt will equal $112 billion.
d.   investment spending will decline by $222 billion and government debt will equal $112 billion.
e.   investment spending will decline by $112 billion and government debt will equal $100 billion.

5.   Ricardian equivalence means that:

a.   a society should be indifferent between the central bank purchasing government debt and the public purchasing government debt.
b.   budget deficits and budget surpluses are equivalent in terms of their effect on savings and investment.
c.   investment spending is crowded out by an amount equal to the increase in the budget deficit.
d.   savings rise by an amount equal to the budget deficit.
e.   (c) and (d).

6.   Supppose you believe in Ricardian equivalence. You would assert that:

a.   a budget deficit of $10 billion will generate $10 billion more worth of savings.
b.   a budget deficit of $10 billion will reduce consumption spending by $10 billion.

c.   a budget deficit will create capital deepening.
d.   a budget deficit imposes a burden on the current generation.
e.   (a), (b), and (d).

7.   Which one of the following would NOT be a warning sign that the level of national debt is too high?

a.   hyperinflation.
b.   a low level of investment.
c.   an increase in foreigners' share of the purchase of government bonds.
d.   debt service that is increasing rapidly.
e.   all of the above are warning signs.

8.   Which one of the following statements is true?

a.   if the government decides that in the year 2050, social security benefits will be cut by 25%, the current budget deficit will be reduced.
b.   the full-employment deficit will increase if personal income tax rates are cut.
c.   the full-employment deficit will increase if the economy goes into a recession.
d.   countries with bigger budget deficits (as a percentage of GDP) have higher levels of investment (as a percentage of GDP).
e.   states typically balance their capital budgets.

9.   A balanced budget amendment:

a.   could limit the use of fiscal policy during recessions.
b.   may not be enforceable because the government could always impose mandates or requirements on businesses to carry out actions where the balanced budget amendment restricts the government.
c.   may not really create a balanced budget because Congress will find loopholes and other ways of presenting the appearance of a balanced budget when in fact there is not one.
d.   may lead to legal challenges by various interested parties.
e.   all of the above.

10.   Which one of the following statements is true?

a.   a trade deficit implies that a country is lending some of its savings to foreign countries.
b.   a budget deficit is more likely to lead to a trade deficit when an economy is operating below the full-employment (potential) level of output.
c.   the U.S. has seen the emergence of the twin deficits in the 1990s.
d.   a budget deficit does not necessarily cause crowding out if a country is able to borrow from foreign countries.
e.   a country with a large budget deficit and a high level of savings is more likely to have a trade deficit than a country with a large budget deficit and a low level of savings.

11.   Suppose a country's budget deficit in 1995 was $40 billion and in 1996 was $50 billion. Further, suppose its debt in 1995 was $600 billion, its GDP in 1995 was $800 billion, and its GDP in 1996 was $850 billion. Using these numbers, which one of the following statements is correct?

a.   in 1996, debt as a percentage of GDP is 71.8%.
b.   in 1996, the deficit as a percentage of GDP is 5.9% and the debt as a percentage of GDP is 76.5%.
c.   in 1995, the debt as a percentage of GDP is 5% and in 1996 is 39.4%.
d.   in 1995, the deficit as a percentage of GDP is 5% and in 1996 is 10.6%.
e.   in 1996, the deficit as a percentage of GDP is 18.75%.

VI.   PRACTICE EXAM: ESSAY QUESTIONS

1.   Discuss the balanced budget amendment. Which budget do you think the amendment should apply to -- the full-employment (structural) budget or to the actual budget?

2.   What might explain the ability of some countries to run budget deficits yet maintain trade surplusses? Be sure to explain the link between investment and savings.

VII.   ANSWER KEY: MULTIPLE CHOICE QUESTIONS

1.   Correct answer: a.

Discussion: Monetization of the budget deficit occurs when the government sells bonds to the central bank. The central bank's purchase of the new issue of government bonds leads to an increase in the money supply, much like a central bank purchase of existing government bonds held by households and businesses leads to an increase in the money supply. (See PET #2 above for review.)

Statement b is not correct; monetization has nothing to do with the relationship between the full-employment and actual budget deficit. Statement c is not correct based on the discussion above. Statement d is not correct; in fact, if the debt is monetized on a continuous basis, hyperinflation is likely to emerge. That is, debt monetization can be destabilizing to an economy. Statement e is not correct. Currently, there is no Congressional approval required on the sale of government bonds to the Fed.

2.   Correct answer: a.

Discussion: Automatic stabilizers are government programs and tax sources that do not require action by the Congress to be changed, either increased or decreased. The amount spent on government programs rises with the downturns in the business cycle and falls with upturns in the business cycle. The amount of tax revenue collected by the government rises with upturns in the business cycle and falls with downturns in the business cycle. Thus, the budget deficit increases because government spending increases and tax revenues decline as the economy's unemployment rate increases (economy goes into a recession).

Statement b is not correct because the full-employment deficit takes out the effects of automatic stabilizers on calculating the budget deficit. That is, when the economy goes into a downturn, the full-employment budget deficit should not change whereas the actual budget deficit will increase. Statement c is not correct; the full-employment budget deficit, not automatic stabilizers, provide a more accurate picture of the stance of fiscal policy. Statement d is not correct as mentioned in the discussion above. Statement e is not correct because statements b, c, and d are not correct.

3.   Correct answer: e.

Discussion: A decrease in the national debt means that the government is borrowing less money from household and businesses (who lend their savings). The reduction in government borrowing eliminates reduces the competition that businesses have to face when trying to sell their bonds to households and other businesses. Thus, businesses will find that there is a larger pool of savings available to them that can be borrowed and used to fund purchases of plant and equipment (investment). This means that there is "crowding in" (an increase in business investment as the national debt is reduced). The increased investment also means that the capital stock will increase, i.e., there will be capital deepening. Furthermore, with less debt outstanding, interest payments on the national debt will decline. That is, debt service will be reduced. Also, with a lower debt service and a bigger capital stock, the burden of the debt on future generations will be reduced. Thus, all of the above statements are correct.

4.   Correct answer: b.

Discussion: If the government has never run a budget deficit up until now, its debt up until now is zero. However, the budget deficit of $222 billion means that the government issues $222 billion worth of government bonds (IOUs). Thus, government debt rises to $222 billion. Some of the debt is owed to the central bank (since they purchased $100 billion) and some of it is owed to households and businesses (since they purchased $122 billion). The fact that households and businesses buy $122 billion of the government debt means that they reduce their purchases of corporate bonds by $122 billion. This means that businesses' spending on plant and equipment (investment) will be reduced by $122 billion.

Based on the above discussion, statements a, c, d, and e cannot be correct.

5.   Correct answer: d.

Discussion: The proposition of Ricardian equivalence means that households increase their savings by an amount equal to the budget deficit. They do this because they anticipate that the interest payments on the debt (debt service) arising from the current budget deficit will be paid for by higher taxes in the future. Thus, in order be able to pay for the higher taxes, households increase their savings today (in an amount equal to the budget deficit). The increase in savings also means that households must cut back on consumption. So, there is a burden on the current generation -- they must reduce their consumption expenditures. Consumption expenditures are thus "crowded out."

Statements a and b are not correct. They do not define or describe Ricardian equivalence. Statement b is not correct. Statement c is not correct. Ricardian equivalence means that there is no crowding out associated with the increased budget deficit. That is, investment spending does not decline when the government runs a budget deficit; however, consumption spending does decline. Statement e is not correct because statement c is not correct.

6.   Correct answer: e.

Discussion: As discussed in the answer to question (5) above and in PET #6 of this chapter, a budget deficit of $10 billion will raise savings by $10 billion. If savings increase by $10 billion, consumption must decrease by $10 billion. Thus, statements a and b are correct. Statement d is correct; the burden on the current generation is the reduction in consumption expenditures that they must make in order to save enough to pay for the future taxes they anticipate paying to service the debt.

Statement c is not correct. Capital deepening occurs if the level of net investment (gross investment spending minus depreciation) increases. Ricardian equivalence only suggests that the level of gross investment spending will not be reduced as a result of the budget deficit. It does not say anything about net investment or even whether net investment will increase.

7.   Correct answer: c.

Discussion: An increase in foreigners' share of purchase of government bonds is not a warning sign. For example, an increase in foreigners' purchases of U.S. government bonds from 5% to, say, 25%, does not mean that national debt is too high. In fact, if foreigners are willing to purchase our government debt, they must have confidence that the government can pay it off. This suggests that the national debt is not "too high."

Statements a, b, and d are all warning signs of national debt that is too high. When national debt is too high, a country's central bank may be forced to buy the government's debt because households and businesses will not. Central bank purchases of government debt create increases in the money supply and can lead to inflation. When national debt is too high, a country's level of investment is typically quite low (Ricardian equivalence is not assumed to hold nor is there empirical evidence that it does.) That is, continuous budget deficits which increase national debt also crowd out investment. If debt service is increasing rapidly, the national debt must be growing quite rapidly, as well.

8.   Correct answer: b.

Discussion: The full-employment deficit reflects the fiscal stance of the government taking out any business-cycle-induced effects (i.e., the effects of the automatic stabilizers on the budget position). A cut in personal income tax rates is not an automatic stabilizer. The approval of Congress is required in order to cut tax rates and as such, reflects a change in the policies of the government. It will also show up as a change in the fiscal stance of the government. With the cut in personal income tax rates, the government will likely collect less in tax revenues. Without any change in government spending programs, the budget deficit will increase. This is an increase in the full-employment budget deficit since, even when the economy is operating at full employment, the budget deficit will be bigger than before since tax rates have been cut.

Statement a is not correct. The current budget deficit will not reflect the 25% cut in social security benefits that will take place in the year 2050. Furthermore, workers who are currently paying in to the social security trust fund will continue to contribute the same amount since their social security taxes are being used to fund current social security payments, not payments in the year 2050. Statement c is not correct. The full-employment deficit should not change when the economy goes into a recession since the effects of the recession on the budget deficit are not included in the full-employment deficit. However, the actual deficit will get bigger. Statement d is not correct. Typically, countries with big budget deficits have low, not high, levels of investment spending. Statement e is not correct. States balance their operating budgets and are permitted to borrow (issue bonds) to finance their capital budgets. Capital budgets are spending on highways, schools, telecommunications, and other types of investment.

9.   Correct answer: e.

Discussion: Without escape clauses, having to balance the budget could limit the use of fiscal policy during recessions. Automatic stabilizers act to increase the budget deficit during recessions. If the effects of the automatic stabilizers on the budget position must be offset so as to keep the budget in balance, the government may find itself having to raise taxes or cut government spending in order to keep the budget balanced.   These actions could actually worsen the recession.   If the objective of a balanced budget amendment is to limit the tax and spend nature of the government, a balanced budget amendment could still proved to be unenforceable.   In effect, the government could balance its budget, say be reducing government spending on, e.g., research and development, but then mandate companies to place a certain some of money into a research and development fund for national uses. Loopholes are always discovered as a way to get around a law politicians may not like to deal with. Thus, some government spending programs may be taken "off budget" meaning that they will not show up as a government expense. In that way, the government's budget will be easier to balance. A balanced budget amendment might also invite legal challenges, particularly by groups most affected by the balancing budget act. If the government decides to balance the budget by raising taxes 100% on alcohol and tobacco and reducing government spending on the space program, you can bet that the affected parties will show up in Washington to fight the changes. Thus, all of the above statements are correct.

10.   Correct answer: d.

Discussion: When a country is able to borrow from abroad, savings from other countries comes into the deficit country.   The savings provided by foreigners helps to counteract the crowding out effects on investment caused by the government budget deficit.   Thus, a country that is able to borrow from abroad (which happens when the country runs a trade deficit) is better able to maintain a given level of investment spending. (See PET #7 of this chapter for review.)

Statement a is not correct. A trade deficit implies that a country is borrowing from abroad, not lending to foreigners. Statement b is not correct. A budget deficit is more likely to lead to a trade deficit when an economy is operating at the full employment (potential) level of output, not below it. Statement c is not correct. The twin deficits (budget and trade deficits) emerged in the early 1980s. Statement e is not correct. A country with a large budget deficit and a high level of savings is less, not more, likely to have a trade deficit than a country with a large budget deficit and a low level of savings. This is because the high savings country is able to lend a more significant amount of money to both corporations and the government than is a low savings country.

11.   Correct answer: b.

Discussion: The deficit as a percentage of GDP in 1996 is ($50 billion/$850 billion) X 100 = 5.9%. The debt in 1996 is equal to the debt in 1995 plus the budget deficit incurred in 1996. Thus, the level of debt in 1996 is $650 billion. Since GDP in 1996 is $850, the debt as a percentage of GDP is ($650 billion/$850) = 76.5%. Based on these calculations, none of the others are correct. You may wish to review PETs #1 and #3 of this chapter.

VIII. ANSWER KEY: ESSAY QUESTIONS

1.   The balanced budget amendment is an amendment to the Constitution that requires that the U.S. government (Treasury) spend no more (for all programs -- defense, education, interest on the national debt, welfare, etc.) than is collected in tax revenues. Basically, the amendment restricts the government from spending in excess of its "income" (tax revenues). In practice, a balanced budget amendment is not so simplistic since the government does not know with certainty in any given year exactly how much it will

collect in tax revenues and how much it will have to pay out for all the different programs. In part, the uncertainty stems from not knowing what the health of the economy will be in any given year. For example, the government may forecast that tax revenues for 1997 will be $1 trillion based on predictions about the health of the economy in 1997. Thus, the government would limit its expenditures to $1 trillion. However, if the economy goes into a recession, the automatic stabilizers will kick in and the government may end up spending more than $1 trillion and collecting less than $1 trillion in tax revenues. This is why some economists suggest that the balanced budget amendment should apply to the full-employment budget, not the actual budget. Some economists would go even further and say that a balanced budget amendment ties the hands of the government in using fiscal policy were the economy to enter a recession or worse. Others respond that the balanced budget amendment could then be written with "escape clauses" that specify the conditions under which the amendment does not have to be abided by. One condition might be an economic recession. Proponents of the balanced budget amendment argue that politicians need some external constraint on their ability to spend. Without the constraint of a balanced budget amendment it is argued, politicians will always spend too much. However, a critic might argue that a balanced budget amendment does not necessarily imply that government spending will be constrained (or kept at a reasonable level). A country can have a very high level of government spending and still have a balanced budget. The government could pay for its excessive government spending by imposing high tax rates. Other critics of the balanced budget amendment argue that politicians will find some way to present to the public an appearance of a balanced budget by using gimmicks and other accounting methods. For example, if national defense is taken "off budget" because, say, national defense is considered a program we ought to fund regardless of our tax revenues, then national defense will not show up as an expense of the governnment against the tax revenues it collects. In this way, the government's budget balance will improve. In fact, state and local governments practice this sort of accounting -- they have operating and capital budgets. The operating budgets are paid for by tax revenues whereas the capital budgets are paid for by borrowing (issuing bonds). Some economists would argue that since capital spending is an investment in the future of the economy, borrowing to fund it should be permitted. From that perspective, the federal government should have two budgets -- an operating budget and a capital budget. The operating budget is what should be kept in balance whereas government debt should be allowed to be issued to fund capital expenditures (government spending on highways, telecommunications, research and development, etc.).

2.   The link between budget deficits and trade deficits depends on the relationship of investment to savings. The following equation gives the relationship:

$$(S - I) + (T - G) = (EX - IM)$$

where S = private savings, I = investment spending by businesses, T = tax revenues, G = government spending, EX = exports, and IM = imports. (T-G) is the government budget balance and (EX-IM) is the trade balance. (See PET #8 of this chapter for review.)

The equation above shows that countries that save, in total, an amount equal to investment spending by businesses will have budget and trade balances that are exactly the same amount. That is, if a country's total savings are $50 billion and investment is $50 billion while the government runs a budget deficit of $170 billion (i.e., T-G = -$170 billion), the country's trade balance will also be -$170 billion (i.e., trade deficit of $170 billion).

When the total savings of a country is greater than investment spending, the trade balance will be less than the budget balance. For example, if total savings are $150 billion and investment spending is $50 billion while the budget deficit is $125 billion, the country's trade deficit will be $25 billion. If savings are $200 billion and investment spending is $50 billion while the budget deficit is $125 billion, the country will, in this case, have a trade surplus of $25 billion. The example shows that a country that "saves a lot" relative to investment or "has a low level of investment spending relative to savings" will have a trade deficit that is less than its budget deficit. In some cases, where savings are very high relative to investment (or investment very low relative to savings), a country may have a budget deficit alongside a trade surplus. The reason that high-savings countries (or low-investment countries) may be able to run trade surplusses despite the government budget deficit is that the country, as a whole, saves more than enough to fund businesses' investment spending and the government's budget deficit. The excess savings are then lent to foreign countries. Countries that lend abroad (as you will see in a later chapter) are countries that have trade surplusses.

Take It to the Net

We invite you to visit the O'Sullivan/Sheffrin page on the Prentice Hall Web site at:

http://www.prenhall.com/osullivan/

for this chapter's World Wide Web exercise.

CHAPTER 32
INTERNATIONAL TRADE AND PUBLIC POLICY

I.   OVERVIEW

In this chapter, you will learn why trade can be mutually beneficial to countries. You will re-encounter the principle of opportunity cost and use it to determine comparative advantage. You will learn that free trade can lower the price that consumers would pay for goods compared to the prices they would pay if they did not trade (autarky). You will also learn that there are resource movements from one industry to another associated with moving from a position of no trade (autarky) to a position of free trade. These resource movements mean that free trade will, in the short run, create employment losses and factory closings in some industries but expansion in others. You will learn about policies that restrict trade -- tariffs, bans on imports, quotas, and voluntary export restraints. You will learn that protectionist trade policies are typically designed to protect job losses in specific industries. However, protectionist trade policies impose costs on consumers. Thus, you will see that protectionism creates some winners and losers within a country. You will learn that protectionist trade policies initiated by one country may invite retaliation by a trading partner. You will learn about the rationale for protectionist trade policies and criticisms of these arguments. You will learn about some recent trade policy debates over foreign producers "dumping" their products in the U.S., over the impact of trade agreements on the environment, and about whether freer trade causes income inequality. You will also learn about some recent trade agreements.

II.   CHECKLIST

By the end of this chapter, you should be able to:

√   Explain the benefits from specialization and trade as compared to autarky.
√   Use an output table to calculate the opportunity costs of production in two countries for two different types of goods and determine in which good a country has a comparative advantage.
√   Draw a production possibilities curve using information from an output table. Explain what the different points on the production possibilities curve represent.
√   Explain what determines the range of terms of trade that would be mutually beneficial to two countries.
√   Draw a consumption possibilities curve using information about the terms of trade. Explain what the different points on the consumption possibilities curve represent.
√   Describe the employment effects of free trade.
√   Explain who the winners and losers are from free trade.
√   List the different types of protectionist trade policies.
√   Explain how the different protectionist trade policies work and their effects on import prices.
√   Compare and contrast the effects of an import ban to an import quota on equilibrium price and quantity using demand and supply curves.
√   Compare and contrast an import quota to a tariff.
√   Explain how the threat of retaliation by one country can persuade another country to loosen its protectionist policies.
√   Explain why import restrictions might lead to smuggling.
√   Define the Smoot-Hawley Tariff Bill.
√   Discuss some arguments (or rationales) for protectionist trade policies.
√   Describe the practice of dumping and predatory dumping (pricing).

√ Explain why some firms might dump their products in other countries.
√ Discuss why trade policy and environmental issues have become linked.
√ Explain how trade might cause income inequality to widen.
√ Discuss some recent trade agreements.

III. KEY TERMS

Production possibilities curve: a curve showing the combinations of two goods that can be produced by an economy, assuming that all resources are fully employed.

Comparative advantage: the ability of one nation to produce a particular good at an opportunity cost lower than the opportunity cost of another nation.

Consumption possibilities curve: a curve showing the combinations of two goods that can be consumed when a nation specializes in a particular good and trades with another nation.

Autarky: a situation in which each country is self-sufficient, so there is no trade.

Terms of trade: an indication of the rate at which two goods will be exchanged.

Import quota: a limit on the amount of a good that can be imported.

Voluntary export restraint (VER): a scheme under which an exporting country "voluntarily" decreases its exports.

Tariff: a tax on an imported good.

Learning by doing: the knowledge gained during production that increases productivity.

Infant industry: a new industry that is protected from foreign competitors.

Dumping: a situation in which the price a firm charges in a foreign market is lower that [a] the price it charges in its home market or [b] the production cost.

IV. PERFORMANCE ENHANCING TIPS (PETS)

PET #1

In autarky, a country is constrained to consume what it produces. With trade, a country is able to consume a bundle of goods different from what it produces. Trade permits consumption beyond the production possibilities frontier and thus makes a country potentially better off.

PET #2

Opportunity cost calculations used to determine comparative advantage should be based on a per unit comparison.

(This is a review of PET #1 from Chapter 3.) Suppose you are given the following information:

	Country A	Country B
Wood products per hour	10	8
High-tech products per hour	15	4

The information in the table tells you that Country A can produce 10 units of wood products in one hour (with its resources) and 15 units of high-tech products in one hour. Country B can produce 8 units of wood products in one hour (with its resources) and 4 units of high-tech products in one hour. How can this information be used to determine which country has a comparative advantage in wood production and which country has a comparative advantage in high-tech production?

The easiest way to compute comparative advantage is to determine what the opportunity cost of production is for each good for each country, on a per unit basis. To do this, you must first answer how much Country A must give up if it were to specialize in the production of wood. For every additional hour of effort devoted to producing wood products, Country A would give up the production of 15 units of high-tech products. (Of course, it is then able to produce 10 more units of wood products.) On a per unit basis, Country A must give up 1.5 units of high-tech products for each 1 unit of wood products = (15 high-tech products/hour)/(10 wood products/hour) = 1.5 high-tech products/1 wood product. You would read this as "for Country A, the opportunity cost of 1 wood product is 1.5 high-tech products." For Country B, for every additional hour of effort devoted to producing wood products, it must give up 4 units of high-tech products. (Of course, it is then able to produce 8 more units of wood products.) On a per unit basis, Country B must give up 0.5 units of high-tech products for each 1 unit of wood products = (4 high-tech products/hour)/(8 wood products/hour). You would read this as "for Country B, the opportunity cost of 1 wood product is 0.5 high-tech products." Thus, Country B has the lower opportunity cost of producing wood products since it has to give up fewer high-tech products.

Since Country B has the lower opportunity cost of wood production, it should specialize in wood production. (Wood production is "less costly" in Country B than in Country A). If this is true, then it must also be true that Country A has the lower opportunity cost of high-tech production and thus should specialize in producing high-tech goods.

Let's see if this is true using the numbers from the table above. For Country A, the opportunity cost of producing more high-tech products is that for every additional hour of producing high-tech products, it must give up producing 10 units of wood products. (Of course, it is then able to produce 15 more units of high-tech products). On a per unit basis, Country A must give up 0.67 wood products for every 1 high-tech product = (10 wood products/hour)/(15 high-tech products per hour). You would read this as "for Country A, the opportunity cost of 1 high-tech product is 0.67 wood products." For Country B, the opportunity cost of producing more high-tech products is that, for every additional hour of producing high-tech products, it must give up producing 8 units of wood products. (Of course, it is then able to produce 4 more units of high-tech products.) On a per unit basis, Country B must give up 2 wood products for every one unit of high-tech products = (8 wood products/hour)/(4 high-tech products/hour). Thus, Country A has the lower opportunity cost of producing high-tech products since it has to give up fewer wood products. (High-tech production is "less costly" in Country A than in Country B.)

PET #3

Opportunity cost calculations used to determine comparative advantage are also used to determine a range for the terms of trade that would create mutually beneficial exchanges between two countries.

In PET #2 above, the opportunity cost in Country A of producing wood products is 1.5 high-tech products (i.e., 1.5 high-tech products/1 wood product). In Country B, the opportunity cost of producing wood products is 0.5 high-tech products (i.e., 0.5 high-tech products/1 wood product). Thus, the terms of trade range that would be beneficial to both countries must be between 0.5 high tech/1 wood product and 1.5 high-tech products/1 wood product.

For example, a mutually beneficial terms of trade might be 1 high-tech product/1 wood product. Country A would only have to give up (trade) 1 high-tech product in return for 1 wood product if it trades. If Country A produces for itself, it will have to cut production by 1.5 high-tech products to get back 1 wood product. The extra 0.5 high-tech product the country "saves" can then be used to buy more from the foreign country. Thus, Country A gains from trade. On the other hand, Country B would give up (trade) 1 wood product to Country A and get in return 1 high-tech product. If Country B produces for itself, it will only get back 0.5 high-tech products by reducing wood production by 1 unit. Thus, Country B gains, as well.

PET #4

Trade protection reduces the total supply of a good in a country. The reduced supply will increase the price a country pays for the protected good.

Your textbook mentions different types of trade protection -- import bans, import quotas, voluntary export restraints, and tariffs -- all of which act to raise the price of the goods and services that a country imports from other countries. Protectionist trade policies effectively reduce the total supply of a good (where the total supply comes from domestic production plus foreign imports) by restricting the amount of foreign imports. Thus, in terms of supply and demand analysis, protectionist trade policies shift the supply curve to the left. A leftward shift in the supply curve raises the price of a good. (See the box in PET #7 in Chapter 4 for review.)

V.   PRACTICE EXAM: MULTIPLE CHOICE QUESTIONS

1.   Use the table below to answer the question. Assume that each country can use its resources to produce either stuffed animals or pineapples.

	Country A	Country B
Stuffed Toys (per day)	200	300
Pineapples (per day)	400	900

a.   Country B has a comparative advantage in the production of both goods.
b.   Country A has a comparative advantage in the production of stuffed toys and Country B has a comparative advantage in the production of pineapples.
c.   Country B has a comparative advantage in the production of stuffed toys and Country A has a comparative advantage in the production of pineapples
d.   Country A has a comparative advantage in the production of both goods.
e.   neither country has a comparative advantage in the production of stuffed toys.

2.   Suppose the opportunity cost of producing one unit of lumber in Canada is 3 units of auto parts and that the opportunity cost of producing one unit of lumber in Japan is 6 units of auto parts. If the terms of trade are one unit of lumber for 8 auto parts, then:

a.   Canada and Japan will be able to engage in mutually beneficial trade.

b.   Japan will benefit from trade but Canada will not.
c.   Canada will benefit from trade but Japan will not.
d.   Canada will specialize in the production of auto parts.
e.   (a) and (d).

3.   Use the graph below to answer complete the following question.

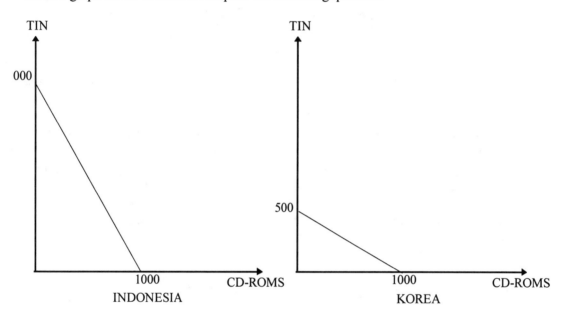

a.   Indonesia will specialize in tin production.
b.   a terms of trade of 250 units of tin for 100 CD ROMs will lead to greater consumption possibilities for Indonesia than its consumption possibilities in autarky.
c.   a mutually beneficial terms of trade would be 1.5 units of tin for 1.0 units of CD ROMs.
d.   if trade occurs, workers in the CD ROM industry in Korea will become unemployed.
e.   (a) and (c).

4.   Which one of the following is NOT an example of a protectionist trade policy?

a.   ban on imports.
b.   voluntary export restraint.
c.   tariff.
d.   import quota.
e.   all of the above are protectionist trade policies.

5.   Which one of the following trade policies would create the biggest increase in the price of the protected good?

a.   an import ban.
b.   a voluntary export restraint.
c.   an import quota.
d.   a tariff.

e.   a WTO license.

6.   Which one of the following would NOT be a result of a tariff imposed by the U.S. on footwear imported from Brazil?

a.   U.S. footwear firms will be winners.
b.   employment in the U.S. footwear industry will be higher than compared to a situation of free trade.
c.   the price that U.S. consumers pay for footwear produced in the U.S. will be lower than compared to a situation of free trade.
d.   U.S. citizens should prefer a tariff on footwear to an import quota.
e.   all of the above would result from the tariff on Brazillian footwear.

7.   Which one of the following statements is true?

a.   under an import quota, if the government sells import licenses to importers, then importers may not make money from the quota.
b.   Japan's agreement to a voluntary export restraint on its automobile exports to the U.S. resulted in a decrease in the price of U.S.-made automobiles.
c.   the threat of retaliation may persuade a country to impose harsher protectionist trade policies on its trading partners.
d.   the Smoot-Hawley Tariff bill was designed to gradually lead to the removal of tariffs around the world.
e.   the NAFTA agreement turned a U.S. trade surplus with Mexico into a U.S. trade deficit.

8.   Which one of the following would NOT be a likely result of protectionist trade policies?

a.   retaliation.
b.   smuggling.
c.   consumers paying a higher price for the protected good.
d.   unemployment in the protected industry.
e.   inefficient production.

9.   Which one of the following statements is true?

a.   protectionist trade policies often obtain Congressional approval because of the lobbying efforts of a limited group of people most likely to benefit from the protection.
b.   the infant industry argument for trade protection is that it promotes learning by doing and thus can enable a new industry to be able to compete with other producers from around the world.
c.   a problem with granting trade protection to an infant industry is that the protection is not likely to be removed as the industry matures.
d.   by protecting infant industries from foreign competition, trade protection may lead to inefficient production by the protected industries.
e.   all of the above are true.

10.   Which one of the following is a problem with a government subsidizing an industry in the hope of establishing a world-wide monopoly?

a.   the taxpayers ultimately pay for the government subsidy.

b.   there is no guarantee that country will be able to profit from securing the monopoly.

c.   another country may also grant a subsidy to the same industry.

d.   the government may end up subsidizing an industry in which there are not economies of scale.

e.   all of the above are problems.

11.   Which one of the following statements is NOT true?

a.   dumping occurs when a firm charges a price in a foreign market that is below its cost of production.

b.   dumping is illegal under international trade agreements.

c.   predatory dumping is an attempt to drive competitors out of the industry so that the dumping firm can gain monopoly status.

d.   countries are permitted to restrict imports from other countries if the production methods used by other countries cause harm to the environment.

e.   the wages of skilled labor in the U.S. have risen relative to the wages of unskilled labor as world trade has increased.

VI.   PRACTICE EXAM: ESSAY QUESTIONS

1.   Suppose the U.S. initially has no trade restrictions on imports of copper. Explain how a tariff on copper creates winners and losers within the U.S. Where might resources (labor and capital) move after the tariff is imposed? Be sure to address the government's use of the tax revenues earned by the tariff. Use demand and supply analysis to show the effects of the tariff.

2.   Discuss some of the arguments made in favor of trade protection.

VII.   ANSWER KEY: MULTIPLE CHOICE QUESTIONS

1.   Correct answer: b.

Discussion: Country A's opportunity cost of producing 1 stuffed toy is 2 pineapples (i.e., 400 pineapples per day/200 stuffed toys per day = 2 pineapples/1 stuffed toy). That is, in order to produce 1 more stuffed toy, Country A would have to take resources out of pineapple production and put them into stuffed toy production. Thus, pineapple production would decrease by 2 units. Country B's opportunity cost of producing 1 stuffed toy is 3 pineapples (i.e., 900 pineapples per day/300 stuffed toys per day = 3 pineapples/1 stuffed toy). That is, in order to produce 1 more stuffed toy, Country B would have to take resources out of pineapple production and put them into stuffed toy production. Thus, pineapple production would decrease by 3 units in Country B. Thus, it "costs" less to produce stuffed toys in Country A (in terms of what must be given up) than it does in Country B. Since Country A has the comparative advantage in stuffed toy production, Country B must have a comparative advantage in pineapple production. To assure yourself that this is true, you can invert the ratios above so that Country A must give up producing 1/2 stuffed toy in order to produce 1 more pineapple whereas Country B must give up producing 1/3 stuffed toy in order to produce 1 more pineapple. Thus, pineapple production is less "costly" (in terms of what must be given up) in Country B than in Country A.

Based on the above discussion, none of the other statements are correct.

2.   Correct answer: c.

Discussion: A mutually beneficial terms of trade must be between 3 auto parts/1 unit of lumber and 6 auto parts/1 unit of lumber. Since Canada's opportunity cost of producing lumber is less than Japan's opportunity cost of producing lumber, Canada has a comparative advantage in lumber production and thus should trade lumber for autoparts. Japan should do the reverse. At a terms of trade of 8 auto parts/1 unit of lumber, Canada will benefit since in autarky, she could only exchange one unit of lumber for 3 auto parts; with trade she would get 5 **more** auto parts per unit of lumber. However, at a terms of trade of 8 auto parts/1 unit of lumber, Japan will not benefit since in autarky, she would have to give up 6 auto parts in order to produce one unit of lumber whereas with trade, she would have to give up 2 **more** auto parts in order to purchase lumber from Canada. Thus, Japan would be worse off with trade than producing lumber for herself. (See PET #3 above for review.)

Statement a is not correct. For trade to benefit both countries, the terms of trade must range between 3 auto parts/1 unit of lumber and 6 auto parts/1 unit of lumber. Otherwise, one country will gain and the other country will lose. Statement b is not correct based on the discussion above. Statement d is not correct because Canada will specialize in lumber production. Statement e is not correct because neither statement a or d are correct.

3.   Correct answer: e.

Discussion: The slope of the production possibilities curve gives the opportunity cost of producing tin (or CD ROMs). The slope of the production possibilities curve for Indonesia shows that the production of 1 CD ROM "costs" 2 units of tin. For Korea, the opportunity cost of producing 1 CD ROM is 0.5 units of tin. Since CD ROMs incur a lower opportunity cost in Korea than Indonesia, Korea will specialize in and export CD ROMs while Indonesia will specialize in and export tin. Thus, statement a is correct. Since the terms of trade are between 0.5 units of tin/1 CD ROM and 2 units of tin/1 CD ROM, trade can be mutually beneficial. Thus, statement c is correct.

Statement b is not correct. Statement b implies a terms of trade of 2.5 units of tin/1 CD ROM. While this terms of trade would be beneficial to Korea, it would not be beneficial to Indonesia. (See PET #3 above for review.) Statement d is not correct. Since Korea will specialize in CD ROM production, labor and capital will have to move to the CD ROM industry. Thus, workers will become, at least temporarily, unemployed in the tin industry, not in the CD ROM industry.

4.   Correct answer: e.

Discussion: None necessary.

5.   Correct answer: a.

Discussion: An import ban completely eliminates any imports of the good. For example, an import ban on cigarettes imposed by the U.S. would mean that no cigarettes produced in foreign countries would be permitted into the U.S. Thus, the total supply of cigarettes available to the U.S. market would be reduced. In this case, the total supply of cigarettes available to the U.S. market would have to come solely from U.S. production of cigarettes. The import ban would thus be represented by a leftward shift in the supply curve where the new supply curve would now be that attributed to domestic production only. Since this policy is the most restrictive on imports, the increase in the price of cigarettes will be the biggest of any of the policies.

Statement b, c, and d are not correct. An import quota and a voluntary export restraint do not drive imports to zero but instead simply restrict the amount of imports to sum number (greater than zero). A tariff is a tax on the price of the imported good and also act to reduce the supply of the imported good, but not to zero. Statement e is not correct. There is no such thing as a WTO license.

6.   Correct answer: c.

Discussion: Statement c is not correct. A tariff on footwear from Brazil will raise the price to U.S. consumers of footwear, regardless of whether the footwear is produced in Brazil or the U.S.

Statement a is correct. U.S. footwear firms will be winners in the sense that they will be able to get a higher price for the footwear that they sell to U.S. consumers. Statement b is correct. In free trade, there would be less production of footwear by U.S. producers and more by foreign producers. Thus, under free trade, employment in the U.S. footwear industry would be lower than when footwear is subject to a tariff which is to say employment in the U.S. footwear industry would be higher with the tariff than in free trade. Statement d is correct. A tariff raises the price of the protected good (footwear in this case) less than does an import quota. Moreover, the government collects tariff revenue that the government could then use to fund government programs that benefit consumers (or to even give them tax refunds!).

7.   Correct answer: a.

Discussion: When the government establishes an import quota, it gives licenses to importers which dictate how much of a good they are permitted to import. Naturally, importers are aware that they can profit by having an import license because they can buy the good from the foreign Country At the unrestricted price and sell in the home Country At the quota-induced price which is higher. However, if importers have to pay for the import licenses, then some of the profit that they expect to make from the import quota will be "eaten up" by the cost of the import license. That is, paying for the import license is a cost that an importer would have to consider in determining how profitable it would be to have the license.
Statement b is not true. Japan's agreement to a voluntary export restraint (VER) on its automobile exports to the U.S. resulted in a higher, not lower price of U.S.-made automobiles. U.S. consumers paid approximately $660 more for a U.S.-made automobile after the VER. Statement c is not true. The threat of retaliation may persuade a country to impose less harsh (i.e., less restrictive) protectionist trade policies on its trading partners, not harsher policies. Statement d is not correct. The Smoot-Hawley Tariff bill raised U.S. tariffs by an average of 59% and is pointed to as a policy that may have worsened the U.S. depression of the 1930s. Statement e is not correct. The devaluation of the peso is much more likely to have turned the U.S. trade surplus with Mexico into a U.S. trade deficit. The devaluation of the peso effectively made Mexican products much cheaper than U.S.-made products.

8.   Correct answer: d.

Discussion: Protectionist trade policies are "protectionist" because they protect workers in the domestic industry from job losses that might occur were the industry left open to foreign competition. Thus, protectionist trade policies typically (at least in the short run) enhance employment in the protected industry.

All of the others may be a result of protectionist trade policies.

9. Correct answer: e.

Discussion: None necessary.

10. Correct answer: e.

Discussion: When a government subsidizes an industry, it gives money to the industry. The money the government has to give to the industry is ultimately provided by taxpayers. There is no guarantee that a country will be able to profit from securing a monopoly in a particular industry since other governments, may have, at the same time, chosen to subsidize the same industry. In this case, one or both countries may end up earning losses. The government also may choose to subsidize an industry thinking that the industry has large economies of scale (low average cost of production at very large levels of output) and thus is much more likely to exist as a monopoly (single producer). However, if it turns out that the industry is actually able to exist with more than one producer, the government subsidized industry may find itself having to compete with producers from other firms around the world. In this case, monopoly profits anticipated by the government may not materialize.

11. Correct answer: d.

Discussion: Statement d is not true. Countries are NOT permitted to restrict imports from other countries if the production methods used by other countries cause harm to the environment. For example, suppose that Chile produces aluminum using a method that creates a lot of air pollution (more than what would be permitted under U.S. standards). Under World Trade Organization (WTO) laws, the U.S. would not be permitted to restrict the importation of Chilean aluminum into the U.S. even though the production methods used by Chilean producers would be outlawed in the U.S.

VIII. ANSWER KEY: ESSAY QUESTIONS

1. First of all, one might wonder why the U.S. decided to institute a tariff on a previously freely traded good. There are a few explanations. One explanation might be that the U.S. imposed the tariff as a retaliatory action to its trading partner's decision to impose a tariff on a U.S. good(s). The retaliation may be used as a device to prompt the trading partner to remove their tariff on a U.S. good(s). An alternative explanation might be that workers in the U.S. copper industry felt threatened by the competition from copper producers in foreign countries. Fearing that the competition might mean that U.S. copper producers would lose their market to foreign producers (and thus jobs and profits), workers/management in the U.S. copper industry may have lobbied Congress for trade protection.

When a tariff is introduced on foreign imports of copper, there will be winners and losers in the U.S. The winners will be the copper producers and workers in the copper industry. The price at which producers can sell copper will increase (as the graph below shows) and thus their profits may increase as well.

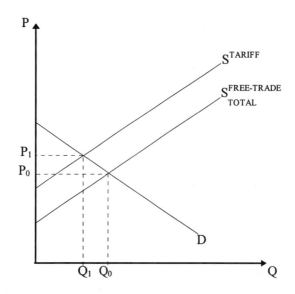

More workers and capital may now be needed in the copper industry, so resources may be taken out of other industries and moved into copper production. Thus, workers with skills in the copper industry will benefit. However, since the tariff raises the price of copper, users (buyers) of copper will lose.

Since the tariff generates tariff revenue for the government, the government may be able to use the revenue to offset some of the higher costs to copper users (i.e., subsidize copper users). Alternatively, the government may be able to use the tariff revenue to reduce income taxes on all workers, i.e., all workers might be given a tax refund. Or, the government could use the tariff revenue to help pay for other government programs that the citizens of the country feel are worth supporting.

2.   There are several arguments made in favor of trade protection. One argument is that trade protection should be granted to industries that are just starting out -- so-called "infant industries." The argument is that the infant industries need protection from international competition in the early stages of development so that they become competitive themselves. Without the protection, the industry may not be successful, so the country loses out on establishing an industry that it may want. Another argument made in favor of trade protection is that trade protection "keeps jobs at home." Here, the argument is that without trade protection, the industry will be unable to compete against foreign competitors and so the domestic industry will go out of business. Thus, by granting protection to a domestic industry, a government can prevent the industry from going out of business and thereby prevent any attendant job losses that would result. Another argument made in favor of protection is that monopoly profits may be obtained. In this case, protection would be granted to industries which are likely to survive as monopolies. By granting protection to a monopoly industry, the country becomes the sole producer of the industry output and may thus be able to extract monopoly profits from sales around the world. The government may encourage this if it is able to share in the profits with the producer. Another argument that can be made in favor of protection is that it can be used to get trading partners to loosen their trade restrictions. For example, a country may threaten to or actually impose stiff tariffs against a good or set of goods imported from another country to prompt the country to reduce its tariffs. The U.S. used this type of threat against Japan and was successful in getting Japan to loosen some of its trade restrictions against the U.S. Another argument made in favor of protection is that it will "level the playing field." This is a tit-for-tat application of protectionism. For example, if one country's government subsidizes a particular industry, then its production costs are unfairly low relative to the production costs of the same industry in other country that

is not subsidizing the industry. Thus, to compete on a level ground, trade protection is considered to be a fair response.

This discussion provides arguments made in favor of trade protection. To be sure, there are many arguments that can be made against trade protection.

Take It to the Net

We invite you to visit the O'Sullivan/Sheffrin page on the Prentice Hall Web site at:

http://www.prenhall.com/osullivan/

for this chapter's World Wide Web exercise.

CHAPTER 33
THE WORLD OF INTERNATIONAL FINANCE

I.   OVERVIEW

In this chapter, you will learn how movements in the value of currencies affect economies around the world. You will use a supply and demand model to understand what causes the value of currencies to change. You will learn how to convert foreign currency prices to U.S. dollar equivalents using the exchange rate. You will also learn how to convert U.S. dollar prices to foreign currency equivalents using the exchange rate. You will learn how changes in interest rates and prices in the U.S. can lead to changes in the value of the dollar against other currencies. You will re-encounter the reality principle which requires that you consider movements in the exchange rate after adjusting for inflation, i.e., movements in the real exchange rate. You will learn about the relationship between the real exchange rate and a country's net exports. You will learn about the law of one price and purchasing power parity. You will learn about current account and capital account transactions and the relationship between the two. You will learn about fixed exchange rate systems where countries agree to keep the value of their currencies fixed against others. You will learn that fixed exchange rate systems require intervention by governments (or central banks) in the market for foreign exchange. You will consider the pros and cons to a fixed versus a floating exchange rate system. You will learn a little of the history of the U.S. experience with different exchange rate systems. You will learn about the European Union's plans to have a single currency much like the fifty states of the U.S. pay for transactions with a single currency. You will learn about the Mexican financial crisis of 1994 and what steps were taken to manage the crisis.

II.   CHECKLIST

By the end of this chapter, you should be able to:

√   Explain what a currency appreciation and depreciation is.

√   Explain how a currency appreciation or depreciation might affect exports and imports.

√   Use an exchange rate to convert the foreign currency price of a good to an equivalent price in U.S. dollars (or another currency besides the U.S. dollar).

√   Use an exchange rate to convert the U.S. dollar price of a good to an equivalent price in foreign currency.

√   Use demand and supply analysis to show how changes in the demand and supply of a currency affect its price (the exchange rate).

√   Explain how an increase in the prices and interest rates of a country may affect the price of its currency. Use demand and supply analysis to illustrate.

√   Define and compute a real exchange rate.

√   Define an appreciation and depreciation of the real exchange rate. Give a numerical example.

√   Describe the law of one price.

√   Describe purchasing power parity and its implications for the real exchange rate.

√   Explain the relationship between inflation in one country relative to another and the exchange rate between the two countries.

√   Define the current account and the capital account.

√   Describe the types of transactions that give rise to a deficit and those that give rise to a surplus.

√   Describe the relationship between the current account and the capital account.

√   Explain why the balance of payments must sum to zero under a flexible exchange rate system.

√   Explain how foreign exchange market intervention works to keep exchange rates stable.

√   Describe what actions a country would have to take to keep its currency's value from increasing or decreasing.

√   Explain what actions a government must take to keep its exchange rate fixed if it has a balance of payments deficit or surplus.

√   Explain what actions besides foreign exchange market intervention a country may need to take in order to eliminate a persistent balance of payments deficit or surplus under a fixed exchange rate system.

√   Discuss the U.S. experience with fixed and floating (flexible) exchange rates.

√   Discuss the Mexican financial crisis of 1994.

III.   KEY TERMS

Exchange rate: the rate at which we can exchange one currency for another.

Appreciation: an increase in the value of a currency.

Depreciation: a decrease in the value of a currency.

Real exchange rate: the market exchange rate adjusted for prices.

Multilateral real exchange rate: an index of the real exchange rate with a country's trading partners.

The Law of One Price: the theory that goods which are easily tradeable across countries should sell at the same price expressed in a common currency.

Purchasing Power Parity: a theory of exchange rates that states that the exchange rate between two currencies is determined by the price levels in the two countries.

Current account: the sum of net exports (exports minus imports) income received from investments abroad, and net transfers from abroad.

Capital account: minus the value of country's net acquisition (purchases less sales) of foreign assets. A purchase of a foreign asset is a deficit item on the capital account while a sale of a domestic asset is a surplus item.

Net international investment position: holdings of foreign assets minus holding of domestic assets.

Foreign exchange market intervention: the purchase or sale of currencies by governments to influence the market exchange rate.

Flexible rates: a currency system in which exchange rates are determined by free markets.

Fixed exchange rates: a system in which governments peg exchange rates.

Balance of payments deficit: under a fixed exchange rate system, a situation in which the supply of a country's currency exceeds the demand for the currency at the current exchange rate.

Balance of payments surplus: under a fixed exchange rate system, a situation in which the demand of a country's currency exceeds the supply for the currency at the current exchange rate.

Devaluation: a decrease in the exchange rate to which a currency is pegged in a fixed rate system.

Revaluation: an increase in the exchange rate to which a currency is pegged.

IV.   PERFORMANCE ENHANCING TIPS (PETS)

PET #1

The exchange rate is the price of one currency in terms of another. It can be thought of just like the price of any good or service.

Think about the price of any good or service, say a painting priced at $200, i.e., $200/painting. The item in the denominator is what is being priced. So, too, for an exchange rate. Suppose the exchange rate is expressed as 0.50 U.S. dollars/1 German mark. In this case, the currency that is being priced is the mark. Its price is 50 cents. The inverse of this exchange rate would be 2 German marks/$1 U.S. dollar. Now, the currency that is being priced is the dollar. One dollar is priced at (or costs) 2 German marks.

If the price of a painting rises, we would say the painting has appreciated in value. If the price of a painting falls, we would say the painting has depreciated in value. So, too, for an exchange rate. If the exchange rate decreased from 0.50 U.S. dollars/1 German mark to 0.40 U.S. dollars/1 German mark, we would say that the mark has depreciated since it now worth 40 cents instead of 50 cents. If the German mark has depreciated against the dollar, then it must be true that the U.S. dollar has appreciated. To see this, the inverse of 0.40 US dollars/1 German mark is 2.5 German marks/1 U.S. dollar. Thus, the dollar has appreciated in value since it is now worth 2.5 marks instead of 2 marks.

PET #2

You can think of the terms "U.S. assets" and "foreign assets" as referring largely to U.S. financial assets and to foreign financial assets.

Financial assets include stocks, mutual funds, corporate bonds, and government bonds (securities, bills). For example, suppose a U.S. resident purchases a Treasury bond issued by the British government. We would say that the U.S. resident has acquired a foreign asset. Alternatively, if a German resident purchases a U.S. corporate bond, we would say that the German resident has acquired a U.S. asset.

PET #3

A U.S. resident's purchase of a foreign asset means that the U.S. resident is lending his savings to the foreign country. A foreign resident's purchase of a U.S. asset means that the foreign resident is lending his savings to the U.S.

PET #4

The real exchange rate defines how many units of a U.S. good can be exchanged for a unit of the foreign good.

The equation for the real exchange rate is [exchange rate X price of good in U.S/ price of good in foreign country] where the exchange rate is foreign currency/U.S. dollar.

Suppose the exchange rate is 5 French francs/$1 and a bottle of wine in the U.S. is priced at $9 and an equivalent bottle of wine in France is priced at 15 francs per bottle. The real exchange rate would be:

$$= (5 \text{ Ffr}/1\$ \text{ X } \$9/\text{bottle of U.S. wine})/15 \text{ Ffr/bottle of French wine}$$
$$= 3 \text{ bottles of French wine}/1 \text{ bottle of U.S. wine.}$$

(since $ and Ffr cancel out and "bottle of U.S. wine" is in the denominator whereas "bottle of French wine" is in the denominator of the denominator (which moves it to the numerator)).

Thus, the real exchange rate measures how many bottles of U.S. wine can be exchanged for bottles of French wine. An increase in the real exchange rate would be called a real appreciation of the dollar since one bottle of U.S. wine would be worth more bottles of French wine. A decrease in the real exchange rate would be called a real depreciation of the U.S. dollar since one bottle of U.S. wine would be worth fewer bottles of French wine.

PET #5

If %Δexchange rate = foreign inflation rate - U.S. inflation rate, then, %Δreal exchange rate = 0.

(where exchange rate is expressed as foreign currency/U.S. dollar)

For example, suppose the exchange rate is 2 marks/U.S. dollar and rises to 2.2. The percentage change in the exchange rate is 10%. If the German inflation rate is 12% and the U.S. inflation rate is 2%, the percentage change in the real exchange rate will be zero.

PET #6

An increase in the **net** *foreign assets of Country A means that Country A's purchases minus sales of foreign assets is greater than foreigners' purchases minus sales of the Country A's assets (and vice-versa for a decrease in the net foreign assets of Country A). An increase in net foreign assets held by Country A also means that Country A is on net lending to foreign countries; this also means that Country A is running a* **capital** *account* **deficit** *(not surplus).*

For example, suppose that in 1995 Country A's residents purchased $100 billion worth of foreign assets and sold $20 billion of foreign assets (acquired in previous years). Country A's purchases minus sales of foreign assets (i.e., net purchases) will be $80 billion. If the residents of foreign countries purchase $150 billion worth of Country A's assets and sell $30 billion of Country A's assets (acquired in previous years), foreign countries' purchases minus sales of Country A's assets (i.e., net purchases) will be $120 billion. Now, since Country A has, on net, purchased $80 billion of foreign assets and foreign countries have, on net, purchased $120 billion of Country A's assets, we would say that there was a **decrease** in the **net** foreign assets of Country A equal to $40 billion (80 - 120). We would also say that foreign countries are on net, lending to Country A, i.e., Country A is on net borrowing from foreign countries. We would also say that Country A has a capital account surplus.

PET #7

A current account deficit (surplus) of $X means that the capital account must be in a surplus (deficit) of $X.

For example, suppose that Japan has a current account surplus of 50 billion yen against the United States. Japan's capital account must be in a deficit of 50 billion yen against the United States. The deficit on the **Japanese** capital account means that Japan's net acquisition (purchases less sales) of U.S. assets are greater than the United States' net acquisition (purchases less sales) of Japanese assets. In effect, this means that **on net**, Japan lends 50 billion yen to the U.S. That is, Japan is acquiring more U.S. assets than the U.S. is acquiring of Japanese assets -- the U.S. net foreign asset position must be declining. (See PET #6 above.)

If Japan has a current account surplus of 50 billion yen with the U.S, then it must be the case that the U.S. has a current account deficit of 50 billion yen with Japan. The U.S. current account deficit of 50 billion yen is thus financed by Japan lending 50 billion yen to the U.S. through the capital account.

PET #8

If the price of a currency (i.e., the exchange rate) is fixed below its equilibrium value, there will be an excess demand for the currency. If the price of a currency is fixed above its equilibrium value, there will be an excess supply of the currency.

For example, suppose the exchange rate is $0.50/German mark at which it is fixed. First of all, the currency that is being priced is the German mark. Its price is $0.50. Thus, the demand and supply curves drawn below represent the demand and supply of German marks.

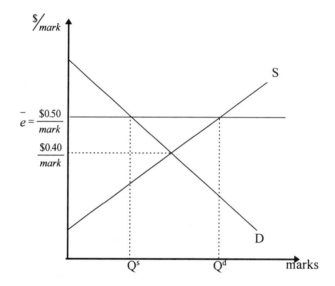

Since the equilibrium price of a mark is $0.40/German mark, the quantity of marks supplied must exceed the quantity of marks demanded at the fixed rate. That is, there is an excess supply of German marks. This also means that there must be an excess demand for dollars.

V.   PRACTICE EXAM: MULTIPLE CHOICE QUESTIONS

1.   Suppose the current franc/deutschemark rate is 4.1. If this rate changed to 3.80, we would say that:

a.   the deutschemark has depreciated.
b.   the franc is now worth fewer deutschemarks.
c.   the demand for francs must have decreased.
d.   the supply of deutschemarks must have decreased.
e.   (b) and (c).

2.   Suppose the price of a Swedish crystal vase is 80 Swedish krona and the current exchange rate is 6 Swedish krona per U.S. dollar. Which one of the following statements would be true?

a.   an increase in Swedish interest rates will reduce the dollar price of the crystal vase.
b.   an increase in U.S. interest rates will reduce the dollar price of the crystal vase.
c.   the current dollar price of a Swedish crystal vase is $480.

d.   if the price of a U.S. crystal vase is $30, then Swedish crystal vases cost more than U.S. crystal vases.
e.   none of the above.

3.   Suppose that prices in Austria fall relative to those in the U.S. Which one of the following would be expected to happen?

a.   the shilling/dollar exchange rate will fall.
b.   the demand for shillings will fall.
c.   the supply of dollars will fall.
d.   Austria's net exports will increase.
e.   (a) and (d).

4.   Which one of the following statements is true?

a.   the U.S. multilateral real exchange rate decreased during the early to mid 1980s.
b.   the law of one price applies to nontradeable goods like houses and haircuts.
c.   purchasing power parity calculations may provide a reasonable guide to setting an appropriate exchange rate for countries that have experienced hyperinflation.
d.   an increase in the U.S. real exchange rate will be associated with an increase in U.S. net exports (U.S. exports minus U.S. imports).
e.   all of the above are true.

5.   Which one of the following items is NOT classified as a current account transaction?

a.   exports.
b.   imports.
c.   purchases of foreign assets.
d.   income earnings paid to foreign holders of U.S. assets.
e.   net transfers.

6.   Which one of the following transactions would give rise to a supply of foreign currency from the U.S perspective?

a.   income earnings from foreign investments in the U.S.
b.   U.S. imports.
c.   a foreigner's purchase of a U.S. asset.
d.   U.S. aid to a foreign country.
e.   none of the above.

7.   Which one of the following statements is true?

a.   if the U.S. has a capital account surplus, it will have a current account surplus, too.
b.   if the U.S. has a capital account surplus, it will have a current account deficit.
c.   a surplus on the U.S. current account generates an excess demand for foreign currency.
d.   a surplus on the U.S. capital account generates an excess demand for foreign currency.
e.   (b) and (d).

8.   If the current yen/$ exchange rate is 135 and the U.S. government believed that the exchange rate was too high, the U.S. government:

a.   might sell dollars to the private market.
b.   might buy dollars from the private market.
c.   might buy yen from the private market.
d.   fix the exchange rate.
e.   (a) and (c).

9.   Which one of the following statements is true of the foreign exchange market?

a.   the Federal Reserve has official responsibility for conducting foreign exchange market intervention.
b.   when a country runs a balance of payments surplus under a fixed exchange rate system, its holdings of foreign exchange will decrease.
c.   Europe has plans for a single currency named the "european currency unit" or "ecu."
d.   foreign exchange intervention may not be successful at changing a currency's value because the dollar amount of intervention is very small relative to the trillions of dollars traded on the foreign exchange market by private market participants.
e.   today, all countries participate in flexible exchange rate systems.

10.   Which one of the following statements is NOT true?

a.   under the Bretton Woods system, all currency values were fixed in terms of an SDR (special drawing right).
b.   fixed exchange rate systems and the free (unrestricted) flow of capital are typically incompatible.
c.   for fixed exchange rate systems to work, countries must maintain similar inflation rates and interest rates.
d.   President Nixon effectively took the U.S. out of the Bretton Woods system.
e.   political events can sometimes lead to an international financial crisis.

VI.   PRACTICE EXAM: ESSAY QUESTIONS

1a.   Suppose you have $1,000 to invest and are considering buying either a 1-year U.S. treasury bond which has an interest rate of 7% per year or a German treasury bond which has an interest rate of 10% per year. The current exchange rate is 1.60 marks/dollar. If you expect the mark/dollar rate to be 1.68 in one year, where might you invest and why?

1b.   Suppose that, one year from now, the mark/dollar rate is 1.62; did your decision based on your expectation in part (1a) turn out to be a good decision? Explain.

2a.   Consider the market for French francs (Ffr) where the current equilibrium exchange rate is $0.20/Ffr. What will happen to the exchange rate if the price of French goods declined relative to the price of U.S. goods? Use supply and demand analysis to answer the question.

2b.   Suppose that the U.S. and France wanted to prevent any change in the exchange rate, i.e., they want to keep it fixed at $0.20/Ffr. What will happen to France's balance of payments given your answer to (a)? What will the U.S. and French governments have to do?

VII.   ANSWER KEY: MULTIPLE CHOICE QUESTIONS

1.   Correct answer: a.

Discussion: Since the exchange rate is expressed as francs/deutschemarks, the currency that is priced is the deutschemark; its price is 4.1 francs. If the exchange rate changes to 3.80, we would say that the price of a deutschemark has declined. It is now worth only 3.80 francs. That is, the deutschemark has depreciated in value. (See PET #1 above for review.)

A depreciation in the value of the deutschemark means that the franc has appreciated in value. To see this, invert the exchange rate. In this case, the initial price of a franc would be 1 deutschemark/4.1 francs = 0.24 deutschemarks/franc and the new price would be 1/3.8 = 0.26 deutschemarks/franc. Thus, the franc is now worth more deutschemarks, not fewer deutschemarks. Thus, statement b is not correct. We could also say that the franc has appreciated in value. Statement c cannot be correct. A decrease in demand for francs would mean that the price of a franc would decline, i.e., it would depreciate in value. However, the change in the exchange rate implies that the franc has appreciated in value. Statement d cannot be correct. A decrease in the supply of deutschemarks would increase the price of a deutschemark, i.e., the deutschemark would appreciate in value. However, the change in the exchange rate implies that the deutschemark has depreciated in value.

2.   Correct answer: b.

Discussion: Statement b is correct and requires that you understand that the increase in U.S. interest rates will increase the value of the U.S. dollar, say from 6 krona/dollar to 8 krona/dollar. At the current exchange rate, a Swedish vase costing 80 krona will, in terms of dollars, cost 80 krona/(6 krona/dollar) = $13.33. Since the increase in U.S. interest rates increases the value of the U.S. dollar, the dollar price of the Swedish vase will be reduced. If the exchange rate changes to 8 krona/dollar, the Swedish vase will cost, in terms of dollars, $10 (= 80 krona/(8 krona/dollar)).

Statement a is not correct. An increase in Swedish interest rates will increase the value of a krona (appreciate the krona) and decrease the value (depreciate) the dollar. That is, the exchange rate may change from 6 krona/dollar to 4 krona/dollar. In this case, the dollar price of the Swedish vase will increase from $13.33 to $20, not decrease. Statement c is not correct. The current dollar price of a Swedish vase is $13.33. Statement d is not correct. If a U.S. crystal vase costs $30 and the current dollar price of a Swedish crystal vase is $13.33, then Swedish crystal vases are less expensive than U.S. crystal vases, not more expensive.

3.   Correct answer: e.

Discussion: If prices in Austria fall relative to those in the U.S, Austrian-made goods become relatively less expensive than U.S-made goods. This will increase the demand for Austrian-made goods and reduce the demand for U.S-made goods. Thus, Austria's net exports will increase, so statement d is correct. (Also, a decrease in the price of Austrian-made goods reduces Austria's real exchange rate. A lower real exchange rate is associated with an increase in net exports). To buy the goods, U.S. consumers must convert their dollars to Austrian shillings. That is, U.S. consumers will demand Austrian shillings (and correspondingly supply their dollars in exchange). Thus, statements c and d are not correct. The increase in demand for

Austrian shillings will increase the price of a shilling (appreciate the shilling) and correspondingly decrease the price of the dollar (depreciate the dollar). That is, the shilling/dollar exchange rate will decline. Thus, statement a is correct.

4.   Correct answer: c.

Discussion: For countries that experience hyperinflation, purchasing power parity calculations may provide a reasonable guide to setting an appropriate exchange rate.

Statement a is not correct; the U.S. multilateral real exchange rate (a weighted average of the real value of the U.S. dollar against a basket of other currencies) increased in value during the mid-1980s, not decreased in value. Statement b is not correct. The law of one price applies to tradeable goods, but not to non-tradeable goods. Statement d is not correct. An increase in the U.S. real exchange rate will be associated with a decline in U.S. net exports. This is because an increase in the real value of the dollar makes U.S. exports more expensive to foreign countries and U.S. imports from foreign countries less expensive. Thus, U.S. exports will decline and U.S. imports will rise. That is, net exports will decline.

5.   Correct answer: c.

Discussion: Purchases of foreign assets are classified as a capital account transaction. A purchase of a foreign asset (e.g., a U.S. resident's purchase of a Japanese corporate bond) is considered as a capital outflow from the U.S. It is a capital outflow because some U.S. savings are flowing out of the country to purchase the Japanese bond.

6.   Correct answer: c.

Discussion: When a foreigner purchases a U.S. asset, he must buy the U.S. asset with U.S. dollars. Thus, the foreigner must convert his foreign currency to U.S. dollars before purchasing the asset. Thus, the foreigner supplies foreign currency (and correspondingly demands U.S. dollars).

Statement a is not correct. If a foreign resident has made an investment in the U.S. (i.e., purchased a U.S. asset), the investment income will be paid in terms of U.S. dollars (since it is a U.S. asset). The foreign resident, of course, will want to convert the U.S. dollar proceeds into foreign currency. Thus, U.S. dollars will be supplied and foreign currency demanded. Statement b is not correct. When a U.S. resident imports goods from a foreign country, the goods must be paid for with foreign currency. The U.S. resident must convert dollars to foreign currency to make the payment. Thus, imports into the U.S. create a demand for foreign currency and a supply of U.S. dollars. Statement d is not correct. When the U.S. gives foreign aid to another country, it gives the Country Aid in terms of the foreign country's currency. Thus, the U.S. government must convert U.S. dollars to foreign currency. That is, the U.S. supplies dollars and demands foreign currency.

7.   Correct answer: b.

Discussion: If the U.S. has a capital account surplus, it is on net, borrowing foreign currency. That is, the U.S. is borrowing more from abroad than it is lending to foreign countries. (See PET #6 above). This means that, through capital account transactions only, foreigners are supplying their currency to the U.S. in excess of the U.S. demand for foreign currency. That is, there is an excess supply of foreign currency and correspondingly an excess demand for dollars arising from capital account transactions. Thus, statement d is not correct. The surplus on the U.S. capital account is used to finance a deficit on the U.S. current account. That is, a deficit on the U.S. current account means that the U.S. demand for foreign currency exceeds the supply of foreign currency arising from current account transactions. The excess demand for foreign currency is alleviated through the U.S. capital account surplus (which generates the necessary supply of foreign currency). Thus, statement b is correct (and statement a is not). Statement c is not correct because a surplus on the U.S. current account corresponds to an excess demand for dollars (and an excess supply of foreign currency). This is because a current account surplus means that on net, foreigners are buying more U.S.-made goods and services than the U.S. is buying of foreign-made goods and services, i.e., the U.S. is a net exporter.

8.   Correct answer: e.

Discussion: If the U.S. government believed that 135 yen/$ was too high, the government would take action to push down the exchange rate, i.e., reduce the (yen) price of a dollar say to 125 yen/$. A decrease in the price of a dollar could be accomplished by increasing the supply of U.S. dollars on the private market. That is, the government would sell dollars to the private market. At the same time, a decrease in the price of a dollar (which means an increase in the price of a yen) could be accomplished by increasing the demand for yen (i.e., buying yen). Thus, statements a and c will both work to reduce the exchange rate (i.e., reduce the yen price of a dollar).

9.   Correct answer: d.

Discussion: Statement d is true; there is limited evidence that foreign exchange market intervention can actually alter, in any substantial way, the value of one currency against another.

Statement a is not true. The U.S. Treasury has official responsibility for conducting foreign exchange market intervention although it may act in concert with the Fed. Statement b is not true. A country that runs a balance of payments surplus (sum of current account plus capital account) is on net earning foreign exchange. That is, the country's foreign reserves will increase, not decrease. Statement c is not true. While Europe does have plans for a single currency, the name of the currency is to be the "euro." Statement e is not correct. Some countries participate in fixed exchange rate systems. Many countries in Europe currently participate in a fixed exchange rate system known as the "exchange rate mechanism."

10.   Correct answer: a.

Discussion: Statement a is not true. Under the Bretton Woods system, all currency values were fixed in terms of the U.S. dollar (and the U.S. dollar's value was fixed in terms of gold, i.e., $35 per ounce of gold).

Statement b is true. For countries to successfully operate a fixed exchange rate system, it is often the case that they must also impose capital controls (taxes, etc.) on the movement of capital into and out of their countries. Statement c is true. Fixed exchange rate systems may break down when countries are not able to keep interest and inflation rates amongst themselves similar. Statement d is true. Nixon suspended convertibility of U.S. dollars into gold in August 1971 and thereby effectively ended the Bretton Woods system of fixed exchange rates. Statement e is true as the case study in your textbook about Mexico reveals.

VIII.   ANSWER KEY: ESSAY QUESTIONS

1a.   While the 10% interest rate on the German bond makes it seem a more appealing investment than the U.S. bond, I must take into account any losses (or gains) on currency conversions required to purchase (and then redeem) the German treasury bond. To purchase the German treasury bond, I must convert my $1,000 to marks. Since the current exchange rate is 1.60 marks/dollar, I will be able to exchange $1,000 for 1,600 marks. Then, I will invest the 1,600 marks in the German bond, where I will earn a 10% return, i.e., 0.10 X 1,600 = 160 marks. At the end of the year, I will thus receive 1,760 marks. Since I expect the exchange rate to be 1.68 marks/dollar (dollar appreciation/mark depreciation), I expect to convert the 1,760 marks to dollars at 1,760 X ($1/1.68 marks) = $1,047.62. So, I expect $1,000 investment to yield $1.047.62 which is less than I could earn if I used my $1,000 to buy the U.S. bond. In one year, the U.S. bond will yield $1,070 ($1,000 X 1.07). It would thus be wiser to invest in the U.S. bond since I expect it to earn more than the German bond.

1b.   My decision in (1a) to invest in the U.S. bond was based on what my expectation of the exchange rate would be in one year (which may turn out to be wrong). If the exchange rate one year later is 1.62 marks/dollar, then had I invested in the German bond, I would have converted 1,760 marks back to dollars at this exchange rate. That is, I would have gotten back $1,086.14 = (1,760 marks X $1/1.62marks). If I had known that the exchange rate would be 1.62 marks/dollar in one year, then I would have invested in the German bond since I could have earned a higher return ($1,070 versus $1,086.14). Hindsight is always accurate!

2a.   A decrease in the price of French goods relative to U.S. goods will increase the demand for French goods (from both French and U.S. residents). The increased demand for French goods by U.S. residents translates into an increase in the demand for French francs (and correspondingly, an increase in supply of U.S. dollars on the foreign exchange market) since U.S. residents need the French francs in order to purchase the French goods. The increase in demand for French francs will increase the price of the French franc, i.e., the exchange rate expressed as $/Ffr will increase above, say, $0.20/Ffr. That is, the French franc will appreciate (and the dollar will depreciate). For example, the French franc may rise in value to $0.25/Ffr. The demand and supply diagram for French francs below shows how the increase in demand for French francs raises the price of the franc.

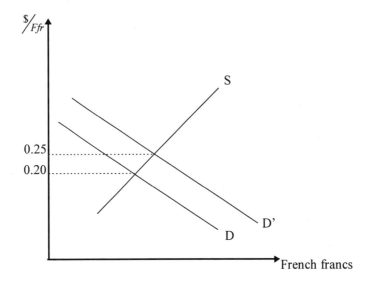

2b.   France's balance of payments will (assuming it started at zero) move toward a surplus.   The increase in demand for French francs with the exchange rate fixed will create a situation of an excess demand for French francs at the $0.20 price. (See diagram below.) An excess demand for French francs corresponds to a balance of payment surplus for France.

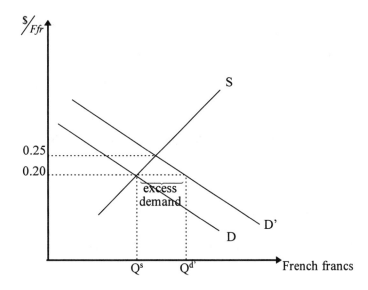

The governments must intervene in the foreign exchange market to prevent the French franc from appreciating to $0.25/Ffr. They must take action to keep the exchange rate fixed at $0.20/Ffr. Since the demand for French francs has increased (and correspondingly, the supply of dollars has increased), the governments must supply the market with the French francs they desire (and buy up the supply of dollars, i.e., take dollars off of the market). Thus, the U.S. government will lose French francs (since the U.S. government will be supplying them to the foreign exchange market (and taking in U.S. dollars)). The French central bank will gain U.S. dollars (since the French government will be buying up the supply of dollars from the foreign exchange market (and giving out French francs in return)).

Take It to the Net

We invite you to visit the O'Sullivan/Sheffrin page on the Prentice Hall Web site at:

http://www.prenhall.com/osullivan/

for this chapter's World Wide Web exercise.

APPENDIX
BASIC ALGEBRAIC RULES

1a.　　The negative of a negative value is positive.

　　　　Example:　-(-b) = b

(You can put in a number, say 3, for "b," if you prefer to use numbers rather than variables.)

What is really going on is that the negative sign in front of (-b) is really -1. So another way to think of the rule is:

1b.　　Multiplication of a negative value by a negative value returns a positive value.

　　　　Example: $(-a) \cdot (-b) = a \cdot b$.

(Here again, if you prefer, you can put in numbers for a and b.   If a = 1 and b = 3, then $(-1) \cdot -3 = 3$.)

1c.　　Multiplication of a negative value by a positive value returns a negative value.

　　　　Example: $(-a) \cdot (b) = -a \cdot b$.

(Here again, if you prefer, you can put in numbers for a and b.   If a = 4 and b = 3, then $(-4) \cdot 3 = -12$.)

2.　　　When moving variables in an equation from one side of the "=" sign to the other, the sign of the variable will change. If the variable was positive, it will now have a negative sign in front of it. If the variable was negative, it will now have a positive sign in front of it.

　　　　Example: $Y = a - b \cdot X$

can also be written as:

　　　　　　$Y - a = b \cdot X$

In the example above, "a" was eliminated from the righthand side of the equation by effectively subtracting it from each side of the equation (as long as you do the same thing to both sides of the equation, its meaning is not altered). That is:

　　　　　　$Y - a = a + b \cdot X - a$.

Since a - a = 0, the "a" on the right hand side of the equation is eliminated.

Other ways in which the equation $Y = a - b \cdot X$ can be written are:

　　　　　　$Y + b \cdot X = a$
　　　　　　$Y - a + b \cdot X = 0$.

3.　　　A variable multiplied by its reciprocal equals 1.

Example: $J \cdot (1/J) = 1$.

4.   If two variables are multiplied by each other, separation of them requires division.

Example: $Y \cdot Z = H$

can also be written as:

$Y = H/Z$.

In the example above, Z is effectively eliminated from the left hand side of the equation by dividing the left and righthand side of the equation through by Z. (As long as you do the same thing to both sides of the equation, its meaning is not altered.) Since $Z/Z = 1$, Z is eliminated from the lefthand side of the equation.

5.   Division by a variable is equivalent to multiplying by the reciprocal of the variable.

In the example to rule 4 above, Z was eliminated on the lefthand side of the equation by dividing through each side of the equation by Z. You can also think of this as multiplying each side of the equation by 1/Z. (As long as you do the same thing to both sides of the equation, its meaning is not altered.) That is:

$1/Z \cdot Y \cdot Z = H \cdot (1/Z)$

Since $1/Z \cdot Z = 1$, the equation becomes $Y = H/Z$.

6.   When a set of variables is multiplied (or divided) by a common variable, the common variable can be factored out.

Example: $Z - d \cdot Z + h \cdot Z$

can also be written as:

$Z \cdot (1 - d + h)$

where Z is the common variable.

Example: $k/q - d/q + h/q$

can also be written as:

$1/q \cdot (k - d + h)$

where 1/q is the common variable.

7.   When given two equations with a common variable, substitions can be made.

Example: $Y = a + b \cdot X$ and $X = z - v \cdot U$

You may substitute for X from the second equation into the first equation to get:

$$Y = a + b \bullet (z - v \bullet U)$$
$$Y = a + b \bullet z - b \bullet v \bullet U$$

Factoring the "b" out of the two last terms on the righthand side of the equation yields:

$$Y = a + b \bullet (z - v \bullet U)$$

8.   Common variables that appear on both sides an equation should be moved to the same side where factoring can be done.

Example: $Y = a + b \bullet z - b \bullet v \bullet Y$

The common variable is Y. By moving the Y term on the righthand side (along with any variables that it is multiplied or divided by) to the lefthand side (see rule #2 above), the equation becomes:

$$Y + b \bullet v \bullet Y = a + b \bullet z$$

Factoring out the "Y" on the lefthand side (see rule #6 above) gives:

$$Y \bullet (1 + b \bullet v) = a + b \bullet z.$$

The term $(1 + b \bullet v)$ can be eliminated from the lefthand side of the equation by dividing through both sides by $(1 + b \bullet v)$. (See rule #4 above). This yields a "solution" for Y as:

$$Y = [a + b \bullet z] / [1 + b \bullet v]$$